Understanding and Preventing

Violence

Volume 4
Consequences and Control

Albert J. Reiss, Jr., and Jeffrey A. Roth, eds.

Panel on the Understanding and Control
of Violent Behavior
Committee on Law and Justice
Commission on Behavioral and Social Sciences
and Education
National Research Council

NATIONAL ACADEMY PRESS
Washington, D.C. 1994

NATIONAL ACADEMY PRESS 2101 Constitution Avenue, N.W. Washington, D.C. 20418

NOTICE: The project that is the subject of this report was approved by the Governing Board of the National Research Council, whose members are drawn from the councils of the National Academy of Sciences, the National Academy of Engineering, and the Institute of Medicine. The members of the committee responsible for the report were chosen for their special competences and with regard for appropriate balance.

This report has been reviewed by a group other than the authors according to procedures approved by a Report Review Committee consisting of members of the National Academy of Sciences, the National Academy of Engineering, and the Institute of Medicine.

The panel study on understanding and preventing violence was supported by grants from the National Science Foundation, the Centers for Disease Control and Prevention of the U.S. Department of Health and Human Services, and the National Institute of Justice of the U.S. Department of Justice. Additional funding to support publication of the commissioned papers was provided by the John D. and Catherine T. MacArthur Foundation, the National Institute of Mental Health of the U.S. Department of Health and Human Services, and the National Institute of Justice.

Library of Congress Cataloging-in-Publication Data

Understanding and preventing violence.
    "Panel on the Understanding and Control of Violent
Behavior, Committee on Law and Justice, Commission on
Behavioral and Social Sciences and Education, National
Research Council."
    Includes bibliographical references and index.
    Contents: v. [1]. [without special title] — v. 4.
Consequences and control.
    1. Violence—United States. 2. Violence—United
States—Prevention. 3. Violent crimes—United States.
I. Reiss, Albert J. II. Roth, Jeffrey A., 1945-
III. National Research Coucnil (U.S.). Panel on the
Understanding and Control of Violent Behavior.

HN90.V5U53 1993 v. 4   303.6   92-32137
ISBN 0-309-04594-0 (v. 1)
ISBN 0-309-05079-0 (v. 4)

Printed in the United States of America.

First Printing, May 1994
Second Printing, November 1994

Contents

Foreword   vii

Public Perceptions and Reactions to Violent
Offending and Victimization
  Mark Warr   1

The Costs and Consequences of Violent Behavior
in the United States
  Mark A. Cohen, Ted R. Miller, and Shelli B. Rossman   67

Violence and Intentional Injuries: Criminal Justice and
Public Health Perspectives on an Urgent National Problem
  Mark H. Moore, Deborah Prothrow-Stith,
  Bernard Guyer, and Howard Spivak   167

Predicting Violent Behavior and Classifying Violent
Offenders
  Jan Chaiken, Marcia Chaiken, and William Rhodes   217

Incarceration and Violent Crime: 1965-1988
  Jacqueline Cohen and José A. Canela-Cacho   296

Index   389

Foreword

In cities, suburban areas, and even small towns, Americans are fearful and concerned that violence has permeated the fabric of their communities and degraded the quality of their lives. This anxiety is not unfounded. In recent years, murders have killed about 23,000 people annually, while upward of 3,000,000 nonfatal but serious violent victimizations have occurred each year. These incidents are sources of chronic fear and public concern over the seeming inability of public authorities to prevent them.

Because of this concern, three federal agencies requested the National Research Council to carry out a comprehensive review of research applicable to the understanding and control of violence. Within the general topic of violence, the three sponsors expressed somewhat different sets of priorities. The National Science Foundation's Law and Social Science Program sought a review of current knowledge of the causes of violent behavior and recommendations about priorities in funding future basic research. The other two sponsors were more concerned with the application of that knowledge to the prevention and control of violence. The National Institute of Justice sought advice on how to prevent and control violent crimes, using the combined resources of criminal justice and other agencies. The National Center for Injury Prevention and Control of the Centers for Disease Control and Prevention sought assistance in setting priorities in efforts to prevent injuries and deaths from violent events.

In response, the Commission on Behavioral and Social Sciences and Education, through its Committee on Law and Justice, established the Panel on the Understanding and Control of Violent Behavior and took primary responsibility for shaping the specific mandate and composition of the panel. Two features of its mandate carried particular weight. First, to draw implications from past research and to chart its future course, the perspectives and models of biological, psychological, and social science research on violence should be integrated. Second, as a matter of science policy, the panel's work should orient the future allocation of research and evaluation resources toward the development and refinement of promising strategies for reducing violence and its consequences.

Early on, the panel recognized that the extraordinary breadth of its mandate demanded the mobilization of expertise beyond that of its own members and staff. Therefore, in addition to preparing a number of internal review memoranda, it commissioned a number of reviews and analyses by experts in certain specialized topics. Although the commissioned papers reflect the views of their authors and not necessarily those of the panel, all were valuable resources for the panel. From the entire set, the panel selected 15 for publication in supplementary volumes because it found them particularly useful. The panel is grateful to all the authors and to the discussants who prepared comments for the panel's Symposium on Understanding and Preventing Violence.

This volume contains five of the panel's commissioned reviews and analyses concerning the consequences of violence and strategies for controlling them. Mark Warr reviewed the research literature on public perceptions and reactions to violence. Mark Cohen, Ted Miller, and Shelli Rossman developed estimates of the costs of violence. Panel member Mark Moore, collaborating with Deborah Prothrow-Stith, Bernard Guyer, and Howard Spivak, explored the commonalities and complementarities of criminal justice and public health responses to violence. Jan Chaiken, Marcia Chaiken, and William Rhodes reviewed the results of efforts to reduce violence through the prediction and classification of violent offenders. Panel member Jacqueline Cohen and José Canela-Cacho analyzed the relationships between trends in violence and in prison populations during a period of extraordinary increase in the use of incarceration. The panel members believe that, like themselves, others will find these papers to be valuable sources of knowledge and insights.

Understanding and Preventing

Violence

Volume 4

Consequences and Control

Public Perceptions and Reactions to Violent Offending and Victimization

Mark Warr

INTRODUCTION

During their life course, individuals will normally come to learn about violence through at least one of two distinct processes. Some will themselves become victims of violence and may draw on those experiences in reaching conclusions about the nature and circumstances of violent behavior. Others will never experience violent victimization directly but will instead learn of such events indirectly, through the social networks in which they participate, through news and other depictions of violence in the mass media, or from other sources. Still others will learn about violence through a mixture of direct and indirect information.

In the same way that learning about violence can be characterized as direct or indirect, the consequences of violence for an individual or a population can be direct or indirect. Some individuals will undergo short- or long-term changes in their lives as a consequence of being personally victimized. For others, the mere prospect of becoming a victim will be sufficient to produce voluntary or involuntary changes in behavior or lifestyle.

The distinction between direct and indirect experience with violence is of utmost importance, because the ratio of these two

Mark Warr is at the Department of Sociology, University of Texas at Austin.

is one of the features that most distinguishes violence from other social problems or adverse life events. In the United States, the proportion of citizens who suffer a violent victimization each year is rather small (e.g., U.S. Department of Justice, 1992; Federal Bureau of Investigation, 1993). In American culture, however, news and other forms of communication about violence are ubiquitous and unrelenting, with the result that one is far more likely to hear about, read about, or watch violent events than to experience them. To use an example, the crude annual probability of being murdered in the United States is roughly 1 in 10,000 (9.3 per 100,000 in 1992 according to Federal Bureau of Investigation data). According to the 1988 General Social Survey (National Opinion Research Center, 1988), approximately 10 percent of the adult population of the United States personally knew a victim of homicide during the year preceding the survey. The probability of knowing a victim of homicide is therefore about three orders of magnitude (or 1,000 times) greater than the probability of being a victim. Similarly, the proportion of Americans who worry about being murdered (22% by one estimate; see McGarrell and Flanagan, 1985) is far greater than the proportion who will actually be murdered.

These observations have two immediate implications. First, the social consequences of violence cannot be fully understood by focusing exclusively on victims; investigators must look beyond those who are directly victimized to those who suffer forms of indirect victimization. Although the plight of victims is not to be discounted, an exclusive emphasis on victims is a little like rushing to aid those caught in an apartment fire and ignoring those who jumped from the windows. Secondly, because indirect information on violence is far more prevalent than direct information, it is imperative that investigators examine the information on violence to which the general public is exposed, including the sources, accuracy, and consequences of such information.

This paper examines the current state of evidence on public perceptions and reactions to violent offending and violent victimization. The first topic on our agenda is public fear of victimization, including the individual and social consequences of fear. Next, we examine the images and information on violence to which the general public is exposed. Following this, we consider social evaluations of violent behavior, specifically, the perceived seriousness of offenses. Then we conclude with an examination of public opinion concerning legal sanctions and criminal justice.

The literature we consult in this paper falls for the most part in the domain of criminology and, as such, pertains primarily to violent crime. And although our principal interest lies in violent offending and victimization, when appropriate, we examine violence as a special case within the larger context of criminal behavior.

FEAR OF VICTIMIZATION

In *The Challenge of Crime in a Free Society*, the President's Commission on Law Enforcement and Administration of Justice (1967:3) offered this observation: "The most damaging of the effects of violent crime is fear, and that fear must not be belittled." By adopting this position and by commissioning research on fear, the commission granted legitimacy to an area that had largely been ignored or dismissed by criminologists. Since the commission's report, however, research on what has come to be known as fear of crime has increased markedly, and measures of fear have come to be included routinely in national polls and recognized as important social indicators. Although much research on fear of crime has been merely descriptive, the area is gradually acquiring a more theoretical and cumulative character. After considering some conceptual issues pertaining to fear, we examine the current state of knowledge about fear of crime.

CONCEPTUAL ISSUES

There is no conventional definition of fear of crime, and the term has been equated with a variety of emotional states, attitudes, or perceptions (including mistrust, anxiety, perceived risk, fear of strangers, or concern about deteriorating neighborhoods). In psychology and certain of the life sciences, however, the term fear is more uniformly used to denote a specific emotional state that is phenomenologically familiar to most people, that is, a feeling of alarm caused by an awareness or expectation of danger (see Sluckin, 1979). This affective state is frequently (though not necessarily) associated with certain physiological changes, including increased heart rate, rapid breathing, sweating, decreased salivation, and increased galvanic skin response (Thomson, 1979). Although fear of criminal victimization differs from other forms of fear (e.g., fear of falling, separation fear, fear of predators) in the object (stimulus) of fear, there is no evidence that fear of crime is qualitatively different from other forms of fear.

Fear of crime may be evoked by a clear and present danger, as when an individual is confronted by an armed assailant or is issued a verbal threat of violence. This type of intense, immediate fear appears to be what some have in mind when they speak of fear of crime. As sentient and symbolic beings, however, humans have the ability to anticipate or contemplate events that lie in the future or are not immediately apparent. Hence people may experience fear merely in anticipation of possible threats or in reaction to environmental cues (e.g., darkness) that imply danger. Psychologists commonly use the terms fear and anxiety to differentiate reactions to immediate threats (fear) from reactions to future or past events (anxiety). This terminological clarity has not been adopted in research on fear of crime, but it appears that most measures of fear are designed to capture anxiety rather than fear of victimization. This approach evidently rests on the assumption that anxiety about possible victimization is more common among the general public than fear resulting from actual encounters with crime. In view of the high ratio of indirect to direct experience with crime, that assumption would seem to be eminently warranted, but there is no direct evidence for it. Another justification for emphasizing anxiety rather than fear is the possibility that anxiety about possible victimization commonly leads people to avoid places or situations in which the threat of actual victimization (and hence fear) is likely. Although we retain the conventional phrase "fear of crime" in this paper, the term fear is understood to include anxiety about future victimization, unless otherwise noted.

Fear of crime is sometimes portrayed as a discrete variable, much like a switch that can be turned off or on. However, the range of English-language terms commonly used to describe states of fear (terror, worry, alarm, apprehension, dread), as well as self-reports and physiological measures of fear, indicate that fear is a quantitative or continuous rather than a discrete variable (Sluckin, 1979). Consequently, fear in a human population is characterized both by its prevalence (the proportion of a population that experiences fear during some reference period) and its magnitude or intensity (the degree of fear experienced by fearful individuals). Hence one population may have small but intensely fearful subgroups, whereas another suffers from widespread but moderate fear. In addition to magnitude and prevalence, fear is also characterized by its duration, both among individuals and within social units (e.g., communities). Because criminal events (or exposure to immediate signs of danger) are commonly fleeting, episodes of fear (strictly defined) are likely to be relatively brief. Anxiety, on the other hand, is by no means so short-lived and may become a chronic or obsessive condition (Sluckin, 1979).

When individuals are confronted with an ostensibly dangerous environment, they may quite naturally experience fear for their own personal safety. In addition, however, they may also fear for others (e.g., children, spouses, friends) whose well-being they value. Fear of crime is sometimes broadly construed to include fear for others, extending even to one's neighborhood, city, or nation. If investigators have been generous in defining fear, however, the fact is that virtually all research in the United States has concentrated on personal fear. This is most unfortunate because it is entirely possible that fear for others is at least as prevalent as personal fear and may have consequences that are distinct from, or that amplify, those arising from personal fear. Furthermore, measuring fear for others would permit investigations into the sociometry of fear in social units. For example, in family households, do wives fear for their husbands as much as husbands do for wives? Do they share equal fear for their children?

MEASURING FEAR

Fear can be measured by eliciting self-reports from subjects or by direct measurement of physiological indicators of fear (see Sluckin, 1979). In principle, physiological measures of fear are preferable to self-reports because they eliminate many of the problems associated with self-reports and survey methodology in general (e.g., demand effects, errors in recall, reluctance to admit fear, question-wording effects). Physiological measures have their own problems and limitations, however. Because they sidestep cognition, physiological measures of fear cannot reveal the object of fear (i.e., the persons, things, or events to which the subject is reacting), nor can they distinguish fear of crime from other forms of fear. This may present few problems in controlled laboratory experiments (as when subjects are presented with slides of dangerous or innocuous scenes) because the cues or stimuli of interest can be isolated and confounding cues eliminated or controlled. However, the number and variety of cues that appear in natural settings suggest that physiological measures of fear are of limited value in nonexperimental research. Another problem with physiological measures of fear is that the physiological changes commonly associated with fear are not unique to that emotion and may accompany other emotional states as well (Mayes, 1979). Thus, for example, there appears to be no physiological basis for distinguishing between persons who react to a violent threat with anger and those who react with fear.

SURVEY RESEARCH ON FEAR

Survey research on fear of crime is extensive, but investigators have employed a bewildering variety of questions to measure fear. Indeed, more than 100 distinct questions have been employed in studies of fear during the past two decades (see Ferraro and LaGrange, 1987; DuBow et al., 1979). Much of this diversity stems from variation in the context stipulated in survey questions. Some questions measure fear during the day; others, at night. Some pertain to fear at home, whereas others question respondents about fear in their own neighborhood or in their city. Still others ask respondents about fear when alone or with others. Such sensitivity to context among researchers is admirable but is of little value unless the contextual variables are fully and systematically varied, and their effects assessed within the same, well-defined populations. Unfortunately, this is rarely the case, and the variety of survey questions and samples used in measuring fear makes it difficult to assess the prevalence or magnitude of fear in the United States as a whole.

Only one measure of fear has been applied routinely to national samples: Is there any area around here—that is, within a mile—where you would be afraid to walk alone at night? The question stipulates a rather narrow, if relatively clear, context. That is, the respondent is alone, it is nighttime, and the location is outside the home but within its general vicinity. The response categories (yes or no) permit only a crude assessment of the magnitude of fear among respondents, meaning that the question is better suited for measuring the prevalence rather than the magnitude of fear.

The question has appeared intermittently in both the Gallup survey and the General Social Survey (GSS) since 1965 (Gallup, 1983; National Opinion Research Center, 1988). Figure 1 shows the response distributions (i.e., the percentage answering yes) from 1965 to 1988. Inspection of the plot reveals that fear of criminal victimization is quite prevalent in the general population. From year to year, roughly one-third to one-half of Americans are afraid of their local environment. The most striking feature of the plot, however, is the relative constancy of fear through the 1970s and 1980s. From 1965 to 1972, fear rose moderately, from a low of 31 percent in 1967 to 42 percent in 1972. During the 1970s and

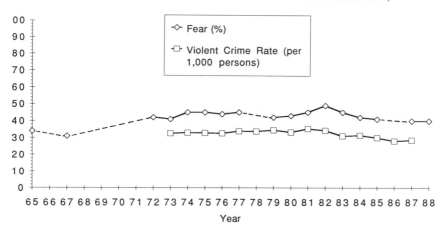

FIGURE 1   Percentage of respondents afraid to walk alone at night, 1965-1988, and NCS violent crime rate, 1973-1987. SOURCE: Gallup (1983), National Opinion Research Center (1988), Jamieson and Flanagan (1989).

1980s, however, the range of variation in fear is merely 9 percent, and only 5 percent if 1982 is excluded. If the prevalence of fear is rather high, then, it has also remained quite stable during the past two decades.

Data on trends in fear naturally invite comparisons with trends in crime rates. However, data from the Federal Bureau of Investigation (FBI) Uniform Crime Reports (UCR) and from the National Crime Survey (NCS) do not concur closely as to recent trends in crime, and in any event, there are too few observations in the fear series for a rigorous time-series analysis. Nevertheless, it is worth noting that the violent crime rate as measured by the NCS has been remarkably constant since 1973 (the first year of the NCS), as the lower plot in Figure 1 demonstrates. If we assume that the crimes that people fear outside the home (as stipulated in the Gallup/GSS question) are offenses against the person, then there appears to be no major disparity between trends in fear and trends in violent crime as measured by the NCS.

Offense-Specific Fear

General measures of fear of the sort used in the GSS and Gallup surveys serve a useful purpose, but they suffer a major limitation. Although such measures tell us how afraid individuals or groups are, they do not tell us what they are afraid of. That is, such measures do not tell us the crime or crimes that individuals have in mind when they report fear. Consequently, two individuals may report identical levels of fear, but that fear may arise in response to quite different crimes.

An alternative to such omnibus measures of fear is to ask respondents to report their fear of a variety of specific crimes. Such data permit answers to one of the most critical questions about fear of crime: In any given population, what crimes are feared most, and which least? If the crimes that occur in our society were arranged according to the degree to which they are feared, which offenses would head the list, and how would the remaining crimes be arranged?

The answer to that question has important policy implications (see below), but the question was unfortunately ignored for years because the answer seemed self-evident. That is, investigators largely assumed that crimes are feared in direct proportion to their seriousness, implying that violent crimes are feared more than property crimes. Although seemingly plausible, this argument is far less compelling than it first appears. As a general rule, the incidence and the seriousness of crimes are inversely related; the more serious an offense, the less frequently it occurs (cf. Erickson and Gibbs, 1979). Hence, if the seriousness of crimes were the only determinant of fear, individuals would fear most exactly those offenses that are least likely to happen to them. To use an analogy, this is a little like fearing injury from lightning strikes more than rush hour traffic.

The seriousness of crimes, then, is not likely to be the sole determinant of fear. Drawing on this observation, Warr and Stafford (1983) proposed a model stipulating the degree to which different crimes are feared. According to this model, the degree to which a crime is feared depends on two factors—the perceived seriousness of the offense and the perceived risk of the offense (i.e., the subjective probability that it will occur). Neither of these factors, however, is itself a sufficient condition for fear. A serious crime will not be highly feared if it is viewed as unlikely, nor will a seemingly inevitable offense be highly feared if it is not serious. To provoke high fear, an offense must be viewed as both serious *and* likely, meaning that fear is a multiplicative function of perceived risk and perceived seriousness, that is, $\overline{F}_j = a\overline{R}_j^{b1}\overline{S}_j^{b2}$, where $\overline{F}_j$ is the mean fear of the *j*th offense, and $\overline{R}_j$ and $\overline{S}_j$ are the mean perceived risk and seriousness, respectively, of the *j*th offense.

The multiplicative model of fear was tested by asking a sample of Seattle residents to report their everyday fear of becoming victims of different crimes, as well as the perceived risk and perceived seriousness of each crime. Table 1 shows the mean fear scores (on a scale from 0 to 10) of the 16 offenses from the Warr and Stafford (1983) study, along with the mean perceived risk and perceived seriousness of the offenses (also rated on scales of 0 to 10). The most striking feature of these data is the order in which the offenses are feared. As the multiplicative model implies, there is no strong direct correlation between fear of the offenses and either perceived seriousness (R^2 = .31) or perceived risk (R^2 = .03). For example, murder, although perceived to be the most serious offense, ranked 10 among the 16 offenses on fear because of the very low perceived risk attached to murder. Indeed, respondents were more afraid of having juveniles disturb the peace than of being murdered. On the other hand, "having someone break into your home while you are away" was the offense most feared by Seattle residents, even though it carries no risk of personal injury. The high fear attached to residential burglary stemmed from the fact that it was viewed as both moderately serious and relatively likely to occur.

The multiplicative model of fear proved to be a very accurate predictor of fear for these data, with R^2 = .93. In addition, the standardized coefficients for perceived risk (1.02) and seriousness (1.05) were each quite close to 1.0, meaning that risk and seriousness carry essentially identical weight in producing fear. Other offense-specific data suggest that the hierarchy of offenses found in the Warr and Stafford study is not unique to Seattle. Data from a 1987 survey of Dallas residents show a close match with the Seattle data in the order in which offenses are feared (Warr, 1988), as do data from a recent national Gallup survey (Warr, 1993).

Although the order in which crimes are feared is intrinsically interesting, it also has direct implications for public policy, particularly police policy. Suppose, for example, that to counteract public fear of crime, the police in a particular metropolitan area are given additional resources (e.g., manpower, hardware, salary) for the purpose of reducing crime and thereby (presumably) reducing fear. Where should these resources go? Public officials often seem to assume that the general public is most afraid of violent crime. Yet if the police decided to invest in the prevention of homicide, for example, their efforts would be largely wasted because homicide is not highly feared. A much more productive strategy would be to invest the money in reducing residential burglary.

Reducing fear is not the only purpose of crime reduction, however, and that goal must be balanced against other goals or values (re-

TABLE 1 Mean Fear, Perceived Risk, and Perceived Seriousness of 16 Offenses Among Seattle Respondents

Description of Offense	Fear		Perceived Risk		Perceived Seriousness		Expected Fear (PR = 5)[a]	
	Mean	Rank	Mean	Rank	Mean	Rank	Mean	Rank
1. Having someone break into your home while you are away	5.86	1	4.50	2	7.20	8	7.26	8
2. Being raped[b]	5.62	2	2.51	11	9.33	2	9.86	2
3. Being hit by a drunk driver while driving your car	5.11	3	3.57	6	7.66	5	7.81	5
4. Having someone break into your home while you are home	4.49	4	2.72	8	7.72	4	7.88	4
5. Having something taken from you by force	4.05	5	2.61	9	7.48	7	7.59	7
6. Having strangers loiter near your home late at night	4.02	6	3.83	5	4.35	13	4.01	13
7. Being threatened with a knife, club, or gun	4.00	7	2.57	10	8.25	3	8.52	3
8. Having a group of juveniles disturb the peace near your home	3.80	8	4.25	3	4.30	14	3.95	14
9. Being beaten up by a stranger	3.59	9	2.12	14	7.63	6	7.77	6
10. Being murdered	3.39	10	1.29	15	9.66	1	10.27	1
11. Having your car stolen	3.35	11	2.72	8	5.77	10	5.59	10
12. Being cheated or conned out of your money	2.50	12	2.16	13	5.55	11	5.34	11
13. Being approached by people begging for money	2.19	13	6.73	1	2.15	16	1.74	16
14. Receiving an obscene phone call	2.07	14	3.87	4	3.18	15	2.77	15
15. Being sold contaminated food	1.96	15	2.24	12	5.53	12	5.32	12
16. Being beaten up by someone you know	1.04	16	0.83	16	6.17	9	6.05	9

[a]PR = perceived risk.
[b]Female respondents only.

SOURCE: Warr and Stafford (1983).

ducing personal injury, enforcing community moral standards) that generally give priority to violent offenses. Moreover, although it is true that violent crimes are not uniformly feared more than other offenses, it would be a serious mistake to ignore such crimes because of the enormous fear they are *capable* of producing. The last column in Table 1 shows the expected fear score for each of the offenses under the multiplicative model, with perceived risk set to an arbitrary constant (i.e., 5). If all crimes were perceived to be equally likely, as in this example, violent crimes would clearly outweigh all other forms of crime in the fear they evoke. That is an unlikely scenario, to be sure, but the point is that even moderate increases in the perceived risk of violent victimization have the potential to increase fear enormously.

Social Distribution of Fear

One of the most distinctive features of fear of victimization is that fear, like victimization itself, is not randomly distributed in the population. Evidence accumulated over the past two decades consistently indicates that fear is particularly pronounced in two groups: females and older individuals (Hindelang et al., 1978; Warr, 1984; Skogan and Maxfield, 1981; Baumer, 1978; Clemente and Kleiman, 1977; DuBow et al., 1979). In their three-city survey, for example, Skogan and Maxfield (1981) found that the proportion of respondents who felt "very unsafe" walking alone in their neighborhood at night rose from 7 percent among those aged 18-20 to 41 percent among those over 60, and although 6 percent of males reported such fear, the figure increased to 23 percent among females. Hindelang et al. (1978) report much the same results, but they also note that the association between fear and age is much stronger among males than among females. These patterns are quite evident in the GSS data. The sex difference in responses to the fear item is very large, with 22 percent of males and 60 percent of females responding yes in the cumulative (1972-1987) file. Among females, this proportion is rather constant across age groups, varying no more than 6 percent. Among males, however, the age gradient is much more marked, increasing from 14 percent among those under 20 to 32 percent among those over 60.

How can such large sex and age differentials in fear be explained? One possible explanation is that females and the elderly are more afraid than others because they face the greatest objective risk of victimization. In fact, however, exactly the opposite is true. Although they have the greatest fear, females and the elderly are actually at substantially lower risk of victimization than males and the young for most crimes (e.g., Hindelang et al., 1978; Flanagan and Jamieson, 1988), a situation that is sometimes called the paradox of fear (e.g., Stafford and Galle, 1984; Warr, 1984; Skogan and Maxfield, 1981).

If females and older individuals are not at greater objective risk than others, perhaps their fear stems from higher perceived risk. However, Warr (1984) found that the perceived risk of victimization for different crimes is not consistently higher among females and the elderly. Indeed, for some crimes, females and the elderly are more afraid than their counterparts even when their perceived risk is lower.

How, then, can we explain the greater fear of females and older individuals? Much of the answer appears to lie in age- and sex-related differences in what can be called sensitivity to risk. To illustrate, suppose that we were to plot the relation, among individuals, between fear of a particular offense and the perceived risk of victimization for that offense. As shown in Figure 2, the relation has three primary features: the threshold of fear (the intercept), the slope of fear (the rate at which fear increases with

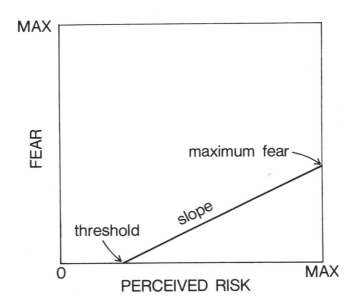

FIGURE 2 Parameters of the fear/perceived risk relation.

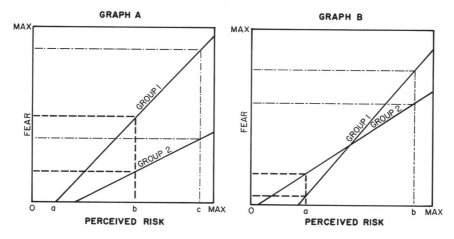

FIGURE 3   Some illustrative relations between fear and perceived risk for two groups.

perceived risk), and the maximum fear that the offense is capable of producing (i.e., at maximum perceived risk). Once this relation has been established, we can predict the degree of fear that will result at each level of perceived risk.

Now suppose that we were to plot the same relation for two different groups (e.g., males and females). If the relation were identical in both groups, then any given degree of perceived risk would produce the same degree of fear in both groups. Suppose, however, that the relation between fear and perceived risk is not the same for the two groups, as in Figure 3A. In this case, an equivalent level of perceived risk would produce quite different levels of fear in the two groups, meaning that the groups differ in their sensitivity to risk. Not only will a fixed level of risk produce different levels of fear under this condition, but it is entirely possible for one group to exhibit greater fear than another even when their perceived risk is lower (compare the fear of groups 1 and 2 at points b and c in Figure 3A). Group differences in fear may even be reversed at different points along the risk continuum (see Figure 3B). Using data from a sample of Seattle residents, Warr (1984) found substantial age and sex differences in sensitivity to risk across a variety of crimes. Moreover, the observed age and sex differences in fear were largely attributable, not to differences in perceived risk, but rather to differences in sensitivity to risk among these groups.

The notion of sensitivity to risk helps to explain sex and age differences in fear, but at the same time it raises a larger question: Why do females and older persons display greater sensitivity to risk? Part of the answer seems to lie in rather small age- and sex-related differences in the perceived seriousness of crimes (Warr, 1984), but there appears to be a much more important reason. That is, females and the elderly seem to perceive crime in a way that is fundamentally different from males and the young. Specifically, among females and older individuals, different crimes are subjectively linked in a way that is not true for other groups. In examining the correlations between fear of different crimes, Warr found strong correlations between certain crimes. Examined closely, these configurations of offenses typically consisted of crimes that can (logically or empirically) occur contemporaneously or in continuous sequence (e.g., robbery and murder, burglary and rape), and the strong correlations between fear of these crimes suggested that they were in fact viewed as likely to occur together as part of the same criminal event. The frequency and strength of these subjective linkages were much greater among females than males and among older, rather than younger, individuals (Warr, 1984, 1985, 1987). Taken together, they suggest that circumstances or events that appear innocuous or comparatively minor to males or younger persons are apt to be viewed as more dangerous to females and the elderly because of the offenses they imply or portend.

One offense that looms large for women but not men, of course, is rape. Using data from the Seattle study, Warr (1985) found that (1) rape is feared more than any other crime among women under 35; (2) rape is viewed by women as approximately equal in seriousness to murder; (3) the highest sensitivity displayed by any age/sex group to any crime is that of young women to rape; (4) fear of rape is closely associated with a variety of other offenses for which rape is a possible outcome (e.g., burglary, robbery, receiving an obscene phone call) or precursor (e.g., homicide); and (5) fear of rape is strongly associated with certain lifestyle precautions (e.g., going out alone). For many women, then, fear of crime may be synonymous with fear of rape.

OTHER CORRELATES

Although age and sex have been the most thoroughly documented and closely examined correlates of fear, there are others as well. The prevalence of fear appears to be substantially greater among blacks than whites, and unlike age and sex differences in fear, black/white differences in fear are quite consistent with objective risk (Hindelang et al., 1978; Skogan and Maxfield, 1981; DuBow et al., 1979; Garofalo, 1977). Not surprisingly, fear is a largely urban phenomenon, although the degree of inter-city variation in fear is striking. In the Law Enforcement Assistance Administration (LEAA) surveys of 26 cities conducted during 1972-1974, the proportion of respondents who reported feeling "very unsafe" or "somewhat unsafe" when alone in their neighborhood at night ranged from a low of 26 percent in San Diego to a high of 58 percent in Newark (see Skogan and Maxfield, 1981; Garofalo, 1977). Finally, fear is inversely related to family income, and the relation holds among both blacks and whites (Hindelang et al., 1978; Garofalo, 1977; Skogan and Maxfield, 1981).

CUES TO DANGER

One of the proximate causes of fear, as we have seen, is the perceived risk of victimization. Although perceived risk is essential to explaining fear, explanations of fear based solely on perceived risk beg the larger question: How do individuals estimate or form impressions of their risk of victimization? One way to address the question is to examine the environmental stimuli, or cues to danger, that individuals confront in their everyday lives. The number and variety of such cues are probably enormous. Some cues may be encountered only occasionally and thus affect only situational or short-term perceptions of risk. Others may be routine if not constant reminders of danger and thus may be more likely to affect long-term perceptions of risk.

Relatively little work has been done on identifying cues to danger or assessing levels of exposure to such cues. However, the current state of evidence does permit some general conclusions.

Dangerous Places

There is strong evidence that people commonly perceive crime in geographic terms, meaning that they typify areas as dangerous or, alternatively, as safe zones. All cities, for example, seem to have widely understood folklore about dangerous areas of the city. These danger zones may be small, as in the case of particular parks, beaches, or neighborhoods, or they may extend to entire sections or regions of a city.

In an ingenious study of the perceptual geography of crime, Ley (1974) asked residents of the Monroe area of Philadelphia to draw lines on a map indicating the routes they would take when walking between their home and different destinations on the map. When the routes drawn by respondents were overlaid, a clear picture of the "stress surface" of Monroe emerged, showing the spatial segmentation of the area into safe and dangerous zones. Ley did not directly question residents about their reasons for avoiding certain areas, but an inspection of the areas revealed a number of potential cues to danger, such as gang graffiti, abandoned buildings, and the presence of prostitutes and junkies.

Ley's work demonstrates the existence of microzones of danger (blocks, street corners), but larger areas may be feared as well. The downtown or central business districts of cities, for example, are often regarded as potentially dangerous places (DuBow et al., 1979; Pyle, 1980; Smith and Patterson, 1980). Pyle (1980) asked a sample of Akron residents to rate the crime problem in 10 geographic areas of the city and then used these perceptual data to construct a three-dimensional cognitive map of the city. The major distinction recognized by respondents was between the central city and the suburbs, with the central city rising like a mountain range from the plains of the suburbs. Although central-city areas actually displayed substantial variation in reported crime rates, respondents largely failed to differentiate among areas within the central city, perceiving it to be uniformly dangerous.

The downtown or central business districts of cities, however, are not necessarily perceived to be their most dangerous areas. In a 1987 survey of Dallas residents conducted by the author[1], respondents were asked, "What area or place in Dallas do you think is most dangerous when it comes to crime?" Only 12 percent of respondents mentioned the downtown area, but a substantial majority named South Dallas or Fair Park, two largely residential areas that abut the central business district. The total rate of UCR index offenses in these areas, although high, was not markedly different from several other areas of Dallas. However, the rate of violent offenses (homicide, rape, and aggravated assault) was distinctly higher, suggesting that violent offenses are most important in defining areas as "dangerous places." This may be true because violent offenses carry the greatest fear potential, but it is also true that persons traveling outside the home are more susceptible to personal crimes than to property crimes (see Hindelang et al., 1978). The propensity to view these two areas of Dallas as dangerous places also increased with the number of years that respondents had lived in the city, which suggests that people come to learn the reputations of areas as they acquire greater familiarity with their city.

Some environments pose a threat only to certain populations, and some are uniquely frightening because they must be faced on a routine basis. One environment that exhibits both these features is the school. In the National Institute of Education's Safe School Study (1978), one-fifth of secondary school students reported that they were afraid at school at least sometimes, although only 3 percent said they were afraid most of the time. Among junior high school students (who were more afraid than high school students), 22 percent reported avoiding three or more locations in the school (the most common being restrooms), a figure that rose to 33 percent among students in large cities. Among the latter group, 8 percent said that they had actually stayed home at least one day during the previous month because someone might hurt or bother them at school. A study of black Philadelphia students by Savitz et al. (1977:22) also demonstrates, in their words, the "dangerousness of the entire educational enterprise" and reveals something about the geography of fear in schools. The classroom itself appears to be the safest place in students' minds; only 21 percent of students thought there was a high risk of being beaten or robbed in the classroom. The hallways, however, were perceived to be more dangerous (34% feared them), and the school yard more dangerous yet (44%). More than half (54%) of the students regarded the streets leading to and from school as dangerous.

If certain locations are commonly perceived to be dangerous, what areas are perceived to be safe? One answer has repeatedly appeared in research on fear of crime. Using data from the attitude supplement to the National Crime Survey, Hindelang et al. (1978:168) found that "respondents were much more likely to view their own neighborhoods as safer, rather than more dangerous, than other neighborhoods in the metropolitan area." The same pattern was also observed by Reiss (1967) using data from Boston and the District of Columbia. Surveys conducted by the author in Dallas and Seattle (see note 1) also lead to the same conclusion. Whereas 64 percent of Dallas residents rated their city as "not very safe" or "not safe at all," only 23 percent described their own neighborhood that way. In Seattle, the corresponding figures were 34 percent and 15 percent, respectively.

Why should home and neighborhood be so widely regarded as safe? One possible answer is simply cognitive consistency; the notion of home as a dangerous place is not an easy one to live with. There is, however, another possible explanation. Warr (1990) has shown that a key cue to danger is novelty; novel or unfamiliar environments evoke fear of criminal victimization. For most individuals, of course, home and the surrounding neighborhood are the environments that they are most familiar with (e.g., Holahan, 1982) and, hence, should fear least.

The fact that home is typically perceived to be comparatively safe, however, does not mean that it is perceived to be risk free. Not all individuals feel safe at home (see Skogan and Maxfield, 1981), and residential burglary, as we have seen, is among the most feared crimes. Although areas away from home may be especially feared, the large number of hours that people commonly spend in their home and neighborhood means that any risks in those environments are amplified by exposure to risk. Also, as a "storehouse" of valued possessions (and persons), the home is a uniquely vulnerable location.

Dangerous Persons

If crime is commonly perceived in geographic terms, it is also perceived in social terms. That is, there appear to be widely accepted images of dangerous persons, with the result that some persons in the population are feared more than others. Although the personal attributes that signify danger might appear to be subtle and numerous, that is not necessarily the case. Using data from a factorial survey, Warr (1990) found that two immediately apparent features of persons combine to form a potent cue for eliciting fear. The most frightening persons, quite simply, are *young males*. Young males are particularly frightening to females, but even young males are often frightened of other young males. Moreover, few cues or combinations of cues are more powerful in eliciting fear than a *group* of young males. This finding is corroborated by evidence that adults commonly avoid groups of "teenagers" (e.g., DuBow et al., 1979), but Warr's work indicates that it is young males (even when alone), rather than females, who provoke fear.

The question of dangerous persons, of course, raises one of the most sensitive questions of our day. Granted that young males are frightening, what about young *black* males? Are blacks more frightening than whites? Using data from residents of three cities, Graber (1980:55) reports that respondents "viewed crime largely as the work of young males, black or belonging to other minority races." In a detailed investigation of Chicago neighborhoods, Taub et al. (1984) found substantial proportions of residents who believed that the in-migration of blacks into their neighborhoods would result in higher crime rates. In a 1982 national survey conducted for ABC News, 30 percent of respondents (32% of whites and 16% of blacks) agreed with the statement "a black person is more likely to commit a crime than a white person." None of these studies directly measured fear, and it remains unclear whether or how racial attitudes are translated into outright fear. Still, these findings suggest that blacks (or, most probably, young black males) are frequently typified as criminals or potential criminals and, as a consequence, are feared more than others.

Other Cues

Apart from geographic and social cues to danger, two other cues appear to be important in situational assessments of danger. One of these cues, not surprisingly, is darkness. Fear of crime is generally higher at night, and many Americans report that they avoid going out at night due to fear (see below). Indeed, Warr (1990) reports evidence that darkness is the single most important cue in evoking fear of crime in outdoor situations; an activity or situation (e.g., walking to an appointment) that is utterly innocuous during the day is apt to be much more frightening after dark. The second cue is the presence of bystanders or companions; the presence of others normally acts to reduce or alleviate the fear that individuals would feel if alone (Warr, 1990). However, this calming effect, as one might suspect, does not operate if those "others" are perceived to be dangerous persons.

FEAR AND PRIOR VICTIMIZATION

One of the most intuitively compelling hypotheses about fear is the notion that persons who have been victims of crime should display greater fear than those who have not. Numerous studies, however, have shown little or no difference in fear between victims and nonvictims, and the issue has remained something of a conundrum among researchers (see Hindelang et al., 1978; DuBow et al., 1979; Skogan and Maxfield, 1981). One possible explanation is that many criminal events are minor, have little salience to victims, and are quickly forgotten (e.g., DuBow et al., 1979). However, the absence of positive evidence for the hypothesis may be due to a common methodological deficiency in studies of the consequences of victimization. Most investigations of the victimization/fear relation have failed to control for the confounding effects of demographic variables in comparing victims to nonvictims. As we have seen, victimization rates and fear show strong—but opposite—correlations with age and sex. Consequently, crude comparisons between victims and nonvictims may fail to reveal the effects of victimization experiences.

Skogan and Maxfield (1981) found only small initial differences in fear in comparing victims of crime with nonvictims, but when they controlled for the confounding effects of demographic variables, the differences increased substantially. In addition, the largest differences in fear between victims and nonvictims occurred in cases where the victim had suffered a violent offense that required medical attention. This evidence, along with arguments we consider later, suggests that investigators may have failed to detect what could be substantial effects of prior victimization.

CONSEQUENCES OF FEAR

Much of the increased attention devoted to fear of crime in recent years stems from a deep concern among social scientists, public officials, and the media with the social consequences of fear. As Skogan and Maxfield (1981:186) have noted, "It is widely believed that fear of crime has enormous consequences for the way we live." Claims that the United States has become a "fortress" society or a society "paralyzed by fear" are common, if rather alarmist, expressions of such concern. Yet if the American public has not quite reached the point of panic, there is abundant evidence that fear does indeed affect the lives of Americans to a substantial degree.

Reactions to fear take many forms, but they can be classified under some general rubrics. Avoidance behaviors are those actions "taken to decrease exposure to crime by removing oneself from or increasing the distance from situations in which the risk of criminal victimization is believed to be high" (DuBow et al., 1979:31). Thus, a fearful person may avoid certain locations or certain kinds of people that are perceived to be dangerous, or may avoid certain activities (e.g., shopping) during certain times. Reducing exposure to risk through avoidance behaviors, however, is not always possible. An individual may have no choice but to pass through a dangerous area on the way to work and may not have the option of moving his or her home to a safer neighborhood. Where avoidance is not an option, individuals may engage in protective or precautionary behaviors, that is, strategies designed to reduce the marginal risk of victimization if avoidance is not feasible or acceptable. Thus, for example, a person who must navigate a dangerous environment may alter their mode of transportation (taking a taxi rather than a public bus or driving rather than walking) or seek companions for the journey. Similarly, a person living in a neighborhood with a high rate of residential burglary may invest in home security precautions or purchase a weapon.

Apart from reducing their risk through avoidance or precautionary behaviors, people may also seek to minimize the costs or damages that they will incur in the event of a victimization (what DuBow et al., 1979, call insurance strategies). To illustrate, some persons carry little or no money outside the home in anticipation of potential robberies, whereas others insure or engrave their property in the home or simply refrain from keeping valuable property at home altogether.

Survey Data on the Consequences of Fear

A large number of surveys designed to measure public responses to fear of crime have been conducted in recent years. Although the samples and methodologies of these surveys vary widely, certain findings appear with sufficient regularity to warrant some general conclusions. First, among the most common responses to fear of crime in the United States is spatial avoidance, meaning that individuals commonly report that they avoid areas perceived to be dangerous. Spatial avoidance typically ranks in frequency above most or all other responses to fear in social surveys, at least among those responses that occur outside the home (DuBow et al., 1979; Research and Forecasts, 1980; Skogan and Maxfield, 1981). For example, 77 percent of a sample of Dallas residents reported that they avoided "certain places in the city," as did 63 percent of Seattle residents (Warr, 1985).

As noted earlier, there is a strong tendency among individuals to perceive crime in geographic terms; hence the tendency to avoid "dangerous places" is not surprising. So prevalent is spatial avoidance, however, that it is reasonable to assume that the ecology of U.S. cities is regulated to some extent by such avoidance patterns. Neighborhoods that are perceived to be dangerous places are likely to be find themselves socially isolated, and retail businesses that are located in ostensibly dangerous areas may suffer a shortage of customers (Conklin, 1975; Skogan and Maxfield, 1981). For example, after naming the most dangerous place(s) in their city, respondents in the Dallas survey (see note 1) were asked, "Do you go near or through this area regularly?" More than four-fifths (82%) answered no, and approximately three-quarters (73%) said that they did not know the area well, suggesting a long-standing pattern of spatial avoidance.

If people commonly avoid dangerous places, they also avoid dangerous times, the most obvious example being nighttime. As noted earlier, darkness is a principal cue to danger (Warr, 1990), and substantial proportions of Americans report that they avoid going out at night (DuBow et al., 1979; Warr, 1985; Skogan and Maxfield, 1981). There may well be other periodicities to fear, however. Godbey et al. (1979), for example, report a tendency among some elderly persons to return to their homes in the late afternoon, when schools let out and the streets fill with adolescents.

Another common response to fear is to employ precautionary measures when traveling outside the home. Among the most common is to seek the company of others during one's journey. In surveys of Dallas and Seattle conducted by the author (see note 1), 29 percent and 26 percent of respondents, respectively, reported that they avoided going out of the house alone. In surveys of Chicago, Philadelphia, and San Francisco, approximately 30 percent of respondents in each city reported that they take an escort "most of the time" when leaving home after dark (Skogan and Maxfield, 1981). Traveling by foot is also commonly avoided by urban Americans in favor of the safety of automobiles (Skogan and Maxfield, 1981), and a small percentage choose to carry a weapon or some other form of protection (e.g., a whistle or dog) outside the home (Skogan and Maxfield, 1981; DuBow et al., 1979; Warr, 1985; Research and Forecasts, 1980).

The foregoing responses to fear all pertain to situations outside the home, but although the home is generally regarded as safer than areas away from it, the large majority of Americans nevertheless take precautions, if frequently only minor ones, to protect their dwelling and its occupants. Skogan and Maxfield (1981) report that fully 96 percent of the households interviewed in San Francisco, Chicago, and Philadelphia reported at least one home security precaution. In accordance with other research (e.g., DuBow et al., 1979; Research and Forecasts, 1980), they found that the most common precautions (typically in excess of 80% of households) are such simple steps as locking doors, leaving a light on, asking neighbors to watch the house, identifying persons before letting them in, or stopping mail delivery when away for extended periods. Such precautions, of course, require little financial investment or time. More expensive and time-consuming precautions, however, are not rare. Although estimates vary, roughly 25-40 percent of American households have invested in such measures as window bars or grates, improved locks, property engraving, alarm systems, improved lighting, or theft insurance (see generally DuBow et al., 1979; Research and Forecasts, 1980; Skogan and Maxfield, 1981). The most reliable national data come from the 1983 Victim Risk Supplement to the National Crime Survey (U.S. Department of Justice, 1987), in which household informants were questioned about the steps they had taken "to make [their home] safer from crime." Burglary alarms were present in 7 percent of U.S. households; 34 percent of households had engraved or marked valuables; 42 percent had a gun or firearm "for protection"; and 58 percent had a dog.

Among household security measures, the most controversial is gun ownership. According to repeated GSS surveys, approximately one-half of U.S. households contain one or more firearms (National Opinion Research Center, 1988), but the purpose of those firearms has been the subject of vigorous debate. In a review of the literature on fear of crime and gun ownership, Wright et al. (1983:101) conclude that "there is no credible study anywhere in the literature that shows, clearly and unmistakably, a fear . . . effect in the weapons trend," and argue that firearms are primarily purchased for hunting and recreational purposes. Two subsequent studies, however, cast some doubt on this conclusion. Using survey data from 59 neighborhoods in three standard metropolitan statistical areas (SMSAs), Smith and Uchida (1988) found that the probability of purchasing "a gun or weapon for your protection" was significantly related to respondents' perceived risk of victimization, prior victimization experiences, and perceptions of neighborhood crime trends. Like McDowall and Loftin (1983), they found that the probability of purchasing a weapon increased when the police were perceived to be ineffective. (For related research, see Smith and Uchida, 1988).

Apart from their frequency, perhaps the most striking feature of public responses to fear is their age and sex distribution. As Skogan and Maxfield (1981:195) have observed, "Every analysis of crime-related behavior indicates that women and the elderly are more likely to avoid exposure to risk and to take numerous measures to reduce their chances of being victimized." These differences appear to be most pronounced with respect to avoidance and precautionary behaviors outside the home. For example, whereas 42 percent of women in a Seattle sample reported that they avoid "going out alone," only 8 percent of men reported this precaution. And whereas 40 percent of women reported that they avoid "going out at night," only 9 percent of men did so. The sex difference diminished substantially, however, when it came to spatial avoidance, with 67 percent of women and 58 percent of men reporting that they avoid "certain places in the city" (Warr, 1985). Even males, it seems, avoid dangerous places.

COLLECTIVE RESPONSES

The discussion thus far has concentrated on those avoidance and precautionary behaviors undertaken by individuals. One of the major developments in public responses to crime in recent years, however, has been the rise of collective, organized efforts within communities to reduce or prevent crime or fear of crime. These efforts have taken many forms, including (1) neighborhood watch programs, (2) citizen patrols, (3) neighborhood escort programs, (4) property-marking projects, (5) police-community councils, and (6) citizen crime-reporting programs (see Rosenbaum, 1986, 1988; Skogan, 1981; Skogan and Maxfield, 1981; DuBow et al., 1979; Garofalo and McLeod, 1989). Although estimates vary, it appears that approximately 10-20 percent of adults in the United States participate to some degree in such organized activities (Rosenbaum, 1988; Skogan and Maxfield, 1981).

Among these community-based programs, neighborhood watch programs appear to be the most prevalent, as well as the most frequently studied, programs. As Garofalo and McLeod (1989:326) have said, "Neighborhood watch has been the centerpiece of community crime prevention in the United States during the 1980s." According to the Victim Risk Supplement to the 1983 National Crime Survey (U.S. Department of Justice, 1987), 20 percent of U.S. householders report the presence of a "neighborhood watch or citizens protective group" in their area, although only 39 percent of these households participate. Drawing on a nationwide study of neighborhood watch programs, Garofalo and McLeod (1989) report that the principal goal of such programs is to increase surveillance of the neighborhood by residents, extending, as it were, the "eyes and ears" of the police. Most programs, they found, are sponsored by local police or sheriffs, and residents are encouraged to observe and report suspicious behavior, but not to intervene. The presence of neighborhood watches is usually announced by signs posted in the neighborhood or by stickers attached to homes or vehicles. Although neighborhood surveillance is the primary goal of neighborhood watch programs, most engage in other activities as well, such as property identification, home security surveys, lighting improvement, and so on.

The rapid rise of neighborhood watch programs in the late 1970s and early 1980s was accompanied by strong claims in the media concerning the effectiveness of such programs in reducing crime and fear of crime, as well as high expectations among community activists and some researchers (Lurigio and Rosenbaum, 1986; Rosenbaum, 1988). However, the current state of evidence seems to support the rather pessimistic assessment of Garofalo and McLeod (1989) and others. Much of the evaluation research cited in support of neighborhood watch programs suffers from severe methodological deficiencies, and the most rigorous quasi-experimental studies indicate that victimization rates and fear are not significantly reduced by such programs (Rosenbaum, 1986, 1988; Skogan and Maxfield, 1981; Lurigio and Rosenbaum, 1986). One reason seems to be that neighborhood watch programs are most likely to arise in those neighborhoods that need them least (e.g., Garofalo and McLeod, 1989; Bennett and Lavrakas, 1989). Another is that the initial interest taken by residents often fades quickly, with the result that many neighborhood programs soon become dormant (Taub et al., 1984; Garofalo and McLeod, 1989). Finally, it is possible that neighborhood watch programs, by drawing attention to or dramatizing local crime, increase rather than alleviate fear among some residents.

Fear in Broader Context

There can be little doubt that fear of criminal victimization affects the lifestyles and quality of life of U.S. citizens. In assessing the social implications of fear, however, several points need to be considered. First, much of the current concern with fear of crime arises from an assumption that fear is an intrinsically negative emotion with no redeeming features. In the biological sciences, however, fear is widely regarded as a beneficial rather than a deleterious reaction. Many animal species display apparent fear responses (escape behavior, tonic immobility or freezing, distress calls, crouching, jumping) when confronted by predators and other dangers, or exhibit forms of caution such as neophobia (reluctance to enter a novel area). Far from being dysfunctional, such behaviors are generally regarded as highly adaptive because they reduce individual or collective exposure to risk and maximize the probability of survival in the face of lethal risks (see Sluckin, 1979).

An organism with no fear of predators, after all, is one that is unlikely to live long enough to reproduce. The point is not that fear in humans is a desirable state; a society that feels safe and secure is surely to be preferred over one that does not. However, in the face of real danger, fear may lead individuals to take precautions that reduce their (or others') risk and thereby save them from injury.

A second issue concerns the extent to which fear of crime actually prevents citizens from engaging in normal everyday activities. Drawing on their findings from the National Crime Surveys, Hindelang et al. (1978) offer a provocative argument. Fear of criminal victimization, they argue, typically results in relatively subtle lifestyle changes. Rather than altering what individuals do, fear of crime is more likely to change the way they do it. Instead of forgoing shopping altogether, a fearful person may change their hours for shopping, alter the route or means of transportation employed in getting there, or choose to go shopping with companions. The argument would seem to understate the consequences of fear for some individuals, for whom fear does appear to be a profoundly debilitating condition (e.g., Skogan and Maxfield, 1981). For many Americans, however, it may well be true that fear is less of an outright obstacle than a hindrance in their daily activities.

Beyond the consequences of fear for individuals, however, lie questions about the consequences of fear for social institutions and American society as a whole. In recent years, a number of social commentators have charged that fear of crime has torn the very social fabric of the United States, making individuals afraid to leave their homes or strike up a conversation with a stranger. In a widely cited book, for example, Silberman (1980:7) argued that "fear of crime is destroying the network of relationships on which urban and suburban life depends." Such broad charges, although easy to make, are difficult to verify. Yet it is true that many of the most common avoidance and precautionary behaviors (e.g., not going out at night, spatial avoidance) seem specifically designed to avoid social interaction, particularly with strangers, and such behaviors are sufficiently common to have affected the overall sociability of American life.

Against this rather gloomy assessment, however, stands a quite different view. In one of the most famous of sociological arguments, Emile Durkheim (1933:102) asserted that crime is functional for societies because it unites people against a common threat, thereby increasing rather than decreasing social solidarity:

> Crime brings together upright consciences and concentrates them. We have only to notice what happens . . . when some moral scandal has just been committed. . . . [People] stop each other on the street, they visit each other, they seek to come together to talk of the event and to wax indignant together.

Viewed this way, the effect of fear of crime is not socially disintegrative, but rather integrative (see Conklin, 1975). Although it may be difficult to believe that violence has any positive consequences, Durkheim's position is supported by the nationwide growth of neighborhood watch programs and other community crime prevention organizations in the United States. Regardless of how effective these programs may be in reducing crime, the fact is that millions of Americans have joined such voluntary organizations. Ironically, then, the social consequences of fear may be contradictory, with fear reducing sociability in some domains of life while increasing it in others. Whether these countervailing trends cancel one another out and whether they are simultaneously occurring within the same subpopulations are clearly matters for further investigation.

There is another potential consequence of violence, however, about which there is less reason to be sanguine. The mere presence of violence in a society can, by itself, be construed as a failure of social institutions, most immediately those that have direct responsibility for controlling violence (police, courts, prisons), but also those that are perceived to be at least indirectly implicated (family, church, schools). When citizens come to perceive certain institutions as ineffective, those institutions stand to lose their traditional authority or legitimacy among the general public, a possibility that does not augur well for a society. For example, both the inception and the periodic resurgence of vigilantism in this country seem to have coincided directly with a loss of public confidence in law enforcement. Says historian Richard Brown (1979:154):

> Vigilantism arose as a response to a typical American problem: the absence of effective law and order in a frontier region. It was a problem that occurred again and again beyond the Appalachians, and it stimulated the formation of hundreds of frontier vigilante movements. On the frontier, the normal foundations of a stable, orderly society—churches, schools, cohesive community life— were either absent or present only in rough, makeshift forms. The regular, legal system of law enforcement often proved to be woefully inadequate for the needs of the settlers.

Today the frontiers of law and order are more likely to be found on an inner-city block than in a western territory, and despite the popularity of persons like Bernhard Goetz (see Fletcher, 1988), Americans seem more interested in helping the police than in usurping their power. However, as we see later, public confidence in the criminal justice system (or, more precisely, certain parts of that system) seems to be very low indeed.

SOURCES OF INFORMATION ON VIOLENCE

Violence is a phenomenon that Americans routinely hear about, read about, talk about, and through the medium of television, watch. To understand public perceptions and reactions to violence, therefore, we must examine the indirect sources of information on violence to which the general public is exposed. One of the principal ways in which Americans learn of violence is through news coverage of crime in the mass media. Crime news, as we shall see, not only is remarkably plentiful, but also gives special attention to violence.

News Coverage of Crime

When a crime occurs, knowledge of that event is initially limited to the immediate participants in the event (i.e., victim, offender, and perhaps witnesses). If a crime is reported to the police, however, news of the crime becomes public information and is available to reporters who handle the "crime beat" (e.g., Sherizen, 1978; Ericson et al., 1987). If the crime is selected from the daily pool of crimes for reporting, news of the event may ultimately reach audiences in the thousands or millions. The mass media are thus a powerful amplifying mechanism; information known only to a few may within hours or days become common knowledge.

In the United States, crime and justice stories constitute a large and relatively steady portion of the daily news diet, in both the print and the broadcast media. In perhaps the most comprehensive study of crime news, Graber (1980) coded more than 75,000 news stories from the three network television news programs (CBS, ABC, and NBC), two local newscasts (the CBS and NBC affiliates in Chicago), and three newspapers (the *Chicago Tribune*, *Daily News*, and *Sun-Times*). Crime and justice stories constituted 22 percent to 28 percent of all news stories in the three newspapers, 20 percent of local television stories, and 13 percent of national television offerings. The attention devoted to crime was particularly remarkable when compared to other news topics. In the *Chicago Tribune*, stories of individual crimes "received nearly three times as much attention as the presidency or the Congress or the state of the economy" (Graber, 1980:27). Even national television news, which had the smallest proportion of crime news, placed stories of individual crimes "on a par with the presidency and Congress" (Graber, 1980:27). Drawing on a content analysis of eight newspapers in three metropolitan areas (Philadelphia, San Francisco, and Chicago), Skogan and Maxfield (1981:128) report that "every day each paper reported at least one story about a violent crime in a prominent position." The number of violent crime stories averaged 4.4 to 6.8 stories per paper per day, with half of the stories devoted to homicides.

Although crime stories are a staple of media news coverage, this fact means little if the general public is not exposed to or is not attentive to such information. However, Skogan and Maxfield (1981) found that more than three-quarters of respondents in the three cities surveyed reported watching or reading a crime story on the previous day (44% had read a newspaper crime story, 45% had watched a crime story on television, and 24% had done both). Fully 95 percent of respondents in Graber's (1980) study cited the media as their primary source of information on crime, although 38 percent cited other sources (conversations or, more rarely, personal experience) as well. Not all media information, however, was absorbed. Only 48 percent of respondents claimed to pay "a lot" of attention to crime stories, and checks on newspaper reading habits showed that crime stories were often read only partially, ignored, or forgotten. Even so, crime stories were both read and recalled more frequently than stories on other topics.

CRITICISMS OF MEDIA NEWS COVERAGE

The prevalence of crime stories in media news coverage is scarcely surprising. Apart from the frequency of crime in our society, the inherent human interest character of crime stories means that it is a perpetually newsworthy topic. Yet if the media cannot be faulted for reporting crime, the manner in which they report it is open to scrutiny. Indeed, many critics have argued that news coverage of crime, although seemingly factual and objective, actually presents a badly distorted picture of crime. Some of these criticisms date back to the days of nineteenth-century yellow journalism, though they can be applied to the modern media of mass communication (e.g., television and radio).

Perhaps the most common criticism of media crime coverage pertains to what may be called the "mirror image" model. Although crime statistics or summaries are sometimes reported in the news, most crime news consists of reports of particular crimes, either as they are occurring (as in the case of a bank robbery in progress) or shortly after they have occurred (Graber, 1980; Fishman, 1981). Because the "supply" of crimes to be reported is virtually unlimited, choices must be made as to which to report. Like any other kind of potential news material, the central criterion for choosing crime stories is "newsworthiness." In the case of crime, newsworthiness translates into seriousness; the more serious a crime, the more likely it is to appear as a news story (Skogan and Maxfield, 1981; Sherizen, 1978; Sheley and Ashkins, 1981; Roshier, 1973; Graber, 1980). The brutal homicide is thus more likely to be reported than the nonviolent residential burglary. This standard is not in itself unreasonable, but it is at odds with a sociological reality. As noted earlier, crimes occur in inverse proportion to their seriousness; the more serious a crime, the less frequently it occurs (Erickson and Gibbs, 1979). Hence, by using seriousness as a criterion, the media are most likely to report precisely those crimes that are least likely to occur to individuals.

The image of crime presented in the media is thus a reverse image of reality; the most frequent crimes are the least frequently reported, and the least frequent crimes are the most frequently reported. For example, Graber (1980) reports that whereas murders constituted only 0.2 percent of UCR index offenses in Chicago in 1976, they accounted for 26 percent of crime stories in the *Chicago Tribune*. In a study of media crime coverage in New Orleans, Sheley and Ashkins (1981) found that violent crimes constituted 68 to 87 percent of the crime stories in local television and newspaper outlets, but only 20 percent of the offenses known to police. Skogan and Maxfield (1981) report that murder and attempted murders constituted 50 percent of all newspaper crime stories in the cities examined. Indeed, these investigators found that the number of homicide stories did not closely parallel the actual homicide rates of the cities examined, suggesting that the amount of space devoted to crime is determined less by the "supply" of crime than by the size of the "newshole" allocated to crime stories.

An alien who knew our world only through news coverage, then, might have a peculiar idea of the relative frequency of crimes and might well conclude that violent crime is the most frequent form of crime. The point is not that the presentation of crime news is deliberately distorted, but rather that a standard editorial practice has an inadvertent consequence.

Another source of distortion that may appear in media crime coverage is the practice of using crime news as filler material (e.g., Graber, 1980; Gordon and Heath, 1981). Crime news, of course, is rarely in short supply. When other news (e.g., politics, foreign affairs, the economy) is slow, column space or air time may be filled in with crime stories. If crime news is routinely employed in this way, then the amount of time or space devoted to crime over time will not bear any constant relation to the actual number of crimes occurring. Graber (1980), for example, reports an inverse relation between crime news and political news, suggesting that crime news conforms to a version of Gresham's Law. Crime news may also be increased in an effort to raise circulation or viewership, or it may be heavily featured in order to appeal to a certain kind of audience (Gordon and Heath, 1981; Dominick, 1978). In addition, certain crimes (e.g., drug offenses, gang violence) may be selectively pulled from the larger daily pool of crimes and emphasized for journalistic purposes, resulting in what Fishman (1978) has aptly called a "media wave."

There are a number of other ways by which the media, wittingly or not, may present a distorted image of crime through news coverage. Annual increases in the number of crimes in a city, for example, may be reported without converting the figures into rates or without reporting changes in population. To illustrate, a reported 10 percent increase in the number of crimes in a city, although a potentially frightening statistic, might be considerably less frightening if the recipient of the news were also informed that the population of the city had also grown by 10 percent, meaning that the probability of being victimized had in fact remained constant (Biderman et al., 1967). Similarly, a television story announcing a substantial increase in crime might be unnecessarily frightening if the story did not also inform readers of the types of crime that had actually increased. An increase in shoplifting, for example, is not the same as an increase in robbery or homicide. Furthermore, the media, which frequently rely on FBI crime figures, do not always inform readers of well-known problems with those data.

CRIME AS ENTERTAINMENT

However accurate it may be, news coverage serves the ostensible purpose of informing the general public about crime, but much of the information on crime promulgated in the mass media—in motion pictures, television crime dramas, and crime fiction—is designed for purposes of entertainment or commercial return, and makes little pretense toward objectivity. Crime fiction, for example, has been a major element of Western literature at least since Holmes and Watson appeared in the late nineteenth century, and remains so popular that entire sections of bookstores are frequently devoted to it. Crime-related themes or plots are also a staple of motion pictures, from the sophisticated Hitchcock classics to ultraviolent films like *The Texas Chainsaw Massacre* and *Friday the 13th*. The market for such entertainment, however, pales in comparison to that of television crime dramas, which constitute a large portion of prime-time television programming and may draw audiences in the tens of millions on a single night. Crime and "cop" shows have been a staple of television fare almost since the advent of television itself, owing no doubt to the immense public demand for such shows and to the fact that crime shows, with their emphasis on action, tension, and moral dilemma, are ideal dramatic settings for writers and producers.

Like news coverage of crime, television crime dramas have been subjected to withering criticism for misrepresenting the realities of crime and law enforcement. In one study, for example, investigators coded information on every prime-time crime-related program that appeared during six weeks of the 1980-1981 television season, yielding a total of 263 programs, 250 criminals, and 417 crimes (Lichter and Lichter, 1983). As in media news coverage, murder was by far the most commonly portrayed crime on television dramas, and television crime was much more violent than real crime. Offenders were correctly shown to be typically male, but the television offender was substantially older (usually over 30) than actual offenders and was frequently portrayed as either a businessman (or his flunkee) or a professional criminal. Private detectives were given considerable prominence as law enforcement agents and were frequently portrayed as more effective than the police in controlling crime. And, quite unlike the real world, virtually all offenders were caught and punished. Other research has supported these findings and pointed to other forms of distortion that appear in crime dramas (cf. Elias, 1986; Dominick, 1973).

EFFECTS OF MEDIA COMMUNICATIONS

As we have seen, there is reason to believe that the image of crime presented in the media, either in news coverage or in dramatic presentations, does not closely conform to reality. In view of that evidence, a number of investigators have concluded that public beliefs about crime are seriously distorted (e.g., Conklin, 1975; Quinney, 1970). Such a conclusion, however, is highly premature. Even if the media do not accurately portray crime, it does not necessarily follow that the images of crime that appear there are readily accepted and adopted by the general public. On the contrary, claims about the accuracy of public beliefs about crime cannot be supported without direct measurements of such beliefs, and even if some public beliefs about crime are inaccurate, such inaccuracy is not necessarily attributable to the media. The causal influence of media crime coverage cannot be established without simultaneous measurements of (1) media content, (2) public exposure to that content, and (3) the postexposure effects of media communications. Such research is difficult to conduct in natural settings because of the enormous quantity and variety of media (and other) messages on crime to which the public is exposed (e.g., Graber, 1980).

One study that approaches an ideal design was conducted by Heath (1984), who questioned samples of newspaper readers in 36 cities and examined their fear of victimization in light of the characteristics of the newspapers they read. Heath found that fear was higher among readers of newspapers that emphasized local crimes and crimes that were sensational (bizarre, violent) or random (apparently unprovoked). However, reports of sensational or random crimes reduced fear if those crimes were nonlocal. Evidently, readers were reassured by learning that such crimes were occurring to other people in other places.

Heath's study suggests that fear of crime can be influenced by the character of news coverage. Other research, however, suggests that media influence does not extend to all public perceptions or reactions to crime. For example, although the media present a reverse image of the frequencies of offenses, the general public seems well aware of the relative frequencies of crimes (Warr, 1980). Graber (1980) also reports a number of differences between public conceptions and media depictions of criminals, as well as evidence that crime news is not accepted uncritically by the public. Accordingly, she rejects the notion that "the public is a mere blotter for media images, absorbing them in rough outline." Although Skogan and Maxfield (1981) found an association between exposure to television news coverage and fear, the association proved to be spurious: both fear and exposure to media news were strongly associated with certain demographic characteristics (most notably age). The exposure/fear association disappeared when these confounding variables were held constant.

INTERPERSONAL DIFFUSION OF CRIME NEWS

The mass media, of course, are not the sole sources of information on crime in the United States. Individuals may learn about crime by talking with friends, neighbors, family members, or coworkers. Crime is in fact a rather frequent topic of conversation among Americans. In surveys of three U.S. cities, Skogan and Maxfield (1981) found that 43 percent of respondents had talked with someone else about crime "in the past week or two." A survey of Seattle residents by the author (see note 1) found that 38 percent of respondents discussed crime at least once a week, and 74 percent at least once a month. Interviews with victims of street robberies suggest that crime victims frequently discuss their experiences with others (Lejeune and Alex, 1973).

Somewhat surprisingly, the propensity to talk about crime is quite general, meaning that it is not associated with such personal characteristics as age, sex, or race (Skogan and Maxfield, 1981). On the other hand, neighborhood characteristics strongly affect conversation about crime. Those who live in neighborhoods where crime is perceived to be a problem are more apt to talk about crime, and conversations among neighbors are more common in socially integrated neighborhoods (Gubrium, 1974; Skogan and Maxfield, 1981).

Everyday conversations about crime may cover a variety of topics, of course, but one of their functions is to transmit information about victimization experiences. As in the homicide example in the introduction, the multiplying effect of interpersonal networks in spreading news of crime can be stunning. Table 2 presents some additional evidence on the multiplying effect of interpersonal networks. The data come from a 1982 survey of 2,464 Americans conducted for ABC News (Inter-University Consortium for Political and Social Research, 1982). In the survey, respondents were asked to indicate whether they had been a victim of each of several offenses during the previous year, and whether these offenses had happened during the previous year to "anyone you personally know in your neighborhood." The first column in Table 2 shows the proportion of respondents who had been victimized by each offense, and the second column shows the proportion who knew neighborhood victims. As we would expect, respondents were much more likely to know a victim of each

TABLE 2 Diffusion Ratios for Some Offenses ($n = 2, 464$)

Offense	Percentage of Respondents Victimized	Percentage of Respondents Who Know Victims in Neighborhood	Diffusion Ratio
Having your car or some other property vandalized	16.1	32.3	2.0
Having the home burglarized	4.7	30.3	6.4
Being robbed of money or valuables on the street	2.2	14.0	6.4
Being physically injured by a burglar in the home	0.5	6.0	12.0
Being physically injured by a robber on the street	0.6	8.0	13.3
Being raped	0.1	4.9	49.0

SOURCE: Inter-University Consortium for Political and Social Research (1982).

offense than to have experienced victimization themselves. As indicated in column 3, however, the ratio of "vicarious" victimizations to direct victimizations (i.e., the diffusion ratio) is far from constant across offenses. For example, respondents were two times more likely to know a victim than to have been a victim of vandalism, but compared to their own chances of being victimized, they were about 13 times more likely to know someone injured in a robbery and 49 times more likely to know a victim of rape.

These data, then, suggest that interpersonal diffusion of crime news is not constant from one crime to the next, but rather increases with the seriousness of the crime. News of violent crime, especially, travels farther through social space than other crimes. Similar results are reported by Skogan and Maxfield (1981), whose analysis was not limited to knowledge of neighbors. Fully 66 percent of respondents in their city surveys reported knowing a victim of burglary, personal theft, stranger assault, or rape. When compared to property crimes, however, the proportions of respondents who knew victims of rape or assault were much greater than the relative frequencies of those crimes would suggest. The salience of violent crime was further demonstrated when Skogan and Maxfield asked respondents whether there was any particular crime that they "had read, seen, or heard about" in the last couple of weeks. Nearly all (95%) of the offenses mentioned by respondents were violent crimes, and nearly half were murders or attempted murders. In their words, "the processes which lead victims' stories to 'get around' seem to accentuate the apparent volume of personal as opposed to property crime" (Skogan and Maxfield, 1981:155).

Earlier we noted that the propensity to talk about crime does not vary significantly among sociodemographic groups. However, if talking about crime is a rather general phenomenon, it does not necessarily follow that knowledge of victims is also distributed equally in the population. Rather dramatic evidence of this fact comes from the 1988 General Social Survey. Whereas 10 percent of respondents reported that they personally knew a victim of homicide during the previous year, blacks were fully three times more likely to know at least one victim of homicide than whites (24 versus 8%). These same data also indicate that the social channels through which crime news passes can be very restrictive indeed. Of the homicide victims known to blacks, fully 98 percent were black. Of those victims known to whites, only 4 percent were black. Social differentials in the propensity to know victims were also detected by Skogan and Maxfield (1981:156), who found that "personal contact with victims increased toward the bottom of the income ladder and among Blacks." Higher-income respondents, however, were more likely to know victims of burglary, evidently reflecting the wider social distribution of burglary victims.

Does knowing (or knowing about) crime victims increase people's personal fear of victimization? Three studies designed to answer this question (Klecka and Bishop, 1989; Skogan, 1977; Skogan and Maxfield, 1981) all provide affirmative answers. However, Skogan and Maxfield (1981) note that the effect of knowing victims on fear is most pronounced among those who know local victims (e.g., neighbors or family members). Fear is also enhanced, they report, when individuals and the victims they know share similar characteristics (i.e., age and sex). Fear was most strongly associated with knowing victims of robbery, but knowledge of burglary victims was more common and, consequently, affected a larger number of individuals.

Although knowing crime victims appears to increase fear, firm conclusions on this matter are not yet warranted. The reason is that the probability of knowing crime victims in one's neighborhood, block, or city is likely to be affected by the crime rate, which may itself affect fear through mechanisms other than interpersonal diffusion of crime information. Unfortunately, no study has as yet controlled for such confounding effects; hence the unique effect of interpersonal diffusion on fear is yet to be established.

PERCEIVED SERIOUSNESS OF OFFENSES

Many of the most fundamental questions concerning public perceptions of violence are questions that pertain to social judgments of the *seriousness* of acts. For example, do Americans perceive a rape to be more serious than an armed robbery, or vice versa? Is the murder of a stranger more serious than the murder of a spouse or a son, and is the murder of an adult as serious as the murder of a child? Are violent acts always more serious than nonviolent acts (e.g., theft) and, if so, by how much? To what extent do Americans agree on the seriousness of different acts?

Answers to such questions are important because they speak to the cultural interpretations of violence that Americans hold. Judgments of seriousness are also important because they are closely tied to a variety of other public perceptions and reactions to violence. Judgments about seriousness, as we have seen, affect the degree to which different crimes are feared (Warr and Stafford, 1983) and are the principal determinants of public beliefs concerning appropriate punishments for crimes (see below). In addition, it appears that individuals attend to the seriousness of crimes in judging such things as the certainty of punishment or the relative frequencies of crimes (Warr, 1980; Erickson et al., 1977) and in deciding whether to report a crime to the police (e.g., Skogan, 1984). Ultimately, assumptions about the seriousness of acts are expressed or implied in criminal law, and thus constitute a crucial element of public policy.

At first glance, seriousness appears to be an objective property of crimes, in the same way that mass or volume are objective properties of physical objects. Unlike physical objects, however, there is no natural metric common to all crimes, although certain metrics (e.g., degree of injury, property loses in dollars) can be applied to some subsets of crime (Cohen, 1988). Yet even if all crimes could be gauged against some common objective metric, the value of such a scale would be debatable. The reason is that there is no necessary relation between the objective seriousness of crimes and their perceived seriousness. Individuals or cultures may disagree about the seriousness of an act or about the emphasis or weighting they place on features of the act (e.g., the dollar loss in a burglary). Moreover, there is no reason to presume that the perceived seriousness of crimes is invariant over time. Consequently, seriousness is conventionally treated as a perceptual property of crime (i.e., one that can be measured only by soliciting the opinions of a population).

The largest and most comprehensive study of perceived seriousness to date has been the National Survey of Crime Severity (NSCS) (Wolfgang et al., 1985). Conducted as a supplement to the National Crime Survey in 1977, the NSCS obtained magnitude estimations of the seriousness of 204 offenses from a stratified random sample of 60,000 Americans. An unusually wide variety of offenses was covered in the survey, and the degree of injury, weapon used, and dollar loss were systematically varied for some offenses.

Table 3 presents all of the 204 offenses rated by respondents in the NSCS, along with the seriousness scores for each offense. The seriousness scores are ratio scores, meaning that they express the ratio of each offense (i.e., its geometric mean) relative to a modulus or standard offense ("A person steals a bicycle parked on the street") with a fixed score of 10. Scanning the entire list reveals a rather bewildering variety of crimes, often with little apparent order or pattern. However, a careful examination of the list shows that the scale can be viewed as a set of overlapping regions containing particular types or classes of crime. The overlapping character of these regions, along with the sheer number and variety of offenses, makes it difficult to spot transitions from one region to the next, but they can be identified through close inspection.

The single most important transition in Table 3 occurs between violent offenses (i.e., offenses against persons) and other offenses. The range of the seriousness scale is quite large (from 0.2 to 72.1), but roughly 80 percent of the entire range of the scale (i.e., the upper range) is occupied almost exclusively by violent crimes. Nonviolent offenses do not appear with any frequency until the seriousness scores drop to about 13-14.

Within the violent portion of the scale, homicides receive the highest scores. Of the ten most serious offenses, nine are forms of homicide, either simple homicides or homicides that occur in conjunction with some other crime (e.g., robbery/homicide, rape/homicide). The next several offenses following homicide include crimes in which death was a likely, if not the actual, consequence of the act (e.g., planting a bomb in a public building).

The remainder of the violent portion of the scale covers a variety of violent offenses including rape, aggravated assault, kidnapping, robbery, arson, toxic pollution, and terrorist acts (e.g., bombings). Of these, rape is among the most serious; the upper boundary of the rape "region" overlaps with the lower boundary of homicide. Even when the rape/homicide—which ranks second among all crimes—is excluded, at least one instance of rape ("A

TABLE 3 Seriousness Scores of 204 Offenses from the National Survey of Crime Severity

72.1	A person plants a bomb in a public building The bomb explodes and 20 people are killed.
52.8	A man forcibly rapes a woman As a result of physical injuries, she dies.
47.8	A parent beats his young child with his fists As a result, the child dies.
43.9	A persons plans a bomb in a public building The bomb explodes and 1 person is killed.
43.2	A person robs a victim at gunpoint The victim struggles and is shot to death.
39.2	A man stabs his wife As a result, she dies.
39.1	A factoy knowingly gets rid of its waste in a way that pollutes the water supply of a city. As a result, 20 people die.
35.7	A person stabs a victim to death.
35.6	A person intentionally injures a victim As a result, the victim dies.
33.8	A person runs a narcotics ring.
33.0	A person plants a bomb in a public building The bomb explodes and 1 person is injured but no medical treatment in required.
32.7	An armed person skyjacks an airplane and holds the crew and passengers hostage until a ransom is paid.
30.5	A person plants a bomb in a public building The bomb explodes and 20 people are injured but no medical treatment is required.
30.0	A man forcibly rapes a woman Her physical injuries require hospitalization.
27.9	A woman stabs her husband As a result, he dies.
26.3	An armed person skyjacks an airplane and demands to be flown to another country.
25.8	A man forcibly rapes a woman No other physical injury occurs.
25.2	A man tries to entice a minor into his car for immoral purposes.
24.9	A person intentionally sets fire to a building causing $100,000 worth of damage.
24.8	A person intentionally shoots a victim with a gun The victim requires hospitalization.
24.5	A person plants a bomb in a public building The bomb explodes but no one is injured.
24.5	A person kidnaps a victim A ransom of $1,000 is paid and the victim is returned unharmed.
22.9	A parent beats his young child with his fists The child requires hospitalization.
22.3	A person intentionally sets fire to a building causing $500,000 worth of damage.
21.7	A person pays another person to commit a serious crime.
21.2	A person kidnaps a victim.
21.0	A person robs a victim of $1,000 at gunpoint The victim is wounded and requires hospitalization.
20.6	A person sells heroin to others for resale.
20.1	A man forcibly rapes a woman Her physical injuries require treatment by a doctor but not hospitalization.

Table 3 continued

TABLE 3 (Continued)

19.9   A factory knowingly gets rid of its waste in a way that pollutes the water supply of a city. As a result 1 person dies.

19.7   A factory knowingly gets rid of its waste in a way that pollutes the water supply of a city As a result 20 people become ill but none require medical treatment.

19.5   A person smuggles heroin into the country.

19.5   A person kills a victim by recklessly driving an automobile.

19.5   A high school boy beats a middle-aged woman with his fists She requires hospitalization.

19.0   A person intentionally shoots a victim with a gun The victim requires treatment by a doctor but not hospitalization.

18.3   A man beats his wife with his fists She requires hospitalization.

18.0   A person stabs a victim with a knife The victim requires hospitalization.

17.9   A person robs a victim of $10 at gunpoint The victim is wounded and requires hospitalization.

17.8   Knowing that a shipment of cooking oil is bad, a store owner decides to sell it anyway Only one bottle is sold and the purchaser dies.

17.8   A person intentionally shoots a victim with a gun The victim is wounded slightly and does not require medical treatment.

17.7   A person, armed with a gun, robs a bank of $100,000 during business hours No one is physically hurt.

17.7   An employer orders one of his employees to commit a serious crime.

17.5   A high school boy beats an elderly woman with his fists She requires hospitalization.

17.1   A person stabs a victim with a knife The victim requires treatment by a doctor but not hospitalization.

16.9   A legislator takes a bribe of $10,000 from a company to vote for a law favoring the company.

16.9   A man drags a woman into an alley, tears her clothes, but flees before she is physically harmed or sexually attacked.

16.8   A person, using force, robs a victim of $1,000 The victim is hurt and requires hospitalization.

16.6   A person, using force, robs a victim of $1,000 The victim is hurt and requires treatment by a doctor but not hospitalization.

16.5   A person robs a victim of $1,000 at gunpoint The victim is wounded and requires treatment by a doctor but not hospitalization.

16.4   A person attempts to kill a victim with a gun The gun misfires and the victim escapes unharmed.

15.9   A teenage boy beats his mother with his fists The mother requires hospitalization.

15.7   A county judge takes a bribe to give a light sentence in a criminal case.

15.7   A person robs a victim of $10 at gunpoint The victim is wounded and requires treatment by a doctor but not hospitalization.

15.6   A person, armed with a lead pipe, robs a victim of $1,000 The victim is injured and requires hospitalization.

15.5   A person breaks into a bank at night and steals $100,000.

14.6   A person, using force, robs a victim of $10 The victim is hurt and requires hospitalization.

TABLE 3 (Continued)

14.5	A company pays a bribe of $100,000 to a legislator to vote for a law favoring the company.
14.1	A doctor cheats on claims he makes to a federal health insurance plan for patient services.
13.9	A legislator takes a bribe from a company to vote for a law favoring the company.
13.7	A person, armed with a lead pipe, robs a victim of $1,000 The victim is injured and requires treatment by a doctor but not hospitalization.
13.5	A doctor cheats on claims he makes to a federal health insurance plan for patient services He gains $10,000.
13.4	An employer orders his employees to make false entries on documents that the court has requested for a criminal trial.
13.3	A person, armed with a lead pipe, robs a victim of $10 The victim is injured and requires hospitalization.
13.0	A factory knowingly gets rid of its waste in a way that pollutes the water supply of a city.
12.7	A person intentionally sets fire to a building causing $10,000 worth of damage.
12.2	A person pays a witness to give false testimony in a criminal trial.
12.0	A person gives the floor plans of a bank to a bank robber.
12.0	A police officer takes a bribe not to interfere with an illegal gambling operation.
11.9	A person intentionally injures a victim The victim is treated by a doctor and hospitalized.
11.8	A person stabs a victim with a knife No medical treatment is required.
11.8	A man beats a stranger with his fists He requires hospitalization.
11.7	Ten high school boys beat a male classmate with their fists He requires hospitalization.
11.4	A person knowingly lies under oath during a trial.
11.3	Three high school boys beat a male classmate with their fists He requires hospitalization.
11.2	A company pays a bribe to a legislator to vote for a law favoring the company.
10.9	A person steals property worth $10,000 from outside a building.
10.8	A person steals a locked car and sells it.
10.5	A person smuggles marijuana into the country for resale.
10.4	A person intentionally hits a victim with a lead pipe The victim requires hospitalization.
10.3	A person illegally sells barbiturates, such as prescription sleeping pills, to others for resale.
	10.3 A person operates a store where he knowingly sells stolen property.
10.3	A person threatens to harm a victim unless the victim gives him money The victim gives him $1,000 and is not harmed.
10.0	A government official intentionally hinders the investigation of a criminal offense.
9.7	A person breaks into a department store, forces open a safe, and steals $1,000.

Table 3 continued

TABLE 3 (Continued)

9.7 A person breaks into a school and steals equipment worth $1,000.

9.7 A person robs a victim of $1,000 at gunpoint No physical harm occurs.

9.7 A person walks into a public museum and steals a painting worth $1,000.

9.7 A person breaks into a display case in a store and steals $1,000 worth of merchandise.

9.6 A person breaks into a home and steals $1,000.

9.6 A police officer knowingly makes a false arrest.

9.4 A public official takes $1,000 of public money for his own use.

9.4 A person robs a victim of $10 at gunpoint No physical harm occurs.

9.3 A person threatens to seriously injure a victim.

9.2 Several large companies illegally fix the retail prices of their products.

9.2 A person knowingly makes false entries on a document that the court has required for a criminal trial.

9.0 A city official takes a bribe from a company for his help in getting a city building contract for the company.

9.0 A person, armed with a lead pipe, robs a victim of $1,000 No physical harm occurs.

8.9 A person intentionally hits a victim with a lead pipe The victim requires treatment by a doctor but no hospitalization.

8.6 A person performs an illegal abortion.

8.5 A person sells marijuana to others for resale.

8.5 A person intentionally injures a victim The victim is treated by a doctor but is not hospitalized.

8.3 A person illegally gets monthly welfare checks of $200.

8.2 Knowing that a shipment of cooking oil is bad, a store owner decides to sell it anyway Only one bottle is sold and the purchaser is treated by a doctor but is not hospitalized.

8.0 A person steals an unlocked car and sells it.

8.0 A person, using force, robs a victim of $1,000 No physical harm occurs.

7.9 A person trespasses in a railroad yard and steals tools worth $1,000.

7.9 A teenage boy beats his father with his fists The father requires hospitalization.

7.9 A person intentionally hits a victim with a lead pipe No medical treatment is required.

7.7 Knowing that a shipment of cooking oil is bad, a store owner decides to sell it anyway.

7.7 A person conceals the identify of someone that he knows has committed a serious crime.

7.6 A person steals $1,000 worth of merchandise from the counter of a department store.

7.5 A person, armed with a lead pipe, robs a victim of $10 No physical harm occurs.

7.4 A person illegally gets monthly welfare checks.

7.3 A person threatens a victim with a weapon unless the victim gives him money The victim gives him $10 and is not harmed.

7.3 A person beats a victim with his fists The victim is hurt but does not require medical treatment.

7.3 A person breaks into a department store and steals merchandise worth $1,000.

TABLE 3 (Continued)

7.2	A person willingly hides a bank robber.
7.2	A person signs someone else's name to a check and cashes it.
7.1	A person, armed with a lead pipe, robs a victim of $10 The victim is injured and requires treatment by a doctor but it not hospitalized.
6.9	A person beats a victim with his fists The victim requires hospitalization.
6.9	A person breaks into a public recreation center, forces open a cash box, and steals $1,000.
6.9	A factory knowingly gets rid of its waste in a way that pollutes the water supply of a city As a result, 1 person becomes ill but does not require medical treatment.
6.9	A person steals property worth $1,000 from outside a building.
6.8	Because of a victim's race, a person injures a victim to prevent him from enrolling in a public school No medical treatment is required.
6.7	A person, using force, robs a victim of $10 The victim is hurt and requires treatment by a doctor but not hospitalization.
6.6	A person does not have a weapon He threatens to harm a victim unless the victim gives him money The victim gives him $10 and is not harmed.
6.6	A person steals $1,000 worth of merchandise from an unlocked car.
6.5	A person uses heroin.
6.4	An employer refuses to hire a qualified person because of that person's race.
6.4	A person gets customers for a prostitute.
6.3	A person, free on bail for committing a serious crime, purposefully fails to appear in court on the day of his trial.
6.2	An employee embezzles $1,000 from his employer.
6.2	A person beats a victim with his fists The victim requires treatment by a doctor but not hospitalization.
6.1	A person runs a prostitution racket.
6.1	A person cheats on his federal income tax return and avoids paying $10,000 in taxes.
5.7	A theater owner knowingly shows pornographic movies to a minor.
5.5	A person runs a place where liquor is sold without a license.
5.4	A person has some heroin for his own use.
5.4	A real estate agent refuses to sell a house to a person because of that person's race.
5.4	A person threatens to harm a victim unless the victim gives him money The victim gives him $10 and is not harmed.
5.3	A person loans money at an illegally high interest rate.
5.1	A man runs his hands over the body of a female victim, then runs away.
5.1	A person, using force, robs a victim of $10 No physical harm occurs.
5.0	A person knowingly buys stolen property from the person who stole it.
4.9	A person snatches a handbag containing $10 from a victim on the street.
4.7	A man exposes himself in public.
4.6	A person carries a gun illegally.
4.5	A person cheats on his federal income tax return.

Table 3 continued

TABLE 3 (Continued)

4.4	A person steals an unlocked car and later abandons it undamaged.
4.4	A person picks a victim's pocket of $100.
4.4	A person robs a victim The victim is injured but not hospitalized.
4.3	A person breaks into a public recreation center, forces open a cash box, and steals $10.
4.2	A person attempts to break into a home but runs away when a police car approaches.
3.8	A person turns in a false fire alarm.
3.7	A labor union official illegally threatens to organize a strike if an employer hires nonunion workers.
3.6	A person attempts to break into a parked car, but runs away when a police car approaches.
3.6	A person knowingly passes a bad check.
3.6	A person steals property worth $100 from outside a building.
3.5	A person runs a place where he permits gambling to occur illegally.
3.3	A person breaks into a department store, forces open a cash register, and steals $10.
3.3	A person picks a victim's pocket of $10.
3.3	A person attempts to rob a victim but runs away when a police car approaches.
3.2	A person breaks into a building and steals property worth $10.
3.2	An employer illegally threatens to fire employees if they join a labor union.
3.1	A person breaks into a home and steals $100.
3.1	A person forces open a cash register in a department store and steals $10.
3.1	A person breaks into a school and steals $10 worth of supplies.
2.9	A person steals property worth $50 from outside a building.
2.8	A person breaks into a department store and steals merchandise worth $10.
2.4	A person knowingly carries an illegal knife.
2.2	A person trespasses in a city-owned storage lot and steals equipment worth $10.
2.2	A person steals $10 worth of merchandise from the counter of a department store.
2.1	A person is found firing a rifle for which he knows he has no permit.
2.1	A woman engages in prostitution.
1.9	A person makes an obscene phone call.
1.9	An employee embezzles $10 from his employer.
1.9	A store owner knowingly puts "large" eggs into containers marked "extra large."
1.7	A person under 16 years old is drunk in public.
1.7	A person is a customer in a place where he knows gambling occurs illegally.
1.7	A person steals property worth $10 from outside a building.
1.6	A person is a customer in a house of prostitution.
1.6	A male, over 16 years of age, has sexual relations with a willing female under 16.
1.6	A person is a customer in a place where he knows liquor is sold without a license.

TABLE 3 (Continued)

1.6	A person breaks into a parking meter and steals $10 worth of nickels.
1.5	A person takes barbiturates, such as sleeping pills, without a legal prescription.
1.5	A person intentionally shoves or pushes a victim No medical treatment is required.
1.4	A person has some barbiturates, such as sleeping pills, for his own use without a legal prescription.
1.4	A person smokes marijuana.
1.4	A person trespasses in a railroad yard and steals a lantern worth $10.
1.3	A person has some marijuana for his own use.
1.3	Two persons willingly engage in a homosexual act.
1.1	A person disturbs the neighborhood with loud, noisy behavior.
1.1	A person takes bets on the numbers.
1.1	A group continues to hang around a corner after being told to break up by a police officer.
1.1	A person under 16 years old illegally has a bottle of wine.
0.9	A person under 16 years old is reported to police by his parents as an offender because they are unable to control him.
0.8	A person under 16 years old runs away from home.
0.8	A person knowingly trespasses in a railroad yard.
0.8	A person is drunk in public.
0.7	A person under 16 years old breaks a curfew law by being out on the street after the hour permitted by law.
0.6	A person trespasses in the backyard of a private home.
0.5	A person takes part in a dice game in an alley.
0.3	A person is a vagrant That is, he has no home and no visible means of support.
0.2	A person under 16 years old plays hooky from school.

SOURCE: Wolfgang et al. (1985).

man forcibly rapes a woman. Her injuries require hospitalization") is perceived to be more serious than one form of homicide ("A woman stabs her husband. As a result, he dies"). Even a rape without additional injuries is perceived to be quite serious.

Certain drug offenses (e.g., smuggling or selling heroin) are also perceived to be highly serious, with one such offense ("A person runs a narcotics ring") falling within the lower boundary of homicide. Robbery, on the other hand, is a rather unusual crime, covering much of the range of the seriousness scale and crossing the border between violent and nonviolent offenses. A look at the robbery cases in Table 3 indicates that this wide dispersion is attributable to the large variability of robbery with respect to degree of injury, weapon employed, and dollar losses.

As we leave the region of the scale that is exclusively violent, offenses against the person appear only infrequently and are largely limited to simple assaults (see those offenses between 11.3 and 11.9) and less injurious robberies. Burglary (which first appears just below 10.0 on the scale) and other forms of property crime (e.g., larceny, fraud, auto theft, fencing, forgery, picking pockets) abound in the region extending from about 2.0 to 10.0. White-collar and corporate crimes (e.g., embezzlement, price fixing, insurance fraud) are generally scattered among the more serious property crimes. However, one such offense ("A legislator takes a bribe of $10,000 from a company to vote for a law favoring the company") falls within the lower range of violent crimes, and another ("A factory knowingly gets rid of its waste water in a way that pollutes the water supply of a city. As a result, 20 people die") ranks seventh among all 204 offenses. Approaching the bottom of the scale (especially below 2.0), several classes of offenses begin to predominate, including public order offenses (e.g., loitering, public drunkenness, trespassing, disturbing the peace), status offenses (e.g., truancy, curfew violation), victimless offenses (homosexuality, prostitution, illegal gambling), and numerous forms of petty theft.

As the NSCS and other studies (e.g., Rossi et al., 1974) clearly demonstrate, violent crimes are quite literally a class unto themselves when it comes to social judgments of the seriousness of offenses. But apart from their sheer heinousness, violent crimes are also distinctive for another reason. Because they involve a social interaction between two or more parties, violent crimes naturally raise certain sociological questions. First, does the relation between the victim and the offender affect the perceived seriousness of a crime? No study has been specifically designed to answer this question, but the large variety of offense descriptions typically included in seriousness studies provides some evidence for an affirmative answer. In their survey of Baltimore residents, Rossi et al. (1974:227) noted the tendency for "crimes involving persons known to the offender to be regarded as less serious than crimes committed against strangers." For example, whereas "forcible rape of a stranger in a park" ranked thirteenth among all offenses, "forcible rape of a neighbor" ranked twenty-first, and "forcible rape of a former spouse" ranked sixty-second. Similarly, "being beaten up by a stranger" was perceived to be more serious then "being beaten up by someone you know" among Warr and Stafford's (1983) respondents (see Table 1). More recently, Warr (1989) found that the existence of a standing social relationship between the victim and the offender (e.g., wife, classmate, girlfriend, child) reduced the perceived wrongfulness—but not the perceived harmfulness—of criminal acts.

Apart from the relation between the victim and the offender, do other characteristics of the victim or offender (e.g., their age, sex, or occupation) affect seriousness ratings? The evidence on this question is limited, but highly suggestive. Drawing on the NSCS, Wolfgang et al. (1985:30) conclude that the "more vulnerable or weaker the victim is viewed as compared to the offender, the greater the severity of the act." Thus, for example, a man stabbing his wife to death is perceived to be more serious than a wife who does the same to her husband (39.2 versus 27.9). Both offenses, however, are perceived to be less serious than the death of a child at the hands of a parent (47.8).

The notion that judgments of seriousness are affected by the relative vulnerability of the victim is not surprising, particularly in view of the fact that statutory definitions of crimes often consider the victim's vulnerability (e.g., age, sex, and physical or mental handicap) in determining the seriousness (e.g., degree) of the offense and the attendant penalties. However, it remains unclear why stranger offenses should be perceived as more serious than nonstranger offenses. Perhaps individuals typically presume that violence between intimates is more likely to have been provoked than violence between strangers or that violence between intimates is often the outcome of deep and long-standing disputes. Perhaps, as Rossi et al. (1974) note, stranger offenses are simply less "understandable" than violence between intimates.

Much of the seriousness literature has been aimed at assessing the degree of social consensus on the seriousness of crimes. Because legal and social reactions to crimes are so strongly contingent on their seriousness, it is important to determine the extent to which the general public shares similar perceptions of the seriousness of crimes. Evidence from a variety of sources (see especially Rossi et al., 1974; Hamilton and Rytina, 1980; Wolfgang et al., 1985) has consistently indicated a high degree of social consensus on the relative seriousness of crimes. That is, the seriousness ratings assigned to crimes by any one population subgroup (e.g., males, blacks, the young) tend to be highly correlated with those of other subgroups. However, although the ordering of crimes is largely invariant from one group to the next, some differences in the absolute values of seriousness scores have been observed for certain crimes or demographic groups. Summarizing their analysis of the NSCS, Wolfgang et al. (1985:vi) report that "blacks and members of other racial groups in general assign lower scores than whites. Older people found thefts of large amounts to be more serious than people in younger age brackets. Men and women, however, did not differ in any significant way in their overall scoring pattern. As might be expected, victims assign higher scores than nonvictims."

Although these differences appear to undermine the consensus argument, such intergroup differences are generally small and are dwarfed by the differences between crimes. Like most investigators, Wolfgang et al. (1985) strongly concur with the conclusion of Rossi et al. (1974:234-235) that "subgroup characteristics contribute only moderately to the overall ratings of crime seriousness," particularly when "compared to the overarching influence of the . . . crime being rated." Still, some investigators remain unconvinced by the evidence for consensus, arguing that such apparent consensus may be a methodological artifact arising from instructional bias (i.e., the designation of acts as crimes in seriousness questions), the overrepresentation of certain types of offenses (primarily violent crimes) in seriousness studies, or inappropriate statistical measures of consensus (Miethe, 1982; Rossi and Henry, 1980). Others have raised questions about the properties of seriousness scales themselves, including the additivity of offense components, bounding or compression effects produced by categorical scales, and perhaps most important, differences in the meanings that respondents attach to the term "seriousness" (Gottfredson et al., 1980; Wolfgang et al., 1985; Warr, 1989).

PUBLIC OPINION ON CRIMINAL JUSTICE

One of the most revealing methods of obtaining insights into public attitudes toward violence is to examine public opinion on legal sanctions for crimes and criminals. Because legal sanctions have an expressive as well as a utilitarian function, public opinion on legal sanctions can be construed as an expression of social sentiment concerning crime and criminals.

Although it is tempting to characterize public opinion on punishment in simple terms (e.g., as punitive, tolerant, or indifferent), the complexity of legal punishment means that there are numerous facets of public opinion that require attention. First, investigators must consider normative evaluations of punishment, or public opinion as to what legal punishments ought to be. According to the general public, for example, how severe should the punishments be for different offenses? What form(s) of punishment should be administered for any particular offense? How should offenders of different kinds (e.g., habitual offenders, young offenders, retarded offenders) be treated? Second, what are the ethnopenologies, or folk theories of punishment, that guide public choices? Is the general public largely guided by a desire for retribution or by a concern for deterrence, rehabilitation, restitution, or incapacitation? Third, how knowledgeable is the general public when it comes to criminal justice? Do most individuals in our society, for example, have a realistic conception of the certainty of punishment for crimes, or are they aware of the statutory (or actual) penalties for different crimes? Finally, how does the general public appraise the effectiveness of the criminal justice system? Are the police perceived to be effective and, if so, what about the courts or prisons?

Answers to such questions are of course critical for public policy. A society that has lost faith in its courts and police is poised for trouble, as is a society in which social and legal norms of justice are sharply divergent. Moreover, as numerous legal and social scholars have observed, social norms of justice are among the most telling characteristics of cultures. A society that strongly favors execution, for example, is not the same as one that abjures it, and a society that favors public safety over individual liberties is fundamentally different from one that does not.

Normative Evaluations of Punishment

During the past decade, a number of survey studies have appeared in which respondents were asked to report the punishments they preferred for a variety of criminal offenses. Although the methodologies and samples employed in these studies vary widely, they nonetheless concur closely on certain points. First, there appears to be overwhelming support in our society for the principal of proportionality, or the notion that the severity of the punishment must be proportional to the seriousness of the crime. Numerous studies report extremely strong correlations (usually in excess of .9) between the perceived seriousness of crimes and the severity of punishments that individuals assign to those crimes (Blumstein and Cohen, 1980; Hamilton and Rytina, 1980; Warr et al., 1982, 1983; Jacoby and Dunn, 1987; White, 1975). Indeed, so strong is the relation between preferred punishments and perceived seriousness that the two are sometimes regarded as substitutable if not outright identical variables.

Another consistent finding concerns the form of punishment that individuals assign to crimes. Simply put, Americans overwhelmingly regard imprisonment as the appropriate form of punishment for crimes. Although the proportion who prefer imprisonment increases with the seriousness of the crime (Blumstein and Cohen, 1980; Warr et al., 1982), imprisonment is by far the most commonly chosen penalty across crimes. For example, in their report on the National Survey of Punishment for Criminal Offenses, Jacoby and Dunn (1987:1-2) state that "respondents overwhelmingly supported the use of imprisonment as the most appropriate punishment for criminal offenses. Over all offense types, 71 percent of respondents said the appropriate punishment included prison. Other types of punishments (probation, a fine, or restitution) were most often combined with imprisonment, rather than being substitutes for imprisonment." Similar findings come from Warr et al. (1982), and Blumstein and Cohen (1980). It seems clear, then, that the Enlightenment conception of imprisonment as a general or "all-purpose" form of punishment continues to hold sway among the U.S. public.

Data on publicly preferred penalties for crimes naturally invite comparisons between public preferences and actual penalties (i.e., those sentences that are stipulated in statutes, imposed by judges and juries, or actually served by offenders). The evidence on this matter is not extensive, but it is consistent. Blumstein and Cohen (1980) compared the average prison sentences preferred by a sample of residents from Allegheny County (which includes Pittsburgh) with the average sentences actually served by state prison inmates. The preferred prison sentences for most crimes were substantially longer than the actual time served for those crimes, with ratios (preferred/actual) generally on the order of 2:1. The largest discrepancies between preferred and actual penalties occurred for violent offenses, narcotics offenses, and drunk driving, and the ratios of preferred to actual sentences were significantly larger for repeat offenders (typically 2-4:1) than for first-time offenders. Quite similar results were obtained in the National Punishment Survey (Jacoby and Dunn, 1987), where the prison sentences preferred by a national sample were compared with the average times served in 13 states. Across crimes, the average sentences preferred by respondents exceeded actual time served by ratios ranging from approximately 2:1 to 6:1, with the largest ratios again occurring for violent crimes and drug offenses.

It is possible, of course, that the longer sentences desired by the general public stem from knowledge that offenders frequently serve only a portion of their full sentence. However, at least in the Blumstein and Cohen (1980:229) study, this does not appear to be the case, because respondents were specifically instructed that the sentence they selected was to be "the actual amount of time you want the convicted offender to spend in prison."

Although there are marked differences between public preferences with respect to prison sentences and the actual time served by offenders, the same is not necessarily true when it comes to statutory punishments or the sentences imposed by judges. Blumstein and Cohen (1980) report considerably greater congruence between preferred prison sentences and those imposed by judges in Pennsylvania. Warr et al. (1982) found that the median prison sentences selected by samples of four Arizona cities were typically below the statutory maxima, although this occurred in part because the statutory maxima include life for a rather large number of offenses in Arizona.

VICTIM, OFFENDER, AND RESPONDENT CHARACTERISTICS

If the perceived seriousness of offenses is the major determinant of preferred punishments, there is evidence that individuals also attend to characteristics of the offender and victim in deciding on appropriate punishments for crimes. The punishments recommended for juveniles are consistently lower than those for adults (Warr et al., 1982, 1983; Jacoby and Dunn, 1987), although elderly offenders are treated with somewhat greater lenience than other adults (Jacoby and Dunn, 1987). Male offenders are given more severe sentences than females (Jacoby and Dunn, 1987), and repeat offenders are treated more harshly than first-time offenders (Blumstein and Cohen, 1980; Jacoby and Dunn, 1987). The most severe penalties are also reserved for crimes in which the victim is very young or very old, and in which the victim is female (Jacoby and Dunn, 1987).

In addition to features of the victim and offender, respondent characteristics influence the severity of preferred punishments. Sanction severity increases with the age of the respondent and declines with educational attainment. Whites tend to assign more severe sanctions than blacks (particularly when it comes to the death penalty; see Vidmar and Ellsworth, 1982), and there is limited evidence that males desire more severe sanctions than females, although not for all offenses (see Jacoby and Dunn, 1987; Vidmar and Ellsworth, 1982; Blumstein and Cohen, 1980; Thomas et al., 1976).

Although the punishments desired by the general public are affected by characteristics of the offender, victim, and respondent, it is important not to lose sight of the fact that such variables have rather modest effects when compared to the seriousness of the act. A homicide committed by a young female first offender is still a homicide, and although features of the victim, offender, or evaluator will influence the absolute severity of recommended sanctions, they are unlikely to change the order of offenses with respect to sanction severity (see especially Blumstein and Cohen, 1980; Thomas et al., 1976).

ETHNOPENOLOGIES

When Americans decide on appropriate punishments for offenses, what theories of punishment do they rely on? As we have seen, there appears to be wide social consensus on the principle of proportionality between offense seriousness and sanction severity. Because the principle of proportionality is a central tenet of retributive theories of punishment, this would seem to indicate that the general public is guided by a desire for retribution or just deserts, and some investigators concur with that conclusion (Hamilton and Rytina, 1980; Blumstein and Cohen, 1980). That conclusion has been strongly questioned, however, on the grounds that the principle of proportionality is not unique to retributive theories of punishment and because individuals may invoke seriousness in judging appropriate punishments for reasons having nothing to do with retribution (Warr, 1981; but see Hamilton and Rytina, 1981).

A less inferential method for measuring public theories of punishment is to question individuals directly about their reasons or justifications for punishment. For example, Warr and Stafford (1984) asked a sample of Seattle residents to choose the most important reason for imprisonment from among a list of phrases describing the major theories or justifications of punishment. Retribution was the single most common justification of punishment (42%), followed by incapacitation (20%), rehabilitation (17%), specific (9%) and general (7%) deterrence, and normative validation (5%). This "direct" method has been employed in other studies as well (e.g., Jacoby and Dunn, 1987), but wide variation in question wording and in the choice of theories and crimes (see Vidmar and Ellsworth, 1982; Warr and Stafford, 1984) makes it difficult to reach any general conclusions. One conclusion that does appear to be warranted, however, is that there is no single dominant ideology of punishment among the U.S. public. When asked, individuals commonly invoke or support more than one theory of punishment, and no one theory appears to dominate public thinking about punishment.

PUBLIC CONFIDENCE IN THE CRIMINAL JUSTICE SYSTEM

How do Americans rate the performance of their criminal justice system? One indication comes from responses to a survey question that has been routinely included in the General Social Survey: In general, do you think the courts in this area deal too harshly or not harshly enough with criminals? Responses to this question have been remarkably consistent and uniformly negative in recent years. From 1975 to 1987, the proportion responding "not harshly enough" has fallen within a narrow band, from 79 to 86 percent. As we might deduce from these numbers, there is a great deal of consensus across subgroups of the population. Although younger persons and minority members are less negative in their evaluation of the courts, the differences are quite small, typically no more than 5-10 percent (see Flanagan and Jamieson, 1988). The GSS question does not probe respondents about their sources of dissatisfaction with the courts, but it is reasonable to surmise from our earlier discussion that the principal source of dissatisfaction lies with the sentences meted out to offenders.

If Americans appear to have little confidence in the courts, the same is not true when it comes to the police. Survey evidence consistently indicates that Americans tend to hold favorable attitudes toward the police. In four Gallup surveys conducted between 1977 and 1985, no less than 85 percent of respondents rated the "honesty and ethical standards" of policemen as "average" to "very high" (Gallup, 1985). In a 1986 Media General/Associated Press poll, 59 percent of respondents rated the performance of the police in their community as "good," whereas 31 percent rated it "fair" and 8 percent "poor" (Flanagan and Jamieson, 1988). Such favorable performance evaluations are also typical among those who have had reason to call the police. Data from a 1982 national survey conducted for ABC News show that, of the 35 percent of respondents who had called the police during the prior year, 72 percent reported that the police had responded within "a short time" (McGarrell and Flanagan, 1985). In the same survey, majorities of respondents said that they had a "great deal" or a "good amount" of confidence in the ability of the police to prevent (61%) or to solve crimes (60%).

Although public confidence in the police appears to be quite strong, it is not universal. Blacks (and according to some measures, younger persons) are substantially less likely than whites to hold favorable evaluations of the police (see Walker, 1983). For example, whereas 60 percent of whites in the 1986 Media General/Associated Press poll rated the performance of local police as "good," only 39 percent of blacks offered that evaluation. Although most Americans express confidence in the police, such expressions may have more to do with a sense of gratitude toward or dependency on the police than with an objective assessment of their performance (e.g., Reiss, 1967).

FUTURE RESEARCH

As we have seen in this paper, the state of knowledge on public perceptions and reactions to violence has improved substantially during the past two decades. Although this trend is certainly encouraging, a good deal of both descriptive and analytical work remains to be done.

FEAR OF VICTIMIZATION

Many of the most important unresolved questions concerning fear of victimization are questions of process, meaning that they pertain to the sequence, timing, or duration of events. For example, as a consequence of fear, individuals commonly take steps to reduce their risk, steps that may have the effect of reducing or eliminating the fear that initially provoked them. (Indeed, it may be that people commonly "manage" their fear by taking those steps necessary to reduce it to acceptable levels.) If the adoption of avoidance/precautionary measures is typically followed by a reduction in fear, then conventional cross-sectional measurements of fear may seriously misrepresent the nature of fear in a population. Although such measures may accurately capture instantaneous levels of fear, they overlook the *history* of fear among members of that population. There is a pressing need, then, for longitudinal data to establish the sequential relations between fear and precautionary/avoidance behaviors. In the meantime, cross-sectional measurements of the prevalence of fear might prove to be much more informative if they were to express the proportion of the population "ever afraid" (or, perhaps, afraid during the past six months) as well as the proportion currently afraid.

Longitudinal data would also permit answers to questions concerning the duration of fear or anxiety. For example, in the wake of a frightening event (e.g., a violent attack by a spouse), what is the natural rate (i.e., absent any intervention by the victim or others) at which fear diminishes or decays? How does this rate differ for events of different types (e.g., a rape versus a robbery) and for victims of different types (e.g., males versus females)?

Answers to such questions might help to clarify the rather conflicting state of evidence concerning the relation between fear of victimization and prior victimization. Most studies on this topic report the correlation between current fear and prior victimization without controlling for the time elapsed since victimization or for the nature of the victimization. By failing to hold constant the interval since victimization, such a procedure is bound to capture the natural history of fear at different points in time among respondents.

Perhaps the most daunting task facing investigators is documenting the nature and consequences of what might be called victimization careers. In all likelihood, individuals in a population such as ours experience an enormous variety of patterns of victimization (both direct and indirect) during their life course. Even in the unlikely event that two persons were to experience the same number and types of victimization events, those events would likely differ in the order in which they occurred, the intervals between them, the density or rate of events during a given interval of time, or the ages at which the victims experienced the events. Sorting out such patterns of victimization and establishing their individual and social consequences will require concerted research on *victimization careers*, much in the same way that criminal careers became a major focus of criminological research during the 1980s.

Some additional questions concerning reactions to fear also need to be answered. First, how and why do individuals differ in the avoidance or precautionary measures they undertake? For example, do the size and the composition of households affect their responses to fear? Do lifestyle characteristics (e.g., amount of time spent away from home or amount of time spent with companions) affect such responses? How is the use of security precautions affected by their cost, perceived effectiveness, and the ease with which they can be adopted? Aside from individuals or households, research is also needed on the consequences of fear for businesses, including the reactions of commercial establishments to ostensibly dangerous environments. To what extent does spatial avoidance affect the livelihoods of retail businesses? Are the location and relocation decisions of businesses frequently affected by the reputations of areas and, if so, do such decisions stem from concern about the added costs of security, the danger to employees, or the potential lack of customers? Is the social designation of certain places as "dangerous" areas ultimately a self-fulfilling prophecy? That is, by driving out businesses and curtailing normal forms of social intercourse (shopping, pedestrian traffic), might not such reputations cause or prolong the problems they imply?

Although the focus of this paper has been on fear of victimization among the general public, it would be of interest to examine fear within special populations, such as prison populations; those in mental institutions; or active, violent offenders in the free world. Such data are generally unavailable, with one notable exception. In a multistate survey of imprisoned felons, Wright and Rossi (1986:138) found that the reasons given by felons for purchasing and carrying firearms had less to do with committing crimes than with protecting themselves from the dangerous persons who inhabit their everyday world.

> All the evidence we have assembled, therefore, points to the same conclusion, namely, that gun criminals carried guns at least as much to protect themselves against the uncertainties of their environment as to prey upon the larger population. That these men inhabit a violent and hostile world is easy to demonstrate. Over 70% of them had been involved in assaults; over 50% had gotten into bar fights; about 40% had been stabbed with a knife; 52% reported having been shot at with a gun. . . .

Even when it came to committing crimes, felons reported that a principal purpose of using a firearm was to protect themselves from injury by victims. Judging from Wright and Rossi's work, then, fear of victimization is not limited to the law-abiding segment of the population and, in a strangely ironic twist, may actually be more common or intense among those who employ violence as an occupational tool.

As noted at the outset of this paper, one form of fear that merits special attention is fear for others, or what might be called altruistic (as opposed to egoistic, or personal) fear. Perhaps no aspect of fear deserves more immediate attention than altruistic fear. One reason is that many of the behaviors that investigators commonly construe to be self-protective may in fact be primarily intended to protect others. Home security precautions are an obvious example (as is participation in neighborhood programs), but virtually any avoidance or precautionary behavior may have the intent or effect of protecting significant others. Another reason, noted earlier, is that the consequences of altruistic fear may be quite distinct from those of egoistic fear. The latter, after all, encompasses but a single individual, whereas altruistic fear may extend to a substantial number of persons and, consequently, may provoke more determined and perhaps more extreme safety precautions. Furthermore, although we may surmise that many adults feel some confidence in their ability to protect their own security, it is probably true that they feel considerably less capable of protecting the safety of others, particularly those, such as children, who cannot readily protect themselves. Also, if one social consequence of fear is a loss of confidence in social institutions, then it is entirely possible that concern about the safety of loved ones may do more to erode such confidence than fear for oneself.

Finally, there is a compelling need for routine, nationwide measurements of fear in the United States. Such measurements should be obtained by using survey questions that (1) measure offense-specific fear; (2) capture the magnitude or intensity as well as the prevalence of fear; (3) cover the full range of contexts (e.g., home, work, commuting, shopping) in which fear is experienced; (4) contain both current and retrospective measures of fear; and (5) measure both personal fear and altruistic fear (i.e., by asking respondents to identify the persons—spouse, children—for whom they are afraid and the intensity of fear that they feel for each individual). Such data could be collected on an annual basis in the United States through a supplement to the National Crime Survey. Because fear is not a rare phenomenon (like some forms of victimization), the full NCS sample is not needed; the supplement could be administered to a small subset (perhaps 5%) of the NCS sample each year.

OTHER ISSUES

As we have seen in this paper, Americans are routinely exposed to numerous communications about violence, both through the mass media and through social networks. At present, however, little is known about how these two sources of information differ in their content, frequency, credibility, and consequences. Although it seems likely that people commonly receive information through both channels, investigators have typically focused on one source while ignoring the other. Consequently, there is a need for research that examines *all* of the messages that individuals receive about violence, as well as the ways in which such messages supplement, contradict, or override one another. In addition to media and interpersonal messages about violence, such research must also consider the environmental cues to danger that people encounter in their everyday lives. Exploratory work by the author points to a rather large variety of cues that evoke fear (e.g., liquor stores, litter and garbage, graffiti, abandoned buildings), but beyond merely identifying such cues, several questions about them need to be answered. Is there a general social consensus on the meaning of such cues, or does their meaning vary from one subgroup of the population (e.g, urban residents, victims, males) to the next? Are some cues to danger offense-specific (suggesting a particular offense such as rape or robbery), whereas others are general (nonspecific) signs of danger? How is exposure to such cues distributed in the general population, and can individuals become habituated to such cues?

Another topic that merits more attention is the perceived seriousness of offenses. Perhaps the most striking deficiency in seriousness research is the absence of longitudinal data on judgments of seriousness. In recent years a number of social movements or public campaigns have arisen for the purpose of altering public opinion about certain offenses, including child abuse, drunk driving, rape, spouse abuse, white-collar crime, and drug use (e.g., Rose, 1977; Pfohl, 1977; Ferraro, 1989). For example, one of the principal goals of the women's movement during the past two decades has been to clearly establish rape as a violent crime, and groups such as MADD (Mothers Against Drunk Driving) have sought to increase the perceived seriousness of driving while intoxicated. Yet it is impossible to assess the effects of such movements on public opinion without longitudinal data on the perceived seriousness of crimes. To date, the only longitudinal study is that of Cullen et al. (1982), who found evidence of substantial increases in the seriousness ranking of white-collar crimes during the 1970s.

A second question concerning seriousness is more fundamental. That is, what *is* the perceived seriousness of offenses? When individuals rate the seriousness of an act, what property or attribute of the act are they in fact evaluating? Some investigators equate judgments of seriousness with normative (i.e., moral) evaluations of acts (Rossi et al., 1974), whereas others take them to be factual assessments of the harm or damage suffered by the victim (Wolfgang et al., 1985). Recent evidence indicates that the general public distinguishes between the wrongfulness and the harmfulness of offenses, and that certain classes of crime (e.g., property crime) are perceived to be more wrong than harmful, whereas others (e.g., public order offenses) are perceived to be more harmful than wrong (Warr, 1989). The distinction between wrongfulness and harmfulness may be critical in answering certain questions about the seriousness of crimes. To illustrate, does the general public consider *mens rea* (criminal intent) in evaluating the seriousness of a crime? It is reasonable to suppose that criminal intent has little effect on the perceived harmfulness of an offense (an accidental homicide, for example, is still a homicide), but a good deal to do with moral evaluations of crimes. Similarly, the distinction between wrongfulness and harmfulness may prove critical in assessing the effect of such variables as victim vulnerability and victim/offender relations.

Although there is a good deal of research on both public preferences with regard to criminal penalties and public evaluations of the criminal justice system, there is no comparable body of research on public *knowledge* of the criminal justice system. What little research exists suggests that the American public is largely ignorant of the statutory punishments for crimes and has a limited understanding of the legal elements that constitute or differentiate criminal acts (Gibbs and Erickson, 1979; Williams et al., 1980). Further research in this area is sorely needed, for at least two reasons. First, to the extent that legal punishments serve the purpose of general deterrence, their deterrent effects cannot be realized if the general public is unaware or misinformed about such punishments. A legislature that imposes a five-year minimum mandatory sentence for armed robbery, for example, can scarcely hope for a deterrent effect if the public is unaware of this change. Second, public evaluations of the criminal justice system must be interpreted in light of public knowledge of that system. Public demand for longer prisons sentences, for example, is far more compelling if the public is aware of the costs of imprisonment and is not seriously misinformed about current sentencing practices.

NOTE

1   Some of the research reported in this paper was prepared exclusively for the panel and has not been previously published. The data come from surveys of Seattle and Dallas conducted by the author and described in Warr (1984, 1989, 1990) and related papers.

REFERENCES

Baumer, T.L.
   1978   Research on fear of crime in the United States. *Victimology* 3 (3-4):254-264.
Bennett, S.F., and P.J. Lavrakas
   1989   Community-based crime prevention: An assessment of the

Eisenhower Foundation's neighborhood program. *Crime and Delinquency* 35:345-364.

Biderman, A., L. Johnson, J. McIntyre, and A. Weir
 1967 *Report on a Pilot Study in the District of Columbia on Victimization and Attitudes Toward Law Enforcement.* Field Surveys I of the President's Commission on Law Enforcement and Administration of Justice. Washington, D.C.: U.S. Government Printing Office.

Blumstein, A., and J. Cohen
 1980 Sentencing convicted offenders: An analysis of the public's view. *Law and Society Review* 14:223-261.

Brown, R.M.
 1979 The American vigilante tradition. Pp. 153-185 in H.D. Graham and T.R. Gurr, eds., *Violence in America: Historical and Comparative Perspectives.* Beverly Hills, Calif.: Sage Publications.

Clemente, F., and M. Kleiman
 1977 Fear of crime in the United States: A multivariate analysis. *Social Forces* 56:519-531.

Cohen, M.A.
 1988 Some new evidence on the seriousness of crime. *Criminology* 26:343-352.

Conklin, J.E.
 1975 *The Impact of Crime.* New York: Macmillan.

Cullen, F.T., B.G. Link, and C.W. Polanzi
 1982 The seriousness of crime revisited: Have attitudes toward white-collar crime changed? *Criminology* 20:83-102.

Dominick, J.R.
 1973 Crime and law enforcement on prime time television. *Public Opinion Quarterly* 37:241-250.
 1978 Crime and law enforcement in the mass media. Pp. 105-128 in C. Winick, ed., *Deviance and Mass Media.* Beverly Hills, Calif.: Sage Publications.

DuBow, F., E. McCabe, and G. Kaplan.
 1979 *Reactions to Crime: A Critical Review of the Literature.* Washington, D.C.: U.S. Government Printing Office.

Durkheim, E.
 1933 *The Division of Labor in Society.* Translated by G. Simpson. New York: Free Press.

Elias, R.
 1986 *The Politics of Victimization: Victims, Victimology, and Human Rights.* New York: Oxford University Press.

Erickson, M.L., and J.P. Gibbs
 1979 Community tolerance and measures of delinquency. *Journal of Research in Crime and Delinquency* 17:55-79.

Erickson, M.L., J.P. Gibbs, and G.F. Jensen
 1977 The deterrence doctrine and the perceived certainty of legal punishments. *American Sociological Review* 42:305-317.

Ericson, R.V., P.M. Baranek, and J.B.L. Chan
  1987 *Visualizing Deviance: A Study of News Organization.* Toronto: University of Toronto Press.
Federal Bureau of Investigation
  1993 *Uniform Crime Reports—1992.* Washington, D.C.: U.S. Government Printing Office.
Ferraro, K.J.
  1989 Policing woman battering. *Social Problems* 36:61-74.
Ferraro, K.F., and R. LaGrange
  1987 The measurement of fear of crime. *Sociological Inquiry* 57:70-101.
Fishman, M.
  1978 Crime waves as ideology. *Social Problems* 25:531-543.
  1981 Police news: Constructing an image of crime. *Urban Life* 9:371-394.
Flanagan, T.J., and K.M. Jamieson
  1988 *Sourcebook of Criminal Justice Statistics—1987.* Bureau of Justice Statistics. Washington, D.C.: U.S. Department of Justice.
Fletcher, G.P.
  1988 *A Crime of Self-Defense: Bernhard Goetz and the Law on Trial.* New York: Free Press.
Gallup, G.
  1983 *The Gallup Report, Report No. 210.* Princeton, N.J.: The Gallup Poll.
  1985 *The Gallup Report, Report No. 239.* Princeton, N.J.: The Gallup Poll.
Garofalo, J.
  1977 *Public Opinion About Crime: The Attitudes of Victims and Nonvictims in Selected Cities.* Law Enforcement Assistance Administration. Washington, D.C.: U.S. Department of Justice.
Garofalo, J., and M. McLeod
  1989 The structure and operation of neighborhood watch programs in the United States. *Crime and Delinquency* 35:326-344.
Gibbs, J.P., and M.L. Erickson.
  1979 Conceptions of criminal and delinquent acts. *Deviant Behavior* 1:71-100.
Godbey, G., A. Patterson, and L. Brown
  1979 *The Relationship of Crime and Fear of Crime Among the Aged to Leisure Behavior and Use of Public Leisure Services.* Washington, D.C.: Andrus Foundation.
Gordon, M., and L. Heath.
  1981 The news business, crime, and fear. Pp. 227-250 in D.A. Lewis, ed., *Reactions to Crime.* Beverly Hills, Calif.: Sage Publications.
Gottfredson, S.D., K.L. Young, and W.S. Laufer
  1980 Additivity and interactions in offense seriousness scales. *Journal of Research in Crime and Delinquency* 17:26-41.

Graber, D.A.
  1980 *Crime News and the Public.* New York: Praeger.
Gubrium, J.F.
  1974 Victimization in old age: Available evidence and three hypotheses. *Crime and Delinquency* 20:245-250.
Hamilton, V.L., and S. Rytina
  1980 Social consensus on norms of justice: Should the punishment fit the crime? *American Journal of Sociology* 85:1117-1144.
  1981 On philosophical distinctions and observed judgements. *American Journal of Sociology* 87:435-437.
Heath, L.
  1984 Impact of newspaper crime reports on fear of crime: A multimethodological investigation. *Journal of Personality and Social Psychology* 47(2):263-276.
Hindelang, M.J., M.R. Gottfredson, and J. Garofalo
  1978 *Victims of Personal Crime: An Empirical Foundation for a Theory of Personal Victimization.* Cambridge, Mass.: Ballinger.
Holahan, C.J
  1982 *Environmental Psychology.* Englewood Cliffs, N.J.: Prentice Hall.
Inter-University Consortium for Political and Social Research
  1982 ABC News Poll of Public Opinion on Crime, December 1982. Inter-University Consortium for Political and Social Research, University of Michigan.
Jacoby, J.E., and C.S. Dunn
  1987 National Survey on Punishment for Criminal Offenses: Executive Summary. Paper prepared for the National Conference on Punishment for Criminal Offenses, Ann Arbor, Michigan.
Jamieson, K.M, and T.J. Flanagan
  1989 *Sourcebook of Criminal Justice Statistics—1988.* Bureau of Justice Statistics. Washington, D.C.: U.S. Department of Justice.
Klecka, W.R., and G.F. Bishop
  1978 *Neighborhood Profiles of Senior Citizens in Four American Cities: A Report of Findings to the National Council of Senior Citizens.* Washington, D.C.: National Council of Senior Citizens.
LeJeune, R., and N. Alex
  1973 On being mugged: The event and its aftermath. *Urban Life and Culture* 2:259-287.
Ley, D.
  1974 *The Black Inner City as Frontier Outpost.* Washington, D.C.: Association of American Geographers.
Lichter, L.S., and S.R. Lichter
  1983 *Prime Time Crime.* Washington, D.C.: The Media Institute.
Lurigio, A.J., and D.P. Rosenbaum
  1986 Evaluation research in community crime prevention: A critical look at the field. Pp. 19-44 in D.P. Rosenbaum, ed., *Commu-*

nity Crime Prevention: Does It Work? Beverly Hills, Calif.: Sage Publications.

Mayes, A.
1979 The physiology of fear and anxiety. Pp. 24-55 in W. Sluckin, ed., *Fear in Animals and Man.* New York: Van Nostrand Reinhold.

McDowall, D., and C. Loftin
1983 Collective security and the demand for legal handguns. *American Journal of Sociology* 88:1146-1161.

McGarrell, E.F, and T.J. Flanagan
1985 *Sourcebook of Criminal Justice Statistics—1984.* Bureau of Justice Statistics. Washington, D.C.: U.S. Department of Justice.

Miethe, T.D.
1982 Public consensus on crime seriousness: Normative structure or methodological artifact? *Criminology* 20:515-526.

National Institute of Education
1978 *Violent Schools—Safe Schools: The Safe School Study Report to the Congress,* Vol. I. Washington, D.C.: National Institute of Education.

National Opinion Research Center
1988 *General Social Surveys, 1972-1987: Cumulative Codebook.* Chicago: National Opinion Research Center.

Pfohl, S.J.
1977 The "discovery" of child abuse. *Social Problems* 24:310-323.

President's Commission on Law Enforcement and Administration of Justice
1967 *The Challenge of Crime in a Free Society.* Washington, D.C.: U.S. Government Printing Office.

Pyle, G.F.
1980 Systematic sociospatial variation in perceptions of crime location and severity. Pp. 219-45 in D.E. Georges-Abeyie and K.D. Harris, eds., *Crime: A Spatial Perspective.* New York: Columbia University Press.

Quinney, R.
1970 *The Social Reality of Crime.* Boston: Little, Brown.

Reiss, A.J.
1967 *Studies in Crime and Law Enforcement in Major Metropolitan Areas.* Field Surveys III, Part 1, of the President's Commission on Law Enforcement and Administration of Justice. Washington, D.C.: U.S. Government Printing Office.

Research and Forecasts
1980 *The Figgie Report on Fear of Crime, Part 1: The General Public.* Willoughby, Ohio: ATO, Inc.

Rose, V.M.
1977 Rape as a social problem: A byproduct of the feminist movement. *Social Problems* 25:75-89.

Rosenbaum, D.P.
1986 *Community Crime Prevention: Does it Work?* Beverly Hills, Calif.: Sage Publications.

1988 Community crime prevention: A review and synthesis of the literature. *Justice Quarterly* 5:323-395.

Roshier, B.
1973 The selection of crime news by the press. Pp. 28-39 in S. Cohen and J. Young, eds., *The Manufacture of News.* Beverly Hills, Calif.: Sage Publications.

Rossi, P.H., and J.P. Henry
1980 Seriousness: A measure for all purposes? Pp. 489-405 in M. Klein and J. Teilman, eds., *Handbook of Criminal Justice Evaluation.* Beverly Hills, Calif.: Sage Publications.

Rossi, P.H., E. Waite, C.E. Bose, and R.E. Berk
1974 The seriousness of crimes: Normative structure and individual differences. *American Sociological Review* 39:224-247.

Savitz, L.D., M. Lalli, and L. Rosen
1977 *City Life and Delinquency—Victimization, Fear of Crime and Gang Membership.* Washington, D.C.: U.S. Department of Justice.

Sheley, J.S., and C.D. Ashkins
1981 Crime, crime news, and crime views. *Public Opinion Quarterly* 45:492-506.

Sherizen, S.
1978 Social creation of crime news: All the news fitted to print. Pp. 203-224 in C. Winick, ed., *Deviance and Mass Media.* Beverly Hills, Calif.: Sage Publications.

Silberman, C.E.
1980 *Criminal Violence, Criminal Justice.* New York: Vintage Books.

Skogan, W.G.
1977 Public policy and fear of crime in large American cities. Pp. 1-18 in J.A. Gardiner, ed., *Public Law and Public Policy.* New York: Praeger.
1981 On attitudes and behaviors. Pp. 19-45 in D.A. Lewis, ed., *Reactions to Crime.* Beverly Hills, Calif.: Sage Publications.
1984 Reporting crimes to the police: The status of world research. *Journal of Research in Crime and Delinquency* 21:113-137.

Skogan, W.G., and M.G. Maxfield
1981 *Coping with Crime: Individual and Neighborhood Reactions.* Beverly Hills, Calif.: Sage Publications.

Sluckin, W.
1979 *Fear in Animals and Man.* New York: Van Nostrand Reinhold.

Smith, C.J., and G.E. Patterson
1980 Cognitive mapping and the subjective geography of crime. Pp. 205-218 in D.E. Georges-Abeyie and K.D. Harris, eds., *Crime: A Spatial Perspective.* New York: Columbia University Press.

Smith, D.A., and C.D. Uchida
1988 The social organization of self-help: A study of defensive weapon ownership. *American Sociological Review* 53:94-102.

Stafford, M.C., and O.R. Galle
  1984   Victimization rates, exposure to risk, and fear of crime. *Criminology* 22:173-185.
Taub, R.P., D.G Taylor, and J.D. Dunham
  1984   *Paths of Neighborhood Change: Race and Crime in Urban America.* Chicago: University of Chicago Press.
Thomas, C.W., R.J. Cage, and S.C. Foster
  1976   Public opinion on criminal law and legal sanctions: An examination of two conceptual models. *Journal of Criminal Law and Criminology* 67:110-116.
Thomson, R.
  1979   The concept of fear. Pp. 1-23 in W. Sluckin, ed., *Fear in Animals and Man.* New York: Van Nostrand Reinhold.
U.S. Department of Justice, Bureau of Justice Statistics
  1987   *National Crime Surveys: Victim Risk Supplement, 1983.* Washington, D.C.: U.S. Department of Justice.
  1992   *Criminal Victimization in the United States.* Washington, D.C.: U.S. Department of Justice.
Vidmar, N., and P.C. Ellsworth.
  1982   Research on attitudes toward capital punishment. Pp. 68-84 in H.A. Bedau, ed., *The Death Penalty in America.* Oxford: Oxford University Press.
Walker, S.
  1983   *The Police in America.* New York: McGraw-Hill.
Warr, M.
  1980   The accuracy of public beliefs about crime. *Social Forces* 59:456-470.
  1981   Which norms of justice? A commentary on Hamilton and Rytina. *American Journal of Sociology* 85:433-435.
  1984   Fear of victimization: Why are women and the elderly more afraid? *Social Science Quarterly* 65:681-702.
  1985   Fear of rape among urban women. *Social Problems* 32:238-250.
  1987   Fear of victimization and sensitivity to risk. *Journal of Quantitative Criminology* 3:29-46.
  1988   The Hierarchy of Fear: A Comparison of Two Cities. Unpublished manuscript, Department of Sociology, University of Texas, Austin.
  1989   What is the perceived seriousness of crimes? *Criminology* 27:795-821.
  1990   Dangerous situations: Social context and fear of victimization. *Social Forces* 68:891-907.
  1993   Fear of victimization. *The Public Perspective* 5(1):25-28.
Warr, M., and M.C. Stafford
  1983   Fear of victimization: A look at the proximate causes. *Social Forces* 61:1033-1043.
  1984   Public goals of punishment and support for the death penalty. *Journal of Research in Crime and Delinquency* 21:95-111.

Warr, M., J.P. Gibbs, and M.L. Erickson
  1982 Contending theories of criminal law: Statutory penalties versus public preferences. *Journal of Research in Crime and Delinquency* 19:25-46.
Warr, M., R.F. Meier, and M.L. Erickson
  1983 Norms, theories of punishment, and publicly preferred penalties for crimes. *Sociological Quarterly* 24:75-91.
White, G.F.
  1975 Public responses to hypothetical crimes: Effect of offender status and seriousness of the offense on punitive reactions. *Social Forces* 53:411-419.
Williams, K.R., J.P. Gibbs, and M.L. Erickson
  1980 Public knowledge of statutory penalties: The extent and basis of accurate perception. *Pacific Sociological Review* 23:105-128.
Wolfgang, M.E., R.M. Figlio, P.E. Tracy, and S.I. Singer
  1985 *The National Survey of Crime Severity*. Washington, D.C.: U.S. Government Printing Office.
Wright, J.D., and P.H. Rossi
  1986 *Armed and Considered Dangerous*. New York: Aldine.
Wright, J.D., P.H Rossi, and K. Daly
  1983 *Under the Gun: Weapons, Crime, and Violence in America*. New York: Aldine.

The Costs and Consequences of Violent Behavior in the United States

Mark A. Cohen, Ted R. Miller and Shelli B. Rossman

INTRODUCTION

The purpose of this paper is twofold: first, to set forth a comprehensive theoretical framework in which to evaluate the consequences and costs of violent behavior, and second, to review and update existing estimates of the cost of victimization. At first glance, it might seem that enumerating the consequences of violent behavior is a straightforward task. Take the highly publicized murder of Carol Stuart (whose husband, Chuck, was later found to have been the murderer) and her unborn child in Boston.[1] The direct consequences are obvious—two deaths and enumerable medical costs associated with the interim treatment of both victims. However, many indirect consequences of this murder are not so obvious.

Carol Stuart's family and friends suffered a loss. More than 800 mourners attended her funeral. Aside from the time spent away from work or other activities, some of the mourners no doubt suffered at least transitory psychological injury. It is possible that a close relative suffered post-traumatic stress disorder,

Mark Cohen is at the Owen Graduate School of Management, Vanderbilt University, and Ted Miller is at the National Public Services Research Institute, and Shelli Rossman is at the Urban Institute.

resulting in sleepless nights, withdrawal from social activities, psychological counseling, or even long-term therapy.

Chuck Stuart collected several hundred thousand dollars in life insurance. The insurance companies incurred administrative expenses associated with paying out this money and ultimately attempting to retrieve it after the full story became known.

A massive police investigation followed the murder after Chuck Stuart reported that a black gunman in a jogging suit had attacked their car at a busy intersection. Aside from the cost of employing police officers and other related expenses, it was reported that as many as 150 black men were stopped and frisked every day. Each of those men likely suffered from fear and deprivation of freedom. Other black men who were not stopped by police also suffered from fear under the threat that they too would be detained. Some commuters who normally drove through the area took longer detours or otherwise avoided the neighborhood because of the perceived increase in the risk of victimization. This may have hurt local businesses who otherwise benefited from sales to these commuters. Others who lived in or near the neighborhood might also have taken extra precautions such as staying home at night or buying security systems. Even more subtle and difficult to measure in this particular case is the increased racial tension precipitated by media coverage and apparently illegal police tactics of searching potential suspects.

The police ultimately arrested William Bennett, who was identified in a police lineup by Chuck Stuart. Although a formal indictment was never made (because Stuart's brother went to the police with information implicating Chuck Stuart as the murderer), William Bennett also was a victim of this case, as was his family. Had he been tried or falsely convicted of murder, he would have endured additional costs such as loss of freedom. Further, the government would have incurred the cost of incarceration itself. Had Chuck Stuart (who ultimately committed suicide) lived to be charged with the murders, there would have been additional criminal justice-related costs.

As difficult as it is, the task of enumerating the consequences of violent behavior is considerably easier than attempting to quantify (and monetize) the magnitude of these consequences. Although some costs (such as direct medical expenses) are relatively easy to estimate, others are virtually impossible (such as deprivation of freedom). In between these two extremes, there is a growing economics literature that attempts to place monetary values on pain, suffering, injuries, and death. This paper brings together many disparate sources of information concerning the magnitude of the costs and the consequences of victimization; it also provides a few new and updated estimates.

The empirical side of this paper focuses on the long-term costs and consequences of all personal victimizations in the United States during 1987. Following the definition set forth by the Panel on the Understanding and Control of Violent Behavior, we include all "threatened, attempted or completed intentional infliction of physical harm by persons against persons." However, our primary focus is on the traditional violent crime categories of homicide, robbery, assault, and rape.

For some types of victimizations—notably abuse of children under age 12—and some types of consequences, insufficient data exist to assess the magnitude of either consequences or costs. In such instances, we identify these gaps, and suggest estimation approaches that might be considered in future research.

IMPORTANCE OF ESTIMATING COSTS

Estimating the cost of intentional injury is more than an academic exercise. This section discusses a few of the most important reasons for being concerned with the cost of intentional injury. It also illustrates some of the uses and pitfalls of using cost estimates for policy analysis.

Comparison of Aggregate Crime Costs to Other Social Ills

To the extent that we are successful in estimating the aggregate cost of intentional injury, we can compare this total to the cost associated with other social problems. At a minimum, this would allow one to place the problem of intentional injury in perspective vis-à-vis other social ills (e.g., drug abuse, homelessness). Over time, it might also be possible to compare trends in aggregate costs to determine if these problems are getting worse or better. Whether or not one agrees that this is a useful exercise, various advocacy groups do in fact compare "cost of crime" estimates to other costs in an effort to affect policy decisions (e.g., see Irwin and Austin, 1987:16). Because most of the cost estimates cited in the past have been significant underestimates, more accurate estimates would better inform the policy debate (Cohen, 1988a:538).

However, one cannot simply compare aggregate cost estimates of intentional injury with estimates of the cost of other social ills to arrive at policy recommendations for future public priorities. Suppose, for example, it was estimated that the cost of intentional injury in the United States exceeded the cost imposed by automobile crashes (see, e.g,. Streff et al., 1992). It does not necessarily follow that society should increase expenditures to prevent intentional injuries relative to public spending for preventing such crashes. If one includes the cost of "preventing" intentional injuries and motor vehicle crashes, it might be found (for example) that society is already spending too much on the former and not enough on the latter. Thus, we also need to know the deterrent and incapacitative effect of various sanctions, increased police patrols, etc. More importantly, one needs to know the *marginal* costs and benefits of various policy options designed to reduce crime (or highway crashes)—not just the aggregate costs of current social ills.

If one is really interested in estimating the aggregate cost of intentional injury, the hypothetical question should be posed, "What would life be like without violence?" Not only would there be no victims and no government expenditures on punishing offenders, but "society would be profoundly transformed. Most sorts of organized crime would be eliminated, since it depends on the threat of violence to do business. There would be no more baggage checks in airports. The commercial life of the inner city would be transformed . . . ."[2] This paper does not address these aggregate social costs of intentional injury. Instead, its primary focus is on estimating the cost of individual incidents of intentional injury. This approach is most useful for purposes of conducting benefit-cost analyses of policy options (see below).

Comparison of Harm by Type of Victimization

Without estimates of cost, it is difficult to compare the harm associated with the "average" assault to that of the "average" rape. Although one can tally up the various harms associated with each type of incident (e.g., value of property stolen, frequency of injuries by type of injury, mental health-related injuries), it is difficult to compare these harms objectively without a common metric such as dollars.

Until recently, the only accepted approach to comparing harms has been to survey the public on the perceived seriousness of crime (see Wolfgang et al., 1985; Cullen et al., 1982; Rossi et al., 1974). This approach led to the development of a "crime seriousness index" (Sellin and Wolfgang, 1964).[3] Although surveys are useful as a means of understanding public opinion, they are based on public perceptions concerning the severity of crimes, which may include misperceptions about the frequency of injuries in typical criminal events (see Cohen, 1988b). Moreover, these studies are generally unable to distinguish between the generic harm associated with an injury and the actual consequences of any one victimization. The latter would be particularly important if one were interested in the extent to which the consequences of victimization vary across different segments of the population (e.g., age or sex).

Benefit-Cost Analysis of Policy Options

Society's ability to control criminal behavior is limited by its ability to pay for police, courts, and corrections. In an effort to reduce crime, the severity of its consequences, and the cost of preventing and controlling crime, society has undertaken many criminal justice experiments. Recent examples in corrections include intensive probation (National Institute of Justice, 1987), electronic monitoring of offenders (National Institute of Justice, 1989a), and shock incarceration programs (National Institute of Justice, 1989b). Other criminal justice policy experiments include preventive police patrols and misdemeanor spouse arrest programs for domestic violence (National Institute of Justice, 1988).

One of the advantages of using dollars as a common metric for analyzing criminal victimizations is that we can compare the benefits of reduced victimization to the costs of the proposed policy. If two options have identical crime control effects but differing costs, the choice is simple. Unfortunately, few policy alternatives are so easily compared. In a more realistic case where a new policy reduces crime at some additional expense (or increases crime at a savings), one of the key questions is whether the reduced (increased) crime level is worth its price. Only by monetizing the cost of criminal victimization can one begin to answer that question.

There have been a few attempts to conduct benefit-cost analyses of criminal justice programs. For example, Friedman (1977) concluded that the social benefits of the Supported Work experiment in New York exceeded its social cost. This conclusion was reached despite the fact that the "costs" of crimes averted by this program were largely underestimated due to the state of knowledge prevailing at the time. More recently, the deterrent and incapacitative effects of longer prison sentences were combined with estimates of the monetary cost of crime and the cost of prison to estimate the benefits and costs of various policy options (Cohen, 1988a:549-552; Rhodes, 1988).

Without a full accounting of costs, it is easy to reach erroneous policy conclusions. For example, a study by Austin (1986) found a favorable benefit-cost ratio of an early release program. The savings to the government from releasing prisoners early was determined to exceed costs associated with the slightly higher crime rate caused by recidivists. However, the "cost" of crime in Austin's paper was based solely on direct out-of-pocket victim expenses. In the case of rape, that cost was assumed to be $357, compared to an average auto theft of $2,544 (Austin, 1986:494, Table 37). Cohen (1988a) reestimated the benefit-cost ratios using dollar estimates of the nonmonetary costs of crime (where rape was valued at $51,058) and reached the opposite policy conclusion.

We do not claim that policy decisions should be based solely on benefit-cost analyses, because it will never be possible to adequately monetize *all* costs and benefits. For example, certain policy options might be chosen primarily because they are "fair" or "just." Society clearly values justice, but we have no method of estimating this attribute. In such a case, the benefit-cost analysis can still help policy makers make informed decisions by understanding what it costs society to implement one particular program as opposed to another that might be less fair.

CONCEPTUAL FRAMEWORK FOR
ESTIMATING COSTS AND CONSEQUENCES

Violent behavior imposes many types of costs on society. In determining conceptually whether or not to include an element as a cost, the operational criteria used throughout this paper is whether or not society would be better off in its absence. In other words, we adopt the economist's notion of "social costs" as being any "resource-using activity which reduces aggregate well-being" (Gray, 1979:21). These resources need not be expressed in dollar terms; nor do we require that they be easily measurable.

The economics of crime literature has traditionally distinguished between three types of costs (Demmert, 1979:2-5): (1) those caused directly by violence (i.e., external costs imposed by the offender); (2) those costs society incurs in its attempt to deter or prevent future incidents (through deterrence, incapacitation, or rehabilitation of offenders as well as preventive measures taken by potential victims); and (3) those costs incurred by the offender (such as the opportunity cost of the offender's time while either engaging in the offense or being punished).

To this traditional division of costs, we add (at least conceptually) a fourth—the cost of society's desire to punish socially unacceptable behavior. There is clearly some overlap between this cost and society's desire to deter or prevent future injuries. That is, sending a rapist to jail might simultaneously satisfy the goals of prevention and retribution. Conceptually, one could allocate prison costs (for example) by assuming that "prevention" costs are those for which the social costs of imprisonment are less than the social benefits of imprisonment through reduced crime. Any expenditures beyond those justified by such a cost-benefit analysis would be allocated to "punishment."

Based on the empirical reality that offenders differ in their propensity to commit crimes, Waldfogel (1989) estimated both the marginal costs and the marginal benefits of incarceration. His findings supported the notion that, overall, incarceration "pays for itself" through deterrence or incapacitation. However, at the margin, the results are less clear. It is possible, therefore, that the cost of incarcerating the marginal offender exceeds the benefits of incarceration, which suggest that incarceration may serve a retributive role. Because data limitations make it difficult, if not impossible, to allocate costs between prevention and retribution, all costs of punishment included in this paper are treated as if they were designed for deterrent or preventive purposes.

Monetary Versus Nonmonetary Costs

We can distinguish between two types of costs: monetary and nonmonetary. Monetary costs generally consist of out-of-pocket expenditures, such as medical treatment, property damage and loss, and emergency police or ambulance response. They also consist of lost wages and productivity.

In addition to these monetary costs, injury victims and their families may endure pain, suffering, and reduced quality of life. Since pain, suffering, and quality of life are not normally exchanged in the marketplace, there is no direct method of observing their monetary value. Indeed, the term "cost" is more difficult to conceptualize for nonmonetary losses because one cannot simply "buy" or "sell" pain and suffering.

Suppose for a moment that there were markets for pain and suffering. If person A wants to inflict harm on person B, he must negotiate a mutually acceptable price. For some injuries, person B will be willing to accept this injury in exchange for a high enough price. Alternatively, person B might be willing to pay person A *not* to inflict that harm. These two amounts will place bounds on the ultimate market price. That is, one can bound the value from above by examining the maximum amount a person is willing to pay to avoid an injury—the "ransom" value. The "price" can also be bound from below by using the minimum amount a person would be willing to accept to voluntarily endure the injury—the "compensation" value (see Cook and Graham, 1977).

The ransom value is generally referred to as "willingness to pay" (WTP) because it measures the amount people are willing to pay for avoidance of an injury. The compensation value is generally referred to as "willingness to accept" (WTA) because it examines the amount required to convince a person to accept an injury or death. For marketed goods, WTP and WTA are generally assumed to be equal; otherwise, one could always profit from arbitrage (Merkhofer, 1987:156).

Although WTP and WTA are closely linked, the essential difference between the two is the question of who pays—that is, who has the property rights to the commodity in question. For a commodity that consumers dislike (such as pollution or crime), WTP is likely to be *lower* than WTA for financial,[4] and even psychological or ethical reasons.[5] The difference is most striking when one considers the prospect of a certain death. In such a case, the WTP is bounded by one's own wealth, whereas few people would be willing to accept a certain death at any price.

Which valuation approach should be utilized depends on the policy question being addressed. For example, if one is interested in examining a proposal to reduce the risk of death to a population, a WTP approach might be warranted. However, if one is interested in making a person "whole" as a result of an incident that has already taken place, a WTA approach might be more appropriate.

Finally, it should be noted that many earlier cost of injury and cost of crime studies valued deaths solely on the basis of forgone productivity. This "human capital approach" to valuing life ignores the pain, suffering, and lost enjoyment of life. Instead, it counts the monetary costs of death. This method is appropriate if one is interested solely in the effect of deaths on economic activity, as measured by the gross national product, and on household production.

Interdependency of Cost Categories

It is important to understand that the many different consequences and costs of victimization are interdependent. That is, increasing one type of cost might either increase or decrease another type of cost. Conceptually, victimization (and hence the cost of victimization) can be thought of as being the equilibrium outcome of a "crime market" (Cook, 1986:2). Potential offenders who "supply" crimes are sensitive to both "demand" and cost factors. The demand for crime is based on the vulnerability and exposure of potential victims, partially determined by precautions taken by potential victims. One of the key costs of supplying crime is the expected penalty—the likelihood and severity of punishment.

To illustrate, consider the following simplistic example. Suppose that the violent crime rate in one neighborhood increases. Potential victims will likely take more costly precautionary actions to reduce their exposure to this new increased risk. They might stay at home more often and buy more secure locks—thus raising the cost of prevention. The city might spend money on overtime for police patrols, which will raise the "expected cost" of committing a crime to potential offenders.

The net effect of reducing the demand for and increasing the cost of committing a crime might cause some potential criminals to take more costly actions to avoid capture (such as buying sophisticated equipment or hiring accomplices to watch for police). Alternatively, some potential criminals might decide it is not worth the added risk of failure or capture, and might commit fewer crimes. Thus, it is likely that the crime rate will be somewhat higher than before, but not as high as it would have been if the community had not taken these costly actions in response to the increased criminal activity.

Offsetting Benefits of Victimization

It is possible that intentional injuries will result in offsetting social benefits. For example, suppose a career criminal is robbed at gunpoint and fatally shot. The social cost of this murder might be partially offset by the reduced cost of other future crimes the victim was likely to commit. That is, there might be an "incapacitative" effect of intentional injury (see Cohen, 1983, for a review of the incapacitation literature). Of course, this assumes that no other potential offenders replace the victim's future criminal career by increasing their own violation rate (see Reiss, 1980). Although this might be a reasonable theoretical approach to aggregating social costs of victimization, empirical evidence is too sparse to make any estimates in this paper.

Efficient Versus Inefficient Costs

For a variety of reasons, society often chooses methods of achieving its goals that are not cost minimizing. To the extent that these costs serve no other socially desirable goals, they may be considered wasted resources. For example, Schmidt and Witte (1984:Chap. 16) have estimated the optimal prison size based on actual cost data and found that substantial savings could accrue by building larger-scale prisons. Whether or not the added cost of inefficient prison sizes should be included in the cost of victimization is unclear. To some extent, it is not the offender's "fault" that society spends more than it has to for prisons. On the other hand, because higher than minimum costs are almost inherent in any bureaucracy, it may be reasonable to include such costs. Moreover, we may be paying for other attributes, such as a more humane treatment of prisoners. In this paper, we have included all known costs, regardless of whether there are less expensive ways to achieve the same goal.

Fixed, Average, and Marginal Costs

Although this paper attempts to enumerate and, where possible, monetize virtually all conceivable costs and consequences of violent behavior in the United States, the reader must be careful in using any estimates derived here. As mentioned above, there are many reasons why policy makers might be interested in monetary estimates of the cost of violent behavior. These different reasons often require the use of different estimates. If one is simply interested in the magnitude of the "crime" problem, all costs estimated here should be included. On the other hand, if one is interested in analyzing various criminal justice options, only *marginal* costs and benefits should be considered.

For example, suppose policy makers are considering an increase in the average prison sentence for armed robbers by one year. First, one would need to determine the *marginal* cost of imprisoning one armed robber for a year. The marginal cost of imprisonment does not include the fixed cost of building prisons (unless this new policy requires the use of expanded prison capacity). This amount would be compared to the *marginal benefit* of one additional imprisonment year for an armed robber, which depends on the number of crimes averted (through incapacitation or deterrence), and the cost of each additional crime averted. The cost of each additional crime depends on both the cost to victims and the criminal justice processing costs for each offense.

In some instances, average costs are more readily available than marginal costs. For example, although we might estimate the aggregate cost for private security (and thus derive the average cost of security per crime), we have no evidence on the reduction in private security expenditures that might occur if we reduced the risk of armed robbery. Without such marginal estimates, it would be unrealistic to assume (for example) that a 10 percent reduction in crime rates would result in a 10 percent reduction in prevention expenditures. See Zimring and Hawkins (1988) and Zedlewski (1989) for a discussion of these issues.

Although this paper attempts to distinguish among average, fixed, and marginal costs, it should be acknowledged that this distinction is not always clear cut. For example, one might argue that the marginal cost of imprisonment is the cost of maintaining a prisoner (e.g., food, additional guards) plus the annualized cost of a prison bed. However, if new prisoners are double-celled in jails designed for one prisoner, one might argue that the marginal cost is only the cost of subsistence.

Real Versus Opportunity Costs

Some costs that appear to be fixed are actually marginal opportunity costs. For example, suppose the number of murders in a city is reduced by one. Suppose further that instead of reducing police costs due to less time investigating murders, the effect of this lowered murder rate is to shift police resources into other activities. From an opportunity cost standpoint, these police costs should be counted as part of the cost of a murder. Reducing the need for a police investigation might not reduce police expenditures, but it will certainly free up valuable police resources that will be used for another purpose.

Victim Assistance and Other Cost-Reducing Costs

Some of the costs associated with violent behavior may actually be designed to *reduce* the cost of victimization. For example, victim service agencies provide a variety of psychological treatment programs for victims and assist victims in dealing with the judicial process. At first, it might seem inappropriate to include these as a "social" cost of victimization. After all, victim service agencies really provide a social benefit. However, in the absence of these victim service agencies, the costs of victimization would be even higher—because the pain and suffering endured by crime victims would increase. Thus, attributing the cost of victim service agencies to the cost of the victimization itself seems quite reasonable.

Time Frame for Cost Estimation

Although some injury-related costs are incurred immediately upon injury, others will appear at some future date. Two different methods are generally used to account for this time consideration—the "incidence" and "prevalence" approaches. An incidence-based estimate counts all costs that will result from injuries occurring in a given year, regardless of when the actual cost will be incurred. A prevalence-based estimate counts all costs in a given year, regardless of when the injury actually occurred.

Incidence-based estimates indicate how much could be saved by preventing future incidents; prevalence-based estimates provide insight into the cost savings attainable through improved treatment of existing injuries (Miller and Luchter, 1988). For injuries that are acute (i.e., less than one year's duration), incidence- and prevalence-based cost estimates are roughly identical. However, for serious unintentional injuries, prevalence-based estimates are substantially higher (Miller and Luchter, 1988).[6]

The costs presented here are incidence estimates. They include present and future costs associated with victim injuries that occurred in 1987. However, as explained later, data limitations are likely to cause us to underestimate future costs.

Because some costs occur immediately whereas others accrue in future years, economists achieve comparability among future and present cost flows by converting future costs to present values. Discounted future costs indicate how much would have to be invested today to pay the costs when they arise.

Although most previous cost of injury studies used a discount rate of 6 percent (e.g., Rice et al., 1989), we believe that rate is too high. Instead, the appropriate discount rate is probably between 1 and 3 percent. First, this range is likely to be used by courts in calculating appropriate compensation for injuries, because the U.S. Supreme Court stated that it would not review use of an inflation-free discount rate between 1 percent and 3 percent but would consider reviewing the use of other rates (*Jones and Laughlin Steel Corporation* v. *Pfeifer*, 103 Supreme Court Reporter, 1983:2541-2558). Second, there is evidence that workers apply a 2 percent discount rate when trading off present wages for the risk of future loss of life (Moore and Viscusi, 1990). Third, a Congressional Budget Office review of economic evidence determined that the most appropriate discount rate for public decision making was 2 percent (Hartman, 1990). In this study, we use a discount rate of 2.5 percent.

COSTS AND CONSEQUENCES OF VIOLENT BEHAVIOR

As stated above, we have identified three broad categories of costs: (1) the direct consequences of the injury, (2) society's response to the victimization, and (3) the offender's costs. This section attempts to enumerate all of the possible costs and consequences of these categories.

Direct Consequences of Violent Behavior

Table 1 summarizes the various costs and consequences of violent behavior. Victims incur many direct out-of-pocket expenses such as stolen or damaged property,[7] medical costs, lost wages while away from work, and mental health or other victim-related treatment. Even if medical costs are reimbursed through insurance or employee benefit programs, society bears the cost through higher insurance premiums. In fact, because the provision of insurance requires administrative (overhead) costs, the loss is even higher than the medical cost itself. If the employee receives paid sick leave or workers' compensation during the recovery period, the employer bears the cost of the paid wages and the administrative cost of processing the payments. The employer may even have higher expenses due to lost productivity or the need to hire temporary help or to pay overtime in the interim. Thus, the total "out-of-pocket" portion of injury costs is actually higher than the sum of property losses, medical costs, and lost wages.

In addition to the monetary costs incurred by victims (or paid by third parties), many other nonmonetary costs are no less real but not as easily quantifiable.[8] For example, injuries may result in either a temporary or a permanent inability to do housework.

TABLE 1 Costs of Intentional Injury

Cost Category	Party That Directly Bears Cost[a]
Direct property losses	
(1) Losses not reimbursed by insurance	Victim
(2) Losses reimbursed by insurance	Society
(3) Administrative cost: insurance reimbursement	Society
(4) Recovery by police	Society[b]
Medical and mental health care	
(1) Charges not reimbursed by insurance	Victim
(2) Charges reimbursed by insurance	Society
(3) Administrative overhead of insurance coverage (item 2)	Society
Victim services	
(1) Expenses charged to victim	Victim
(2) Expenses paid by service agency	Society
(3) Temporary labor and training of replacements	Society
Lost workdays	
(1) Lost wages for unpaid workdays	Victim
(2) Lost productivity for paid workdays	Society
Lost school days	
(1) Forgone wages due to lack of education	Victim
(2) Forgone nonpecuniary benefits of education	Victim
(3) Forgone social benefits due to lack of education	Society
Lost housework	Victim and family
Pain and suffering/quality of life	Victim
Loss of affection/enjoyment	Victim's family
Death	
(1) Value of life	Victim
(2) Funeral and burial expenses	Victim's family
(3) Loss of affection/enjoyment	Victim's family
(4) Psychological injury/treatment	Victim's family
Legal costs associated with tort claims	Victim or victim's family
Long-term consequences of victimization	
(1) Future victims	
(2) Future social costs	

[a]Ignores any recovery from offenders through legal action.
[b]See text for discussion of costs borne by society.

Although little or no monetary loss might be associated with lost housework, one can estimate its monetary value.

Lost schoolwork for a student might also be valued. From the victim's perspective, this loss would be at least equal to the present discounted value of future wages forgone by a lack of education. In addition, to the extent that this lost education is not made up and the victim values education beyond the pure monetary benefits from increased earning potential, there might be "psychic" losses. Finally, education is often thought of as a public good— society values an educated population beyond the amount that the average individual would be willing to invest by him/herself. Thus, an additional social component of loss is associated with lost school days.

One of the potentially largest nonmonetary costs associated with victim injury is pain and suffering. Although pain and suffering does not involve a monetary loss, it may be monetized for purposes of comparison with other costs. Related to pain and suffering are the potential costs associated with the inability to continue some enjoyable leisure activities. These might be called "quality of life" costs.

In addition to the victim, the victim's family may incur costs. One obvious cost is any additional expense incurred or time spent by family members doing chores previously performed by the family member who was injured and is no longer able to do them. Another cost, "loss of affection/enjoyment," values spousal and family activities in which the victim can no longer participate due to the injury.

Costs also arise when injured victims die. In addition to the direct costs associated with a premature funeral, the value of the life itself is lost.

In a few instances, victims of violent behavior (or their families) may bring a private tort action against the party who injured the victim or against a third party for negligence (e.g., an unlit parking lot or insufficient hotel room security). These suits involve various legal and court costs.

Finally, we should consider the long-term consequences of intentional injury. For example, there is some evidence that victims of child abuse are more likely to become child abusers themselves. To the extent that a causal connection can be made, one should consider the future cost associated with child abuse to be a cost of today's incident. Of course, one also would need to discount these costs to present value.

Society's Response to Violent Behavior

In addition to the costs imposed directly by the offender, society's response to victimization involves many different types of costs. These costs are summarized in Table 2. Violent behavior also has

TABLE 2 Costs of Society's Response to Intentional Injury

Cost Category	Party That Directly Bears Cost
Fear of crime	Potential victim
Precautionary expenditures/effort	Potential victim
Criminal justice system	Society
(1) Police and investigative costs	Society
(2) Prosecutors	Society
(3) Courts	Society
(4) Legal fees	
(a) Public defenders	Society
(b) Private	Offenders
(5) Incarceration costs	Society
(6) Nonincarcerative sanctions	Society
(7) Victim time	Victim
(8) Jury and witness time	Jury/witness
Victim services	
(1) Victim service organizations	Society
(2) Victim compensation programs	Society
(3) Victim time	Victim
Other noncriminal programs	
(1) Hot lines and public service announcements	Society
(2) Community treatment programs	Society
(3) Private therapy/counseling	Society/offender
Incarcerated offender costs	
(1) Lost wages	Offender/family
(2) Lost tax revenue and productivity	Society
(3) Value of lost freedom	Offender
(4) Psychological cost to family	Family of offender
"Overdeterrence" costs	
(1) Innocent individuals accused of offense	Innocent party
(2) Restriction of legitimate activity	Society
(3) Cost of additional detection avoidance by offenders	Offender
"Justice" costs	
(1) Constitutional protections to avoid false accusations	Society
(2) Cost of increasing detection rate to avoid differential punishment	Society

an impact on people who are not directly victimized, by increasing the level of fear in potential victims. Fear of victimization might also result in increased prevention expenditures on items such as security systems or firearms. It also might lead to changes in behavior, such as taking fewer walks at night.

The most visible cost associated with preventing future victimization is the criminal justice system. This includes government expenditures for police, prosecutors, public defenders, courts, prisons, and other nonincarcerative sanctions. It also includes private expenditures on criminal defense lawyers, as well as the amount of time spent by victims, juries, and witnesses dealing with the criminal justice system. As noted earlier, some of the cost of the criminal justice system might be more properly attributed to retribution than to preventive expenditures.

Some of society's response to violent behavior falls outside the criminal justice arena, with programs such as community treatment facilities and public service announcements.

Some of the costs of violent behavior fall directly on the offender who is apprehended and subject to the criminal justice system. Other costs are borne by the offender's family. For example, if the offender was working prior to incarceration, he/she will suffer from lost wages while in prison. Regardless of whether or not one wants to include the offender's utility as part of "social welfare," those lost wages are a measure of the productivity loss to society. It is also possible that incarceration will reduce the future earning capacity of the offender.

A second potential cost is the value of lost freedom to an incarcerated offender. Beyond the social productivity loss, some would argue that society should consider the impact that prison has on the offender. Even if one wanted to include this as a cost element, it is particularly difficult to monetize.

A related and potentially more troubling cost associated with incarceration of offenders is the risk that the prison experience will increase the propensity of the offender to recidivate. To the extent this is true, if one were to compare the cost of imprisonment to the cost of probation (for example), any marginal increase in future crimes should be attributed to the cost of imprisonment.

Finally, there are two often overlooked categories of costs that we refer to as "overdeterrence" and "justice" costs. Although these costs are likely to be relatively small in terms of the overall cost of victimization, it is important to enumerate them because they have significant policy implications.

Overdeterrence costs are collateral consequences of imposing penalties for violent behavior. First, innocent parties who might be accused of committing a crime will take costly actions to avoid such allegations. Second, violent offenders might increase their level of violence to reduce the risk of capture.

The cost of justice is determined primarily by society's willingness to take costly precautions to ensure that innocent individuals are not accused of crimes. Additional justice costs are incurred to the extent society chooses more costly crime control alternatives than would be required if the concern were solely with minimizing the cost for a given level of deterrence.

Offender Costs

Offenders might spend considerable time or resources committing a violent act. Although all of these costs are borne by the offender directly, society would also benefit from their absence. The most obvious cost would be the opportunity cost of the offender's time. That is, if the offender could be gainfully employed while not engaging in the violent behavior, society has lost that productivity. In addition, one might consider other resource costs, such as expenditures on weapons, that assist the offender in carrying out this behavior.

COST OF CRIME AND INJURY LITERATURE

This section briefly reviews the current state of knowledge in estimating the cost of injury. The literature has generally been focused either on the criminal justice area or on the public health/accident arena. Thus, studies have estimated the cost of such diverse policy concerns as crime, mental health, and automobile crashes.

Approaches to Measuring the Cost of Injury

Measuring the full costs of injury is a particularly difficult task, because many of the costs are not normally exchanged in the marketplace and have no obvious monetary value. This section briefly reviews some of the empirical approaches that have been used to place monetary values on such costs. The conceptual foundations for these various approaches have already been discussed.

We have distinguished between two types of costs—monetary and nonmonetary. Similarly, empirical approaches to estimating the cost of injury fall into two broad categories—direct and indirect. Monetary costs generally can be estimated directly from survey data, especially those that involve direct out-of-pocket losses. Productivity losses also can be estimated directly from data such as wage rates, age, and the educational background of the victim.

Some nonmonetary costs can also be monetized by using direct approaches. "Contingent valuation" surveys ask respondents to place dollar values on various risks and outcomes in order to determine either WTA or WTP values. This survey approach has been used to place dollar values on such nonmarket goods as enhanced visibility and scenic beauty, as well as health-related qualities of air and water (Mitchell and Carson, 1989; Viscusi et al., 1989). Of course, contingent valuation surveys merely *estimate* WTP or WTA. Because respondents do not actually buy and sell the risky commodity, we cannot be certain that their response to a survey question is the same as their behavior would be if actually confronted with a real situation. Although we are unaware of its application to criminal victimization, applying contingent valuation surveys to crime seems like a natural extension of recent work in this area.

Another direct method of estimation is to estimate WTA based on actual jury awards for pain and suffering (Cohen, 1987, 1988a).[9] This method measures the amount that a jury believes is required to compensate a victim in order to make the victim "whole" or indifferent between the two health states—no injury versus injury with compensation. Although this method is based on the same theoretical concept as WTA, since it is a jury's evaluation (and not the victim's) it is only an *estimate* of WTA.

Most nonmonetary costs are monetized by using indirect approaches. The most prevalent approach is "hedonic price estimation," where an observable market transaction is disaggregated into its various attributes—including the "risk" component. Hedonic pricing models have been applied to housing prices to estimate the value of various amenities, including the risk of crime (Thaler, 1978). They have also been applied to wage rates to determine worker willingness to accept an increased risk of injury or death—the so-called statistical value of life. For example, suppose an individual is willing to accept an increased risk of injury of 1 in 100,000 in exchange for $10. Collectively, 100,000 people would thus be willing to accept one additional injury among themselves in exchange for $1 million ($10 × 100,000). Thus, the WTA value for this injury is estimated to be $1 million. Although the latter studies are often referred to as WTP, in reality they are closer to

WTA, because workers voluntarily accept risk in exchange for added compensation. However, since risk is just one attribute of the labor market, we expect WTP and WTA to be the same for these market-determined levels of risk compensation. Similar studies on the purchase of consumer products designed to reduce the risk of death (e.g., smoke detectors) are WTP estimates. Following conventional terminology, throughout the remainder of this paper, we refer to value of life studies as WTP estimates. Reviews of these studies can be found in Fisher et al. (1989) and Miller (1990).

It is important to realize that most of these indirect estimates are attempts to measure the value of a small risk of injury or death—not the value of certain injury or death. The loss in utility due to certain injury or death is *more than* 1,000 times the utility loss due to a 1/1,000 risk of injury or death. Thus, for example, we would expect WTA estimates made by jury awards to be higher than WTA estimates using hedonic pricing estimation. This distinction is most stark when considering the risk of death. Although people often voluntarily accept increased risks of death in exchange for lower prices or higher wages, few individuals would accept any amount of money in exchange for certain death. Thus, the hedonic pricing approach used to estimate WTA and WTP is really only valid for valuing risks—not any one particular injury.

Finally, it should be noted that there is no definitive literature on how these value of life estimates vary by occupation or income (Miller, 1990:18). This is particularly important for purposes of estimating crime costs, because there is some evidence that the average crime victim is *not* representative of the average consumer or worker in the population. For example, unemployed persons have a three times higher risk of being injured by crime than employed persons, and those with annual incomes of less than $10,000 have more than double the risk of injury due to victimization than those with annual incomes of more than $20,000 (Harlow, 1989).

In addition, if victims are themselves involved in criminal activity (e.g., drug dealers or gang members), these individuals might display preferences toward risk that suggest they have a lower value of life than the average population. Indeed, there is some evidence that victims of assaults are more likely than the average population to have committed assaults themselves (Singer, 1981) and that homicide victims are themselves very likely to have a previous arrest record for crimes against the person (Wolfgang, 1958:178). However, not only do we lack adequate evidence on appropriate WTP values for these populations, but a recent study of drug dealers fails to substantiate the hypothesis that their behavior exhibits an extremely low value of life (Reuter et al., 1990).[10]

Cost of Crime Literature

Previous studies of the cost of crime have generally attempted to estimate costs either directly from victim losses or indirectly from market or behavioral data. The direct cost estimates generally have included two components: (1) monetary losses such as property losses, medical expenses, and lost workdays; and (2) private and public expenditures designed to prevent future victimizations. Data on victim losses have come primarily from the National Crime Survey (NCS) (Shenk and Klaus, 1984). Data on public expenditures come from various sources, including the Bureau of Justice Statistics (1989b). For other studies based on these government estimates, see Gray (1979) and Zedlewski (1985, 1987).

One of the main limitations of these earlier studies is that they lacked data on the nonmonetary cost of crime (e.g., pain, suffering, fear, and reduced quality of life). As shown in Cohen (1988a), the dollar value of nonmonetary costs can far exceed the out-of-pocket costs of crime.

One method for estimating dollar values for the nonmonetary cost of crime is to infer property owners' willingness to pay for a safer neighborhood through higher property values. To the extent safety is capitalized in housing prices, we expect higher-crime neighborhoods to have lower housing prices, all else being equal. Several studies have attempted to isolate this effect through hedonic price estimation (Thaler, 1978; Hellman and Naroff, 1979; Rizzo, 1979; Clark and Cosgrove, 1990). Unfortunately, data limitations generally prevent these studies from isolating the cost of any individual crime type (Cohen, 1990). Instead, they estimate the cost of an aggregate measure such as the crime index.

Another method for estimating the nonmonetary costs of crime is to infer society's willingness to pay for reductions in crime from studies of society's willingness to pay for safety or its willingness to accept increased risks. Phillips and Votey (1981) combined these value of life estimates and the out-of-pocket costs of crime with society's perception of the seriousness of crime to arrive at crime-specific monetary estimates. However, their methodology was unable to account for the risk of injury and death for many crimes.

More recently, Cohen (1988a) combined estimates of the value of life with jury award data on the pain and suffering from specific injuries to arrive at a dollar estimate of both the monetary and the nonmonetary costs of individual crimes to victims. The approach used in Cohen (1988a) is a hybrid of direct and indirect cost estimation. Direct costs are taken from NCS data, as well as several additional sources and assumptions where victim surveys are lacking (e.g., psychological counseling). The nonmonetary costs of pain, suffering, fear, and the risk of death are estimated by using indirect techniques. The cost of an increased risk of death is based on value of life estimates, whereas the cost of pain, suffering, and fear due to nonfatal injuries is based on the compensation approach, estimated from jury awards compensating victims for similar injuries.

Although Cohen (1988a) was the first comprehensive attempt to monetize the pain, suffering, and fear caused by individual crimes, because of data limitations, neither its theoretical foundation nor its empirical estimates were entirely satisfactory. The main data limitation was that neither *ex ante* nor *ex post* estimates were available for all costs. Value of life estimates were available only based on *ex ante* risks, whereas pain and suffering associated with specific injuries were available only from *ex post* jury awards. Thus, theoretically, Cohen was forced to use a hybrid of *ex ante* valuation and *ex post* compensation. If one is interested in determining the value to society of reducing crime, costs should be based on *ex ante* measures. However, if the purpose is primarily to determine victim compensation, an *ex post* analysis would be preferable.

Aside from this conceptual problem, Cohen (1988a) was also subject to several important data limitations that probably lowered the cost estimates below their true values. First, as in virtually all previous cost of crime studies—medical costs, property losses, and lost wages were taken from the NCS. This results in an underestimate of victimization costs, because the NCS asks respondents to report on crimes committed during the past six months. On average, therefore, medical costs are limited to the first three months following the incident. The NCS also excludes mental health-related costs. Although the survey asks respondents if they lost time on the job, it fails to ask about lost housework or school days. Also, due to the hierarchical nature of the NCS reports, property losses are likely to be biased. For example, if a person was both raped and robbed, published NCS data would report the property loss under rape—not robbery. Although this might not result in any aggregate bias in the property loss estimate, it certainly does introduce bias in the cost estimates for individual crimes.

A second limitation of the data used in Cohen (1988a) is that nonmonetary costs were estimated by using body part-specific injuries from automobile crashes and other similar injuries. The jury award for pain and suffering was estimated for each type of injury, and applied to the distribution of injuries normally encountered by crime victims (as estimated by the NCS). The problem with this approach is that it is not obvious that a broken arm (for example) resulting from an auto crash and leading to $2,000 in medical costs and lost wages, causes the same pain and suffering as a broken arm resulting from a physical assault. Cohen attempted to adjust for this fact by adding "mental suffering" to the body part pain and suffering estimates. Based on the estimated incidence of mental suffering for each type of crime, jury award estimates for these mental injuries were then added to the pain and suffering for physical injuries.

Cost of Injury Literature

In response to the burgeoning use of health care services and rising national health care expenditures, policy makers have focused increased attention on health resource allocation and cost containment strategies. The first economic studies of illness and disease emphasized methodological issues, such as how to deal with discounting, employment rates, transfer payments, and the value of household labor. Landmark studies (e.g., Rice, 1966; Cooper and Rice, 1976; Hartunian et al., 1981) identified the relevant monetary components in the health sector, such as expenditures for emergency services, hospitalization, physician services, specialized paramedic care, outpatient clinical care, pharmaceuticals, nursing home care, and medical appliances. These studies also examined the nonhealth sector costs (e.g., structural modifications to a patient's home necessitated by long-term impairment, additional expenses for household help, administrative costs of insurance or government-funded health coverage, and legal/court costs) borne directly by patients or by other affected individuals[11] or organizations.

Early cost of illness studies rarely considered injury as a distinct category of illness. However, injury is now acknowledged as the fourth leading cause of all deaths, as well as the leading cause of death for children and adults under the age of 45 (Rice et al., 1989). Nevertheless, aside from annual reports on the costs of consumer product injuries treated in hospitals or emergency rooms (Consumer Product Safety Commission, various years), fewer than two dozen cost of injury studies have been reported in the literature since the 1960s.[12]

Studies have used differing methodologies, such as discount rates that ranged from 4 to 10 percent. Time frames for estimation also varied; some presented incidence costs, whereas others presented prevalence estimates. Some reports detailed only the average costs of injuries; others provided data on the average cost of injury by cause. For example, five studies relate to motor vehicle injury (Smart and Sanders, 1976; Faigin, 1976; Hartunian et al., 1981; National Highway Traffic Safety Administration, 1983, 1987; Miller and Luchter, 1988); two each to unintentional injury (Etter, 1987; Miller et al., 1987) and spinal cord injury (Smart and Sanders, 1976; Bureau of Economic Research, 1985); and one to trauma-related injury (Munoz, 1984). None of these studies specifically addressed the issue of costs due to victim injury.

The most comprehensive and systematic lifetime cost of injury study (Rice et al., 1989) quantified the magnitude of the national injury problem in terms of the major causes of injury, disaggregated by age, sex, and class of injury. The study concluded that the total lifetime cost of treatment, rehabilitation, and lost productivity for the 57 million persons injured during 1985 imposed a $158 billion burden on the U.S. economy, or $2,775 per injured person (Rice et al., 1989:38). This cost estimate includes only the monetary consequences of injury. Rice et al. (1989:109) further estimate the total cost of injuries in 1985, including pain, suffering, and lost quality of life, at $1.1 trillion.

Rice et al. (1989) aggregated the cost of all injuries, which does not permit one to isolate the cost of victim injuries as distinct from those injuries not intentionally caused.[13] Although injury is now perceived as a costly public health problem, little attention has been focused on the explicit role of victim injury in contributing to such costs. The causes, circumstances, and even numbers of victim injuries, such as assaults, are not well known (National Research Council and Institute of Medicine, 1985). A recent review of the progress in injury control initiatives suggested that this area has been slighted due to conventional perceptions that intentionally inflicted injury is largely unpreventable (National Research Council and Institute of Medicine, 1988). In addition, the data needed to examine victim injury separately are limited. For example, roughly 60 percent of the data on hospitalized injury used in Rice et al. (1989) differentiate victim injury, but none of the data on less serious injury make this distinction. Consequently, the study could not estimate the costs of victim injury credibly.

THE COST OF VIOLENT BEHAVIOR

This section reviews and supplements existing cost estimates associated with violent behavior. The cost of society's response to victimization is described in a subsequent section. It should be noted that throughout this paper, we include attempted victimizations and those that do not result in actual physical injury.

COST OF VICTIM TREATMENT AND OTHER DIRECT COSTS

Medical Care

Medical costs are defined as direct medical expenses, including physician, hospital, prescription drugs, and other treatment or appliances for physical injury, regardless of whether such costs have been reimbursed by insurance.

Table 3 presents estimates of the number of victims, together with medical costs, averaged across all injured and uninjured vic-

TABLE 3 Medical Costs Due to Victim Injury, 1987

Offense	Number of Victims	Average Medical Costs per Injured Victim	Number of Injured Victims	Percent Injured	Average Medical Costs per Victim
Rape	147,000	$ 616	90,000[a]	.61[a]	$ 376
Robbery	1,068,500	344	383,000	.36	124
Assault	4,930,000	527	1,412,000	.29	153
Murder	20,100	5,370	20,100	1.00	5,370

[a]Nearly half of these reported no physical injury other than the rape itself.

SOURCES: First-year medical costs for rape, robbery, and assault are taken from the National Crime Survey (U.S. Department of Justice, 1989a). Long-term costs were estimated from worker injury data (National Council on Compensation Insurance). Murder costs are taken from Rice et al. (1989) and include the cost of a premature funeral. The number of victims was obtained from the National Crime Survey and the Federal Bureau of Investigation (for murder). Estimates of rape, robbery, and assault include attempted victimizations.

tims, disaggregated by the type of crime. These estimates are $376 for rape, $124 for robbery, $153 for assault, and $5,370 for murder. Nonfatal crime incidence and medical costs derive from the 1987 NCS, whereas the number of murders is taken from the Federal Bureau of Investigations (FBI) Uniform Crime Report (UCR).

NCS data are dependent on the self-report of individuals in sampled households, queried as to the extent of victimization experienced in the six months preceding the survey.[14] Individuals are asked to recall if they were victimized within the defined time frame. Respondents report all injuries incurred due to victimization, given a listing of possibilities that includes rape; attempted rape; knife or stab wounds; gunshot or bullet wounds; broken bones or teeth knocked out; internal injuries; being knocked unconscious; bruises, black eye, cuts, scratches, swelling, and chipped teeth; and other (U.S. Department of Justice, 1989a). Victims reporting injury are asked if medical care, including self-treatment, was received and the location of such treatment (e.g., at the scene, in a hospital emergency room). Those individuals are further queried as to inpatient hospital duration, if any, and total medical costs, including doctor and hospital bills, medicine, therapy, braces, and other related expenses, regardless of whether such costs were covered by insurance.

The NCS data have several limitations. In addition to sampling and nonsampling errors, the NCS does not include victimization of organizations and commercial establishments, children under age 12, transients, the homeless, individuals in institutional settings such as nursing homes, and military personnel in the sampling frame.[15] The medical costs estimated here do not include any victim injury costs borne by nonsampled populations.

A second limitation of the NCS is the implicit assumption that victims accurately recollect and report incidents that took place within the prescribed time frame (i.e., respondents report all incidents relevant to the time frame and, conversely, do not "telescope in" injuries from earlier time frames). Further, NCS is known to underreport both the incidence and the cost of certain types of crimes, such as domestic violence or assaultive behavior between nonstrangers.[16] Efforts to strengthen NCS data in these areas were beyond the scope of the current analysis.

A closely related issue concerns individuals' abilities to accurately report the degree of injury and the extent of full medical costs. Self-reported injury and medical costs are suspect for several reasons. Victim selections of injury categories from the NCS listing may not accurately reflect actual medical diagnoses. Thus, reported costs may be inadvertently assigned to erroneous injury categories.

A related consideration is that survey respondents, polled every six months, report only costs incurred between victimization and the interview date, which might be only a few days post-victimization. In addition, since the survey limits self-report to a six-month time frame, long-term medical and other costs are not reflected. Further, victims who have suffered minor injuries may forget small costs, whereas those who suffered severe injuries may not know the cumulative costs of present, much less future, treatment by multiple health care providers. Victim-furnished information is also questionable, especially for hospitalized injury, because bills are often sent directly to the insurer without the insured learning of the amount.[17]

Optimally, medical diagnoses of injury and associated costs are captured directly from hospital, physician, and other treatment-related records. Earlier costs of injury/illness studies relied on such independent incidence data sources as the National Electronic Injury Surveillance System (NEISS), the National Accident Sampling System (NASS), the National Hospital Discharge Survey (NHDS), and the National Health Interview Survey (NHIS) (for examples, see Hartunian et al., 1981; Miller and Luchter, 1988; Luchter et al., 1989; and Rice et al., 1989).[18] Unfortunately, potentially relevant data bases (e.g., NEISS, NHDS, or the Comprehensive Health and Medical Program for the Uniformed Services [CHAMPUS]) have not yet been refined for application to victim injury analyses. Such refinement was largely beyond the scope of the present effort.

Despite the limitations noted, the NCS remains the most comprehensive source of information currently available on the incidence and magnitude of harm associated with nonfatal victimization. Therefore, this analysis created a hierarchy of injuries derived from the original NCS data. The data indicated that 61 percent of rape and attempted rape victims reported injury (although nearly half of these had no physical injuries other than the rape itself). Injuries were reported by 36 percent of robbery and attempted robbery victims, and 29 percent of assault and attempted assault victims.

The concern for estimating the cost of longer-term medical care for nonfatal injuries was addressed by extrapolating information from the National Council on Compensation Insurance (NCCI) Detailed Claims Information (DCI) data base.[19] The NCCI data are organized using a two-digit code for body part and a two-digit code for nature of injury: these codes did not always match the NCS injury choices. Where possible, injury categories in the two data bases were conceptually linked based on a series of defensible assumptions, for example, that medical treatment of fractures reported in NCCI was approximately equivalent to treatment of broken bones reported in NCS.

Two caveats should be noted. First, the NCCI data base does not contain categories equivalent to rape or attempted rape. The NCS data reference only the short-term medical costs associated with those injuries, but there are potentially costly long-term effects, as well. Such possibilities include the costs of pregnancy/abortion, venereal disease, and human immunodeficiency virus/acquired immune deficiency syndrome (HIV/AIDS) resulting from rape, as well as mental illness and substance abuse (discussed further below). Data on the incidence and costs of such consequences related to rape/attempted rape are not readily available. Therefore, we applied the most conservative NCCI inflator (i.e., 92% of costs accruing within the first year) to estimate the long-term costs. Thus, our estimate may be significantly underrepresentative of true costs, particularly those associated with recurring sexually transmitted diseases or HIV/AIDS infection.

Second, in some cases, victimization may result in aggravation of preexisting conditions that later manifest in significant health problems. For example, elderly individuals may be at greater future risk of heart attack due to victimization (Burt and Katz, 1985). The NCS data may not capture such delayed-onset effects. To some extent, these effects may be reflected in our estimates of longer-term medical costs, but it is unlikely that all such effects have been included.

Medical costs resulting from murders were based on the assumptions that 50 percent of the victims expire at the scene and receive no medical care; 29 percent are transported to an emergency room, receiving medical care at a charge of $1,590 per fatality;[20] and 21 percent receive emergency care ($1,590) and are admitted to a hospital for an average of 5.85 days in the intensive care unit at a daily cost of $1,697.[21] Medical costs for murder victims also include the additional cost associated with a premature funeral, $2,450 in 1987.[22] With these assumptions, average medical costs per murder victim were an estimated $5,370.

Mental Health Care

Incidence of Mental Health Injury Posttraumatic stress disorder (PTSD) is now well established as a clinical diagnosis often caused by criminal victimization. Among the symptoms are "compulsive repetition" of the traumatic event in the victim's mind, as well as "numbness or unresponsiveness to, or reduced involvement with, the external world" (Horowitz, 1986:244). The cause of posttraumatic stress disorder is usually an event that "lies outside the range of common experiences . . . [such as] . . . rapes, muggings, assaults, military combat, torture, natural disasters, traumatically frightening or painful medical experiences, deaths of loved ones, and accidents such as airplane and car crashes." According to one estimate, in the six months following a traumatic life event, the risk of developing a schizophrenic illness increases by a factor of two to three, the risk of depression increases two- to fivefold, and the risk of a suicide attempt by a factor of six (Paykel, 1978:251).

Despite a large and growing literature on PTSD and the psychological impact of intentional injury on victims, there appear to be no prior estimates of mental health-related expenses for victims of intentional injury. In fact, the National Crime Survey does not ask respondents about mental health treatment, presumably because of the sensitivity of such questions.

Although a large literature documents posttraumatic stress disorder and rape trauma syndrome, few studies have systematically estimated the psychological impact of intentional injury on victims. The few existing studies rely on samples of victims who seek treatment, which likely biases the results in the direction of overestimating the impact of victimization. Few of these studies are able to control for the psychological well-being of the victim prior to victimization. Finally, most of the literature concentrates on rape victims. Few studies have looked at robbery and assault victims.

Another problem with existing studies of psychological injury is that they are more concerned with establishing the causal connection than with quantifying the extent or magnitude of the problem. Even studies that attempt to use a control group compare mean scores on standardized psychological tests. The fact that victimized groups have higher mean scores on these tests supports the hypothesis that victimization causes an increase in psychological injury, but it does little to help us quantitatively measure the frequency and severity of injury.

Based on the few studies that attempted to control for some of the above-mentioned problems, Cohen (1988a:546-547) estimated the rate of traumatic neurosis to be 40 percent in rape victims, whereas the rate of severe psychological injuries was estimated to be 10 percent for rape victims and 2 percent for robbery victims.

More recent studies provide evidence that these earlier estimates were within the correct order of magnitude for rape, but probably too low for other crimes.[23] Wirtz and Harrell (1987) report that high levels of fear, anxiety, and stress persist in crime victims six months after their victimization. They found that physical assault victims (rape, domestic violence, and nondomestic assault) had higher levels of fear, anxiety, and stress than nonassault victims (robbery and burglary).

Kilpatrick et al. (1987) report on the results of extensive interviews with 391 adult females in the Charleston, S.C. area. They found that 27.8 percent of all crime victims experienced PTSD at some point in their lives following the criminal victimization, with rates varying from 11.1 percent for attempted molestation to 57.1 percent for completed rape. Aggravated assault victims reported a 36.8 percent PTSD rate, whereas robbery victims reported 18.2 percent.

Although this is one of the few studies that attempts to estimate the frequency of psychological injury for crimes other than rape, its usefulness is somewhat limited. First, it was a study only of female victims. This is of particular importance in attempting to assign frequency estimates to robbery and assault victims, because we do not know if male victims experience the same levels of psychological injury. There is some limited evidence, however, that elderly male victims of crime exhibit similar rates of fear as elderly female victims—at least in the short term (Berg and Johnson, 1979). Furthermore, Resick's (1987:472-473) preliminary results suggest that both female and male robbery victims report reactions similar to those of rape victims—although some differences are apparent.

Second, the study was not entirely representative of women in Charleston, let alone women in the United States. The "sample members were slightly younger, more likely to be white, and possessed slightly higher incomes than the Charleston County population" (Kilpatrick et al., 1987:483).

Finally, this study does not control for the underlying rate of PTSD and hence is not able to establish a causal connection between a criminal event and PTSD. It is possible, for example, that some of these PTSD episodes were (partially or totally) caused by other life events, such as loss of a family member. It is also possible that PTSD rates are higher after a second victimization (53.7 percent of the sample reported more than one victimization).

The Kilpatrick et al. (1987) study can be compared to the estimates of psychological injury for rape victims in Cohen (1988a) by computing a weighted average PTSD rate for completed and attempted rape. The Kilpatrick study estimates this rate to be 35.2 percent, compared to the 50 percent estimate used in Cohen (1988a). However, this 50 percent estimate includes 10 percent of victims who are assumed to suffer from severely disabling psychological injury and 40 percent who suffer from emotional distress. Many of the latter victims might not have suffered symptoms severe enough to be classified as having PTSD.

Absent better data, we made several assumptions to estimate rates of psychological injury. First, although the Kilpatrick study includes estimates for attempted rapes and molestations, it does not include attempted robberies or assaults. Thus, we assume that the ratio of PTSD injury for completed versus attempted victimizations is about the same as it is for rape and molestation cases. That is, we estimate that victims of completed crimes experience about 3.3 times as many PTSD injuries as victims of attempts. Thus, based on the frequency of attempts versus completed crimes and the rate of PTSD reported in Kilpatrick et al., we can estimate the frequency of PTSD to be 19.0 percent for aggravated assault and 13.8 percent for robbery.

Second, although Cohen (1988a) estimated that the ratio of emotional distress to severely disabling psychological injury is about 4 to 1 in rape victims, this is probably too low for assault and robbery victims. Although we have no evidence of what this ratio should be for other crimes, we assume it is twice as high as rape (i.e., 8 to 1). Table 4 reports these estimates for rape, rob-

TABLE 4 Estimated Rate of Psychological Injury and Potential Mental Health Costs, 1987

Offense	Frequency of Emotional Distress	Frequency of Severely Disabling Illness	Total Cost per Victim[a]	Mental Health Costs[b]	Productivity Costs[b]
Rape	40.0	10.0	$5,250	$3,886	$1,364
Robbery	12.3	1.5	1,200	887	310
Assault	5.6	0.7	550	361	188

[a]Averaged over all victims whether or not they received psychological injury. Based on estimated average mental health cost of $6,500 for emotional distress and $26,500 for severely disabling illness.

[b]Total cost per victim in column 4 is assumed to be apportioned between mental health care and productivity in the same ratio as that estimated for medical care versus productivity loss.

bery, and assault. For example, the 13.8 percent rate for robbery is assumed to be 12.3 percent emotional distress and 1.5 percent severely disabling psychological injury. It should also be noted that the estimate for assault in Table 4 is reduced considerably to account for the inclusion of simple assaults and attempted simple assaults—which are not assumed to cause psychological injury.

Although we are unaware of any random or controlled studies on the incidence of psychological injury in childhood physical and sexual abuse cases, there is ample evidence that these victimizations can lead to serious psychological disorders. For example, it has been reported that among clinical populations of psychiatric patients, childhood sexual abuse was found in 75-90 percent of those with multiple personality disorders and 22-44 percent of female psychiatric inpatients. Incest has been reported in 14-46 percent of female psychiatric patients (Coons et al., 1989:326). Although there is no proof of causal connection, it should be noted that these rates are higher than most estimates of the incidence of sexual abuse in the general population.

Mental Health Costs   For physical injuries, we were able to apply crime-specific estimates of the medical expense and lost wages to arrive at estimates of what a jury would award for the pain and suffering associated with that type injury. Since we have no comparable mental health expense and lost wage estimates for psychological injury, we use the estimates derived from jury award data in Cohen (1988a). If we assume that there were no lost wages or household production, this would translate into about 52 visits at $80 per visit ($4,160) for "traumatic neurosis" and 310 visits ($24,800) for "severely disabling psychological injury."[24] By comparison, data in Harwood et al. (1984) suggest that the average annual costs of an active case of mental illness are roughly $5,000 for medical treatment plus $6,000 in productivity losses. The productivity losses result primarily from suicides. Additional costs result from alcohol and drug abuse associated with mental illness but were not estimated.

Table 4 summarizes the estimated rate of psychological injury and mental health-related costs to victims, including both mental health care and productivity losses. To apportion estimates to the two types of losses, we assume that the ratio of medical to productivity losses is the same for physical injuries as for mental injuries. It should be noted that these estimates are based on only a few studies, most of which exclude male victims. Because of the lack of data, we have excluded child abuse.

One problem with this approach is the assumption that all psychologically injured victims seek mental health treatment. Although this is obviously not true, we have no data that would shed light on the correct percentage. Thus, assuming that the estimated percentage of psychologically injured victims is correct, we have overestimated the monetary mental health costs. Instead, the estimate should be considered the *potential* mental health costs.

There is another important reason for not reducing this estimate to account for those who need psychological counseling but do not receive treatment. In a later section, we estimate the mental pain and suffering associated with victim injury, based on the amount of money spent on mental health care. Individuals who do not receive needed treatment still suffer from pain and suffering. In fact, they probably suffer more than those who ultimately receive needed treatment. Thus, we would underestimate mental pain and suffering if we adjusted the mental health costs downward.

Although the estimates in Table 4 look somewhat "reasonable," we reiterate that this is an area of research in which data are still too sparse to permit any confidence in the actual estimates.[25] Instead, they provide some basis of comparison with the magnitude of more easily discernible costs, such as medical and property losses.

Monetary Losses to Victims: Cash and Property

Table 5 reports NCS data for nonmedical monetary losses to victims of rape, robbery, and assault. Separate estimates are made for cash, property stolen, and property damage. In each case, the average loss is given for those who report losses, along with the percentage of the victim population that incurs that loss. As is clear from these estimates, the cash and property losses associated with victimization involving injury are small relative to many of the other costs estimated here. The average rape victim or assault victim incurs about $10 in cash and property losses, whereas the average robbery (or attempted robbery) victim loses $335.

Indirect Monetary and Nonmonetary Losses

The consequences of victimization can be far reaching. According to Burt and Katz (1985:330), "During the weeks or months following the [rape], women frequently make costly changes in

TABLE 5 Summary of Nonmedical Monetary Losses per Victim, 1987

Offense	Cash Loss per Victim With Cash Loss	Percent Victims With Cash Loss	Property Stolen per Victim With Property Loss	Percent Victims With Property Loss	Property Damage per Victim With Property Damage	Percent Victims With Property Damage	Average Loss Over All Victims
Rape	$207	4	$ 27	5	$ 15	5	$ 11
Robbery	192	38	557	45	157	6	335
Assault	0	0	0	0	200	5	10

NOTE: Attempted rapes, robberies, and assaults are included in these averages.

SOURCE: National Crime Survey data.

their lifestyles; this may involve moving to a 'better' neighborhood, buying expensive security systems, or avoiding work situations which they suddenly perceive as dangerous." It is also possible that nominal dollar losses, such as cash stolen or the value of lost workdays, underestimate the true monetary impact of victimization. For example, a crime victim might be forced into defaulting on a mortgage or lose a job due to lost workdays. An elderly victim on a fixed income might have to temporarily forgo food or heat, leading to detrimental health consequences. However, we are unaware of any studies that attempt to quantify either the incidence of these losses or their monetary value. Future studies of these indirect losses would be of interest.

EMERGENCY RESPONSE TO VICTIMIZATION

This section describes the costs that public agencies incur in responding to victimization and dealing with its immediate consequences. The costs of investigation aimed at capturing and convicting the offender are not included here, because they are primarily costs of preventing future victimizations, as discussed in the next section.

Victim Services

Victim service organizations provide many services to victims of crime, including counseling, temporary shelter, and financial assistance. Although one might argue these costs should be classified with society's response to victimization, we have included them here because they are designed to assist the victim directly. Of course, they may also help prevent future victimization, as in the case of centers for battered women. Since victims are likely to suffer more severe consequences and higher costs in the absence of these services, we include costs of victim services in this section.

According to the Office for Victims of Crime (1988), there are more than 2,000 victim service programs around the country. This may be an underestimate of the actual number of programs: Smith and Freinkel (1988:156) found more than 900 programs for battered women alone in 1986.

Although we do not know how much is spent for victim services by state or local governments or private organizations, there are several ways of arriving at "ballpark" estimates of expenditures. The Victims of Crime Act (VOCA) requires at least a 25 percent match for existing programs, although "soft" matches (e.g., "in-kind" donations, such as volunteer time) are eligible (Office for Victims of Crime, 1988). The 1988 report categorizes program recipients by the percentage of their budget supported by VOCA funds. Assuming that the size distribution of agency budgets is evenly distributed across percentage support, we estimate that VOCA accounted for about 26 percent of all supported agency budgets.[26] At most, VOCA supports 70 percent of victim service agencies (based on the assertion that there are "over 2,000 programs" and the 1,422 programs supported by VOCA). Thus, VOCA funds account for *no more than* 18 percent of all victim service program expenditures. Based on total VOCA funding of $35.4 million, this would imply a lower bound on total expenditures of approximately $200 million.

This estimate implies that the average annual budget of a victim service program is $200,000 ($200 million divided by 2,000 programs). In fact, according to a survey of 36 independent victim assistance programs, the median annual operating budget was $200,000 (Webster, 1988:3). However, the survey noted that the median program relied on 5 full-time staff members, 3 part-time staff members, and 20 volunteers. Thus, if one were to include the value of volunteer time, the opportunity cost of these programs could easily double or triple.

During fiscal year 1986, $35.4 million was granted by states to various victim assistance programs under funds received from VOCA. Table 6 lists these grants by victimization category. Given the assumption that the multiple categories in Table 6 are allocated

TABLE 6 Victim Assistance Program (federal funds)

Offense	Funds	Number of Programs
Sexual assault only	$ 5,129,646	240
Spouse abuse only	8,629,079	427
Child abuse only	4,724,927	219
Sexual assault and spouse abuse	3,391,890	167
Sexual assault and child abuse	1,075,406	30
Spouse abuse and child abuse	1,421,077	34
Sexual assault, spouse abuse, and child abuse	2,688,916	97
Victims in general	6,820,493	226
Other special victims	1,392,383	45
Total	$35,375,806	1,489

SOURCE: Office of Victims of Crime (1988).

TABLE 7 Estimated Victim Service Program Expenditures by Type of Crime

Offense	Expenditures (millions $)	Total Victims	Cost per Victim
Rape	$ 45.9	147,286	$311
Spouse Abuse	66.3		
Child Abuse	38.2		
General/other	149.6		
Total	$200.0		

equally between constituent categories (e.g., funds designated "sexual assault and spouse abuse" are shared equally by the two), Table 7 estimates the total and per victim cost of victim programs. This is based on the earlier assumption that federal funds represent 18 percent of total expenditures.

According to the Office of Victims of Crime (1988:87-90), 41 states reported eligible victim compensation programs in fiscal year 1987. The total amount paid to victims in these 41 states was $101,563,900. Table 8 breaks down average victim compensation per case involving compensation by offenses.

Based on the above estimates, Table 9 estimates the amount of victim compensation *per victim*. Note that no estimate is available for robbery. Also, it is assumed that all sex offenses involve rape, so this estimate is probably too high.

The above discussion of victim services is admittedly very limited. A host of other services directed toward victims are not included. A few examples include foster care for children (e.g., resulting from either domestic violence or single parents who are incarcerated or killed) and victim crisis counseling available at various medical facilities. A comprehensive study of victim services would be desirable.

Police Response Administrative Costs

Table 10 presents estimates of the emergency response costs for police: $78 for rape, $50 for robbery, $30 for assault, and $115 for murder. These estimates *exclude* the cost of investigation, because these costs have been assigned to "society's response to victimization" in the next section of the paper. Police response

TABLE 8 Victim Compensation by Offense, 1987

Offense	Total Compensation	Number of Cases	Average Compensation per Case
Murder	$15,371,643	5,868	$2,620
Sex offenses	5,329,206	4,551	1,171
Assault	57,666,244	24,508	2,353
Child abuse	1,917,658	896	2,140
Child sexual abuse	9,031,115	7,880	1,146
Spouse abuse	232,375	259	897
Other violent	9,275,201	3,987	2,326
DWI/DUI	4,358,973	1,457	2,992
MV assault	1,901,870	696	2,733
Other	5,479,615	6,130	894
Total	110,563,900	56,232	1,966

NOTE: DWI = driving while intoxicated; DUI = driving under the influence; MV = motor vehicle.

SOURCE: Office for Victims of Crime (1988).

TABLE 9 Average Victim Compensation, 1987

Offense	Total Victims	Compensated Victims	Percentage Compensated	Average Payment	Average Compensation Over All Victims
Murder	20,100	5,868	29	$2,620	$765
Rape	147,286	4,551	3	1,171	36
Assault	4,930,149	24,508	0.5	2,353	12

NOTE: Includes attempted rape and attempted assault.

SOURCE: Table 3 (number of victims) and Table 8 (compensation).

times were estimated from a survey we conducted of several police departments (i.e., Dade County, Florida; San Antonio, Texas; San Jose, California). Since these data represent crimes known to the police, the final figures have been adjusted to account for the percentage of crime not known to the police (Bureau of Justice Statistics, 1989a:Table 92).

Unit costs of police response were calculated as salary multiplied by the average time spent on a case per category of crime.

TABLE 10 Police Response Administrative Costs (averaged over all victims), 1987

Offense	Average Number of Hours	Percentage Police Cost per Reported Case	Reported to Police (Table 18)	Cost per Case
Murder	3.5	$115	91.7	$105
Rape	2.4	78	55.7	43
Robbery	1.5	50	44.4	22
Assault	0.9	30	47.7	14

NOTE: Rape, robbery, and assault include attempts.

SOURCE: Number of hours based on survey of Dade County, Fla.; San Antonio, Tex.; and San Jose, Calif. police departments. Dollar costs per hour are taken from Miller and Luchter (1988).

Police salaries, including fringe benefits, were estimated at $22 per hour, based on census data for salaries and a survey of fringe benefit rates in police departments (Miller and Luchter, 1988). To account for officer, supervisory, and support personnel administrative time, the average time spent on a case was inflated by a factor of 1.5. Although some percentage of police time spent on crime investigation is likely to be overtime, due to lack of data we were unable to account for this expense.

The police response estimates do not include all possible police costs associated with victim injury. For example, the cost of injury incurred by police officers during investigation of incidents of violent behavior is not reflected here.[27]

Emergency Transport

Table 11 presents estimates of emergency ambulance costs, disaggregated by crime and distributed across all victims: $6 for rape, $4 for robbery, and $2 for assault. Because no data were available on the frequency of other modes of emergency transportation (such as helicopters), they are not included here. Although NCS includes information on the number of victims requiring hospital treatment, no data on mode of transportation are included. Absent better data, we assume that all individuals who were admitted as hospital inpatients had been transported by ambulance and that no individuals who were treated as outpatients received emergency transportation. Although in reality some victims treated

TABLE 11 Emergency Transport Costs (averaged over all victims), 1987

Offense	Number of Victims	Number of Hospital Admissions	Percentage of Victims Transported	Average Cost of Transport
Murder	20,100		100.0	$465
Rape	147,000	6,400	4.3	6
Robbery	1,068,500	29,800	2.8	4
Assault	4,930,000	60,400	1.2	2

NOTE: Rape, robbery, and assault include attempts.

SOURCE: Hospital admissions taken from the National Crime Survey. Cost assumed to be $145 per transport, from Rice at al. (1989). Murder costs include the cost of coroner.

as outpatients arrived by ambulance and some inpatients were privately transported, we implicitly assume that such cases cancel one another out.

Emergency transport costs for nonfatal injuries were estimated to be $145 per one-way transport (inflated to 1987 dollars from the 1985 National Medical Care Utilization and Expenditure Survey figure reported by Rice et al., 1989).

Data on transport for murder victims were not available. However, approximately 94 percent of motor vehicle crash fatalities are doubly transported; first by ambulance and then by coroners' vehicles (National Highway Traffic Safety Administration, 1983). By assuming similar double transport occurs for 94 percent of murder victims, emergency transport costs per victim were estimated at $465. This includes one-way ambulance charges of $145 for the 94 percent transported by ambulance, plus the National Highway Traffic Safety Administration (1983) estimate of $330 per fatality for coroners costs (in 1987 dollars).

VICTIM PRODUCTIVITY COSTS

Table 12 presents productivity loss estimates related to physical injury. (Table 4 contains estimates of productivity loss due to mental health injuries.) Estimates of productivity losses resulting from victim injuries were based on lost workdays, lost housework days, and lost school days. For those individuals who were nonfatally injured, estimated work loss days due to injury were derived from the NCS data covering the first six-month period postinjury. Vic-

TABLE 12 Estimated Cost of Lost Productivity (averaged over all victims), 1987

| Offense | Due to Medical Reasons | | | Average Lost Productivity Due to Legal Process or Product Repair |
	Average Work Loss	Average Lost Housework	Average Lost Schoolwork for Student	
Rape	$135	$29	$32	$105
Robbery	66	21	25	46
Assault	42	10	27	19
Murder	—————————$610,000—————————			

NOTE: Lost productivity due to mental health-related injuries is reported in Table 4. Rape, robbery, and assault include attempts.

tims who lost days reported average losses of 16 workdays due to rape, 12.5 workdays due to robbery, and 13 workdays due to assault. The percentage of victims reporting lost workdays due to injury was 4 percent for assault, 7 percent for robbery, and 11 percent for rape. The value of lost workdays was estimated to be $75, based on $8.98 per hour for a seven-hour work day, plus 19.7 percent for fringe benefits (Bush, 1990:Tables C24 and C44).

The productivity losses reported here are likely to *underestimate* the true losses for at least two reasons. First, respondents report only work lost from the date of victimization to the date of interview, a period that could vary from one day to six months. Second, the data do not include longer-term work losses, future recurring injury-related work losses, or those associated with permanent impairment. Future studies could be enhanced by additional data on the percentage of injured victims whose work loss and recovery in general require more than six months.

The productivity cost estimate in Table 12 also omits many costs incurred by employers, such as (1) training replacements for victims who never return to work, (2) the loss of unique skills of some workers who do not return, and (3) hiring temporary help or paying overtime to handle the work load of temporarily absent employees.

Because NCS does not query respondents about lost housework days, we made several assumptions to estimate these losses. Primarily, we assumed that injured victims do not return to housework prior to returning to the workplace.[28] For victims who reported lost workdays, we estimated lost housework days at 365/243 (i.e., the ratio of possible housework days to workdays based on a seven-day housework week and a five-day work week) times the number of reported workdays lost. The methodology for estimating these housework losses is contained in Miller et al. (1989a:306).[29] For those who did not report employment and were over the age of 19 (i.e., not assumed to be students), we assumed that lost housework days were the same as for those who reported employment. The mean annual value of housekeeping services was estimated to be $5,170 for the employed and $9,130 for the nonstudent, nonemployed (based on Rice et al., 1989:225).

The NCS also excludes lost school days due to victim injury. Although the data base documents student status, that information was not available to the authors at the time this study was being conducted. Instead, we assumed that 34 percent were students, because 34 percent of the victims were between the ages of 12 and 19. This assumption may overstate the proportion of students among victims, since a fair percentage of late adolescents, who are most at risk for victimization, are no longer in school. Conversely, some older college and graduate students are victimized.

The school year was assumed to equal 166 days. The value of lost school days was calculated by using the average number of lost workdays reported, reduced by 166/243 to account for the seasonality of the school year. The value of each lost school year was estimated to be $3,975, based on the annual cost per pupil in average daily attendance (Bureau of the Census, 1989:Table 229). Dividing by the number of school days per year, the value of a lost school day was estimated as $24. This valuation may be conservative because the economy obtains positive returns from educational investment (Psacharopoulos, 1981).

The NCS also asks respondents the number of lost workdays due either to the legal process or to property repair. Using the above procedure for inferring lost household production from reported lost wages, we estimated the average lost productivity due to victim involvement in the legal process (or property repair). This is also reported in Table 12.

When someone is murdered, all of their future workplace and household productivity is lost. No information was available that would allow us to directly estimate lost productivity to the average murder victim. Instead, the estimated productivity loss per murder victim of $610,000, reported in Table 12, is based on the average productivity loss per firearm-related fatality from Rice et al. (1989), inflated to 1987 dollars and adjusted to the 2.5 percent discount rate used in this study. This estimate includes lost household production. However, lost school days were not included, because losses associated with forgone education are counted in lost wages or lost quality of life.

PROGRAM ADMINISTRATION COSTS

Table 13 summarizes various program administration costs associated with victimization, including health, life, and property insurance and government transfer programs. No cost estimates were available for legal costs associated with lawsuits brought by victims to recover damages.

Health and Life Insurance Claims

Excluding injuries in motor vehicle crashes, approximately 44 percent of the medical costs of injury are covered by private insurance.[30] To compute the administrative costs to process medical claims for victim injury, we multiplied this percentage times the medical costs times the ratio of claims to administrative cost for health insurance, .084.[31] These estimates may be conservative because it was not possible to determine the percentage of privately reimbursed victims reimbursed by workers' compensation, which carries a higher administrative cost of approximately 13 percent. Approximately 32 percent of costs are covered under public health programs such as Medicare and Medicaid for which

TABLE 13 Health Care Administrative Costs (averaged over all victims), 1987

Offense	Average Long-Term Medical Expenses[a]	Health Insurance Administrative Costs	Life Insurance Administrative Costs	Disability Payments	Total Administrative Costs
Murder	$2,920	$155	$3,677	$2,013	$5,846
Rape	376	20	—	0.76	21
Robbery	124	7	—	0.40	7
Assault	153	8	—	0.24	8

NOTE: Rape, robbery, and assaults are averaged over all victims, including attempts.

[a]Excluding premature funerals.

administrative costs are 5 percent of the cost of health claims (Rice et al., 1989). Table 13 indicates that health insurance administrative costs for victim injuries were $20 for rape, $7 for robbery, $8 for assault, and $155 for murder.[32]

Life insurance for murder victims also results in administrative costs. We assume that children do not have life insurance coverage and that the average coverage per adult is $47,500. This figure was computed by dividing the average coverage per household from the Bureau of the Census (1989) by the number of adults per household cited in that same source (Miller, 1989b). This estimate may be high if murder victims had disproportionately lower incomes, because the probability of having life insurance and the amount of coverage increase with income. The percentage of murder victims over age 19 was assumed to be 86 percent (Flanagan and Maguire, 1990:Table 3.129). The administrative expense associated with a life insurance claim was estimated to be 9 percent (Miller, 1989b), implying a cost of $3,677 per murder victim.

Income Transfer Programs

According to Rice et al. (1989) about 14 percent of productivity losses (including lost wages and household production) resulting from nonfatal injuries and 10 percent of those resulting from fatal injuries are reimbursed by public disability benefits. Disability payments probably involve roughly the same 5 percent administrative cost as public medical cost reimbursement. The costs are approximately $0.76 per rape, $0.40 per robbery victimization, $0.24 per assault, and $2,013 per murder. This estimate omits the costs of processing sick leave usage and private disability insurance claims.

Property Insurance Claims

Although NCS asks respondents whether property losses were partially covered by insurance, we did not have access to these data. About 70 percent of all homeowners have property insurance (Insurance Information Institute, 1989). Not all of these losses are likely to be recoverable due to insurance deductibles. About 45 percent of all robbery losses amount to less than $100, whereas 35 percent are more than $250 (Bureau of Justice Statistics, 1989a:76). We assume that 40 percent of all losses are insured and recoverable. The overhead rate for homeowners insurance is 16 percent. Based on these assumptions, the property insurance overhead cost per victim is $1 for rape and assault, and $20 for robbery.

Legal Costs Associated With Tort Claims

Traditionally, victims seldom file legal tort claims for injuries sustained as a result of violent behavior because offenders have few assets to make such suits worthwhile. An exception has been in the case of incidents that occur on third-party premises where there is an allegation of inadequate protection afforded by the third party. These suits often have been directed at businesses such as retail establishments, hotels, and apartment buildings (Carrington, 1978, 1983) and are apparently legally well established in the case of rape (Ballou, 1981).

Sherman and Klein (1984) analyzed tens of thousands of civil tort cases reported from 1958-1982 by the American Trial Lawyers' Association. They found only 186 security-related cases, not all of which involved violent behavior. It should be noted that the Association data set is neither an exhaustive list nor a representative sample of civil tort actions in the United States. Nevertheless, given the several million annual victimizations in the United States, it is clear that few victims sue for damages. There has been some apparent growth over time, however, with about 30 cases per year reported during 1980-1982.

More recently, the number of tort actions brought by victims of rape, sexual assault, or sexual abuse has risen significantly (Jury Verdict Research, 1989). In 1989, Jury Verdict Research, Inc., issued its first handbook devoted solely to such cases. Previously, it was unwilling to make separate estimates for these injuries and instead included them in other, broader categories. Cohen and Miller (1994b) report on nearly 1,000 jury awards to assault victims and 360 awards to rape and sexual assault victims. The median award for assault victims is $59,000, whereas the mean award is $680,000. The median rape or sexual assault award is $430,000, with the mean award being $1.5 million.

Although civil litigation might help compensate some victims, it is not a costless remedy. According to Kakalik and Pace (1986:68-70), legal transaction costs exceeded the total amount of compensation paid through the tort system in 1985. For every $1.00 in compensation awarded to the plaintiff, about $1.13 was spent on legal transaction costs. Moreover, for every $1.00 compensation paid, the plaintiff kept only about 70 cents after paying legal fees and expenses (even less if one includes the value of the plaintiff's time and other expenses such as transportation).[33]

It is possible that larger cases have relatively lower expense to compensation ratios, because there are no doubt some fixed costs of litigation. However, the estimates above are weighted over all tort cases.

Although we offer no concrete estimates of legal transaction fees per victimization, we can examine the likely magnitude of these costs if we make a few assumptions. For example, if 1 percent of all rape victims sued for damages (about 1,500 suits per year), and their typical award was $400,000, the legal transaction cost per rape victim would be about $4,500 ($400,000 × 1% × 1.13 = $972). If only .01 percent of rape victims sued for damages (150 suits per year), the cost per victim would be about $450. However, we simply do not know the frequency of such lawsuits, and no estimates are included in this paper.

Pain, Suffering, and Quality of Life Costs for Nonfatal Victims

In addition to out-of-pocket expenses, such as lost wages and medical expenses, crime victims endure pain, suffering, and reduced quality of life from their injuries. Although there is a conceptual difference between "pain and suffering" and "quality of life" costs to victims, the distinction can sometimes become blurred. Pain and suffering is a monetized value of the physical and mental pain endured by the victim due to the injury. Quality of life costs involve the monetization of enjoyable activities that the victim is no longer able to undertake as a result of the injury. For example, a rape victim's pain and suffering might be thought of as the mental and physical damage caused by the rape, whereas the loss in quality of life might be due to activities the victim no longer feels safe undertaking, such as walking in the park.

Although we can conceptualize these differences, it is often difficult to separate them empirically. Willingness to pay (WTP) studies that estimate how consumers value small changes in the risk of death are likely to include expected lost earnings, lost enjoyment of life, plus an evaluation of pain and suffering likely to be endured after an incident but prior to death. Thus, in fatal injuries, WTP is likely to include a complete accounting of nonmonetary damages. Similarly, if a WTP study estimates the value of a change in risk of a nonfatal injury, that should include both pain and suffering and lost quality of life.

However, few WTP studies have estimated *nonfatal* injuries.

Instead, researchers have attempted to infer WTP for reduced non-fatal injuries by applying WTP estimates for *fatal* injuries to ratings of impairment in nonfatal injuries (see discussion of willingness to pay, below). This approach attempts to account for long-term pain and suffering (which would not be present in fatal cases) by including "pain" in the impairment rating scheme and allowing for fates worse than death (Miller et al., 1989a,b).

It may be possible in the future to distinguish these costs by using the compensation approach, as juries generally specify each component of compensation separately (Miller,1989a:892-893). However, courts are just beginning to recognize "loss of enjoyment" as a distinct category from "pain and suffering." It is not clear whether this distinction will result in increased average awards or whether juries currently include their valuation of lost quality of life when making pain and suffering awards.

In the following discussion, we use the terms *pain and suffering* and *quality of life* interchangeably. Further, we do not distinguish between them in making cost estimates. However, we utilize two different estimation techniques—compensation and WTP. The compensation approach follows Cohen (1988a), and the WTP approach follows the basic methodology in Miller et al. (1989a).

In addition to the *conceptual* differences between WTP and WTA outlined in the first section of this paper, there is an important *empirical* difference between the estimation approaches used here. The WTP estimates are based on values that workers (or consumers) place on small *risks* of injury or death, whereas the compensation estimates are based on actual jury awards for identified individuals who were injured. Thus, the WTP estimates are more relevant for policy analysis of programs designed to reduce the risk of intentional injury, whereas the compensation estimates provide some indication of the amount juries believe is required to make victims "whole." Compensation should be higher than WTP.

Evidence Using the Compensation Approach

Following Cohen (1988a), we estimated the average medical cost and lost wages per type of injury, and combined these with jury award data to estimate the monetary value of pain and suffering. However, unlike Cohen (1988a), the present study does not have to rely on worker injury data for average medical and lost wage estimates. Instead, these data are taken directly from the NCS. Thus, different estimates were made for each type of crime

TABLE 14 Estimated Monetary Value of Pain and Suffering, Nonfatal Injuries (averaged over all victims), 1987

Offense	Due to Physical Injury[a]	Due to Psychological Injury[a]	Due to Fear of Injury[a]	Total Range (WTP and compensation)
Rape	$7,400	$36,600	$ 400	$33,300 - 44,400
Robbery	5,100	9,300	1,800	12,150 - 16,200
Assault	4,800	4,250	2,050	8,325 - 11,100

NOTE: Willingness to pay is estimated at 75 percent of compensation amount. Includes attempted rape, robbery, and assault.

[a]Based on compensation approach.

by type of injury. The first column of Table 14 updates the estimates of pain and suffering caused by physical injuries, using the most recently available data from Jury Verdict Research, Inc.

One could argue that median jury awards are a more appropriate measure of "typical" pain and suffering. Although this argument has some validity, it would not be valid to assume that median jury awards for injuries in personal injury cases (most of which involve motor vehicle crashes) are the same as those caused by criminal victimization. Instead, we want to be able to control for the varying severity of injuries from these disparate causes. Thus, the approach used here is to estimate the functional relationship of "specials" (i.e., the sum of medical costs and lost workdays) to jury awards for pain and suffering. Average medical costs and lost workdays in cases of intentional injury are then used to estimate a pain and suffering award. Thus, the estimates here do not reflect the average jury award. Instead they reflect the average jury award *for a specific amount of medical expenses and lost wages.* In that sense, they are very much like a "typical" award.

In addition to pain and suffering caused by physical injury, a crime victim might suffer psychological injury. The risks of psychological injury, as well as potential mental health care expenditures and lost workdays, are estimated in Table 4. Based on the estimated potential mental health-related costs per victim, we can estimate the pain and suffering damages that a jury would award.

Psychological injuries were categorized as either "traumatic neurosis" or "severely disabling psychiatric injury" in Cohen (1988a). This was consistent with the classifications used by Jury Verdict

Research, Inc. More recent data from Jury Verdict Research, Inc., have similar classifications, with slightly different titles: "emotional distress" and "severely disabling psychological trauma." However, the operational definitions of these categories remain unchanged. Absent better data on actual mental health care costs and lost wages, we rely on the estimation technique used in Cohen (1988a), which yielded the following estimates (in 1987 dollars):

Psychological Injury	Average Medical and LostWages	Average Pain and Suffering
Severely disabling psychological trauma	$26,500	$139,961
Emotional distress	6,500	67,495
Fear with weapon present	—	4,856
Fear without weapon	—	2,398

The pain and suffering estimate for emotional distress is about $9,000 lower than the estimate in Cohen (1988a). It is unlikely that the average award actually decreased in the past few years. The data we have relied on are admittedly very imperfect, and a 15 percent margin of error is certainly possible. On the other hand, pain and suffering awards for severe psychological injury appeared to have increased—from an average of $97,556 to $139,961.[34] Because little is known about the sample sizes or distribution of cases, we have no explanation for this increase. That is, we do not know if this difference is due to one or two "outliers," or if it indicates a significant trend in liability awards. The second column of Table 14 reports the pain and suffering estimate for psychological injury.

For those victims who did *not* receive any physical or psychological injury, we have estimated a "fear" component of pain and suffering. The monetary value of "fear" is one of the least defensible estimates in Cohen (1988a), because it was based on a few jury award cases in Louisiana, in which the courts recognize the right to recover damages for fear without injury.

The data from Jury Verdict Research, Inc. (1989), now include estimates of "emotional distress as the sole injury," typically where "the plaintiff claimed mental anguish, humiliation, depression, anxiety, and damage to reputation . . . that was not accompanied by any physical injury. The psychological trauma was minimal and, in most cases, temporary." The average jury award verdict in cases of this sort with little or no "specials" was $29,646. The median award was $6,000. We are reluctant to use these estimates, because they are based on broader categories of mental anguish than just fear. However, the estimates in Cohen (1988a) were lower than this amount—$4,535 with weapon present and $2,240 without. Thus, our estimates seem quite conservative. These estimates (updated to 1987 dollars) are combined with the frequency of each type of crime that results in no physical or emotional injury and appear in the third column of Table 14. It should be noted that the relatively low estimate for rape does not indicate a low level of fear among rape victims. Instead, the relatively low fear estimate reflects the fact that the percentage of rape and attempted rape victims who suffer from neither mental nor physical injury (and thus suffer only from fear) is very low.

The last column of Table 14 summarizes the pain and suffering estimates: $44,400 for rape, $16,200 for robbery, and $11,100 for assault. It is based on the average cost for all victims—whether they were estimated to have pain and suffering or not. The lower values in this column are based on WTP, discussed in the next section.

Evidence Using Willingness to Pay

Since the first study by Acton (1973), there have been scores of WTP studies for changes in the risk of death and, by extension, the statistical value of an anonymous life. We start with an estimated $2.2 million (1987 dollars) as the WTP or "whole life benefits" of preventing loss of an anonymous life (Miller, 1990). Because only a portion of this amount is due to lost enjoyment of life, Miller (1990) also decomposes the $2.2 million estimate into lost productivity, financial security, and quality of life. The quality of life component of the typical death has a value around $1,750,000, with an uncertainty range from $1,050,000 to $2,450,000. It should be noted that this includes the benefits to the person's loved ones.

Of course, since we all must die sometime, what these studies are really measuring is the value of additional life years. With discounting, the nonmonetary quality of life benefit of a reduced risk of death is about $70,000 per year of life and functioning saved.

For nonfatal injuries, we estimated the percentage impairment associated with injuries, based on physician estimates (see Miller et al., 1989a). We computed average years of impairment per injury for three NCS categories of injury that could also be evaluated by using compensation data. The categories were

(1) broken bones and teeth, based on an average of broken leg, forearm, shoulder, and tooth,
(2) head injury resulting in loss of consciousness, and
(3) internal injury.

The impairment years per injury were multiplied by the nonmonetary value of a life year to estimate the nonmonetary benefits of preventing injuries.

Ratings of impairment were not available for rape, attempted rape, knife wounds, or gunshot wounds. To estimate the nonmonetary component of whole life benefits for these injuries, we assumed that the ratio of whole life benefits to compensation (for nonmonetary losses) was constant across injury types. The whole life cost approach yields nonmonetary benefits equal to about 75 percent of the nonmonetary cost estimates from the compensation approach (with an uncertainty range of ±40 percent, meaning that the upper end of the range would exceed the compensation cost estimates). These lower estimates are reported in the last column of Table 14.

RISK OF DEATH

Throughout this paper, we have made separate cost estimates for murder. In many circumstances, murder occurs as the end result of a less severe underlying crime. In these cases, one can estimate the "risk of murder" and place a dollar value on that risk. Presumably, by reducing the underlying crime we also reduce the risk of murder.

According to the FBI's Uniform Crime Reports, there were an estimated 20,100 murders and nonnegligent homicides in 1987 (Jamieson and Flanagan, 1989:427). The FBI compiles further statistics on the circumstances underlying murder. In 1987, there were 17,963 murders for which the FBI received supplemental information. Of those, the circumstances underlying the murder were known in 13,490 cases.[35] If we assume that the cases with unknown circumstances have the same distribution as those known, we can estimate the total number of murders caused by various underlying crimes and the WTP per victim to avoid the risk of victim fatality (by assuming $2.2 million per statistical life) to be

	Fatal	Nonfatal	Risk of Death	Value
Rape	305	147,286	0.00207	$4,500
Robbery	2,497	1,068,514	0.00233	5,100
Assault	16,654	4,930,149	0.00337	7,400

Later, when we tally the cost of each victimization type, the risk of death is included as part of the cost of the underlying victimization. However, in calculating the aggregate cost of violent behavior, the risk of death is not included. Otherwise, double counting of murders would result.

QUALITY OF LIFE OF FAMILY MEMBERS OF VICTIM

Family members can be affected by victim injuries in several different ways. First, they may be inconvenienced through increased household chores and attending to the needs of the injured victim during recovery. Second, there may be a psychic cost for "loss of companionship." Finally, family members may suffer actual psychological trauma themselves.

Increased Work Load of Family Members

Conceptually, victimization has two different effects on the household duties of family members: (1) replacement of the victim's household services and (2) attending to the physical needs of the victim. The first type of cost has already been attributed to the victim's losses and is estimated in Table 12. Since we are unaware of any data on attending to the physical needs of the victim, we have not included any related cost estimates here. Note that these costs could be incurred directly by family members through their own labor or through the hiring of outside help.

A related area of research has shown that family caregivers of disabled elderly often "experience physical, emotional and social burden as a result of meeting this responsibility" (Mohide et al., 1988:475). Care of relatives with cognitive deficiencies was more burdensome than care of relatives with physical deficiencies. However, we are unaware of any related studies on crime victims or of studies that would allow us to infer the frequency of these problems in crime victims.

Loss of Companionship/Consortium

Although loss of companionship is more likely to occur in death cases, it also may be a concern in cases of severely disabling physical injury and, possibly, in cases of sexual assault and rape. One method of estimating this loss is to examine jury awards for loss of services/consortium. According to 1988 Jury Verdict Research, Inc., data, the median award for catastrophic injury or death to a husband or wife is about $500,000. Median awards for serious injuries (such as fractures, internal injuries, or other injuries with permanent impairment) ranged from $25,000 to $50,000, whereas those for minor injuries range from $5,000 to $10,000.

An alternative approach is to decompose the WTP estimate of the value of a statistical life in order to estimate the nonmonetary component borne by the victim's family. This is done in Miller (1989a:896), where family losses are estimated to be $400,000–$700,000 when an adult is killed, with death of a young child resulting in an even greater loss.

Although the awards to family members in cases of catastrophic injury (including death) are extremely large, it would not necessarily be reasonable to add these to the cost of deaths. Nor would it be reasonable to add family members' mental health-related costs or pain and suffering. We have used a statistical value of life of $2.2 million, which is based primarily on wage rate differentials for risky jobs. Because wage earner's salary is shared by the entire family, to a large extent this value of life estimate represents the loss to the family unit.

Psychological Injury to Family Member

Finally, there might be psychological injury to a family member, especially one who actually witnesses a victimization. Although few studies have tried to assess the long-term mental health consequences to the family of a victim of crime, a good deal of literature describes the mental health effects on spouses and parents of victims of other causes of sudden death. The family's recovery process is apparently much slower when the victim suffered an unexpected death as opposed to being forewarned (e.g., chronic illness).

Lehman et al. (1987) compared a sample of 80 individuals who had lost a spouse or child in a motor vehicle crash from four to seven years earlier, to a matched control group of 80 similar individuals who had not experienced this type of loss, as well as to national norms and a group of female psychiatric outpatients. An additional 20-30 percent of the bereaved group reported depression beyond the rates of the control group.

A more recent survey of 214 family members of homicide victims and 105 randomly sampled nonvictim controls found that 23.4 percent of family members of homicide victims developed homicide related PTSD at some time following the death (Amick et al., 1989; Kilpatrick et al., 1989). However, "in terms of general psychological distress, survivors were no more symptomatic than nonvictim controls." This finding suggests that most family members who did develop PTSD recovered substantially prior to the interview. We do not know the frequency of psychological counseling or treatment. Moreover, we do not know if there are differences in PTSD frequency depending on whether the family member witnessed the victimization, whether the offender was related to the family, etc. (Amick-McMullan et al., 1989).

Pynoos and Eth (1985:20) report on more than 100 child witnesses to the murder of a parent, rape of a mother, or suicidal act of a parent. They found that nearly 80 percent had PTSD. Unfortunately, little is known about the selection process for this sample or if the percentage varies by type of incident.

Pynoos and Eth (1985:21-22) also report that "the Sheriff's Homicide Division of Los Angeles County estimates that dependent children witness between 10 to 20 percent of the approximately 2,000 annual homicides in their jurisdiction." In addition, virtually all of the 50 child homicide witnesses interviewed experienced PTSD (Pynoos and Eth, 1985:29).

Finally, Pynoos and Eth (1985:22) report that a child (or children) directly views a mother being raped in about 10 percent of all rapes reported to the police in Los Angeles County. Nationally, they report that about 40 percent of all rapes occur at home, and that 40 percent of all rape victims are of childbearing age. In addition, they report that a child witnessed or knew about marital rape in 11 percent of these incidents.

Based on the above, it is estimated that 10 percent of the children of homicide victims suffer from PTSD, whereas the rate for spouses and parents of young victims is 20 percent. Of course, to estimate the cost averaged over all victims, one must multiply these rates by the fraction of homicide victims who have children and the fraction who are married. Although we do not have such data, we can make some ballpark estimates based on several assumptions. For example, if we assume that 100 percent of homicides involve victims who either have a child or a spouse, or are youths themselves, and that the ratio of emotional distress to severely disabling injury is 4 to 1, the average homicide involves lost wages, medical costs, and pain and suffering of about $28,000. As the percentage of victims who have dependents decreases, this figure would decrease accordingly. Although a significant consequence for those who are affected, this cost is relatively small in comparison to the $2.2 million value we place on homicide itself. Moreover, because the lost quality of life to family members is partially accounted for in the $2.2 million value of life, we have not included this as a cost element.

In cases of rape, we estimate that 10 percent involve a child witness and that 80 percent of these witnesses experience PTSD. Because we have no evidence on the severity of these PTSD cases, we assume the same ratio of emotional distress to severely disabling injury as for rape cases (i.e., 4 to 1). Thus, over all rape victims, it is assumed that 6.4 percent (10% of rape incidents × 80% PTSD rate × 80% of PTSDs being less severe) involve a child witness who suffers from emotional distress, and 1.6% (10% × 80% × 20%) involve a severely disabling injury to a child witness. Based on jury awards for these psychological injuries, it is estimated that the average rape involves child victim-related losses of about $10,000. Given the sparse evidence we relied on to make this estimate, it should be considered tentative at best. The important point, however, is that it appears this is not a trivial cost relative to the other costs of rape.

Family member injury is likely to occur in other situations of violent behavior, particularly incidents involving domestic violence. Examples of likely psychological trauma include children witnessing spouse or child abuse, and spouses who must deal with child abuse by the other spouse. Further research in this area no doubt would be of interest.

Except in the case of rape (where we assume a $10,000 loss per incident), we have *not* included separate quality of life estimates for family members.

Psychological Trauma to Witnesses of Violent Behavior

In addition to family members, other witnesses of violent behavior might suffer from psychological trauma—especially in cases of severe injury or death. According to NCS data, 69 percent of all violent crimes were witnessed by more than one person—either other victims, family members, or bystanders (Bureau of Justice Statistics, 1989e:4). Unfortunately, we do not know the percentage in each witness category.

Although little research has been done specifically on the psychological effects of witnessing a violent act, both transitory fear and more severe PTSD are possible outcomes in some instances. Since we have no estimates of the frequency of such injury, no cost estimates are included here. However, if frequency estimates were made, the psychological trauma costs mentioned in the earlier section on family members could be applied.

INJURIES CAUSED BY EARLIER VICTIMS

For more than 25 years, social science literature has posited that family violence, such as spousal assault and child abuse, promotes additional violence directed intergenerationally within families or externally toward society in general. This "cycle of violence" is difficult to quantify. A recent review of the literature noted that "our knowledge of the long-term consequences of abusive home environments remains limited" (Widom, 1989:252).

A recent study by Widom (1989) compared a group of adults with documented histories of being abused or neglected to a control group. Abused and neglected subjects were more likely to have an adult criminal record and a substantially higher rate of arrest for violent offenses than the matched control group. Despite these findings, the relationship between childhood victimization and adult criminality is not inevitable: 29 percent of abused and neglected subjects evidenced adult criminal records; however, 71 percent did not. Consequently, Widom suggests that reassessment of the cycle of violence hypothesis is needed to develop more complex and comprehensive models of the relationship.

To the extent that child abuse causes later violent behavior by former victims, the costs of the later violence stem from the earlier violence and should be attributed to it. Proper attribution would make it clear that prevention of the initial victimization will pay extra dividends through reduced future victimization. Unfortunately, we were unable to assemble enough reliable data to take this approach.

COST OF SOCIETY'S RESPONSE TO VIOLENT BEHAVIOR

This section details the costs associated with society's response to violent behavior. Some of these costs are incurred by society in an effort to deter and punish offenders (e.g., criminal justice costs); others are designed to prevent victimization (such as precautionary expenditures by potential victims). Finally, some costs such as "fear" are by-products of the actual victimization and are not related to efforts to reduce crime.

Because most criminal justice statistics refer solely to aggravated assaults, the cost estimates developed in this section do *not* include simple assaults.

Precautionary Measures and Fear of Crime

Individuals and firms take many precautionary measures to reduce their likelihood of becoming crime victims. In some cases, these precautions involve monetary expenditures for such items as handguns, security systems, and private guards. However, many of these precautions involve more subtle costs, such as taking fewer walks at night.

Monetary Expenditures for Crime Prevention

According to a 1985 poll, 42 percent of all households own at least one "gun or revolver," and 20 percent of those respondents claim they own their firearms "mainly for protection reasons" (Bergan, 1985). Thus, about 8.4 percent of all households (42% × 20%) own firearms primarily for protection. Following Zedlewski (1985), based on 89.5 million households and an average cost of $75 per firearm, this amounts to $564 million spent on protective firearms. However, because a portion of these expenditures would have to be apportioned to the prevention of household burglary, we cannot attribute all of these costs to violent crime.

The last known estimate of private security costs for commercial and government establishments was $21.7 billion in 1980 (Cunningham and Taylor, 1985:14). In 1987 dollars, this would be about $30 billion. Once again, it is impossible to allocate these expenditures to protection against violent crime (such as armed robbery), as opposed to those designed to control employee theft and shoplifting. We are also unaware of any estimates of private residential security expenditures.

Zedlewski (1985:774) includes an estimate of the annual cost of maintaining guard dogs. Updating his estimates to 1987 dollars (and number of households) yields an annual expenditure estimate of $5.1 billion. In addition to the problem of allocating these costs between violent and nonviolent crimes, to the extent that owners derive pleasure from these pets, it would not be correct to allocate the full cost to protection.

Although some precautionary expenditures or steps can be measured, others are more subtle. For example, Sherman (1989) argues that high crime rates (particularly for armed robberies) and the high cost of security have diminished the number of small neighborhood businesses. This has an impact on employment opportunities in the inner cities, as well as decreasing the quality of life for those who live nearby and have to travel further for goods and services.

Crime Prevention Behavior

According to a recent Gallup Poll, 43 percent of the American people live within a mile of an area where they are "afraid to walk alone at night," and 10 percent say they do not feel "safe and secure" at home at night (Gallup, 1989:8). People who fear being crime victims are likely to change their behavior. They might take fewer walks at night, buy more expensive locks and security systems, etc. These are preventive measures designed to reduce the likelihood of victimization by reducing exposure to risky situations.

A survey of households in Washington, D.C., in 1971 (Clotfelter, 1977:502), found the following reported rates (percent) of self-protective behavior:

Usually locked house when at home	84.9
Usually left lights on when away	65.8
Ever stayed home at night because of crime	43.8
Installed additional locks	42.7
Ever took taxis because of crime	28.6
Carried something for protection	15.0
Obtained watchdog	12.4
Put bars on windows	5.9
Installed burglar alarm	2.7

Other studies and examples of protective behavior are cited in Clarke (1983). However, we are unaware of any attempts to place monetary values on these behavioral changes. Clotfelter and Seeley (1979:222-224) conceptualize the cost of modified behavior in terms of the opportunity cost of increased social contact or activity. In theory, many of these behavioral changes could be valued if one were to conduct an in-depth study. For example, a contingent valuation survey might elicit the value to homeowners of being able to walk outdoors at night. More detailed interviews could also help elicit quantitative information that might be used to measure out-of-pocket costs, such as the cost of additional taxi rides, additional electricity usage for increased lighting, or alarm installation and monitoring.

Fear of Crime

Potential victims will continue to purchase security devices and change their behavior until the marginal costs of these precautionary measures just equal the perceived marginal benefits in terms of reduced crime risk. Thus, at some point, it becomes "rational" to accept fear instead of spending more resources trying to reduce that fear.

Interestingly, many studies suggest that fear is negatively related to the risk of victimization. For example, "elderly women, who are most afraid, are the least frequently victimized. Young men, who are least afraid, are most often victimized" (Moore and Trojanowicz, 1988:3; see also Skogan, 1986; Skogan and Maxfield, 1981). Nonetheless, this fear is a social cost, because people who are afraid of victimization would be willing to pay to reduce that fear. Moreover, this phenomenon is actually quite consistent with rational behavior. We may observe low victimization rates among groups that are most fearful precisely because these are highly vulnerable groups that have taken preventive measures to reduce their exposure to potential victimization (Cook, 1986:6-8; Balkin, 1979:345). To date, there have been few attempts to place a dollar value on the fear of crime. Conceptually, one could use the hedonic pricing technique to estimate property value differences based on the risk of crime. However, data limitations make it very unlikely that one could isolate the fear component of housing price differentials, much less the fear of each individual crime type. One would need to have data on housing prices, crime rates, and security expenditures that are likely to be capitalized into the housing price itself. An alternative approach might be to apply the contingent valuation survey approach, discussed earlier.

CRIMINAL JUSTICE SYSTEM COSTS

Total criminal justice expenditures for 1986 were reported to be $53.5 billion (Jamieson and Flanagan, 1989:2), allocated as follows:

Police protection	$26.25 billion
Judicial and legal	11.50 billion
Corrections	15.75 billion
Total	53.50 billion

The bulk of these expenditures (56 percent) were made at the local level, whereas states spent 32 percent and the federal government only 12 percent.

For purposes of this study, the above estimates are virtually useless. Police protection encompasses many types of duties related to law and order, including traffic safety. Even the "criminal justice" component of police protection involves a significant amount of nonviolent crime. The same problem exists for the other two cost categories. A more appropriate method of estimating criminal justice-related costs would be to estimate the cost of each stage of the process and apply these estimates to individual crime types. This disaggregated approach is attempted below.

Investigation, Prosecution, and Court-Related Costs

There are numerous stages of the criminal justice system, including police investigation, prosecution, court costs, and pretrial detention. We are unaware of any previous studies that estimate costs systemwide. Instead, previous cost studies have generally focused on one stage of the process in one city (Weller and Block, 1979; Toborg, 1981; Chabotar, 1987:11).

In 1979, the Administrative Office of the Courts conducted a study of the amount of time spent by federal district court judges on each type of case (Flanders, 1980). These estimates include court time, as well as time spent by judges in conferences, research, etc. They are averaged over all cases in that category—whether they resulted in a guilty plea, dismissal, or trial.[36] To convert hours into dollars, several assumptions must be made. As a lower bound, we could multiply the time spent by the average salary of state general trial judges, currently $68,935 per year (Jamieson and Flanagan, 1989:109). However, this ignores all other court-related costs. Another item that can be added is the average cost of filing a case in court, estimated to be $124 (Judicial Conference, 1989). This can be added to judicial wage costs to arrive at a lower bound. As an upper-bound estimate, we have used the estimated cost for state court time, about $4 per minute in 1982 (Bureau of Justice Statistics, 1988d:123). Table 15 summarizes these estimated ranges for judicial costs per arrested offender.

TABLE 15 Estimated Costs of Court-Related Time per Arrested Offender, 1987

Offense	Hours of Judicial Time	Minimum Cost (judge's wages plus filing costs)	Maximum Cost (assumes 100% court time)
Homicide	13.2	$550	$3,700
Rape	7.3	350	2,075
Robbery	5.1	300	1,450
Assault	3.7	250	1,050

SOURCE: Hours taken from Flanders (1980).

One of the most comprehensive criminal justice tracking systems is employed by the Metropolitan Dade (Metro-Dade) County Department of Justice Assistance in Florida. They collect data from about 40 different local agencies to determine the cost of each stage of the process—from police investigation through final disposition.[37] Table 16 computes the average cost of each stage of the criminal justice process for Metro-Dade in 1987.

These estimates include all adult felonies—both Part I offenses and drug-related crimes. Thus, we can estimate only the average cost for all felonies, by each stage of the process. However, we do know how many of each crime type entered each stage of the process.

Table 17 combines these estimates with the proportion of murder (and manslaughter), rape, robbery, and aggravated assault cases that reach the same stage. It also includes an estimate for "other felonies" (which includes child and sexual abuse cases). The estimates in Table 17 are per case known to police rather than per case reported in the NCS.

Because offenders "drop out" at various stages of the criminal justice system, we need estimates of the percentage of total offenses that involve each stage of the process. One of the problems with estimating these drop-out rates is that estimates of total victimization come from the NCS, whereas the number of investigations and arrests comes from the Uniform Crime Reports. These sources often have different crime definitions. For example, the NCS includes only households, whereas UCR includes crimes against business. However, since this study excludes property crimes, the difference between the two surveys is of somewhat less importance. In theory, the main problem would

TABLE 16 Average Cost Per Criminal Justice Processing Stage, Metropolitan Dade County, 1987

States	Aggregate Cost	Number of Cases	Average Cost per Case
Investigation and arrest	$94,153,376	$200,000	$ 477
Booking	7,713,658	41,572	186
Pretrial jail	34,987,532	33,958	1,030
Screening and prefiling process	4,853,614	45,687	106
Arraignment	15,694,845	42,629	368
Pretrial hearings	26,071,280	20,977	1,243
Trial	17,294,310	573	30,182
Sentencing	5,615,097	15,925	353
Posttrial jail	14,431,618	3,831	3,767
Conditional release	8,734,319	9,541	915

SOURCE: Metropolitan Dade County Department of Justice Assistance, Dade Justice Improvement Model.

TABLE 17 Average Criminal Justice Cost per Crime Known to Police, Metropolitan Dade County, 1987

Crime	Average Cost
Murder/homicide	$5,925
Rape	2,050
Robbery	1,125
Aggravated assault	1,225
Other felonies (excluding drug-related)	3,325

NOTE: Costs of each stage of the process (Table 16) are not estimated on a crime-specific basis; they are averaged over all crimes. However, the percentage of offenses that reach each stage is based on crime-specific data.

appear to be in the case of robbery—where the UCR presumably includes many business crimes.

Table 18 illustrates two methods of estimating the percentage of crimes reported to police. The first column lists the percentage of victims in the National Crime Survey who claim they reported the incident to the police (Bureau of Justice Statistics, 1989a:80). The second column shows the number of estimated crimes, also taken from NCS data (except homicide, which was provided by

TABLE 18 Percentage of Victimizations Reported to Police, 1987

Offense	From NCS (%)	Number of Total Victims (NCS)	Number of Known to Police (UCR)	Implied by UCR/NCS (%)
Homicide	—	20,100	18,430	91.7
Rape	53.2	147,286	81,980	55.7
Robbery	56.1	1,068,514	474,713	44.4
Assault	46.4	4,930,149	—	—
Aggravated	59.6	1,631,673	778,889	47.7
Simple	39.5	3,298,476	—	—

the FBI). The third column is the number of offenses known to police from the UCR (as reported in Jamieson and Flanagan, 1989:510). The last column computes the implied rate of reporting by comparing columns 2 and 3. The two estimates are fairly close for rape. For robbery, we would expect the reporting rates implied by comparing NCS to UCR data to be higher than that in the NCS itself, because business crimes are included in UCR. However, the opposite appears to be true. Since we need to use UCR data on the percentage cleared by arrest, we are using the last column of Table 18 to estimate the percentage of robberies reported to police. The UCR data do not include simple assaults, which apparently have a lower reporting rate. Thus, we have used the lower NCS estimate of 39.5 percent for simple assaults.

Based on Table 18 and estimates of the "clearance" rate by arrest and the final disposition of the case, we can estimate the percentage of victimizations that eventually lead to each stage of the criminal justice process. This is done in Table 19.

Combining the criminal justice processing costs per offense known to police from Table 17 with the estimate of offenses reported to police from Table 18 yields an estimated criminal justice processing cost per offense, shown in Table 20. Processing costs are estimated to be $5,750 for murder, $1,150 per rape, and $500 each for robbery and assault. These estimates are averaged over all offenses (including attempts), even those not reported to police.

Legal Fees Associated With Criminal Justice System

In 1986, an estimated $991 million was spent by all levels of government on indigent defense, whereas the average cost per

TABLE 19 Percentage of Victimizations Disposed of at Each Stage of Criminal Justice System

Offense	NCS Estimate[a]	Reported to Police[b]	Cleared by Arrest[c]	Dismissed[d]	Guilty Pleas[d]	Guilty Verdicts[d]	Acquittal[d]
Homicide	20,100	97.1%	67.9%	18.5%	28.2%	16.4%	4.7%
Rape	147,286	55.7	29.5	12.3	13.8	2.4	1.1
Robbery	1,068,514	44.4	11.8	4.9	6.0	0.7	0.2
Assault	4,930,149	42.2	24.9	12.2	11.6	0.7	0.4
Aggravated	1,631,673	47.7	28.1	13.7	13.1	0.8	0.4
Simple	3,298,476	39.5	23.3	11.4	10.9	0.6	0.4

[a]From the National Crime Survey, except homicide, which is the number of murders and nonnegligent homicides from the Uniform Crime Report, as reported in Jamieson and Flanagan (1989:427). It should be noted that the homicide estimate is higher than the number of homicides known to police—it is the FBI's reported estimates.

[b]Taken from Table 18; see text.

[c]Column 2 multiplied by percentage of offenses known to police that are cleared by arrest, from the Uniform Crime Report, as reported in Jamieson and Flanagan (1989:510). Note that because no clearance rate is available for simple assaults, it is assumed to be the same for as aggravated assault.

[d]Column 3, the fraction cleared by arrest, multiplied by the estimated fraction of arrests resulting in each type of plea in six jurisdictions in 1986, from Boland et al. (1989). Note that the estimates in Boland et al. (1989) refer only to felony convictions. Because no comparable estimates are available for simple assaults, they were assumed to have the same disposition as aggravated assaults.

TABLE 20 Criminal Justice Processing Costs per Criminal Offense, 1987

Offense	Cost per Offense Reported to Police (Table 17)	Percentage Reported to Police (Table 18)	Cost per Offense
Murder/manslaughter	$5,925	91.7	$5,430
Rape	2,050	55.7	1,150
Robbery	1,125	44.4	500
Assault[a]	1,225	47.7	580

[a]Based on costs for all felony cases and the processing stages for aggravated assault (no estimates available for simple assaults).

case was about $230 in 1987 dollars (Bureau of Justice Statistics, 1988c:4-5). Although no published crime-specific estimates are available, we can estimate the cost by crime type, based on a few additional pieces of information. From Table 15, we estimate the weighted average time spent by judges per case to be 4.05 hours. This implies an average cost of indigent defense of $57 per hour of judicial time.

Spangenberg et al. (1986:33) reported that 48 percent of all felony cases require indigent defense. No estimates are available on the cost to defendants who hire their own legal counsel. However, given the relatively low fees paid for indigent defense, privately funded legal defense costs are likely to be higher. Absent other data, we assume that the private cost per case is the same as the indigent defense cost estimated above.

Assuming that indigent defense time is proportional to judicial time and that the cost of private defense is the same as indigent defense, we can estimate the average cost per case, as shown in Table 21.

Cost of Sanctions

Convicted offenders are subject to a variety of sanctions such as jail or prison, probation, community service, and fines. According to the Bureau of Justice Statistics (1989c), incarceration is imposed in 95 percent of murder, 75 percent of rape, 76 percent of robbery, and 45 percent of aggravated assault convictions. Expected time served in prison for newly incarcerated offenders and

TABLE 21 Cost of Legal Defense per Case Filed in Court, 1987

Offense	Hours Spent on Case	Indigent Defense ($57/hour)	Percent Arrested (Table 19)	Cost per Incident
Homicide	13.2	$750	67.9	$500
Rape	7.3	415	29.5	125
Robbery	5.1	290	11.8	35
Aggravated assault	3.7	212	28.1	60

NOTE: Of these costs, 48 percent are borne by governments through indigent defense programs. The remaining 52 percent are paid for by the offender.

actual time served in jail for recently released prisoners are available from the Bureau of Justice Statistics (1989c, 1988f). However, no estimates are available for the average time served for persons sentenced to life in prison. Because the median age of prisoners convicted of violent crimes is 28 (Bureau of Justice Statistics, 1988b), a full life term could average 40 years or more. However, parole is generally granted in life sentences—usually after 20 years or less. Absent better data, we assume that the average life sentence results in 20 years in prison.

Table 22 computes the average time served by type of offense. The first column shows the average time served per convicted offender—including those who receive no jail time. The second column is the percentage of offenses that result in convicted offenders (taken from Table 19). The third column is thus the average time served *per offense*—the "expected" time served for all offenders. The last column compares these estimates to a recent study by Kleiman et al. (1989) of "imprisonment-to-offense ratios," which were computed by comparing prison populations to the number of offenses committed. These two methods yield very similar results for murder and robbery. However, Kleiman et al.'s estimates are considerably lower for aggravated assault and rape. Although we cannot reconcile the two estimates, one possible explanation is that the imprisonment-to-offense ratio tends to underestimate the true time served in periods of rising prison populations (Kleiman et al., 1989:7). For this paper, the time served per offense estimates are used instead.

The cost of incarceration varies widely by type of facility and by state (Bureau of Justice Statistics, 1988d:123). The distribution of state facilities is about 44 percent maximum security, 44 percent medium security, and 12 percent minimum security (Bureau of Justice Statistics, 1987:6). Since we do not know the distribu-

TABLE 22 Estimated Time Served by Convicted Felons (days)

Offense	Time Served per Convicted Offender	Percentage of Offenders Convicted (Table 19)	Time Served per Offense	"Imprisonment-to-Offense Ratio" (Kleiman et al., 1989)
Murder	3,496	44.6	1,559	1,278
Rape	1,812	16.2	293	117
Robbery	1,447	6.7	97	115
Aggravated assault	644	13.9	90	31

tion of security levels for incarcerated offenders by type of crime, it is assumed to be the same for all offenders. The average annual operating costs (updated to 1987 dollars) were $12,300 for a state prisoner and $10,650 for a jail inmate (Bureau of Justice Statistics, 1988d). The American Correctional Association estimates the annual cost of incarceration to be about $41 per day or $15,000 per year (Zedlewski, 1985). A recent report on a privately operated minimum to medium security facilities estimated the daily cost of incarceration at about $25 per day (National Institute of Justice, 1989c). For this paper, we assume the daily cost of incarceration to be $35 per day (about $12,500 per year).

In 1987, about 82 percent of the offenders released from prison received some form of supervision, such as parole (Bureau of Justice Statistics, 1988g). We assume that the average releasee is supervised for two years, at an annual cost of $740 (Bureau of Justice Statistics, 1988d).

The percentage of convicted offenders sentenced to probation is also available by type of crime (Bureau of Justice Statistics, 1989c). The annual cost of probation is estimated to be $625 (Bureau of Justice Statistics, 1988d). We assume that the average length of probation is three years.

The death penalty is imposed in about 2 percent of murder convictions (Bureau of Justice Statistics, 1989c). Although we do not know how many death penalties were imposed for other offenses, there has not been an execution in the United States for an offense other than murder since 1967 (Jamieson and Flanagan, 1989:672). Thus, we assume that the only death penalty sentences are for cases of murder.

The cost of imposing the death penalty is quite high when the entire legal process is taken into account. Estimates of the cost per death penalty case vary considerably from state to state, from

TABLE 23 Estimated Cost of Imposing Sanctions per Offense, 1987

Offense	Prison or Jail	Parole or Probation After Release	Probation Only	Death Penalty	Total
Murder	$47,700	$450	$ 70	$26,750[a]	$74,970
Rape	5,100	140	180	—	5,420
Robbery	3,400	60	220	—	3,680
Aggravated assault	3,150	110	475	—	3,735

[a]Includes the entire criminal justice processing cost of imposing the death penalty.

$1.4 million in New York and $3.0 million in Florida (Spangenberg and Walsh, 1989:56), to as high as $15 million in California (Tabak, 1989:136). If the average cost per conviction is assumed to be $3 million, the cost per murder (after discounting for those not involving a conviction) is $26,750.

Table 23 summarizes the above estimates. The cost of sanctions per offense is estimated to be $74,970 for murder, $5,420 for rape, $3,680 for robbery, and $3,735 for aggravated assault. These are average costs based on current levels of conviction and incarceration—including offenses that do not lead to prosecution or conviction.

Alternatives to incarceration such as intensive probation (National Institute of Justice, 1987) and home detention (National Institute of Justice, 1989a; Hofer and Meierhoefer, 1987) are less costly than prison. For example, the average probationer in Georgia's intensive probation program costs the state $6,775 less than comparable incarcerated offenders (National Institute of Justice, 1987). Because most of these programs are still rather small, we have not estimated their costs here. To the extent that they replace incarceration, the average cost per offense will be reduced. Of course, one must also account for any increase (or decrease) in crime rates caused by the alternative sanction program.

Victim and Witness Interaction With Criminal Justice System

One cost that has received little or no attention in the literature on crime costs is the amount of time spent by victims and witnesses with police and the criminal justice system. In some cases, this might involve no more than a few minutes being interviewed by a police investigator. At the other extreme, it might involve police lineups to identify suspects or even several days in court testifying before a grand jury and as a prosecution witness.

Roughly half of all violent crimes are reported to police. After initial contact with the police, 16-33 percent of victims reported later contact, including personal visits, telephone conversations and correspondence; 11-20 percent reported contact with other authorities; and 10-13 percent with victim assistance programs (Bureau of Justice Statistics, 1989a; Whitaker, 1989). However, we do not know the amount of time spent at each stage of the process.

Some of these costs were included in Table 12, which reported on an NCS estimate of lost workdays due either to victim involvement in the legal process or to the need to repair or replace property. Those estimates per offense were quite small. We know of no estimates of the number of witnesses per case or of the time spent by witnesses at various stages of the legal process.

OTHER NONCRIMINAL JUSTICE PROGRAMS

In addition to the criminal justice system's response to criminal activity and precautionary expenditures by potential victims, a host of social and neighborhood programs are intended partially to reduce the exposure to victimization (demand) or the propensity of people to commit offenses (supply).

On the supply side, one possibility is to rehabilitate known offenders. However, few such programs have been successful (Sechrest et al., 1979). The few programs that have proven successful have been "designed to improve labor market performance or to ensure a supportive family-type environment" (Witte, 1989:5).

Instead of targeting offenders, some evidence suggests that "habilitation" of high-risk groups is more successful than rehabilitation of known offenders. Early intervention programs with high-risk groups (e.g., Head Start and the Job Corps) have been shown to reduce criminal behavior (Witte, 1989:6). Some feel that programs designed to educate students about our legal system and values might have beneficial effects on reducing violence (Donahue, 1990). Because these programs all have multiple goals, their costs should not be entirely apportioned to the prevention of crime, yet alone violent behavior. In addition, more research is needed to determine the long-term effects of these programs.

Other programs have been designed to reduce the "demand"

side of victimization, by reducing the exposure of certain neighborhoods or groups. About 600 U.S. cities have adopted "crime stoppers"-type programs, where rewards are offered for anonymous tips leading to the arrest and conviction of criminals (Rosenbaum et al., 1987). Although we do not know of any estimates of the cost of these programs, we can identify the cost categories to be (1) time spent by law enforcement officers, (2) media time and space donated to the project, and (3) volunteer time by board members and other workers. Although no data exist on the resources devoted to these programs, one survey found that 80 percent of the programs have "an active board of directors that meets once a month" (Rosenbaum et al., 1987:31). Of course, the crime stoppers program is designed to deal with all types of crimes. An estimated 16 percent of the tips received deal with personal crimes such as rape, robbery, assault, and homicide (Rosenbaum et al., 1987:30).

Many neighborhoods have established "neighborhood watch" programs where volunteers engage in various crime prevention activities. One national survey "found that over 90 percent of police and sheriffs' departments had established formal crime prevention programs such as Neighborhood Watch. In California, over 5,000 such programs serve 85 percent of the State's population." (Cunningham and Taylor, 1985:2). A recent survey sent questionnaires to 2,300 neighborhood watch programs around the country (Garofalo and McLeod, 1988). Although there are no data on the number of hours spent by volunteers or the dollar expenditures, the study found that many of these programs involve the expenditure of funds on projects such as emergency telephones, street lighting improvements, and hired guards.

INCARCERATED OFFENDER COSTS

In addition to paying for the cost of incarceration, society loses the productive capacity of individuals who are incarcerated. These productivity losses are true social costs that should be taken into account when examining the costs and benefits of incarceration. Some would argue that the value of lost freedom to the offender should also be considered (Becker, 1968:179-180).

According to the Bureau of Justice Statistics (1988b), 31 percent of all state prisoners were unemployed at the time of their incarceration; the corresponding estimate for jail inmates is 46.7 percent (Bureau of Justice Statistics, 1985). Weighted by population estimates, approximately 37 percent of all inmates were unemployed prior to their offense.[38] Unfortunately, no published estimates are available on the distribution of employment or earnings by offense type. It is possible, for example, that property offenders are more likely to have been unemployed than violent offenders.

Few published reports document the earnings of offenders prior to incarceration. A 1978 study of jail inmates (Bureau of Justice Statistics, 1980) found the median income to be $6,750 (in 1987 dollars). A study of state prison inmates in 1986 (Bureau of Justice Statistics, 1988b) reported on the distribution of income prior to arrest. If we annualize the earnings of those who were incarcerated for part of the year prior to their most recent incarceration, the average state prison inmate was earning an estimated $8,800 in 1987 dollars.

Only a part of this income could be considered lost productivity due to incarceration. For example, the 1983 survey of local jail inmates found that only about 60 percent of inmates' main source of income came from wages (Bureau of Justice Statistics, 1988b:Table 2). About 24 percent of the inmates received social security, unemployment, welfare, or an educational scholarship as their main source of income. The remaining 16 percent received income from family members, illegal sources, or "other" unspecified sources.

Although we do not know how income was distributed across these various sources, if we assume it was evenly distributed, the average incarcerated offender costs society about $5,285 in lost productivity per year of incarceration. Combining this estimate with the average time served per offense from Table 22 yields the following lost productivity estimates:

Murder	$22,600
Rape	4,200
Robbery	1,400
Aggravated assault	1,300

Not only is there no consensus on whether society should be "concerned" about the lost freedom to offenders, there are virtually no estimates of the value of lost freedom. In theory, one might be able to estimate the trade-off between fines and imprisonment by examining the rate of offenses in jurisdictions with different levels of fines and imprisonment (Posner, 1980:413). However, we are unaware of any such studies. Moreover, it is not obvious that sufficiently rich data exist to undertake such a study.

One possible measure of the value of lost freedom would be jury awards for false imprisonment. Although false imprisonment data are not available, according to Jury Verdict Research, Inc., the mean award for false arrest by police is $85,000, with the median being $60,000.

In addition to the freedom lost by imprisonment, convicted felons are denied many civil rights such as voting, juror service, public employment, and firearm ownership (Burton et al., 1987).

One potential social cost of incarceration is the disruption of lives for the family of an offender. Incarceration no doubt places a financial and emotional burden on the remaining spouse and children. To some extent, these are "innocent victims" of the offense as well. Although few studies exist on the impact of incarceration on family members of the offender, only about 20 percent of all jail and state prison inmates are reported married at the time of their incarceration (Bureau of Justice Statistics, 1980, 1988b). On the other hand, more than 40 percent are reported to have dependents.

It is also possible that sending offenders to jail will "train" them to become more hardened criminals (Irwin and Austin, 1987:17). To the extent that this is true, society incurs an additional cost associated with increased future criminal activity. This is a particularly difficult proposition to test empirically, because we generally do not permit randomized experiments in such criminal justice settings. One study of probation versus prison suggests that prisoners have a slightly higher recidivism rate than similar probationers but concludes that "the results presented here are only suggestive and should not be used to support specific policy recommendations" (Petersilia and Turner, 1986:iii).

Finally, one potential cost associated with jailing offenders is the higher rate of injury and death in prison. In 1987, the average state and federal prison population, plus local jail population, was about 847,000 (Jamieson and Flanagan, 1989:605, 612). During the same year, the total number of suicides in these institutions was 498, a rate of 0.00059. This compares to a nationwide suicide rate of about 0.0002 (Bureau of Justice Statistics, 1988d:24). Another 339 deaths in state and federal correctional facilities were caused either by "another" person or by an "unspecified" cause (Jamieson and Flanagan, 1989:662). Based on a total prison population of about 557,000, this death rate is about 0.00061, compared to a nationwide homicide rate of about 0.0001.

However, one cannot simply compare suicide and murder rates in prisons to those outside without controlling for the background level of suicide and murder for incarcerated individuals. For example, both the suicide and the homicide rates are significantly higher for males aged 18 to 44 (and particularly those between 25 and 34), which are also the groups with the highest criminal participation rates. Although we are unaware of studies directed specifically at these issues, Gaes (1985) reviews existing literature on the effect of overcrowding on prison illness and violence. However, without further study, we cannot conclude that jailed offenders have a higher rate of injury or death than their nonjailed cohorts.

Cost of "Overdeterrence"

Overdeterrence might affect either those who commit an offense or those who are completely innocent. In the case of those who commit an offense, the concept is generally applied to non-violent offenses, where the benefit to the offender exceeds the cost to society. For example, we would not want to impose so severe a penalty on double parking that a woman about to give birth parks three blocks away from a hospital to avoid the penalty (if that was the only spot available). Similarly, we might not want to deter a person from cheating on his income taxes if that is the only viable way for him to afford the medical expenses needed to save his wife's life (Shavell, 1985).

It is also possible to overdeter violent offenses. For example, if we imposed a mandatory death penalty for rape, those few individuals who are still not deterred might choose to kill their victims to reduce the probability of detection (because the penalties for rape and murder would be identical). As a second example, the increased sophistication of forensic technology might cause violent offenders to resort to arson to cover up any possible identifying evidence. The concern here is that there is adequate "marginal deterrence" to keep offenders from escalating the violence and harm caused by the crime they commit (Stigler, 1970).

Overdeterrence costs are also imposed on innocent people. In some cases, a criminal defendant may be falsely accused of committing a crime. Even if eventually found not guilty, the person accused of the crime may bear significant psychological and reputational costs. If found guilty and incarcerated, the costs obviously escalate. Moreover, there are few social benefits from false convictions. For example, convicting a mentally incompetent offender has little deterrent value.

We are unaware of any studies that specifically quantify the extent of false imprisonments or accusations. It has been reported, however, that between 5 and 8 percent of all child sexual abuse allegations are false (Blodget, 1987). One way to estimate the monetary cost of a false accusation would be to use jury award data on false arrests. As mentioned earlier, the mean award for false arrest by police is $84,987, with the median being $60,000. This does not include the cost associated with false imprisonment.

In addition to the cost imposed on the innocent party accused of wrongdoing, a related cost is imposed on all innocent people who might *potentially* be accused in the future. These individuals might take costly actions or change their behavior in some manner to avoid being falsely accused of committing a crime. For example, it is possible that the risk of being falsely accused of child abuse will cause some legitimate day care providers to close down and will reduce the attractiveness of this line of work for potential new entrants, thereby raising the cost of day care. Although we would like to think this is not a significant problem given the high legal standards of proof in criminal cases, there is a growing concern over this problem in the case of child sexual abuse. Indeed, there have been reports of day care centers closing due to the inability to obtain insurance against child abuse claims (Wickenden, 1985). This problem is less likely to occur in cases of injury normally associated with "street crime."

COST OF "JUSTICE"

There are two types of costs associated with justice. First, the extensive constitutional protection afforded accused defendants may be thought of as imposing a justice cost. In many ways, this can be thought of as the opposite of the overdeterrence cost mentioned above, because these provisions are designed primarily to protect innocent parties from being falsely accused.

Second, one can often identify less expensive ways of accomplishing current levels of crime control that our society would still not prefer on grounds of justice. For example, in theory, one could considerably reduce police resources and catch fewer criminals, while at the same time imposing much more severe penalties on those few criminals who are caught (Polinsky and Shavell, 1979). To the extent society deems this unacceptable, it could be considered a cost of justice. Although we have no method of estimating the costs of justice, these costs are implicitly included in the cost of the criminal justice system estimated elsewhere in this paper.

OFFENDER COSTS

In an earlier section, we discuss the cost of sanctioning offenders, which includes the lost productivity and freedom of the offender, as well as potential costs to the offender's family. However, even if an offender is not held accountable for his or her actions, considerable time and resources may have been devoted to committing an act of violence. These costs are best thought of as the opportunity costs associated with criminal activity. Although the primary cost is likely to be lost productivity for offenders who would otherwise be engaged in legal and gainful employment, an additional cost might include the purchase of products to assist in the criminal activity (e.g., firearms).

One question of concern to many researchers is the extent to which crime and work are substitutes in the minds of potential offenders. The underlying hypothesis has been that if we increase job opportunities for the poor, crime will be reduced. Although we have not extensively surveyed the literature, it appears that this issue is still unsettled. For example, Cook and Zarkin (1985) find that burglaries and robberies increase somewhat with the unemployment rate, whereas motor vehicle thefts actually decrease. Witte et al. (1989) find that individual participation in crime is negatively related to *both* work and school. They also cite other studies that find wage rates do not appear to affect levels of criminal activity and that "a legitimate use for time (school or work) rather than income is most strongly associated with lower levels of criminal activity" (Witte et al., 1989:18). They interpret these findings to suggest that most people view crime as an *inferior* alternative to work, and that people who are inclined to go to school and work are inherently less likely to commit crime.

As noted above, about 37 percent of incarcerated offenders were unemployed prior to their conviction. Of course, judges may partially select candidates for incarceration based on prior history. Thus, the true unemployment rate of violent offenders may be considerably less.

SUMMARY OF COST ESTIMATES

This section combines all of the previous cost estimates and presents aggregate estimates per crime. It should be noted that all of the estimates are in 1987 dollars. To increase to 1994 dollars, these estimates should be increased by approximately 25-

30 percent. Table 24 summarizes the victim-related cost estimates in this paper. It is based on the WTP approach to valuing reduced quality of life. The average victim-related cost of rape (including attempted rape) is estimated to be $54,100 (in 1987 dollars). The average robbery or attempted robbery cost $19,200, whereas the average assault or attempted assault (including simple and aggravated) cost $16,500. (If compensation estimates are used for valuing reduced quality of life in nonfatal injuries, the estimates increase to $65,200 for rape, $23,200 for robbery, and $19,300 for assault.) As noted in Table 24, many costs are excluded due to data limitations. Thus, the true cost of violence is higher than reported here.

It is important to realize that the bulk of these cost estimates—roughly 85 percent—can be attributed to *nonmonetary* losses such as pain, suffering, and the reduced quality of life. The remaining 15 percent include direct monetary losses to victims, lost productivity, emergency response, and program administration.

The estimates in Table 24 are based on all attempted and completed victimizations—including those that result in no physical injuries. If we adjust these estimates to account for only those victims who suffer physical injury, victim costs are considerably higher: $85,700 to $104,000 for rape, $44,300 to $55,400 for robbery, and $38,8000 to $48,400 for assault.

Table 25 summarizes the cost of society's response to violent behavior disaggregated into the categories of murder, rape, robbery, and aggravated assault. Unlike victimization costs, we are unable to estimate the cost of society's response to *simple* assaults.

Table 26 estimates the measurable aggregate costs of violence in the United States in 1987. It excludes murder because these incidents are apportioned to the underlying crime. In 1987, it was estimated that the cost of victimization was $8.0 to $9.6 billion for rape, $20.5 to $24.8 billion for robbery, and $81.3 to $95.2 billion for assault.

Table 27 aggregates society's response to victimization over all incidents in 1987. We estimate total measurable costs of society's response to rape to be $1.6 billion; robbery, $6.3 billion; and aggravated assault, $10.1 billion. These estimates include about $2 billion spent in response to murder where the underlying crime was either rape, robbery, or assault.

TABLE 24 Summary of Estimated Costs: Violent Behavior (averaged over all victimizations—including attempts), 1987

Cost Category	Murder	Rape[a]	Robbery[a]	Assault[a]
Direct victim losses				
Medical costs (Table 3)	$ 5,370[b]	$ 376	$ 124	$ 153
Mental health costs (Table 4)[c]	n.a.	3,886	887	361
Property costs (Table 5)	n.a.	11	335	10
Indirect monetary losses	—	—	—	—
Emergency response				
Victim services (Table 7)	—	311[d]	—	—
Police response (Table 10)	105	43	22	14
Emergency transport (Table 11)	465	6	4	2
Victim productivity	610,000			
Due to medical (Table 12)	n.a.	196	112	79
Due to mental health (Table 4)	n.a.	1,364	310	188
Due to legal process (Table 12)	n.a.	105	46	19
Program administration (Table 13)				
Health and life insurance	3,832	20	7	8
Government transfer programs	2,013	1	1	1
Insurance/overhead (property)	n.a.	1	20	1
Legal costs for civil suits	—	—	—	—
Pain, suffering and quality of life				
Pain and suffering: victim (Table 14)[e]	1,590,000	33,300[h]	12,200[h]	8,300[h]
Risk of death: victim	n.a.	4,500[f]	5,100[f]	7,400[f]
Quality of life for family	g	10,000[h]	—	—
Psychological trauma to witnesses	—	—	—	—
Injuries caused by earlier victims	—	—	—	—
Total	2,212,000	54,100	19,200	16,500

NOTE: — indicates no estimate is available; n.a. indicates data are not applicable.

[a]Includes attempts and deaths resulting from underlying crime.

[b]Includes premature funeral and related expenses.

[c]Assumes 100 percent of those in need receive mental health care; see text.

[d]This is known to be an underestimate. Only those costs that can be reasonably estimated were included.

[e]These estimates are based on WTP values. Compensation estimates are $44,400 for rape, $16,200 for robbery, and $11,100 for assault.

[f]Risk of death is equal to the victim cost of death ($2.2 million) times the fraction of each crime type that results in murder. These figures must be taken out of the aggregate estimates if one includes murder; otherwise there is double counting.

[g]Although loss to the family is not insignificant in the case of murder, it may be accounted for partially in the $1.59 million estimate of quality of life costs to murder victims; see text.

[h]This estimate has a higher degree of uncertainty than many others presented here.

TABLE 25 Summary of Estimated Costs: Society's Response to Violent Behavior (averaged over all victimizations—including attempts), 1987

Cost Category	Murder	Rape	Robbery	Aggravated Assault
Precautionary measures and fear				
Monetary expenditures for prevention	—	—	—	—
Crime prevention behavior	—	—	—	—
Fear of crime	—	—	—	—
Criminal justice-related costs				
Criminal justice processing (Table 20)	$ 5,430	$1,150	$ 500	$ 580
Legal defense (Table 21)	500	125	35	60
Sanctions (Table 23)	74,970	5,420	3,680	3,735
Victim and witness interaction	—	a	a	a
Other noncriminal justice programs	—	—	—	—
Incarcerated offender/productivity	22,600	4,200	1,400	1,300
Overdeterrence costs	—	—	—	—
Justice costs	—	—	—	—
Offender costs	—	—	—	—
Total	103,800	10,900	5,600	5,600

NOTE: — indicates no estimate is available.

[a]Some of these costs have been included in Table 24, under lost victim productivity.

TABLE 26 Aggregate Cost of Violent Behavior

	Rape	Robbery	Assault
Cost of victimization	$ 54,100	19,200	16,500
Number of victims	147,000	1,068,500	4,930,000
Aggregate cost (billion $)	8.0	20.5	81.3

NOTE: These estimates are based on the WTP approach. If pain and suffering for nonfatal injuries is valued by the compensation method, aggregate costs would increase to $9.6 billion for rape, $24.8 billion for robbery, and $95.2 billion for assault.

TABLE 27 Aggregate Cost of Society's Response to Victimization

	Murder	Rape	Robbery	Aggravated Assault	Total
Cost ($)	103,800	10,900	5,600	5,600	—
Number of victims	20,100	147,000	1,068,500	1,630,000	—
Aggregate cost (billion $)	2.1	1.6	6.0	9.1	18.8
Aggregate cost with murder allocated to underlying crime[a] (billion $)	—	1.6	6.3	10.1	18.8

[a]Allocates 19,456 of the estimated 20,100 murders to rape, robbery, and assualt. The remaining murders are connected with property crimes such as burglery, arson, and motor vehicle theft. Their aggregate cost is less than $0.1 billion.

WHO PAYS FOR VICTIM INJURIES?

Victims and government agencies appear to bear most costs of victim injuries. Nonmonetary costs associated with pain, suffering, and reduced quality of life constitute major costs, as presented in Table 24. These costs are borne by victims and their families.

The costs of medical treatment and lost productivity for victim injuries are paid by different sources. We estimate that 32 percent of the medical costs of victim injuries (and other injuries) are paid by government, 44 percent by private insurers, 5 percent by charity, and 19 percent by victims and their families.[39] Data from the Bureau of the Census (1989) suggest that employer premium payments ultimately cover about 72 percent of the private insurance premiums and that consumers cover the rest. Government and charity provide additional funding for victim services and shelter programs, as well as for institutional care of victims who suffer severe physical or mental injuries.

Government also pays an estimated 16.5 percent of the wage losses, plus contributions to victim compensation funds in some states. Life insurance covers 9 percent of the wage losses in murders. A large, but unknown, proportion of the remaining wage losses for nonfatal injuries are covered by employers through sick leave. Victims and their families bear 78 percent of the wage losses resulting from murders and much of the wage losses resulting from permanently disabling victim injuries. They bear virtually all the costs of lost household production, about 24 percent of total productivity losses. Private insurance premiums cover about 70 percent of the administrative costs of insurance reimbursement, and government covers the remainder. State and local governments also bear nearly all costs of emergency response to victimization.

Actions to reduce fear and the likelihood of victimization include both public investments in police services and private investments in self-protective measures. Clotfelter (1977:502-503) estimated the demand for self-protective measures as a function of household income and the neighborhood crime rate, and found that

> the probability of taking protective measures increases with the average victimization rate for the area and also is higher for black households . . . [and] low income households are more likely than other households to respond to crime by simply staying at home and forgoing whatever the alternative activities might be.

There is considerable interest in shifting some of the monetary burden imposed by crime back to the offenders. Some examples include "Son of Sam" laws, private tort actions, and government programs requiring restitution or partial payment for the cost of imposing alternative sanctions. An important area for future research would be to examine the extent to which these programs have shifted costs back to offenders.

SUMMARY OF RESULTS AND SUGGESTIONS FOR FUTURE RESEARCH

This paper sets forth a comprehensive theoretical foundation for characterizing the costs and consequences of victimization. It also reviews and updates existing monetary estimates of the cost of criminal victimization. In some instances, the costs estimated here are no more than ballpark estimates. Other costs are simply not estimated due to lack of data. Accordingly, the reader should refer to the relevant section of the paper to determine the source and strength of each estimate. Although there is considerable uncertainty surrounding each estimate, we deliberately have not attempted to estimate ranges. Provision of consistent probability ranges around these estimates would have further complicated the analysis.

Although future research no doubt will reduce some of that uncertainty, it can never be eliminated. We have argued earlier that making cost estimates is a policy imperative because, in their absence, policy decisions are made on a less informed and arbitrary basis. However, that does not mean that all policy decisions should be based on simple benefit-cost comparisons. Indeed, given the uncertainty in estimating both the benefits and the costs of various policy outcomes, it is incumbent upon the analyst to attempt to account for the uncertainty in these estimates when comparing policy options. Thus, for example, one could construct ranges of costs and benefits based on various plausible assumptions to determine how often the benefit-cost ratio exceeds 1 and to estimate the mean ratio (Hofler and Witte, 1979).

It is interesting to compare the cost estimates developed here to aggregate U.S. expenditures on crime and justice. For example, the total cost of sanctions associated with murder, rape, robbery, and aggravated assault implied by Table 25 is about $12 billion, compared to the $15.75 billion total estimated for the United States in 1986 (Jamieson and Flanagan, 1989:2). This suggests that a good portion of the cost of sanctions in the United States is associated with punishment of violent offenders. This is consistent with the fact that about 55 percent of all prison inmates are serving time for violent offenses.

On the other hand, total criminal justice costs (police and courts) for the crimes estimated here are only about $1.9 billion compared to total U.S. costs of $37.75 billion. There are several reasons why violent offenses account for such a small part of the total police and court costs. First, a good portion of police expenditures are preventive in nature or related to traffic safety and control. (Although police expenditures designed to prevent crimes are not included here, some portion could be allocated to violent offenses—at least in theory.) Second, although violent offenders receive relatively more severe sentences, they are much fewer in number than other criminal offenders. Arrests for violent crimes account for only about 20 percent of FBI crime index arrests. Arrests for violent crimes (including simple assaults) account for only about 12 percent of all arrests nationwide. Thus, violent behavior is a major factor in the cost of corrections, but much less a factor in the cost of the rest of the criminal justice process.

There are several major gaps in the literature on the costs and consequences of violent behavior. In terms of offense types, we have not included kidnappings, bombings, arson, or child abuse. Although few estimates are available for these offenses, the methodology used here could also be applied to them. Cohen (1988a) provides some preliminary estimates of victim costs in the case of kidnapping, bombing, and arson. Although we know of no cost estimates made for child abuse, Daro (1988) provides some evidence on the cost of victim treatment and family intervention programs. These are certainly areas worthy of future research.

There are also several major cost categories in need of further research. First, little is known about the effect that fear of victimization has on behavior. We have identified several categories of injury, including both the indirect monetary losses suffered by victims who make costly lifestyle or job changes as a result of their victimization and the cost to potential victims.

Second, more research is needed to assess systematically the psychological impact of victimization on victims, their families, and witnesses. The estimates in this paper are based on only a few isolated studies. Although there is a growing literature in the mental health field, much of that work is clinical. Some recent studies are attempting to find control groups and to estimate the incidence of psychological injury. More interdisciplinary work clearly needs to be done in this area—not only in assessing the incidence of injury, but also in understanding its severity. In addition, the growing trend toward bringing legal damage claims against offenders or third parties in the case of rape and child sexual abuse might prove to be a useful source of information on society's evaluation of these injuries.

Third, surprisingly little is known about the cost of victim service or other noncriminal justice programs for offenders and victims. A comprehensive survey could easily assess these costs if it was properly designed to include volunteer time and other costs not directly budgeted by nonprofit and government groups.

Finally, although we provide estimates of the cost of medical care and lost productivity due to injuries, the data sources generally available to the criminal justice community are highly suspect. Alternatives to the NCS could provide more realistic information on medical costs (and also improve our estimates of pain and suffering).

ACKNOWLEDGMENTS

Support for this research was provided by the Dean's Summer Research Fund, Owen Graduate School of Management, Vanderbilt University and by The Urban Institute. The authors are grateful to Colin Loftin and Brian Wiersema for providing us with National Crime Survey data, and to Philip J. Cook, Wendy Max, and other members of the Panel on the Understanding and Control of

Violent Behavior who provided comments on an earlier version of this paper. All remaining errors are solely the responsibility of the authors.

NOTES

1   The following details of the case are taken from "A Murderous Hoax," *Newsweek*, January 22, 1990, pp. 16-22.

2   Comments by Philip J. Cook on earlier draft of this paper, April 1, 1990.

3   See Maltz (1975) for a critique of the crime seriousness index, as well as suggestions for improvements in crime classification schemes. Maltz also proposes that other objective measures of crime seriousness be explored, such as the amount of time until recovery from temporary physical injuries, as well as the possible monetizing of physical injuries and death.

4   This is due to the "wealth" effect (Cook and Graham, 1977). That is, because the marginal utility of money declines with wealth, people are willing to pay less to avoid an injury than would be required to accept one. To the extent that the wealth effect is the only difference, then WTA and WTP are likely to be fairly close if they amount to a relatively small portion of a person's wealth.

5   Fischhoff and Cox (1986:62) cite various reasons for this disparity. From a psychological standpoint, individuals who own a commodity might have a better idea of its value. Ethically, one can argue that someone who owns the commodity must be compensated considerably for its loss.

6   The incidence of serious unintentional injury has been declining over time, and treatment promoting recovery has been improved. As a result, prevalence-based unintentional injury estimates, which represent a cross-sectional snapshot, tend to be higher, because they capture higher than normal injury rates, including such costs as those associated with treating disabled American veterans from the Vietnam War.

7   It has been argued that even though the victim involuntarily transfers money or property to the offender, or even if the property is eventually recovered, the value of this property can be used as a proxy for resources devoted by the offender (as well as intermediaries such as fencing operations) and are thus a social cost (Becker, 1968:171, note 3). However, Demmert (1979:9) argues that if the "market" for crime is not competitive, the value of stolen property is higher than the thief's actual cost; thus, the

value of stolen property should be viewed as an upper bound on its true social cost.

8   The term "nonmonetary" is used throughout this paper to describe costs that are not normally traded in the marketplace, such as pain, suffering, and fear. Although they are called nonmonetary, one can attempt to place dollar values on these costs, which is the subject of the following discussion.

9   Cohen (1987) contains more detail on the methodology and assumptions than Cohen (1988a). Throughout the remainder of this paper, future references to both papers are cited as Cohen (1988a).

10   According to that study, the risk of death due to drug dealing in Washington, D.C. is 1.4 percent per year (Reuter et al., 1990:104). If we assign the same value of life to these individuals as to the average in the population—$2.2 million—that suggests a required risk compensation of $30,800 per year. Because the average drug dealer in that population earned $55,000 (Reuter et al., 1990:93), we cannot rule out the possibility that these dealers have a value of life within the range of the average population.

11   Losses (costs) may be generated not only by patients, but also by family members, friends, and coworkers, because such individuals may lose time from work, school, or housekeeping activities or may suffer reduction in productivity associated with the patient's condition. Hartunian et al. (1981) regard such output losses as a secondary component of indirect costs. Such costs are significant; however, because of the empirical difficulties associated with data collection and attribution of cause, these costs are virtually never estimated.

12   Rice et al. (1989:84) present a listing of cost of injury studies, including source; study period and methodology; total costs, as well as direct, indirect, and other related costs; and discount rate used.

13   Of some relevance, they do indicate that the lifetime monetary costs of firearm injuries average $54,000, with fatalities responsible for 84 percent of the costs (Rice et al., 1989:46, 49).

14   The NCS, which is sponsored by the U.S. Department of Justice, is a household survey that has been implemented by the Bureau of the Census since the early 1970s. The data base, which includes both crimes known to the police and those not reported, provides the only nationally representative estimates of nonfatal criminal victimization and the harms associated with victimization due to rape, robbery, assault, personal and household larceny,

burglary, and motor vehicle theft (see U.S. Department of Justice, 1989b, for an expanded discussion of NCS data and methodology).

15   In some respects, the undercounting of children, transients, and the homeless represents an important omission because these persons are at greatest risk of victimization.   Further, the omission of institutionalized cohorts is troubling because persons who sustained very severe injury due to victimization may be institutionalized, receiving ongoing care for long-term temporary or permanent impairment.   The costs for such care can be extremely high and probably are not reflected in this analysis.   Finally, although this is not a study of incidence of victim injury, calculations of costs per victimization are affected by the accuracy of incidence estimates because the number of incidents serves as the denominator when costs of injury are distributed across all victims.

16   Estimates of domestic violence, child abuse, and nonstranger victimizations vary considerably.   Some victims do not report such incidents for a variety of reasons: for example, nonstranger victimization may not be regarded as a crime; the incident may be viewed as a private matter; or the offender may be present during the survey interview, thus constraining discussion.   It may be possible to triangulate estimates of such offenses to improve existing incidence data.   Cost estimates could also be refined based on the distribution of injuries associated with adult assault and child abuse captured by hospital trauma registries and data bases.

17   One measure of the possible underreporting of medical costs by victims is represented by gunshot wounds.   The NCS data document an average medical cost per injury that ranges from $816.87 (for robbery—gunshot, conscious) to $13,000 (for rape—gunshot, conscious).   These figures are significantly different from the $33,159 average medical cost of firearm injury per hospitalized victim and the $458 average medical cost for injured, nonhospitalized victims reported by Rice et al. (1989:xxviii).

18   They used data on length of hospital stay from NHDS or NASS, or medical cost data from the National Medical Care Utilization and Expenditure Survey, the National Council on Compensation Insurance's Detailed Claims Information data base, or the Comprehensive Health and Medical Program for the Uniformed Services.

19   This data base contains data on nearly 500,000 injured people. Once a claim enters the sample, all medical costs are tracked until the workers compensation insurer is able to sell the claim

to a health insurer. The amount that the health insurer charged for paying all future medical costs is added as a final cost.

20   This represents the weighted average in 1987 dollars of the costs per patients who die within one hour of arriving at a Washington, D.C. emergency room, having presented with central nervous system or cardiovascular injuries (Rice et al., 1989).

21   This is based on an average cost of $1,235 plus a factor of 1.40 to allow for physician and professional fees. These assumptions were based on documentation provided by Ellen MacKenzie and Ted Miller as a result of their independent contributions to Rice et al. (1989).

22   Because all murder victims would eventually die at some later date, this cost reflects only the difference between a funeral today and the projected value of a funeral at the end of the average expected lifetime.

23   It should be noted that the literature review for the research in Cohen (1988a) was completed in early spring 1986. Due to the time lag associated with completion of the study and publication of results, several important studies published in 1987 and 1988 were not included in that earlier study.

24   According to the American Psychiatric Association (1987:62), the median hourly fee for a psychiatrist in 1985 ranged from $81 per hour in an office to $101 in a hospital setting. Individual psychotherapy fees for social workers and psychologists ranged from $60 to $70 per hour. Although the average number of visits per calendar year is 8.2, the distribution is highly skewed, with about half of the patients having fewer than 3 visits, whereas the upper tenth percentile have 25 or more and account for about half the total expenditures (American Psychiatric Association, 1987:137).

25   As this book goes to press, a new study by Cohen and Miller (1994a) estimated actual mental health care expenditures by victims of crime. Estimates were derived from a survey of mental health care professionals. Actual expenditures are considerably less than reported in Table 4. For example, actual mental health expenditures for rape victims is estimated to be $589 compared to $3,886 in "potential" costs.

26   This may not be a reasonable assumption. According to Kimmich (1985:71-72), most of the private social service agencies that serve children and receive little government support have small total revenues. Most of the larger agencies rely more heavily on government funding. Kimmich goes on to estimate that in 1982, 48-49 percent of all funding for health, mental health and social service agencies for children (excluding day care) was gov-

ernment sponsored. This estimate does not differentiate among federal, state, and local government support.

27   However, because police injuries presumably are included in NCS injury estimates, to include them here would result in double counting when aggregating costs.

28   This is consistent with Waller et al. (1990) who found that despite presumptions that injured workers tend to malinger, such individuals actually do not return to housework or recreational activities before they return to work.

29   As part of an earlier Federal Highway Administration project, through a series of meetings with five federal agencies, a consensus was reached on the conceptual method for valuing lost days of housework (Miller et al., 1989a). Note that a day of housework is not an eight-hour day. It is the number of hours someone works at home, which varies depending on sex, age, household structure, and employment status. The valuation method includes a procedure for averaging values across these parameters.

30   The NCS estimates that 67.3 percent of injured victims had health insurance coverage or were eligible for public medical services (Bureau of Justice Statistics, 1989a:Table 76). However, this does not detail the percentage of victims that fall within each category. Because the different types of coverage involve different administrative rates, reimbursement rates were estimated by using the percentage of medical costs reimbursed for all injuries from Rice et al. (1989). The higher reimbursement rate for injuries in motor vehicle crashes was removed by using survey data from All-Industry Research Advisory Council (1988) and Miller (1989b).

31   The insurance administrative costs were computed using 1987 insurance loss ratios (A.M. Best Company, 1988). Some consumer advocates assert that these published insurance company statistics on loss adjustment expenses include expenses that are not loss specific. Nevertheless, no better estimates of administrative costs of claims are available.

32   For murder, the administrative cost percentage was applied to medical costs excluding funeral costs.

33   Similar ratios of plaintiff legal expenses to compensation are reported by the All-Industry Research Advisory Council (1988).

34   Note that the median awards also increased. The current Jury Verdict Research, Inc. study reports a median award of $68,000, with a verdict range of $13,000 to $750,000. Earlier data used in Cohen (1988a) were based on a median award of $42,000, with a range of $6,500 to $100,000 (in 1982 dollars).

35 These data were provided by the FBI, Uniform Crime Reports division.

36 According to John Shepard, Federal Judicial Center, the reported case weights can be converted to hours by multiplying each weight by 4.

37 The authors wish to thank Robert Santos-Alborna and Jeffrey M. Silbert, of the Metro-Dade Department of Justice Assistance, for providing these data. The data were computed by using the Dade Justice Improvement Model.

38 Although the estimates of employment are for different base years, comparable years for the number of inmates are available. In 1986, there were an estimated 450,000 state prisoners (Bureau of Justice Statistics, 1988b) and 274,000 jail inmates (Bureau of Justice Statistics, 1988a). These numbers were used to arrive at the weighted estimate.

39 Data in All-Industry Research Advisory Council (1988) and Miller (1989b) were used to remove the motor vehicle crash reimbursement from the medical reimbursement data for injuries in Rice et al. (1989).

REFERENCES

Acton, J.P.
  1973 *Evaluating Public Programs to Save Lives: The Case of Heart Attacks.* Santa Monica, Calif.: The RAND Corporation.
All-Industry Research Advisory Council
  1988 *Attorney Involvement in Auto Industry Claims.* Oak Brook, Ill.: AIRAC.
A.M. Best Company
  1988 *Best's Aggregates and Averages, 1987,* 88th ed. Oldwick, N.J.: A.M. Best Company.
American Psychiatric Association
  1987 *Economic Fact Book for Psychiatry,* 2nd ed. Washington, D.C.: American Psychiatric Press.
Amick, A., D.G. Kilpatrick, H.S. Resnick, and B.E. Saunders
  1989 Public Health Implications of Homicide for Surviving Family Members: An Epidemiological Study. Paper presented at the Tenth Annual Meeting of the Society for Behavioral Medicine.
Amick-McMullan, A., D.G. Kilpatrick, and L.J. Veronen
  1989 Family survivors of homicide victims: A behavioral analysis. *Behavior Therapist* 12(4):75-79.
Austin, J.
  1986 Using early release to relieve prison crowding: A dilemma in public policy. *Crime and Delinquency* 32:404-502.

Balkin, S.
  1979   Victimization rates, safety, and fear of crime. *Social Problems* 26(3):343-357.
Ballou, G.M.
  1981   Recourse for rape victims: Third party liability. *Harvard Women's Law Journal* 4:105-160.
Becker, G.
  1968   Crime and punishment: An economic approach. *Journal of Political Economy* 78:169-217.
Berg, W.E., and R. Johnson
  1979   Assessing the impact of victimization: Acquisition of the victim role among elderly and female victims. In W.E. Parsonage, ed., *Perspectives on Victimology*. Beverly Hills, Calif.: Sage Publications.
Bergan, P.
  1985   *ABC News-Washington Post Poll*, Survey No. 0181. (New York: ABC News, January 11-16, 1985), as reported in Flanagan and Jamieson (1988:170).
Blodget, N.
  1987   Spouses use allegations to up the ante in divorce cases. *ABA Journal* 73(May):26.
Boland, B., C.H. Conly, L. Warner, R. Sones, and W. Martin
  1989   *The Prosecution of Felony Arrests, 1986.* Bureau of Justice Statistics. Washington, D.C.: U.S. Department of Justice.
Bureau of Economic Research
  1985   *Economic Consequences of Spinal Cord Injury.* New Brunswick, N.J.: Rutgers University.
Bureau of Justice Statistics (BJS)
  1980   *Jail Inmates: Sociodemographic Findings From the 1978 Survey of Inmates of Local Jails.* Washington, D.C.: U.S. Department of Justice.
  1985   *Jail Inmates, 1983.* Washington, D.C.: U.S. Department of Justice.
  1987   *1984 Census of State Adult Correctional Facilities.* NCJ-105585. Washington, D.C.: U.S. Department of Justice.
  1988a *Jail Inmates, 1987.* Washington, D.C.: U.S. Department of Justice.
  1988b *Profile of State Prison Inmates, 1986.* Washington, D.C.: U.S. Department of Justice.
  1988c *Criminal Defense for the Poor, 1986.* NCJ-112919. Washington, D.C.: U.S. Department of Justice.
  1988d *Report to the Nation on Crime and Justice.* NCJ-105506. Washington, D.C.: U.S. Department of Justice.
  1988e *Capital Punishment, 1987.* Washington, D.C.: U.S. Department of Justice.
  1988f *Time Served in Prison and on Parole, 1984.* NCJ-108544. Washington, D.C.: U.S. Department of Justice.

1988g *Probation and Parole, 1987.* NCJ-113948. Washington, D.C.: U.S. Department of Justice.

1989a *Criminal Victimization in the United States, 1987.* NCJ-115524. Washington, D.C.: U.S. Department of Justice.

1989b *Justice Expenditure and Employment in the United States, 1985.* NCJ-106356. Washington, D.C.: U.S. Department of Justice.

1989c *Felony Sentences in State Courts, 1986.* NCJ-115210. Washington, D.C.: U.S. Department of Justice.

1989d *Households Touched by Crime, 1987.* NCJ-117434. Washington, D.C.: U.S. Department of Justice.

1989e *The Redesigned National Crime Survey: Selected New Data.* NCJ-114746. Washington, D.C.: U.S. Department of Justice.

Bureau of the Census
1989 *Statistical Abstract of the United States, 1989,* 109th ed. Washington, D.C.: U.S. Department of Commerce.

Burt, M.R., and B.L. Katz
1985 Rape, robbery, and burglary: Responses to actual and feared criminal victimization, with special focus on women and the elderly. *Victimology: An International Journal* 10:325-358.

Burton, V.S., Jr., F.T. Cullen, and L.F. Travis, III
1987 The collateral consequences of a felony conviction: A national study of state statutes. *Federal Probation* 51(September):55.

Bush, G.
1990 *Economic Report of the President.* Washington, D.C.: U.S. Government Printing Office.

Carrington, F.
1978 Victims' rights: A new tort? *Trial* 14(6):39-59.
1983 Victims' rights: A new tort? Five years later. *Trial* 19(12):50-53.

Chabotar, K.J.
1987 *Analyzing Costs in the Courts.* National Institute of Justice. Washington, D.C.: U.S. Department of Justice.

Clark, D.E., and J.C. Cosgrove
1990 Hedonic prices, identification, and the demand for public safety. *Journal of Regional Science* 30(1):105-121.

Clarke, R.V.
1983 Situational crime prevention: Its theoretical basis and practical scope. Pp. 225-256 in M. Tonry and N. Morris, eds., *Crime and Justice: An Annual Review of Research,* Vol. 5. Chicago: University of Chicago Press.

Clotfelter, C.T.
1977 Urban crime and household protective measures. *Review of Economic Studies* 59:499-503.

Clotfelter, C.T., and R.D. Seeley
1979 The private costs of crime. Pp. 213-232 in C.M. Gray, ed., *The Costs of Crime.* Beverly Hills, Calif.: Sage Publications.

Cohen, J.
1983   Incapacitation as a strategy for crime control: Possibilities and pitfalls. Pp. 1-84 in M. Tonry and N. Morris, ed., *Crime and Justice: An Annual Review of Research*, Vol. 5. Chicago: University of Chicago Press.

Cohen, M.A.
1987   The Cost of Crime to Victims. Working Paper No. 87-12, Owen Graduate School of Management, Vanderbilt University.
1988a   Pain, suffering, and jury awards: A study of the cost of crime to victims. *Law and Society Review* 22:537-555.
1988b   Some new evidence on the seriousness of crime. *Criminology* 26(2):343-353.
1990   A note on the cost of crime to victims. *Urban Studies* 27:125-132.

Cohen, M.A., and T.R. Miller
1994a   The Cost of Mental Health Care for Victims of Crime. Working paper, Owen Graduate School of Management, Vanderbilt University.
1994b   The Monetary Value of Pain and Suffering Due to Criminal Victimization: Evidence from Jury Awards. Working paper, Owen Graduate School of Management, Vanderbilt University.

Consumer Product Safety Commission
various *Annual Report to Congress*. Washington, D.C.: U.S. Government Printing Office.
years

Cook, P.J.
1986   The demand and supply of criminal opportunities. Pp. 1-27 in M.H. Tonry and N. Morris, eds., *Crime and Justice: An Annual Review of Research*. Chicago: University of Chicago Press.

Cook, P.J., and D.A. Graham
1977   The demand for insurance and protection: The case of irreplaceable commodities. *Quarterly Journal of Economics* 91:143-156.

Cook, P.J., and G.A. Zarkin
1985   Crime and the business cycle. *Journal of Legal Studies* 14:115-128.

Coons, P.M., E.S. Bowman, T.A. Pellow, and P. Schneider
1989   Post-traumatic aspects of the treatment of victims of sexual abuse and incest. *Psychiatric Clinics of North America* 12(2):325-335.

Cooper, B., and D. Rice
1976   The economic cost of illness revisited. *Social Security Bulletin* 39:21-36.

Cullen, F.T., B.G. Link, and C.W. Polanzi
1982   The seriousness of crime revisited. *Criminology* 20:83-102.

Cunningham, W.C., and T.H. Taylor
1985   *Crime and Protection in America: A Study of Private Secu-*

rity and Law Enforcement Resources and Relationships: Executive Summary. National Institute of Justice. Washington, D.C.: U.S. Department of Justice.

Daro, D.
  1988   *Confronting Child Abuse: Research for Effective Program Design*. New York: Free Press.

Demmert, H.G.
  1979   *Crime and Crime Control: What Are the Social Costs?* Technical Report CERDCR-3-79. Center for Econometric Studies of the Justice System, Hoover Institution. Stanford, Calif.: Stanford University.

Donahue, T.S.
  1990   Education in the law: Promoting citizenship in the schools. *NIJ Reports*. National Institute of Justice. Washington, D.C.: U.S. Department of Justice.

Etter, I.B.
  1987   The National Safety Council's estimates of injury costs. *Public Health Reports* 102:634-636.

Faigin, B.M.
  1976   *1975 Societal Costs of Motor Vehicle Accidents*. Washington, D.C.: National Highway Traffic Safety Administration.

Fischhoff, B., and L.A. Cox, Jr.
  1986   Conceptual framework for regulatory benefits assessment. In J.D. Bentkover, V.T. Covello, and J. Mumpower, eds., *Benefits Assessment: The State of the Art*. Dordrecht, Holland: D. Reidel Publishing Company.

Fisher, A., L.G. Chestnut, and D.M. Violette
  1989   The value of reducing risks of death: A note on new evidence. *Journal of Policy Analysis and Management* 8(1):88-100.

Flanagan, T.J., and K. Maguire, eds.
  1990   *Sourcebook of Criminal Justice Statistics—1989*. Bureau of Justice Statistics. Washington, D.C.: U.S. Department of Justice.

Flanders, S.
  1980   *The 1979 District Court Time Study*. Washington, D.C.: Federal Judicial Center.

Friedman, L.S.
  1977   An interim evaluation of the supported work experiment. *Policy Analysis* 3:147-170.

Gaes, G.G.
  1985   The effects of overcrowding in prison. Pp. 95-147 in M.H. Tonry and N. Morris, eds., *Crime and Justice: An Annual Review of Research*. Chicago: University of Chicago Press.

Gallup, G., Jr.
  1989   *The Gallup Report*. Report Nos. 282-3. March/April. Princeton, N.J.: Gallup.

Garofalo, J., and M. McLeod
    1988   Improving the use and effectiveness of neighborhood watch pro-
            grams. *Research in Action*. Washington, D.C.: National Insti-
            tute of Justice.
Gray, C.M., ed.
    1979   *The Costs of Crime*. Beverly Hills, Calif.: Sage Publications.
Harlow, C.W.
    1989   *Injuries From Crime*. Bureau of Justice Statistics special report
            NCJ-116811. Washington, D.C.: U.S. Department of Justice.
Hartman, R.
    1990   One thousand points of light seeking a number: A case study of
            CBO's discount rate policy. *Journal of Environmental Econom-
            ics and Management* 18(2)53-57.
Hartunian, N.S., C.N. Smart, and M. Thompson
    1981   *The Incidence and Economics of Major Health Impairments: A
            Comparative Analysis of Cancer, Motor Vehicle Injuries, Coro-
            nary Heart Disease, and Strokes*. Lexington, Mass.: Lexington/
            Heath.
Harwood, H.J., D.M. Napolitano, P.L. Kristiansen, and J.J. Collins
    1984   *Economic Costs to Society of Alcohol and Drug Abuse and
            Mental Illness: 1980*. Research Triangle Park, N.C.: Research
            Triangle Institute.
Hellman, D.A., and J.L. Naroff
    1979   The impact of crime on urban residential property values. *Ur-
            ban Studies* 16:105-112.
Hofer, P.J., and B.S. Meierhoefer
    1987   *Home Confinement: An Evolving Sanction in the Federal Criminal
            Justice System*. Washington, D.C.: Federal Judicial Center.
Hofler, R.A., and A.D. Witte
    1979   Benefit-cost analysis of the sentencing decision: The case of
            homicide. Pp. 165-186 in C.M. Gray, ed., *The Costs of Crime*.
            Beverly Hills, Calif.: Sage Publications.
Horowitz, M.J.
    1986   Stress-response syndromes: A review of posttraumatic and ad-
            justment disorders. *Hospital and Community Psychiatry* 37(3):
            241-249.
Insurance Information Institute
    1989   *1989-90 Property/Casualty Fact Book*. New York: Insurance
            Information Institute.
Irwin, J., and J. Austin
    1987   *It's About Time: Solving America's Prison Crowding Crisis*.
            San Francisco, Calif.: National Council on Crime and Delin-
            quency.
Jamieson, K.M., and T.J. Flanagan, eds.
    1989   *Sourcebook of Criminal Justice Statistics—1988*. Bureau of Jus-
            tice Statistics. Washington, D.C.: U.S. Department of Justice.

Judicial Conference of the United States
  1989 Report on the Actual Costs of Filing Actions in District Courts.
        Unpublished report to the U.S. Congress, Washington, D.C.,
        August 15.
Jury Verdict Research, Inc.
  1989 Injury Valuation: Tables of Verdict Expectancy Values for Sexual
        Assault, Sexually Transmitted Diseases and AIDS. Jury Verdict
        Research, Inc., Solon, Ohio.
Kakalik, J.S., and N.M. Pace
  1986 *Costs and Compensation Paid in Tort Litigation.* R-3391-ICJ.
        Santa Monica, Calif.: The RAND Corporation.
Kilpatrick, D.G., B.E. Saunders, L.J. Veronen, C.L. Best, and J.M. Von
  1987 Criminal victimization: Lifetime prevalence, reporting to po-
        lice, and psychological impact. *Crime & Delinquency* 33(4):479-
        489.
Kilpatrick, D.G., H.S. Resnick, and A. Amick
  1989 Family Members of Homicide Victims: Search for Meaning and
        Post-Traumatic Stress Disorder. Paper presented at the 97th
        Annual American Psychological Association Convention, New
        Orleans, August.
Kimmich, M.H.
  1985 *America's Children.* Washington, D.C.: Urban Institute Press.
Kleiman, M.A.R., K.D. Smith, R.A. Rogers, and D.P. Cavanagh
  1989 *Imprisonment-to-Offense Ratios.* Bureau of Justice Statistics,
        NCJ-114948. Washington, D.C.: U.S. Department of Justice.
Laibstain, L.S.
  1988 Legal aspects of sex ring crimes against children. Pp. 41-46 in
        A.W. Burgess and C.A. Grant, eds., *Children Traumatized in
        Sex Rings.* Washington, D.C.: National Center for Missing and
        Exploited Children.
Lehman, D.R., C.B. Wortman, and A.F. Williams
  1987 Long term effects of losing a spouse or child in a motor vehicle
        crash. *Journal of Personality and Social Psychology* 52(1):218-
        231.
Luchter, S., B. Faigin, D. Cohen, and L. Lombardo
  1989 Status of Costs of Injury Research in the United States. Paper
        presented at the Experimental Safety Vehicle Conference,
        Gothenbug, Sweden.
Maltz, M.D.
  1975 Measures of effectiveness for crime reduction programs. *Opera-
        tions Research* 23(3):452-474.
Merkhofer, M.W.
  1987 *Decision Science and Social Risk Management.* Dordrecht, Holland:
        D. Reidel Publishing Company.
Miller, T.R.
  1989a Willingness to pay comes of age: Will the system survive?
        Northwestern University Law Review 83:876-907.

1989b *65 MPH: Winners and Losers.* Washington, D.C.: Urban Institute.

1990 The plausible range for the value of life—red herrings among the mackerel. *Journal of Forensic Economics* 3(3):17-40.

Miller, T., and S. Luchter

1988 The socioeconomic impacts of injuries resulting from motor vehicle crashes. Pp. 2.513-2.527 in *Proceedings XXII FISITA Congress Technical Papers on Society of Automotive Engineers.* SAE P-211. Warrendale, Pa.: Society of Automotive Engineers.

Miller, T., A. Hoskin, and D. Yalung-Mathews

1987 Procedure for annually estimating wage losses due to accidents in the U.S. *Journal of Safety Research* 18(3):101-119.

Miller, T., P. Brinkman, and S. Luchter

1989a Crash costs and safety investment. *Accident Analysis and Prevention* 21(4):303-314.

Miller, T., C. Calhoun, and W.B. Arthur

1989b Utility-adjusted impairment years: A low-cost approach to morbidity valuation. *Estimating and Valuing Morbidity in a Policy Context: Proceedings.* AERE Workshop. Washington, D.C.: U.S. Environmental Protection Agency.

Mitchell, R.C., and R.T. Carson

1989 *Using Surveys to Value Public Goods: The Contingent Valuation Method.* Washington, D.C.: Resources for the Future.

Mohide, E.A., G.W. Torrance, D.L. Streiner, D.M. Pringle, and R. Gilbert

1988 Measuring the wellbeing of family caregivers using the time trade-off technique. *Journal of Clinical Epidemiology* 41(5):475-482.

Moore, M.H., and R.C. Trojanowicz

1988 *Policing and the Fear of Crime.* Washington, D.C.: National Institute of Justice.

Moore, M., and K. Viscusi

1990 Discounting environmental health risks: New evidence and policy implications. *Journal of Environment Economics and Management* 18(2):551-561.

Munoz, E.

1984 Economic costs of trauma, United States, 1982. *Journal of Trauma* 24:237-244.

National Highway Traffic Safety Administration (NHTSA)

1983, *The Economic Cost to Society of Motor Vehicle Accidents.* DOT
1987 HS 806-342, January 1983 and 1986 Addendum. Washington, D.C.: U.S. Department of Transportation.

National Research Council and Institute of Medicine

1985 *Injury in America.* Washington, D.C.: National Academy Press.

1988 *Injury Control: A Review of the Status and Progress of the Injury Control Program at the Centers for Disease Control.* Washington, D.C.: National Academy Press.

National Institute of Justice (NIJ)
1987 New dimensions in probation: Georgia's experience with intensive probation supervision. By B.S. Erwin and L.A. Bennett. *Research in Brief.* January. Washington, D.C.: National Institute of Justice.
1988 Policy experiments come of age. By J. Garner and C.A. Visher. *Research in Action.* NIJ Reports No. 211, September/October. Washington, D.C.: National Institue of Justice.
1989a Electronic monitoring of offenders increases. By A.K. Schmidt. *Research in Action.* NIJ Reports No. 212, January/February. Washington, D.C.: National Institute of Justice.
1989b Shock incarceration programs in state correctional jurisdictions— An update. By D.L. MacKenzie and D.B. Ballow. *Research in Action.* NIJ Reports No. 214, May/June. Washington, D.C.: National Institute of Justice.
1989c Comparing costs of public and private prisons: A case study. By C.H. Logan and B.W. McGriff. *Research in Action.* NIJ Reports No. 216, September/October. Washington, D.C.: National Institute of Justice.
Office for Victims of Crime, U.S. Department of Justice
1988 *Victims of Crime Act of 1984: A Report to Congress by the Attorney General.* Washington, D.C.: U.S. Department of Justice.
Paykel, E.S.
1978 Contribution of life events to causaton of psychiatric illness. *Psychological Medicine* 8:245-252.
Petersilia, J., and S. Turner
1986 *Prison Versus Probation in California: Implications for Crime and Offender Recidivism.* Santa Monica, Calif.: The RAND Corporation.
Phillips, L., and H.L. Votey, Jr.
1981 *The Economics of Crime Control.* Beverly Hills, Calif.: Sage Publications.
Polinsky, A.M., and S. Shavell
1979 The optimal tradeoff between the probability and magnitude of fines. *American Economic Review* 69(5):880-891.
Posner, R.A.
1980 Optimal sentences for white-collar criminals. *American Criminal Law Review* 17:409-418.
Psacharopoulos, G.
1981 Return to education: An updated international comparison. *Comparative Education* 17(3):321-341.
Pynoos, R.S., and S. Eth
1985 Children traumatized by witnessing acts of personal violence: Homicide, rape, or suicide behavior. In S. Eth and R.S. Pynoos, eds., *Post-Traumatic Stress Disorder in Children.* Washington, D.C.: American Psychiatric Press.

Reiss, A.J., Jr.
  1980   Understanding changes in crime rates. In S. Fienberg and A. Reiss, eds., *Indicators of Crime and Criminal Justice: Quantitative Studies.* Washington, D.C.: U.S. Department of Justice.
Resick, P.A.
  1987   Psychological effects of victimization: Implications for the criminal justice system. *Crime and Delinquency* 33:468-478.
Reuter, P., R. MacCoun, and P. Murphy
  1990   *Money From Crime: A Study of the Economics of Drug Dealing in Washington, D.C.* Santa Monica, Calif.: The RAND Corporation.
Rhodes, W.M.
  1988   Benefit-Cost Analysis of the Guideline Criminal History Adjustment. Staff Report. U.S. Sentencing Commission, Washington, D.C.
Rice, D.
  1966   *Estimating the Cost of Illness.* Health Economics Series, No. 5, Pub. No. 947-5. Washington, D.C.: U.S. Department of Health, Education and Welfare.
Rice, D., E. MacKenzie, and Associates
  1989   *Cost of Injury in the United States: A Report to Congress.* San Francisco, Calif.: Institute for Health and Aging, University of California, and Injury Prevention Center, The Johns Hopkins University.
Rizzo, M.J.
  1979   The cost of crime to victims: An empirical analysis. *Journal of Legal Studies* 8:177-205.
Rosenbaum, D.P., A.J. Lurigio, and P.J. Lavrakas
  1987   *Crime Stoppers: A National Evaluation of Program Operations and Effects.* Washington, D.C.: National Institute of Justice.
Rossi, P.H., E. Waite, C.E. Boise, and R.E. Berk
  1974   The seriousness of crimes: Normative structure and individual differences. *American Sociological Review* 39:224-237.
Schmidt, P., and A.D. Witte
  1984   *An Economic Analysis of Crime and Justice.* Orlando, Fla: Academic Press.
Sechrest, L., S. White, and E.D. Brown
  1979   *The Rehabilitation of Criminal Offenders: Problems and Prospects.* Washington, D.C.: National Academy of Sciences.
Sellin, T., and M.E. Wolfgang
  1964   *The Measurement of Delinquency.* New York: John Wiley & Sons.
Shavell, S.
  1985   Criminal law and the optimal use of nonmonetary sanctions as a deterrent. *Columbia Law Review* 85:1233-1262.

Shenk, J.F., and P.A. Klaus
1984 *The Economic Cost of Crime to Victims.* Bureau of Justice Statistics. Washington, D.C.: U.S. Department of Justice.

Sherman, L.W.
1989 Small merchants' big burdens. *Wall Street Journal* (October 23):A10.

Sherman, L.H., and J. Klein
1984 *Major Lawsuits Over Crime and Security: Trends and Patterns, 1958-1982.* Institute of Criminal Justice and Criminology. College Park: University of Maryland.

Singer, S.I.
1981 Homogeneous victim-offender populations: A review and some research implications. In *Victims of Crime: A Review of Research Issues and Methods.* Washington, D.C.: National Academy of Sciences.

Skogan, W.G.
1986 Fear of crime and neighborhood change. In A.J. Reiss, Jr., and M. Tonry, eds., *Communities and Crime.* Vol. 8 of *Crime and Justice: A Review of Research.* Chicago: University of Chicago Press.

Skogan, W.G., and M.G. Maxfield
1981 *Coping With Crime: Individual and Neighborhood Reactions.* Beverly Hills, Calif.: Sage Publications.

Smart, C., and C.R. Sanders
1976 *The Costs of Motor Vehicle Related Spinal Cord Injuries.* Washington, D.C.: The Insurance Institute for Highway Safety.

Smith, S.R., and S. Freinkel
1988 *Adjusting the Balance: Federal Policy and Victim Services.* Westport, Conn: Greenwood Press.

Spangenberg, R.L., and E.R. Walsh
1989 Capital punishment or life imprisonment? Some cost considerations. *Loyola of Los Angeles Law Review* 23:45-58.

Spangenberg, R.L., B. Lee, M. Battaglia, P. Smith, and A.D. Davis
1986 *National Criminal Defense Systems Study: Final Report.* Bureau of Justice Statistics, NCJ-94702. Washington, D.C.: U.S. Department of Justic.

Stigler, G.J.
1970 The optimum enforcement of laws. *Journal of Political Economy* 78:526-536.

Streff, F.M., L.J. Molnar, M.A. Cohen, T.R. Miller, and S.B. Rossman
1992 Estimating costs of traffic crashes and crime tools for informed decision making. *Journal of Public Health Policy* 13:451-471.

Tabak, R.J.
1989 The execution of injustice: A cost and lack-of-benefit analysis of the death penalty. *Loyola of Los Angeles Law Review* 23:59-146.

Thaler, R.
1978   A note on the value of crime control: Evidence from the property market. *Journal of Urban Economics* 5:137-145.

Toborg, M.A.
1981   *Pretrial Release: A National Evaluation of Practice and Outcomes.* National Institute of Justice. Washington, D.C.: U.S. Department of Justice.

U.S. Department of Justice
1988   *Report to the Nation on Crime and Justice.* NCJ-105506. Washington, D.C.: U.S. Department of Justice.
1989a   *Criminal Victimization in the United States, 1987.* NCJ-115524. Washington, D.C.: U.S. Department of Justice.
1989b   *National Crime Surveys: National Sample, 1979-1987 (Revised Questionnaire),* 3rd ed. ICPSR 8608. Washington, D.C.: U.S. Department of Justice.

Viscusi, W.K., W.A. Magat, and J. Huber
1989   Pricing Environmental Health Risks: Survey Assessments of Risk-Risk and Risk-Dollar Trade-Offs for Chronic Bronchitis. Working Paper, Center for the Study of Business Regulation, Duke University.

Waldfogel, J.
1989   Does the Criminal Justice System "Pay for Itself" Through Deterrence and Incapacitation? Working paper, Stanford University.

Waller, J.A., S.R. Payne, and J.M. Skelly
1990   Disability, direct cost, and payment issues in injuries involving woodworking and wood-related construction. *Accident Prevention* 22(4):351-360.

Webster, B.
1988   Victim assistance programs report increased workloads. *Research in Action.* Washington, D.C.: National Institute of Justice.

Weller, D., and M.K. Block
1979   Estimating the cost of judicial services. Pp. 149-164 in C.M. Gray, ed., *The Costs of Crime.* Beverly Hills, Calif.: Sage Publications.

Whitaker, C.J.
1989   *The Redesigned National Crime Survey: Selected New Data.* Bureau of Justice Statistics, NCJ-114746. Washington, D.C.: U.S. Department of Justice.

Wickenden, D.
1985   Good-bye day care: The insurance crisis hits preschool. *The New Republic* 193(December 9):14-17.

Widom, C.S.
1989   Child abuse, neglect, and violent criminal behavior. *Criminology* 27:251-271.

Wirtz, P.W., and A.V. Harrell
1987 Assaultive versus nonassaultive victimization: A profile analysis of psychological response. *Journal of Interpersonal Violence* 2:264-277.

Witte, A.D.
1989 Deterrence and Rehabilitation. Paper prepared for the Vanderbilt Institute for Public Policy Seminar Series (January).

Witte, A.D., H. Tauchen, and H. Griesinger
1989 Deterrence, Work and Crime: Revisiting the Issues With Birth Cohort. Working Paper #139, Wellesley College.

Wolfgang, M.E.
1958 *Patterns in Criminal Homicide.* Philadelphia: University of Pennsylvania Press.

Wolfgang, M.E., R.M. Figlio, P.E. Tracy, and S.I. Singer
1985 *The National Survey of Crime Severity.* Bureau of Justice Statistics. Washington, D.C.: U.S. Department of Justice.

Zedlewski, E.W.
1985 When have we punished enough? *Public Administration Review* (November):771-779.

1987 Making confinement decisions. *Research in Brief.* Washington, D.C.: National Institute of Justice.

1989 New mathematics of imprisonment: A reply to Zimring and Hawkins. *Crime and Delinquency* 35(1):169-175.

Zimring, F.E., and G. Hawkins
1988 The new mathematics of imprisonment. *Crime and Delinquency* 34(4):425-436.

Violence and Intentional Injuries: Criminal Justice and Public Health Perspectives on an Urgent National Problem

Mark H. Moore, Deborah Prothrow-Stith, Bernard Guyer, and Howard Spivak

INTRODUCTION

When one person attacks another, and an injury occurs, most citizens view the event as a violent crime. By definition, such crimes inflict physical harms on the victims. But the important social consequences of these attacks go well beyond the immediate trauma to the victim (see Cohen et al., in this volume). The victim suffers psychological damage as well as physical pain. Others in the society may be frightened by the experience of the victim and become concerned that they, too, are vulnerable.

In the past (and, for the most part, still) society has relied primarily on the criminal justice system to respond to such incidents. Part of the reason is a deeply held conviction that such attacks are morally wrong as well as simply harmful, and that those who commit such offenses should be held accountable for their misconduct. In this view, justice demands judgment and punishment for such acts, regardless of the practical effect of punishment on future criminal offending (von Hirsch, 1976).

Yet reliance on the criminal justice system also reflects a practical

---

Mark Moore is at the Kennedy School of Government, Harvard University; Deborah Prothrow-Stith and Howard Spivak are at the School of Public Health, Harvard University; and Bernard Guyer is at the Department of Maternal and Child Health, Johns Hopkins University.

judgment about the best ways of preventing and controlling violent crime. In this view, violent crime is best controlled by relying on arrests and incarcerations to deter, incapacitate, and rehabilitate criminal offenders. It is these responses that the agencies of the criminal justice system are designed to produce (for a discussion of their effectiveness, see Blumstein et al., 1986).

Recently, however, interpersonal attacks have drawn the attention of public health practitioners as well as criminal justice officials (e.g., see Mercy and O'Carroll, 1988; Health Resources and Services Administration, 1986). The reason is that injuries have emerged as one of the principal threats to the nation's health. Moreover, "intentional injuries" (which includes suicides, homicides, and aggravated assaults among other violent episodes) account for a surprisingly large proportion of all injuries (National Committee for Injury Prevention and Control, 1989).

Indeed, among all citizens in the United States, suicides and homicides have become the eleventh leading cause of death. Among citizens aged 15-34, homicides are now the third leading cause of death, and among black males aged 15-34, homicide is now the *leading* cause of death. Moreover, because intentional injuries occur disproportionately among younger Americans, they account for an unexpectedly large proportion of the total "years of potential life lost" in the United States each year (National Committee for Injury Prevention and Control, 1989:192). Behind the statistics on homicides and suicides lies a much larger but less well documented number of less severe injuries that degrade the health of the victims and make substantial claims on the nation's hard-pressed public hospitals (see Cohen et al., in this volume).

In short, the *health* consequences of criminal violence are now large enough to show up as a significant component of the nation's overall health problems. Criminal violence exacts a particularly large toll from the health of those who are least advantaged in the society. These simple facts make violence a concern for the public health community as well as the criminal justice community.

However, there are other reasons for the public health community to become involved in efforts to control criminal violence. Over the years, in controlling epidemics of cholera, smallpox, and polio, and in dealing with other kinds of injuries such as auto fatalities, public health researchers and practitioners have developed analytical and operational approaches that can usefully complement the approaches now being taken by criminal justice researchers and practitioners to control criminal violence (for a discussion of these techniques and approaches, see Friedman, 1987).

For example, public health researchers and practitioners have traditionally concentrated on *preventing* incidents of violence rather than dealing with their consequences after the fact. That is arguably a useful complement to the criminal justice system's predominantly reactive stance.

Similarly, the public health community uses epidemiological techniques to identify specific "risk factors" that increase the risk of violence and then designs programs to eliminate or reduce their effect. This is a useful complement to the criminal justice system's primary focus on the deterrence and control of criminal offenders.

Public health researchers and practitioners are instinctively multidisciplinary and seek to mobilize many different individuals, community groups, and agencies in making an attack on criminal violence. This seems a useful complement to the apparent tendency of the criminal justice system to focus principally on its own internal operations.

In short, criminal violence may usefully be seen as a public health problem not only because the consequences of violent attacks constitute an important health problem, but also because public health methods may expand society's current capacities for dealing with the problem. That is the primary purpose of this paper: to show how the criminal justice system's traditional vision and response to violent crime may be usefully complemented by the public health community's approach to the problem.

Of course, their approaches overlap to a great degree, and these overlaps reveal their commitment to a common cause. However, the areas in which their approaches diverge are both interesting and valuable. Although the differences in approach sometimes create tensions between the two communities, it is precisely in these areas that the most useful contributions are made by the public health community, for it is in those areas that the public health community usefully challenges criminal justice thinking and operationally complements criminal justice capabilities.

Indeed, by synthesizing the somewhat different images of the problem and the solution, society may develop a more accurate and complete picture of violence and be able to fashion a more effective response than is now possible. That, at least, is what our experience of working together has taught us.

In searching for a synthetic view of violence and an effective public response, we have found it useful to compare and contrast public health and criminal justice system approaches to violence in five separate domains:

1. how each community tends to see and define the problem of violence;

2. the analytic frameworks (and implicit assumptions about causation) that each community uses to identify the principal causes;

3. the entering presumptions and biases, rooted in long professional experience and empirical research, that guide each community's search for effective methods of intervention;

4. the principal political and organizational resources that each community can mobilize to deal with the problem; and finally

5. the principal values that each community believes are the most important ones to be advanced and protected in organizing society's response to violence.

From this dialogue, we have seen the possibility of a new conception of violence, and new opportunities for society to deal effectively with it. No doubt, as the dialogue between these two communities develops, we will all learn a great deal more about how to synthesize the complementary views. Still, even at this preliminary stage, a new view of violence and its effective control is worth sketching.

1. Violent crime is a threat to the nation's health and safety as well as to public security. It must be seen and responded to as both a health problem and a crime problem.

2. In reckoning the social consequences of criminal attacks resulting in injury, it is important to consider not only the magnitude of the physical injury, but also the psychological damage and fear that are stimulated by criminal violence.

3. It is important to see that violence that occurs in the context of ongoing relationships (such as within families) is particularly damaging and particularly hard for the criminal justice program to identify or manage. Consequently, it is in these areas that the public health and medical communities have particularly important roles to play.

4. Acts of violence that will be properly labeled by society as criminal attacks emerge from a complex causal system that includes, but is not limited to, the intentions of the offender. Other factors influencing individual incidents and aggregate levels of violence include such things as (a) the availability and use of criminogenic commodities (such as guns, drugs, and alcohol); (b) the density of criminogenic situations (such as ongoing unre-

solved conflicts); and (c) a variety of cultural factors that help to justify and encourage violence.

5.   It follows as a corollary, then, that there are important opportunities to prevent criminal violence beyond those ordinarily relied on by the criminal justice system. Although it is both just and effective to hold offenders accountable for violent attacks, it may also be possible to prevent such attacks or reduce their seriousness by altering the "risk factors" that lead to criminal violence.

6.   In all likelihood, society's main line of attack on criminal violence will continue to come from the nation's criminal justice agencies. They are the ones who have the troops and the most familiar paradigm for defining and attacking the problem. Their efforts can usefully be aided, however, by a partnership with those in public health.

7.   Members of the public health community can enhance the significance of the criminal justice community's efforts by emphasizing that health, as well as security, is at stake. They can widen the perspective of the criminal justice community about the possible causes of violence and the possible lines of attack, and they can mobilize support for antiviolence programs from constituencies that have not previously been involved in dealing with these issues.

How we arrived at such views is described below. Before presenting our analysis, however, two cautionary notes are in order.

First, the analysis uses the literary device of referring to perspectives and views held by the "criminal justice community" and the "public health community." We understand that individuals in these "communities" do not all hold the same views. Indeed, we suspect that the differences in perspective *within* these communities are at least as great as those *between* the two communities. Even worse, our analysis attributes to these communities particular views that are sharply drawn caricatures of the actual views held by members of the communities. Thus, we risk alienating the two communities from our discussion and from one another.

Despite the hazards, we think this device serves our purposes. We believe that each community does have a somewhat distinctive approach and that there is much to be learned by taking the particular *gestalts* seriously, developing their implications, and seeing how each complements the other. In short, we think that at this stage of intellectual development, we are likely to learn more if we work to sharpen the distinctive perspectives and see how they challenge one another, than if we blur the distinctions in easy agreements.

Second, we make a sharp distinction between the views of the "criminal justice *practitioner* community" and the "criminal justice *research* community." One could make a similar distinction for the public health community, but making this distinction seems less important for the latter. The intellectual and professional gulf between practitioners and researchers seems much less in the public health community than in the criminal justice community. In fact, in important respects, the criminal justice *research* community has more in common with the public health research and practitioner community than with the criminal justice *practitioner* community. What unites them is their common interest and commitment to "behavioral sciences."

Most criminal justice practitioners are not "behavioral scientists." They have not been trained to be social science researchers or social engineers. They mete out justice through the operations of the criminal justice system. They work in close contact with the moral sentiments of local communities and with individual cases rather than aggregate phenomena. Their home disciplines are philosophy, law, and the professional arts of police and correctional administration rather than social science.

In making these distinctions, we are not apologizing for the views of criminal justice practitioners. We think that their value commitments and perspectives are important to honor in dealing with criminal violence. Justice is a value society means to preserve in making its response to violence. We simply note that on some important questions (such as the causes of violence or effective methods of prevention), the views of criminal justice practitioners will be somewhat different from those of both criminal justice researchers, on the one hand, and the public health community, on the other.

Third, throughout the discussion, we distinguish between "traditional" and "stereotypical" criminal justice responses to violent crime, and emerging criminal justice practices which have a more preventive focus. We do so to acknowledge that criminal justice practitioners have long been interested in prevention, and that the interest in new forms of prevention is now increasing; but also to recognize that the principal focus of the criminal justice system has been on arresting and punishing offenders once a crime has occurred.

"CRIMINAL VIOLENCE" AND "INTENTIONAL INJURIES": DIFFERENT PERCEPTIONS OF A SHARED CONCERN

In today's hard-pressed communities, a world of trouble awaits attention by public agencies. Precious few resources are available to respond. Thus, common sense dictates that public agencies stay focused on the problems that are central to their responsibilities; they should not stray into new areas. Thus, it is natural to think that criminal justice agencies should remain focused on crime control, and public health agencies on traditional public health concerns.

THE COMMON CONCERN: INTERPERSONAL VIOLENCE

What this view overlooks, however, is that public health and criminal justice agencies *share* a common concern *that is at the center of their respective responsibilities.* Each community, consistent with its own responsibilities, must be intensely concerned about attacks by one citizen against another that produce physical injury (i.e., homicides, rapes, and aggravated assaults).

The criminal justice community must be concerned because these crimes are among the most important for the criminal justice system to address. The public health community must be concerned about such events because they damage the health status of the least advantaged in society.

SIGNIFICANT ASPECTS OF INTERPERSONAL VIOLENCE

Both public health and criminal justice communities initially concern themselves with the nature and magnitude of the injury that results from interpersonal violence. To a degree, the criminal justice community is directed to consider the magnitude of the injury by the provisions of criminal law. If a person *dies* as a result of a criminal attack, the offender is charged with homicide, murder, or manslaughter rather than aggravated assault.

Where the differences are not reflected in law, they are often reflected in formal administrative rules. New sentencing guidelines, for example, typically require judges to consider the extent of injury to the victims in deciding on an appropriate sentence for a given criminal offense (Nagel, 1990).

Where the differences are not reflected in either law or formal procedures, they nonetheless appear in informal practices. Prosecutors, for example, commonly rely on the "seven-stitch rule" to distinguish aggravated assault from simple assault; unless an injury requires more than seven stitches to close, the incident will be treated as a simple rather than an aggravated assault. In these respects, then, the criminal justice community gives attention to the seriousness of the injury to the victim.

Criminal Justice Emphasis on the Offender

What is surprising to public health professionals, however, is how quickly the attention of criminal justice officials shifts from the victim and his injuries, on the one hand, to concerns about the offender, on the other. Once some injury has been established, and some indication of who the offender is has been obtained, criminal justice officials begin to lose interest in the victim as a victim. The victim remains important as a witness in a criminal proceeding against the offender, but the victim as someone who needs continuing attention recedes into the background (for criminal justice neglect of victims, see President's Task Force on Victims of Crime, 1982; Bureau of Justice Statistics, 1983).

Instead, attention begins to focus on the offender. To criminal justice officials, the seriousness of an offense is judged as much on characteristics of the offender as injury to the victim. Indeed, in judging the seriousness of an incident of interpersonal violence, three characteristics of the offender become important. The first is the intention of the offender in the instant case: the more deliberate and calculating the attack, the more serious is the crime.

The second is the "dangerousness" of the conduct that led to the injury. For example, the criminal justice system often treats mere threats from gun-toting offenders more seriously than actual injuries inflicted by offenders armed only with their fists. This reflects the view that the exact nature of the injury emerging from a criminal attack is largely fortuitous. What is morally relevant (and therefore important to criminal prosecution) is the dangerousness of the conduct of the offender.

The third is the offender's prior record of offending. This is important for two slightly different reasons. On the one hand, the offender's prior record is often seen as predictive of future acts of violence: the more violence there is in an offender's past and the more serious it is, the greater is the risk for the future (Chaiken and Chaiken, 1982; Greenwood, 1982).

On the other, the past record of offending is often used by investigators (if not judges and juries) to gauge the intention of the offender in the instant case: the longer the prior record, the less likely it seems that an offense was committed by accident (Moore, 1986).

These concerns about the offender's intent, conduct, and prior record all distract attention from the victim and the magnitude of the injury inflicted. Yet, from the perspective of criminal justice officials, these issues are essential. What is important for the cause of justice is being clear about the heinousness of the crime: care for the victim is less significant.

Public Health Focus on the Victim

In contrast, in looking at instances of criminal violence, members of the public health community initially focused more attention on the victim. Because they were interested in health consequences, it mattered whether a knife wound was deeply penetrating and life threatening, or bloody but easily sutured. They were also concerned with what continuing kinds of care would be required to restore the victim to his or her previous condition. They were particularly concerned, if the victimization involved an on-going relationship, how that continuing relationship would be structured in the future. In short, their medical orientation and preventive concerns kept their attention focused on the victim rather than the offender.

More recently, however, the public health community has begun to share the criminal justice system's interest in the offender. The difference in its orientation to the offender is that, like many in the criminal justice community, it is interested in preventing the emergence of people who are prone to committing violence.

PROBLEMS RELATED TO INTERPERSONAL VIOLENCE

The differing concerns of the two communities also affect each community's perception of what other specific problems are related to the core problem of interpersonal violence, and are therefore part of its responsibilities, and which are not.

At the outset, it seems that there ought to be a fairly clear line of demarcation between the concerns of the two communities. The criminal justice community's terrain is marked out by behavior that is proscribed by criminal statutes. Presumably, the gradients of concern are determined by the seriousness of the criminal offense. The public health community's terrain is marked out by

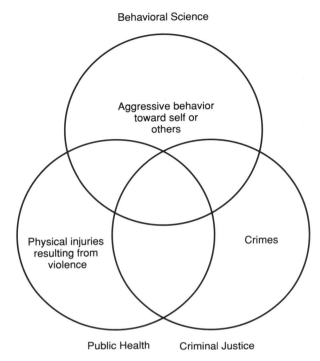

FIGURE 1 Overlapping perspectives of public health, criminal justice, and behavioral science. SOURCE: Adapted from National Committee for Injury Prevention and Control (1989:193).

the occurrence of physical trauma. The gradients of concern involve the seriousness of the injury.

As noted above, these concerns produce an important overlap, but it also seems true that clear boundaries exist. Figure 1 makes this point graphically by using a Venn diagram to show the areas of overlap and of difference.

In practice, however, the clear distinctions begin to blur. The sharp edges that define the concerns of one community begin to shade into the concerns of the other. As a result, the area of overlap becomes much larger. The reasons for this are the following.

Violence and "Nonviolent" Crimes

The concerns of the criminal justice community embrace all criminal offenses—including those offenses that do not necessarily produce violence or physical trauma. Burglary, larceny from the person, even robberies that do not result in injury are all considered important crimes (Bureau of Justice Statistics, 1984). Yet they do not involve violence—at least not in the narrow, literal sense.

Public health practitioners, focused principally on controlling violence, might be less interested in these offenses. They might be concerned about them as citizens, but as public health practitioners they might feel less responsible for them because the offenses do not involve injuries per se. In trying to account for the criminal justice community's interests in such offenses, they might reasonably assume that its concern reflected a concern for protecting property rather than life and safety.

To a degree, the public health practitioner would be correct in these views. The criminal justice community *is* concerned about protecting property as well as protecting life and safety. Yet, in an important sense, the criminal justice community's concerns about these "property offenses" can be seen as deriving from concerns about controlling violence and its consequences as much as from concerns about protecting property. To the extent that this is true, the public health community might be interested in these offenses as well as the more obviously violent crimes.

One reason is that any crime, including property crime, has the potential for creating real violence. The clearest example occurs when household burglaries become robberies because an unanticipated homeowner appears on the scene.

However, this example illustrates a far broader point. When any crime is committed, a potential for violence is created simply because a powerful social norm has been violated. Those who have been wronged (and all their family, friends, and relatives) feel angry and vengeful. In defending themselves against attack, in apprehending the offender, sometimes even in punishing the offender, real violence may occur (Cook, 1981). The point is simply that it is not just literal violence that begets violence, it is the more metaphorical violence to the social order that begets violence. In the language of public health, *any* crime—even property crimes—can be a *risk factor* for violence.

The second reason for the criminal justice community's concern about property offenses is closely related to the first. Precisely because crimes have the potential to escalate into violence, even nonviolent crimes produce a significant amount of fear. Fear is an important problem in its own right. Indeed, it is one of the most important reasons to be concerned about violent crime (Moore and Trojanowicz, 1988; Garofalo, 1981). It impoverishes the daily lives of those who are afraid, and it forces people to stay indoors and to buy locks or guns, with disastrous consequences for the quality of urban life. Because fear is one of the most important reasons to be concerned about violent crime, if nonviolent crimes also produce fear, they too must be taken seriously.

The third reason for the criminal justice community's concern about offenses that do not produce injury or trauma is not only that they produce fear, but also that some of the worst and most degrading offenses work by sustaining a palpable threat of violence over a victim without ever having to produce much injury. This would be true, for example, of the worst cases of domestic violence in which the explicit violence of the husband against the wife is dwarfed in psychological and social significance by the daily threat of violence. It is also true in cases of extortion by organized crime groups or youth gangs (Moore, 1983a).

The point of these observations is simply this: although the domain of the criminal justice community reaches to all crimes, not just those that result in injury, its concerns about nonviolent crimes is broader than a concern for protecting property. Indeed, one might say that its interests in protecting property derive at least partly from concerns about reducing the potential for violence in the society. One can also say that its concerns about nonviolent offenses are fueled by the same concerns that tend to make violent crime its dominant concern: namely, the fact that fear and continuing threats of violence impoverish individual and community lives.

In this sense, the only feature that explicitly violent crimes bring to social concerns about crime in general is physical trauma. That, of course, is significant—particularly because it exacerbates all the less tangible costs of crime as well. Yet it is hardly all that is important about violent crime. Insofar as other crimes share some of these other aspects, they too become important.

Violence and Relationships

As noted above, what initially draws the public health community to the problem of intentional violence is concern for the health consequences of criminal violence. Once in this domain, however, the concerns of the public health community naturally widen to include other offenses (National Committee for Injury Prevention and Control, 1989:192-267). In discussing "intentional injuries," the public health community includes sexual offenses (ranging from rape to child molestation) in which no blood is shed, no bones are broken, and no bruises are left, but intrusive physical contact occurs. It also include offenses such as domestic assault, and child abuse and neglect, where injury is often present and is part of what attracts its attention but is not the most important aspect of the offense.

By including such offenses in its conception of "intentional injury," the public health community departs from a strict preoccupation with injury understood as physical harm and enters a realm in which injury acquires a more metaphorical meaning. There is nothing wrong with this, of course. The interesting question is what particular concerns prompt the public health community's interest in these crimes and what the criminal justice community might learn from these perspectives.

It is not too difficult to understand why the public health community might give special emphasis to sexual offenses. To a degree, one can accommodate this interest within the framework of concern for physical trauma by noting that all sexual offenses involve intrusive physical contact, and most involve other injuries such as abrasions, cuts, and bruises. Still, it is clear that this is not the most important reason that sexual offenses become prominent.

The principal reason the public health community accords sexual offenses such high priority, of course, is that the victim suffers important psychological as well as physical damage (Estrich, 1987). The public health community's concern for the victim and his or her treatment naturally emphasizes this fact. The lesson to be learned is that psychological "injury" must be added to physical injury as an (implicit) public health concern.

Similarly, one can accommodate the interest in domestic violence, child abuse, and child neglect by pointing toward the physical injuries that usually attend such situations. Again, however, that does not account for the importance attached to such offenses. What seem to make these offenses important in the minds of the public health community are five particular features.

First, as in the case of sexual offenses, there is a strong presumption that psychological trauma is an important feature of these cases. In psychological terms, there can be nothing worse than being locked in an ongoing relationship that is supposed to be supportive and nurturing, and instead turns out to be abusive.

Second, in many of these cases there is a pattern of repeat victimization that not only contributes to the psychological damage, but also demands, in the minds of public health practitioners, a preventive response (Police Foundation, 1976).

Third, because many of the cases involve families and violence within families seems to affect the development of the children, the public health community has a special interest in trying to end that violence. Only in this way can a continuing cycle of violence be broken (Dubowitz, 1987).

Fourth, these cases often involve other contributing causes such as alcohol or drug abuse, acute stress, or other forms of mental illness. Consequently, a therapeutic response often seems more promising at the outset than a criminal justice system response.

Fifth, and perhaps most importantly, these cases of psychological and physical violence are more visible to health agencies than to criminal justice agencies. The reasons are that the victims of such offenses are less likely to call criminal justice agencies than they are to appear in doctors' offices and emergency rooms. Moreover, the difficulties of investigating and prosecuting these cases have discouraged many criminal justice officials from doing so even when they have learned of the crimes (Berk et al., 1980, 1982).

Thus, in thinking about "intentional violence" the public health community tends to look beyond those offenses that cause physical injury and to look at offenses that cause psychological injury as well. Also, members of the public health community have special concerns for offenses that occur in the context of ongoing relationships—perhaps because it is in that context that the threat of violence or neglect carries a particularly heavy psychological burden, and perhaps because there is a special opportunity for the public health community to make a contribution to these neglected offenses.

Toward a Synthesis

Viewed from both criminal justice and public health perspectives then, a much wider and deeper understanding can be obtained of what the society has at stake in instances of criminal violence and of what constitutes events that are worth calling by that name. The criminal justice community's vision of violent crimes committed by dangerous offenders is enlarged by concern for the victim, for psychological damage, and for the special problems created by crimes that occur in the context of ongoing relationships. The public health community's vision is enlarged by seeing that property crimes may be risk factors for violence and that fear is an important consequence of many crimes that do not produce physical trauma.

This synthesis suggests that there are even wider domains of common concerns and, therefore, greater opportunities and need for cooperation than first appeared. If the criminal justice system is influenced by the public health community to increase its commitment to healing victims as well as catching offenders, its concerns become far wider. It can no longer view victims merely as witnesses in the drama of criminal prosecution. They become important objects of care and attention. Such a task is particularly challenging in the context of domestic assaults, child abuse, and other crimes involving close relations because the victim of such offenses is not only the person who was injured but the ongoing relationship. The challenging question before the criminal justice system, then, is how it might best respond in these situations to restore the family unit to proper, or at least tolerable, functioning.

Similarly, if the public health community is influenced by the criminal justice community's views of crime, then its own interests in crime will be significantly widened. Its concerns should not be limited only to criminal violence or to physical attacks. The concern for psychological damage, for fear, for the escalation of violence that might come from lesser property offenses widens the domain of public health concerns substantially. Indeed, from this perspective, its concerns might even extend to burglaries and larcenies.

It also becomes apparent that the two communities cannot simply carve up the domain of interpersonal violence into separate spheres and then operate independently within them. The criminal justice community owes a great deal to the public health community for spotting the problem of crimes in ongoing relationships, and for being an important part of the response to such offenses, but it cannot simply cede these cases to the public health or social service community. There are important issues of justice that must be addressed in the handling of these cases, as well as important issues of care and protection of victims.

Similarly, the criminal justice community cannot respond to criminal victimization all by itself: it has always relied on the medical community to suture the victim's wounds, and might now see a greater opportunity and obligation to join with the public health, medical, and psychological communities to heal the psychological damage associated with crime, as well as to relieve the suffering in intimate relationships that have gone astray. In sum, to deal effectively with what can now be seen as a far more complex problem of violence and its consequences, there is urgent need for an effective collaboration between the two communities.

"INTENTIONS OF OFFENDERS" AND "RISK FACTORS FOR VIOLENCE": TWO DIFFERENT CAUSAL PARADIGMS

Just as the criminal justice and public health communities have usefully contrasting views on what is socially significant about interpersonal violence, they also have similar but slightly different ideas about where to look for the causes of the problem. The differences are sharper, here, between the views of criminal justice practitioners on the one hand, and those of criminal justice researchers and the public health community on the other, for it is in this domain that the precepts of "behavioral science" make their strongest claims.

CRIMINAL JUSTICE: THE INTENTIONS OF OFFENDERS

As a philosophical matter, the criminal justice system is committed to finding the primary cause of violent offending in the intentions, motivations, and characters of offenders. Unless there is some such intent, any violence that occurs would be treated as accidental rather than criminal (Kaplan and Skolnick, 1982:1-10). Yet many criminal justice practitioners go beyond this philosophical position and see the intentions of individuals as the primary empirical cause of violence. In this view, if the offenders had not gotten angry, or if they were not so vicious and ruthless, the violent offenses would not have occurred.

If the motivations of offenders are the key causal factors shaping incidents of violence, then an effective policy response would be one that focused on this particular variable. In particular, it would be effective to threaten potential offenders with punishment for violent acts (Zimring and Hawkins, 1973; Blumstein et al., 1978).

It would also be effective if those who had shown themselves willing to commit violent offenses—despite the moral injunctions against such conduct—were kept in circumstances where they could not commit such acts again (Greenwood, 1982).

In addition, it would be effective to try to alter offenders' attitudes and feelings so that they would be less inclined to commit violent acts in the future (Sechrest et al., 1979). Thus, the criminal justice practitioner community's commitment to deterrence, incapacitation, and rehabilitation flows quite naturally from its focus on the intentions of individual offenders as the principal cause of violent acts.

PUBLIC HEALTH: AN EPIDEMIOLOGIC APPROACH

The public health community acknowledges the role of the offender's intentions in causing violence: that is implicit in categorizing assaultive behavior as "intentional injuries." However, the public health community tends to see criminal violence as emerging from a more complex causal system than one dominated solely by the settled intentions of the offender.

According to one commentator, the public health approach to violence prevention and control is based on four interrelated steps:

1. public health surveillance (i.e., the development and refinement of data systems for the ongoing and systematic collection, analysis, interpretation, and dissemination of health data);

2. risk group identification (i.e., the identification of persons at greatest risk of disease or injury and of the places, times, and other circumstances associated with increased risk);

3. risk factor exploration (i.e. the analytic exploration of potentially causative risk factors for disease or death, as suggested by the nature of the high-risk population and other research); and

4. program implementation/evaluation (i.e., the design, implementation, and evaluation of preventive interventions based on our understanding of the population at risk and the risk factors for the outcome of interest) (Mercy and O'Carroll, 1988:290).

These are the basic empirical methods of action-oriented epidemiologists intent on locating and reducing threats to health. The approach is not focused on individual offenses for which offenders must be found and held accountable; rather, it seeks to identify aggregate patterns of violence that might be alleviated by preventive social interventions.

Perhaps the most difficult step in this analytic process is the third: the search for potentially modifiable risk factors for intentional injuries. To aid in this search, public health researchers have developed additional analytic frameworks—based originally on an understanding of how infectious diseases develop, spread, and produce disastrous consequences for afflicted populations, and then adapted for use in analyzing the occurrence of injuries. William Haddon, for example, has proposed the matrix presented in Table 1 as a way of identifying potentially modifiable risk factors in the control of automobile accidents (National Committee for Injury Prevention and Control, 1989:8). It is useful to see how these methods might be applied to the analysis of interpersonal violence.

Vectors, Hosts, and Environments

The public health epidemiological analysis begins by relying on the categories that proved so useful to the public health community in controlling infectious diseases: the concepts of vector, host, and environment. In the context of infectious diseases, the vector is some combination of the disease-generating organism and the mechanism for spreading it: for example, a mosquito carrying malaria, a can of tuna fish infected with botulism, or a needle carrying a residue of AIDS-infected blood.

The host is the organism in which the vector finds a home where it can both stay alive as a threat to others and express itself as a disease-producing agent. In the analysis of human problems, the relevant host is most often a human: for example, a worker digging the Panama Canal around the turn of the century, a family of picnickers on Long Island, or a hospital orderly in New York City.

The environment is meant to be a catchall concept that identifies all those things that might influence either (1) the number and distribution of vectors (such as the number and character of swamps in Panama, quality control mechanisms in tuna-packing plants, or needle disposal procedures in hospitals); or (2) the ways in which vectors come in contact with hosts and spread from one host to another (e.g., the sleeping arrangements of workers on the Panama Canal, the enthusiasm for tuna fish sandwiches among the picnicking family, or needle recovery, sharing, and disposal practices around hospitals in New York City).

These concepts and models are most applicable when one is discussing diseases that are literally rather than metaphorically infectious (e.g., where there are biological mechanisms that pass the illness from one person to another in well-understood, quite predictable ways. For such diseases, it is literally as well as metaphorically true that each person is an important part of the environment of every other person, and that each person's conduct may affect the chances of another person becoming infected.

TABLE 1 The Haddon Matrix

Phase	Host (human)	Vector (vehicle)	Physical Environment	Socioeconomic Environment
Precrash	Driver vision Alcohol intoxication Experience and judgment Amount of travel	Brakes, tires Center of gravity Jackknife tendency Speed of travel Ease of control Load characteristics	Visibility of hazards Road curvature and gradient Surface coefficient of friction Divided highways, one-way streets Intersections, access control Signalization	Attitudes about alcohol Laws related to impaired driving Speed limits Support for injury prevention efforts
Crash	Safety belt use Osteoporosis	Speed capability Vehicle size Automatic restraints Placement, hardness, and sharpness of contact surfaces Load containment	Recovery areas Guard rails Characteristics of fixed objects Median barriers Roadside embankments Speed limits	Attitudes about safety belt use Laws about safety belt use Enforcement of child safety seat laws Motorcycle helmet use laws
Postcrash	Age Physical condition	Fuel system integrity	Emergency communication systems Distance to and quality of emergency medical services Rehabilitation	Support for trauma care systems Training of EMS personnel

SOURCE: National Committee for Injury Prevention and Control (1989:193).

How such concepts work in a less biological, more mechanical or sociological world is less clear. There is nothing that necessarily links one traffic accident to the likelihood of another occurring, one suicide to another, or one violent crime to another. Yet there often seems to be some structure in the occurrence of accidents, suicides, and violence, and that structure often gives clues about causation, even if it does not point directly to spiraling interactions between densely connected hosts and agents.

Moreover, the epidemiological concept does serve to remind us that we are all part of one another's environment and that each individual's actions affect the conditions under which other individuals live—not only materially and concretely, but also normatively and emotionally. Expectations about the proper way to behave and express anger are nurtured and sustained in social encounters, not just in the individual psyche. Emotions such as anger and despair may be "contagious" in the sense that one person's mood affects another, even if there is no biological mechanism that controls the spread of moods (Coleman, 1987).

One could conceive of an epidemiology of violence based not only on empirical methods that discover a structure in an observed pattern of events, but based also on a causal theory. In approaches to injury prevention, for example, safety engineers and public health analysts gradually came to conceive of mechanical energy as the vector of injury. Epidemiologists of violence might begin to conceive of feelings of anger, frustration, or aggression as the relevant agent for interpersonal violence. The size and distribution of this vector might be influenced by biological factors such as genes or situational factors such as frustrating conflicts, fear, or despair. The hosts would be ordinary people who were buffeted by these feelings. Such an analysis would not necessarily deal with *instrumental* violence (which would presumably follow quite different epidemiological rules), but it might allow us to begin to understand *expressive* violence in quite different ways than we now do.

Timing of Interventions

Those who studied injury as a public health problem eventually had to go beyond the categories of vector, host, and environment to fully understand the opportunities to intervene to reduce risk factors. They added the idea of timing—pre-, mid-, and post-crash—to this conception (National Committee for Injury Prevention and Control, 1989:8).

That extension seems appropriate in the case of interpersonal violence as well. One can imagine violence prevention measures that (1) operate prior to the incident of violence (e.g., reducing the availability of guns and alcohol, reducing the number of festering disputes in a community, or reducing the number of people who are inclined to use violence as an expressive act); (2) those that affect the violent encounter as it develops (e.g., training the police who respond to emergency calls with techniques that minimize the use of force and also minimize the chance of escalation); and (3) measures that operate to minimize the damage associated with violence (e.g., effective emergency medical response and trauma centers, or victim assistance programs designed to minimize the psychological harm to victims). Table 2 presents an initial attempt to use something like the Haddon matrix for the identification of risk factors and interventions that might be successful in reducing risk factors for violence.

TABLE 2 Haddon Matrix for Violence Prevention

Phase	Host (potential attackers)	Vector (means and occasions creating opportunities)	Environment (factors influencing hosts and vectors)
Previolence	Teaching parenting skills	Regulating weapons	Reducing poverty
	Teach nonviolent dispute resolving skills	Regulating alcohol	Reducing disorder of cities
	Early psychiatric interventions	Regulating public drunkenness	Using architecture to promote a sense of community
During violent event	Using nonviolent means of control	Eliminating weapons at scene	Police rapid response
	Teaching self-defense to victims	Mobilizing police	Community alertness
After violent event	Emergency medical treatment	Marital counseling in domestic assault	Providing jobs and counseling to poor families
	Incapacitation	Family therapy in child abuse and neglect	Adding street lighting in dangerous areas
	Rehabilitation		

SOURCE: National Committee for Injury Prevention and Control (1989:8).

Complex Sociological Prevention

Other public health analysts, finding these traditional public health models somewhat confining, have shifted to a "behavioral science model" that orients them to "complex social prevention" (Rosenberg et al., 1986:1399-1400). The justification for adopting this perspective has been stated by Rosenberg et al. (1986:1400):

> Public health as a discipline must progress beyond the traditional disease model, with its natural tendency to overemphasize the importance of purely medical problems and interventions . . . . A new terminology must be developed for prevention that allows for multiple levels of determination on the one hand, and, on the other, for interventions that are designed less to change individual behavior or the natural environment than to change social behavior and the social environment.

Although this approach is promising, it looks less like traditional epidemiology and more like sociological and criminological methods for understanding the causes of violence. Indeed, in this conception, the public health analysis of violence comes into almost perfect alignment with criminological and sociological views of the problem.

SOCIOLOGICAL AND CRIMINOLOGICAL ANALYSES

Although it is true that the criminal justice *practitioner* community tends to focus on the character and intention of offenders as the most important causal factor determining incidents of victimization, the criminal justice *research* community has long engaged in analyses of interpersonal violence, and criminal offending more generally, that are in the same spirit as epidemiological analyses carried out by the public health community. It is also true that, increasingly, criminal justice practitioners are joining them in this understanding of criminal violence and are basing their operational strategies on these conceptions.

Spatial and Temporal Location of Crimes

For example, for several decades, sociologists and criminologists have done empirical work disclosing patterns in the incidence of criminal victimization and criminal offending (e.g., see Wolfgang, 1958a; Hindelang et al., 1978). Over the last decades, that work has been enormously advantaged by the routine use of victimization surveys (Dodge, 1981). Such work will also be advanced by recent changes in the Unified Crime Reporting system that will add important information about the nature of crimes reported to police, including data on the magnitude of the losses to victims and the relationship of the offender to the victim (Bureau of Justice Statistics and Federal Bureau of Investigation, 1985; Police Executive Research Forum, no date a,b).

Potentially even more significant is that criminal justice practitioners are increasingly becoming epidemiologists of criminal offending. With the help of researchers, criminal justice practitioners have learned that a relatively small number of offenders account for a large fraction of serious crimes (Petersilia, 1980; Peterson et al., 1981). Such offenders become the focus of particularly intensive criminal justice system attention (Moore et al., 1984). Similarly, researchers and the police have discovered that criminal incidents tend to cluster in particular locations (defined in terms of both time and space). These so-called hot spots can also become the focus of intensive police "problem-solving" efforts (Sherman et al., 1989).

Situational Analyses of Crime Causation

Both researchers and practitioners in the criminal justice community have also become increasingly interested in the idea that many crimes emerge not simply from the evil intentions of criminal offenders but also from criminogenic features of particular situations (Clarke, 1990). An unlighted area around a subway stop may be an invitation for street muggings. A crowded street filled with bank teller machines and check cashing establishments may create favorable conditions for larcenies from the person, and some of these, when resisted, may produce violence. A teenage discotheque next to school may invite vandalism, and next to a housing project for the elderly may produce the kinds of small scuffles and unpleasant encounters that provoke fear among the elderly.

Such situations "produce" crimes not only because they attract people who were already motivated to offend, but also because they facilitate the commission of crimes by people who were less committed to criminal offending. Although as a legal matter this does not reduce the culpability of the offender, as a scientific matter, one can see the situation as a contributing cause and therefore as a potential target for intervention.

Criminogenic Commodities

Not only does the criminal justice community now view situations as criminogenic, it also views some commodities as criminogenic (Moore, 1983b). At the top of everyone's list are drugs such as heroin, cocaine, and alcohol. These drugs are linked to violent criminal offending in many different ways (Fagan, 1990). They seem to have an immediate impact on the level and seriousness of offending. They may also have a developmental influence on young children, drawing them into patterns of criminal offending that they would have resisted had they not become involved with drugs but that, once established, seem to hold firm against other more positive social influences (Jessor and Jessor, 1977).

These drugs, particularly alcohol, seem to affect victims as well as offenders and to increase their vulnerability to attack (Wolfgang, 1958b). They also seem to create situations—in barrooms, crack dens, and shooting galleries—in which disputes can erupt and violence can occur (Police Executive Research Forum, no date a). Of course, the economics of producing, selling, and distributing illegal but desired commodities also creates circumstances in which instrumental and expressive violence are both quite common (Goldstein, 1985).

Guns, too, are increasingly seen as criminogenic and violence inducing (Cook, 1983). There is an argument that guns in the hands of police officers or law-abiding citizens might reduce crime and violence through general deterrence of criminal offenders (Kleck, 1988). However, what is more readily observable is that the widespread availability of guns seems to facilitate violence by providing criminal offenders with a plentiful supply of weaponry; by making it possible for spouses, in a moment of fury, to become murderesses; or by providing the means for protective homeowners to transform a household burglary into a violent encounter in which the burglar, the homeowner, or the late arriving teenage son, mistakenly taken for a burglar, might be killed (Cook, 1983).

In addition, there are some who claim that the widespread availability of weapons, and their use in recreational activities such as hunting and target shooting, tend to sustain a general cultural milieu in which violence is celebrated and therefore facilitated (Kleck, 1984). Without passing judgment on the accuracy of these views, it is sufficient to note that there are many in the criminal justice research and practitioner community who are now prepared to see guns as criminogenic in that they contribute to the overall levels and consequences of crime. To a degree, this view is already enshrined in the nation's sentencing policies, criminal codes, and regulatory regimes—all of which take a dim view of both inappropriate uses of weapons and their possession by those who have been convicted of crimes.

Thus, both the criminal justice and the public health communities see a large number of factors determining the incidence, nature, and outcomes of violence. Both have perspectives on the causes of violence that are to some degree unique and complementary, and to some degree similar and overlapping.

DANGEROUS OFFENDERS AS VECTORS OF VIOLENCE

It is also interesting to note that one could easily incorporate the criminal justice community's focus on criminal offenders in the analytic framework of the public health community. Indeed, one could easily see recidivist, violent offenders as the "vectors" in epidemics of violence. Certainly, that would be appropriate if one discovered a pattern of serial killing in an overall pattern of homicide, or the telltale modus operandi of a well-known sex offender in an overall pattern of rapes, or even the skilled work of a "firebug" in a pattern of arsons. One might then think about how to alter the environment so that fewer such vectors were produced, how to find ways to keep the vectors under control, or how to prepare "hosts" so that they would be less vulnerable to attack.

To some degree, however, the criminal justice framework resists seeing things in these social engineering terms. Instead, it keeps focusing our attention on the individual moral agency of those who commit acts of violence. In some odd ways, this makes the criminal justice approach seem more "human" and less "clinical" than the public health perspective. It focuses our attention on individual crimes, committed by real people with better or worse reasons for their violence. There are both a moral indignation and a hope for redemption in the criminal justice perspective that are to some degree missing, or at least underemphasized, in the more scientific and clinical public health perspective.

WIDENING CRIMINAL JUSTICE CONCEPTIONS OF CAUSATION

On the other hand, the important contribution that public health makes to criminal justice perceptions of violence is to encourage the criminal justice practitioner community to continue the current trends that shift attention away from an exclusive focus on offenders. This is important both for operational reasons (because it opens new lines of attack on the problem) and for common moral intuitions of justice (because it changes our common understandings of who and what are to blamed for criminal offending). The idea that there may be accidental criminal offenses emerging from unfortunate circumstances tempers our general hostility to those that we like to hold responsible for criminal offending. Nobody is suggesting that criminal culpability be eliminated, but it might be reexamined in light of the more sophisticated understanding of the complex ways in which criminal violence can come about. That, too, counts as an important contribution.

FAVORED POLICY APPROACHES

Because the criminal justice and public health communities tend to view the causal factors affecting levels of interpersonal violence in somewhat different terms, it is not surprising that their initial assumptions about effective interventions would also differ. Because the criminal justice community sees the motivation of criminal offenders as the principal cause of interpersonal violence, it tends to focus on things that might be done to change the calculations or motivations of such offenders. Because the public health community sees interpersonal violence as emerging from a far broader and more complex process, its approaches are less exclusively focused on the motivations of offenders.

However, there is more to their differences in perceptions about effective interventions than simply a different conception of causal processes. Different professional commitments, competences, and experiences lead them to prefer some interventions over others. For example, the values and traditions of the law infuse the perceptions of the criminal justice community in a much more powerful way than they do the public health community. On the other hand, the values and traditions of science exercise a far greater influence on the public health community than on the criminal justice practitioner community.

Reactive Versus Preventive Approaches

From the perspective of the public health community, the principal difference between the public health approach to violence and that of the criminal justice system is that the latter's approach is *reactive* whereas the former's approach is *preventive*. The criminal justice system seems to wait until an act of violence occurs before taking action. In contrast, the public health community seeks to find ways to intervene *before* a crime occurs and to prevent it from happening.

To help identify preventive opportunities, the public health community distinguishes among three kinds of prevention.[1]

Primary prevention seeks to prevent the occurrence of disease or injury entirely—usually by operating on broad features of the environment that make the disease or injury possible or likely to occur. *Secondary* prevention is concerned with identifying cases or situations relatively early in some developmental process that will lead to serious problems if not altered. *Tertiary* prevention intervenes after an illness has been contracted or an injury inflicted, and seeks to minimize the long-term disastrous consequences of the disease or injury.

The public health community is strongly oriented to prevention. Indeed, it is one of the important ways in which the public health community distinguishes itself from the medical community, which has as its primary focus the care of those who have become seriously ill or badly injured. Among these forms of preventive interventions, the public health community has a particularly strong commitment to *primary* prevention. It is in this domain that its epidemiological methods seem to have the greatest purchase. It is here too that imaginative and bold policy interventions seem to have the greatest potential for making a difference in the overall level of disease and injury, and have in fact produced significant reductions in illness and injury (Institute of Medicine, 1988).

For these reasons, it is natural for the public health community to see the commitment to prevention in general, and to primary prevention in particular, as something valuable that it brings to any new policy area. Moreover, this seems a particularly important contribution to the criminal justice approach to violence because the latter, like the medical approach to illness and injury, seems to be locked primarily in the domain of tertiary prevention. Like the medical community, the criminal justice practitioner community is focused far too much on individual cases and not on the broader, structural factors that might be shaping the observed pattern of individual cases. Moreover, everything that the criminal justice system does—respond to calls for service, arrest offenders, and so on—seems to occur *after* rather than before an intentional injury has occurred. In these respects, the criminal justice system seems to be limited to *tertiary*, or at best *secondary*, rather than *primary* prevention.

Preventive Approaches in Criminal Justice

To a degree, the criminal justice community would share the public health community's view. Its members, too, think of themselves as largely case oriented and reactive. However, many in the criminal justice community (particularly those attuned to concerns about the intrusiveness of the law and the criminal justice system into ordinary social life) would see these features as virtues rather than limitations of the system. In their view, the reactive, case-oriented focus is a key device for limiting the reach of the criminal justice system. With this approach, the criminal justice system intervenes only in situations where it is urgent that it do so. This preserves vast areas of social life from the intrusions of law, public policy, and the utilitarian concerns of the state. A more proactive or preventive approach—one that is justified in terms of its practical impact on levels of violence—threatens a more intrusive, overreaching, and less principled public intervention in the lives of people than now exists.

Deterrence, Incapacitation, and Rehabilitation

There is an equally important strain in criminal justice thought that sees criminal justice interventions as serving utilitarian purposes. Its proponents believe that the way they handle individual cases has effects on levels of criminal violence that stretch out over time and across social life. In short, the criminal justice community—both practitioners and researchers—believes that the reactive, case-oriented approach also prevents crime.

The principal mechanisms are thought to be (1) general deterrence (i.e., the effect that comes from threatening everyone in the population with criminal prosecution if they violate laws); (2) specific deterrence (i.e., the effect on an individual criminal offender that comes from punishing him for a specific offense); and (3) incapacitation (i.e., the effect that comes from holding an offender under such close supervision that it is impossible for him to commit offenses). In addition, the criminal justice community seeks to use periods of confinement for rehabilitative activities such as psychological counseling, drug treatment, vocational skills training, and general education to reduce the likelihood that offenders will continue to commit crimes in the future (Sechrest et al., 1979).

Although all of these mechanisms depend on some crimes being committed (because they are necessary to create the predicate for action), they are also believed to reduce or prevent crimes in the future. Thus, the criminal justice community thinks of itself as having a preventive as well as a reactive focus.

Juvenile Delinquency Prevention

There is still more to the criminal justice community's preventive efforts. In the early decades of the twentieth century—the same period in which the public health community was gathering strength and making great contributions to the control of infectious diseases through improved municipal sanitation—an innovation in criminal justice institutions swept across the country. State after state authorized the creation of juvenile courts and juvenile justice systems to deal with the problem of crimes committed by children (Platt, 1969).

To a degree, this movement was animated by concerns for justice. It seemed wrong as a matter of principle to hold children accountable for criminal conduct to the same degree, and in the same way, as adults. Arguably, the criminal intent that was necessary to justify both punishment and the adversary process of a trial was less present in cases involving youthful offenders than in cases involving adults.

Yet there were also practical, utilitarian reasons to be interested in treating children differently. The emerging disciplines of sociology, psychology, and criminology focused society's attention on a variety of developmental factors that might influence a child's path toward a life of crime or honesty. Some commentators focused on factors within the child, whereas others emphasized the immediate social circumstances in which the child was being reared, and still others emphasized the broader social factors such as urbanization, poverty, and racial discrimination (Platt, 1969). What all agreed on, however, was that society might be able to prevent future crime by intervening earlier in the process of development that would otherwise produce determined criminal offenders. It was this mission that was given to the juvenile justice system, and it was this institution that carried the criminal justice system's principal secondary prevention effort for most of the twentieth century.

More recently, of course, debate over the propriety and effectiveness of the juvenile justice system has changed a great deal (Moore et al., 1987). The concern that inattentive parents and desperate communities might be producing determined criminal offenders has gradually been supplemented by the view that the juvenile justice system was itself criminogenic: that by overreaching into conduct that was not in itself criminal and by taking children out of their communities, the juvenile justice system might be stigmatizing children and putting them in environments where it was easier for them to become committed to lives of crime and to learn the necessary skills (Sarri and Hasenfeld, 1976). Still more recently, advocates have sought to shift the focus of the juvenile justice system from its rehabilitative purposes to greater reliance on the mechanisms of deterrence and incapacitation to control juvenile crime, that is, to make the system resemble the adult system more closely than it now does (Springer, 1986).

The only point of reviewing this history is to illustrate the fact that the criminal justice community has had a long tradition of thinking about how to prevent crimes by intervening in the development of criminal offenders, and that this tradition has been located principally in debates about the proper jurisdiction and approaches of the juvenile justice system. In all likelihood, this tradition will continue as the criminal justice community ponders what to do with a juvenile justice system that has disappointed everyone, but still seems to be the only institution positioned to intervene forcefully in the development processes that surround children who commit crimes or are themselves the victims of crime (Moore et al., 1987). This position has assumed particular importance as it has become apparent that (1) there are some offenders who are particularly active and can be identified (imperfectly) at relatively early stages of development, and (2) the conditions under which children are now being raised are deteriorating badly.

Controlling Criminogenic Commodities

In recent years, the criminal justice community has also begun to be wooed away from its preoccupation with offenders and to examine other approaches to controlling criminal violence. One focus has been on "criminogenic commodities" - including alcohol, drugs, and guns (Moore, 1983b). In public health language, the widespread availability of alcohol, drugs, and guns has been seen as an important risk factor for violence, and the criminal justice community has sought to establish laws, and enforce existing laws, to reduce the danger of these commodities.

Among these commodities, drugs have been the most consistently favored target of the criminal justice community. Indeed, it is the conviction that drugs are closely tied to criminal violence that has propelled drug control to the forefront of the nation's and the criminal justice community's concerns—despite the fact that a plausible argument can be made that the observed connection between drugs and crime is produced as much by the policies designed to control drug use as by the physiological effects of drugs themselves, and that the drug most commonly associated with violence is alcohol (Chaiken and Chaiken, 1990; Fagan, 1990).

At any rate, seeing drugs as criminogenic has generated a major criminal justice effort to reduce levels of drug consumption through both supply reduction and demand reduction efforts (Office of National Drug Control Policy, 1989-1991). Supply reduction efforts include arrests of traffickers and street level dealers (Moore, 1990; Kleiman, 1990). Demand reduction efforts focus enforcement attention on users. Some police departments, despairing of the competence of educational institutions to communicate the proper message, have established their own efforts in schools to educate children about the use of drugs (Bureau of Justice Assistance, 1988; Kennedy School of Government, 1990).

This major effort to reduce drug use is thus not simply a moral crusade by the criminal justice community but also, in its eyes, a straightforward way of preventing criminal violence by controlling an important risk factor.

Since the repeal of Prohibition, alcohol has been less on the minds of the criminal justice community than drugs, but it has never been entirely absent. Studies of domestic assaults, assaults among strangers in public locations, and sexual assaults among intimates and acquaintances often reveal a disproportionate amount of drinking—by either the offender, the victim, or both (Fagan, 1990).

Thus, one might view drunkenness, and particularly public drunkenness, as criminogenic. Similarly, we know that excessive drinking figures prominently in highway fatalities (National Committee for Injury Prevention and Control, 1989:119-120).

What is interesting, however, is that the society has responded to these facts in quite different ways.

Over the last 20 years, the trend has been to "decriminalize" public drunkenness and to treat it as a medical problem. The intention was to discourage police from arresting people for public drunkenness and instead to transport or refer intoxicated people to medical services. What has actually occurred is that the police have simply stopped paying much attention to public drunkenness (Aaronson et al., 1982).

With respect to drunk driving, the trend over the last 10 years has been in exactly the opposite direction: society is increasingly treating drunk driving as a serious crime. It is stiffening the laws against drunk driving and stepping up its enforcement efforts (Jacobs, 1988).

What the alcohol case illustrates is that the criminal justice community tends to become involved in major violence prevention efforts when there is statutory authority that either requires or allows it to do so. Because the repeal of Prohibition and the creation of state licensing authorities essentially removed the police from any responsibilities for policing the production, distribution, or sale of alcohol, the criminal justice community no longer plays much of a role in regulating the supply of alcohol. Because laws against public drunkenness were removed in the interests of both taking a more therapeutic approach to the problem and saving criminal justice resources for more serious crimes (many of which were at least partially caused by public drunkenness), the criminal justice community also abandoned that field. Because laws against drunk driving were strengthened, however, the criminal justice community was drawn into that important domain of injury and violence prevention.

The criminal justice community has only come lately to taking a strong position on guns. Of course, the criminal justice *research* community had long been interested in the criminogenic effects of widespread gun availability, and many had urged the passage of very restrictive laws regulating the supply, distribution, ownership, and use of guns, particularly handguns (Newton and Zimring, 1969). For reasons that are hard to understand, the criminal justice practitioner community did not, until recently, join the researchers in this crusade. Now, the law enforcement community has entered the fray on the side of more restrictive controls.

Nonetheless, it still seems unlikely that the nation will adopt bans on gun ownership or even bans on production. What does seem possible, however, is that there will be more restrictive controls over weapons that have few legitimate purposes (such as assault weapons or teflon-coated bullets) and over who may own such weapons and how they might be used. Insofar as the criminal justice community is focusing on policies to control the availability and use of weapons, it is engaged in an effort that the public health community would recognize as a classic strategy of secondary prevention.

Situational Approaches to Crime Control

In addition to a focus on criminogenic commodities, the criminal justice community has also begun to see the environment of cities or certain situations as criminogenic, and it has sought to find ways of reducing these risk factors. There was a brief period, for example, when the field focused on the opportunities for controlling crime by altering physical living environments to make it easier for individuals to protect themselves and their property, to identify strangers, and generally to enhance a feeling of community responsibility (Newman, 1972; National Institute of Justice, 1980).

The more sustained trend, however, has been an interest in "situational approaches" to crime. The paradigm case has been domestic violence. It has long been known that repeat violence was common in these situations, and it has long been considered important to find improved methods for reducing the potential for violence in ongoing domestic disputes (Bard and Zacker, 1976). The first efforts in this domain were, once again, to decriminalize the offense and seek to deal with the problem through counseling (Bard, 1969). More recently, evidence has become available that arrests are more likely to reduce future attacks than either ignoring the offense or referral to counseling (Sherman and Berk, 1984). Those experiments are now being replicated with reputedly more equivocal results. The sad reality is that we do not yet know what an effective response to this paradigmatic criminogenic situation is.

More generally, the idea that situations might cause violence and that the best response is to find ways to make the situation less explosive, has recently found expression in the emergence of "problem solving" as a method in policing (Goldstein, 1990). This method encourages officers and police departments not to treat crime calls simply as incidents to be searched for violations of law, but instead to look behind the incident to determine what factors are causing the violence and to search for methods including, but not limited to, arrest of offenders for altering the situation so that it is less criminogenic. There are, by now, many individual examples of successes in problem solving, and the analytic methods and organizational arrangements necessary to support problem solving are becoming more refined, but there is not yet evidence indicating that this approach applied generally across a police department will have a substantial aggregate effect on levels of criminal violence (see Moore, 1992).

It is not strictly true, then, that the criminal justice system is uninterested in prevention. It is interested in preventing future crimes through the mechanisms of general and specific deterrence, incapacitation, and rehabilitation. It has developed an entire institution whose purpose is to intervene in the processes of development that produce criminal offenders, and it has made occasional forays into efforts to prevent crime by resolving criminogenic situations and controlling the supply of criminogenic commodities.

Still, however interested the criminal justice community might be in preventive efforts, its commitment to prevention is not quite like the commitment that the public health community brings. At best, prevention is an additional thought in criminal justice. In the public health community, prevention is everything. At best, the criminal justice community is involved in secondary prevention. The public health community starts with secondary prevention and then goes on to primary prevention.

Violence in the Context of Relations

Moreover, the criminal justice community must acknowledge the enormous contributions that the public health community has made to its efforts to understand and control certain kinds of crime. The latter has played a particularly important role, for example, in focusing attention on such offenses as domestic assault, child abuse and neglect, sexual assaults among intimates, and elder abuse (National Committee for Injury Prevention and Control, 1989:213-251). What is interesting about this list of crimes is that they all involve crimes among people who know one another or are locked in ongoing relationships. These crimes are often hidden to the criminal justice system precisely because they do not produce victims or witnesses who are willing to mobilize the police (Moore, 1983a). They become visible to the public health community because the victims show up in emergency rooms and medical offices. Thus, the public health community has made public a set of crimes that would have remained hidden, and has provided the criminal justice system with both the political support and the operational means to take action against such offenses.

The public health community has also played a particularly important role in identifying and publicizing the problem of child abuse and neglect. It was pediatricians in emergency rooms who encountered this hidden problem and exposed it to public view (Kempe et al., 1962). It was public health officials who saw a large aggregate problem in individual clinical reports and put the issue forward as an important health problem. This problem is important not only because it is bad in itself, but also because being abused and neglected as a child is persuasively linked to future abuse and neglect of children, as well as to criminal offending (National Committee for Injury Prevention and Control, 1989:216). Like domestic violence and drunk driving, this problem is now going through a phase in which it is being "criminalized." Whether that is the most effective response is still to be learned.

Innovative Approaches to Youth Violence

In other domains such as youth and gang violence, the public health community has brought an innovative approach to dealing with the problem. In one of the most innovative experiments in controlling violence among teenagers, the Boston Violence Prevention Program seeks to use hospital emergency rooms as a point of contact for those who are involved in violence as victims or offenders, and to follow up those contacts with interventions designed to teach alternative methods for resolving disputes (Prothrow-Stith, 1987). These individually tailored approaches are supplemented by an educational programs in violence-prone city schools to teach children nonviolent methods for resolving disputes and expressing themselves. This reflects the public health view that individual acts of violence mirror a more pervasive culture that subtly (or not so subtly) encourages violence. Education seeks to counter that culture with an alternative one. There is even a slogan to help sustain a local normative movement against violence: "Friends for Life—Teach Your Friends Not to Fight."

Environmental Approaches to Prevention

In these areas the preventive interests of the criminal justice and public health communities align rather closely, but in other domains their interests diverge more sharply. From the perspective of the criminal justice community the two most important ways in which the public health community's zeal for prevention departs from its approach is in the emphasis on finding technological "fixes" for problems and the effort to determine the broadest social and cultural factors influencing levels of violence.

Some of the public health community's most dramatic successes have been in areas in which technology provided a broad, permanent solution to a problem. For example, municipal sewer and water systems solved the problem of typhoid epidemics (Blake and Feldman, 1986). Immunizations solved the problems of polio and smallpox (Henderson, 1986; Gregg and Nkowane, 1986). Improvements in automobile and road design have ameliorated the problem of traffic accidents to some degree (National Committee for Injury Prevention and Control, 1989:216). The lesson that the public health community learned from these experiences is that if one can find an approach to reducing risk factors that does not depend on widespread behavioral changes, that approach should be the primary one relied upon because we know from experience that changing the attitudes and behaviors of large numbers of people through persuasion or coercion is extremely difficult (e.g., see Dennis and Draper, 1983).

Of course, all technological changes require some people to change their behavior. Somebody had to build the sanitary water systems. Someone had to invent the vaccines, and new people must be persuaded to take them each year. The automobile companies had to be compelled to produce safe cars in a world in which consumers were more impressed by tail fins than safety. So the point is not to eliminate efforts to change behavior, but to minimize them: to focus the responsibility for safety-increasing actions on a relatively small number of people who are likely to be paying close attention to this problem, and to make sure that the actions of such people count because they produce a permanent, physical change in the environment of risks.

This seems to be an important principle. What is unclear is how it might be applied in the world of interpersonal violence. The public health community seems to think that this principle is being applied when it examines the control of criminogenic commodities such as guns and alcohol. These look like consumer products that are unsafe and that might be redesigned or regulated to produce fewer acts of interpersonal violence. To a degree, the analogy to automobiles and other consumer product safety issues is apt.

Yet to say that some commonly used products could be redesigned or regulated to produce less crime is not quite like making safer cars, inventing a vaccine, or building a sanitary water system. There is a much larger behavioral component in interpersonal violence than there is in any of these other domains. Consequently, the effective reach of any particular product change in controlling the level of interpersonal violence is much less.

Take, for example, the issue of guns and their role in interpersonal violence. On one hand, it might be possible to legislate a ban on new production of certain kinds of weapons. Alternatively, it might be possible to design guns that are less dangerous by making them less easy to discharge or less lethal if accidentally discharged. However, these interventions alone, without other behavioral changes, would have a limited effect on the levels of gun violence. The ban on new production would have only limited effect until some behavioral means were found to encourage the 40 million people who now own weapons to turn them in. Safer guns would have an effect only if we could find some way of motivating offenders not to use them in crimes.

The point is not that these interventions are useless. Rather, it is that these "technological" changes must always be joined with efforts to change behavior through laws, educational programs, or mass media campaigns.

The more apt analogies might be those efforts to make the physical environments of cities more "violence resistant." That could include reductions in density, the creation of "defensible spaces," a reduction in the number of bars and liquor stores, or the creation of more effective surveillance and responding systems to mobilize police agencies. Although such efforts may well have promise, they do not look like quick, inexpensive fixes to the problem of violence. It seems that it is hard to get the behavioral element out of a problem that is so closely tied to human devices and desires.

Cultural Approaches to Violence Prevention

The public health community's enthusiasm for reaching out to the broadest social factors affecting crime also creates some consternation in the minds of the criminal justice practitioner community. One part of that argument is familiar to the criminal justice community. When the public health community reports that criminal violence is disproportionately located among the nation's poor minority communities, and concludes that crime must be caused by poverty and racial discrimination and that the only long-term solution is to alleviate these "risk factors," it is merely echoing the conclusions of those in the criminal justice community who have long emphasized the "root causes" of crime (Silberman, 1978; Curtis, 1985).

To some degree, in recent years, many in the criminal justice research and practitioner community have turned away from these concerns, not so much because these observations were judged to be wrong or inaccurate but because they seemed irrelevant to much criminal justice policy making (Wilson, 1983). To have these issues come back before the criminal justice practitioner community as a new approach to crime prevention is not necessarily unwelcome, but it is hardly a new contribution. The question that remains to be answered by the public health community (along with the criminal justice community and society in general) is whether it has any ideas about how to eliminate poverty and racial discrimination. Presumably, any such proposal in any public forum is always in order.

The other part of the public health community's broad, primary prevention approach that is less familiar to the criminal justice community is the focus on broad cultural factors that encourage violence. Some members of the public health community see danger in entertainment and recreational activities that seem to celebrate violence, such as television detective shows, horror movies, ice hockey, and football (for the impact of television on behavior, see Slaby and Roedell, 1982). They also sometimes see danger in such things as corporal punishment or settling disputes through fistfights because these embody a primitive, retributive view of justice and celebrate rather than condemn violence in general. Some in the public health community would like to see such activities reduced so that there is less support for a culture of violence.

Such proposals are greeted with a certain amount of skepticism in the criminal justice practitioner community. The rational reasons are that so far there has been little convincing evidence that these things actually do encourage a culture of violence and that regulating such conduct requires the state to intrude in sensitive areas such as freedom of expression and family privacy. Beneath the rational reasons, however, is probably a deeper skepticism about whether all violence is environmentally or culturally determined.

After all, many criminal justice practitioners have seen truly awful deeds. They have seen savage mutilations, vicious rapes, and horrible injuries. Often, the victims were both innocent and defenseless. They experience such events, and see the people who commit them as evil. The evil they observe *may* be the product of poor social conditions or of a culture of violence or mental illness, but these factors are not always evident on the scene of the crime. Nor are they always seen as morally relevant.

As a consequence, the criminal justice practitioner community tends to accept the inevitability of some evil in the world and the need to combat it. It does not imagine that all tendencies to violence are caused by society, and could be eliminated by altering environmental circumstances. The public health community's reliance on goodness and rationality seems far too hopeful for the world that the criminal justice practitioner community inhabits.

Law Versus Education in Behavioral Approaches

One last point of contrast between the public health and the criminal justice communities' approaches to the primary prevention of violence concerns their slightly different attitudes toward the use of criminal law to regulate conduct. The criminal justice practitioner community believes that it is operating on broad social conditions and attitudes through the moral and instrumental impact of the law. In its eyes, a criminal law—once passed—becomes a general standard of conduct, a moral obligation, binding on all citizens. It is supposed to affect citizens' attitudes and beliefs as well as their calculations. The combination is supposed to produce important changes in behavior.

Many in the public health community are more hesitant about using criminal law to try to affect broad changes in attitudes and behavior. This reluctance reflects a long experience in trying to change behavior in controlling epidemics of such things as sexually transmitted diseases. What members of the public health community have learned in these areas is that when certain forms of conduct are criminalized, the behavior is driven underground and those who engage in it are discouraged from seeking treatment. The net result is to make the epidemics harder rather than easier to control. Thus, in trying to shape attitudes and behavior, the public health community often prefers educational rather than legal approaches.

Members of the public health community are not entirely consistent in this. If there is a law that can be enacted against a producer or an advertiser of a dangerous product, they are often in favor of such a law. If there is a bit of behavior in the general population that seems to have little intrinsic value and poses a harm to health (such as riding a motorcycle without a helmet or owning a gun), they are willing to legislate against such conduct. In general, however, and particularly when the behavior of large numbers of citizens is involved, they would prefer to use *educational* rather than *legal* approaches.

There is nothing wrong with preferring educational approaches over legal approaches. In many cases, it seems entirely appropriate. The error, it seems to us, is in forgetting that the law is often an important instrument of education as well as a device for authorizing state intervention and control. Viewed from this perspective, the two should be seen as complementary, rather than as competitive approaches to the same problem. Sometimes it may be wise for the criminal justice community to seek to widen the effective force of criminal laws by supplementing these laws with educational programs (as we are now doing in the domain of drug abuse). In other cases, it may be wise for the public health community to strengthen its ability to control risk-taking behavior by adding the weight of the criminal law to its educational efforts (as has been done in the domain of drunk driving).

TOWARD A SYNTHESIS

In sum, the criminal justice and public health communities bring different professional intuitions to discussions about what methods might best be used to tackle the problem of interpersonal violence. The criminal justice community brings a preference for a largely reactive, individual case-based focus, whereas the public health community brings a broader, preventive approach to the problem. Although there are some preventive aspects to the ordinary criminal justice system processing of cases, these are not the primary concern of the criminal justice community. To the extent that the criminal justice community is concerned with primary and secondary prevention, it tends to focus on changing the processes of development that produce sustained criminal offenders. In addition, the criminal justice community has sought to control some commodities that it views as criminogenic—principally drugs, but also alcohol and guns. Finally, there have been some efforts to analyze and control criminogenic environments and situations.

The public health community has brought a strong commitment to prevention to discussions about the control of interpersonal violence—not only secondary prevention, but also primary. In the secondary domain, it has alerted the criminal justice community to a set of problems involving violence in ongoing relationships that was largely invisible to ordinary criminal justice system operations, and it has joined the criminal justice community in seeking out effective approaches to reducing the incidence of such offenses. Its members have also brought to the control of interpersonal violence innovative methods that use hospitals as points of contact and seek to alter local attitudes among children about violence. Finally, they have brought renewed interest to efforts to control guns and perhaps alcohol as well.

In the domain of primary prevention, they have resurrected

concerns about the impact of poverty and racial discrimination on offending and victimization, and have brought new concerns about factors that are shaping the culture within which violence can occur. They have also reminded the criminal justice community of the virtue of relying on education as well as laws in seeking to regulate behavior on a large scale.

All of this has stimulated the imagination of the criminal justice community about new opportunities to prevent violence and intentional injury.

RESOURCES: TROOPS, ANALYSTS, AND COMMUNITY LEADERS

One of the important questions a criminal justice practitioner might ask when the public health community offers to join the fight against criminal violence is what additional resources the public health community can bring to the problem, beyond a new appreciation of its significance and a new methodology for exploring causes and lines of attack. As Hitler is reputed to have asked, "How many divisions does the Pope have?"

WHO HAS THE TROOPS?

At first blush, the answer seems to be relatively few. A public health department rarely has an organization focused on "intentional injuries." Indeed, only about two states now have special units in their public health departments. Those that exist are largely analytic and advisory rather than operational. This is broadly consistent with past public health tradition. Public health has always worked in interdisciplinary settings, using the resources of other agencies to make contributions to the solution of health problems. One can imagine, in the future, larger and more powerful public health offices working on the prevention of "intentional violence," but for now, the effort is small. As a result, in the minds of hard-pressed criminal justice officials who are struggling to deal with overwhelming operational problems and are accustomed to measuring resources in terms of the number of troops commanded, there is a real question about what public health can concretely contribute to efforts to deal with intentional injury.

However, this is a quite myopic view for the criminal justice community to take. The public health community is quite clear that it is dependent on the operational capacity of the police and the criminal justice system to accomplish its goals; they provide the muscle and the troops in dealing with violent crime. They are also important in dealing with other items on the public health agenda such as traffic accidents, and they are often called in to support public health initiatives in other areas such as environmental health and safety or the control of some health epidemics. So there is a long history of mutual dependence and cooperation between the criminal justice and the public health communities. That history has largely been forgotten or ignored by the criminal justice community, and to a lesser degree even by the public health community. This is a loss—particularly in a world seeking to cope with AIDS, in which this collaboration may once more be very important. Indeed, it would not be too much to say that the police are an important health-producing as well as law enforcement agency.

The worry in the public health community is that if its dependence on the criminal justice system is fully acknowledged and if it does not bring powerful operational resources to the table, the criminal justice system will simply ignore the interests and the potential contributions that the public health community represents. As we have seen, its interests are in promoting health and safety, and in doing so through preventive efforts. The question is what kind of resources it brings to this enterprise, if not operational troops.

PUBLIC HEALTH CONTRIBUTIONS TO THE FIGHT

The answer to this question is that the public health community brings two key resources to the criminal justice community's attack on violence. The first resource is improved analytical capabilities. The second is a new political constituency for violence prevention and control. An enlightened criminal justice community should acknowledge the great value of both contributions.

Analytically, the public health community is relatively far advanced compared to the usual practice in criminal justice agencies. The traditions and training of the former are much stronger. Most of its practitioners have advanced degrees. They know how to gather and analyze data about problems. They know how to design multidisciplinary programs to deal with specific problems. Although these skills also exist in the criminal justice research and practitioner community, they are less common and less commonly deployed than they are in public health.

Politically, the public health community bring two key assets. First, it brings new values that can be attached to criminal justice efforts. In the past, society was opposed to criminal violence because it was wrong and concentrated unfairly among poor people. What the public health community reveals to citizens is that criminal violence is a major threat to the nation's health as well, which changes the seriousness of the problem. It also changes who pays attention to the problem, which is the second great political contribution that the public health community's interest in violence makes to the criminal justice community.

Once violence is seen as a health problem, a different group of people begins paying attention. As long as crime was viewed as a moral evil to be handled through enforcement and punishment, only a limited constituency was mobilized. The people who paid most attention were those in the criminal justice practitioner community. They were backed principally by those who were concerned with getting crime under control. The dialogue was mostly about the extent to which deterrence, incapacitation, and rehabilitation could be expected to work. Many in the minority community and those employed in "helping" professions, such as educators, psychologists, and social workers, felt excluded from the discussion.

Once the problem becomes a health problem, a much different constituency is mobilized. The minority community, which is most often the victim of criminal offending, finds it much easier to talk about the problem as a health problem than as a crime problem. The health profession, educators, and social workers also find the public health formulation of the problem easier to understand and use. Thus, a new constituency interested in controlling violence is created.

This new constituency for attention to violence is important because the new constituency is visible, articulate, and activist. Its interest will provide a basis for passing new laws, raising additional funds, mobilizing volunteer efforts, and inventing new approaches.

In sum, although the public health community does not necessarily command many troops, like the Pope it does have the power of moral suasion and a large following. That is a valuable asset indeed to bring to the table.

KEY VALUES: JUSTICE VERSUS HEALTH

In the background of much of the technical issues that have been discussed so far is a larger issue—the question of what values society ought to have in mind as it approaches a particular problem. As noted in the introduction, the predominant approach in dealing with interpersonal violence has been one guided by concepts of justice—what people properly owe one another and what should be done in instances where people fail to live up to their responsibilities.

Many view the questions of blame and punishment as primitive ideas of social organization—almost indistinguishable from concepts of vengeance and retaliation. This ignores the fact, however, that victims and citizens are angered not simply because they have been injured but because an injustice occurred. They want reassurances that the social order will be restored and that their expectations about what they are entitled to will also be restored. The ceremonies that recreate expectations and norms are an important part of society's response to interpersonal violence and are performed well by the criminal justice system. To ignore the values associated with doing justice is to miss the key element that distinguishes intentional injury from unintentional injury.

On the other hand, as the public health community consistently reminds us, it is best not to rely too much on blame. It attracts too much emotional heat and blots out reasoning or analysis. Imposing it is not always just, and it will not do all the practical work that it is supposed to do.

The public health approach redirects our attention to care for the victims. It encourages us to see the causes of violence in different places and therefore to resist the natural tendency to want a scapegoat when something bad happens even if that is not always just, and it encourages other lines of attack. It emphasizes persuasion and education over coercion, reason over emotion, analysis over the mobilization of overwhelming force. In these broad ways, the public health community may make its largest and most important contribution to society's understanding of, and attack on, the intertwining problems of criminal violence and intentional injury.

NOTE

1   There is some confusion within the public health community about how these terms should be defined. We are following the definitions offered by Last (1980).

REFERENCES

Aaronson, D.E., C.T. Dienes, and M.C. Musheno
  1982 *Decriminalization of Public Drunkenness: Tracing the Implementation of Public Policy.* Washington, D.C.: National Institute of Justice.
Bard, M.
  1969 Family intervention: Police teams as a community mental health resource. *Journal of Criminal Law, Criminology and Police Science* 60(2):247-250.
Bard, M., and J. Zacker
  1976 *The Police and Interpersonal Conflict: Third-Party Intervention Approaches.* Washington, D.C.: Police Foundation.
Berk, R.A., D.R. Loseke, S.F. Berk, and D. Rauma
  1980 Bringing the cops back in: A study of efforts to make the criminal justice system more responsive to incidents of family violence. *Social Science Research* 9:193-215.
  1982 Throwing the cops back out: The decline of local program to make criminal justice system more responsive to incidents of domestic violence. *Social Science Research* 11:245-279.
Blake, P.A., and R.A. Feldman
  1986 Typhoid fever. Pp. 238-240 in J.M. Last, ed., *Public Health and Preventive Medicine*, 12th ed. New York: Appleton-Century-Crofts.
Blumstein, A., J. Cohen, and D. Nagin, eds.
  1978 *Deterrence and Incapacitation: Estimating the Effects of Criminal Sanctions on Crime Rates.* Washington, D.C.: National Academy Press
Blumstein, A., J. Cohen, J.A. Roth, and C.A. Visher, eds.
  1986 *Criminal Careers and "Career Criminals."* Washington, D.C.: National Academy Press.
Bureau of Justice Assistance
  1988 *An Invitation to Project DARE: Drug Abuse Resistance Education: Program Brief.* Washington, D.C.: U.S. Department of Justice.
Bureau of Justice Statistics
  1983 Victim and witness assistance: New state laws and the systems response. *Bureau of Justice Statistics Bulletin* (May). Washington, D.C.: U.S. Department of Justice.
  1984 The severity of crime. *Bureau of Justice Statistics Bulletin* (January). Washington, D.C.: U.S. Department of Justice.
Bureau of Justice Statistics and Federal Bureau of Investigation
  1985 *Blueprint for the Future of the Uniform Crime Reporting Program: Final Report of the UCR Study.* Washington, D.C.: U.S. Department of Justice.

Chaiken, J.M., and M.R. Chaiken
  1982 *Varieties of Criminal Behavior.* Santa Monica, Calif.: Rand Corporation.
  1990 Drugs and predatory crime. Pp. 203-239 in M. Tonry and J.Q. Wilson, eds., *Drugs and Crime,* Vol. 13 in M. Tonry and N. Morris, eds., *Crime and Justice: A Review of Research.* Chicago: University of Chicago Press.
Clarke, R.V.
  1990 Situational crime prevention: Its theoretical bases and practical scope. Pp. 225-256 in M. Tonry and N. Morris, eds., *Crime and Justice: An Annual Review of Research.* Chicago: University of Chicago Press.
Coleman, L.
  1987 *Suicide Clusters.* Boston, Mass.: Faber and Faber.
Cook, P.
  1981 The effect of gun availability on violent crime patterns. *Annals of the American Academy of Political and Social Sciences* 455.
  1983 The influence of gun availability on violent crime patterns. Pp. 49-89 in Vol. 4 of M. Tonry and N. Morris, eds., *Crime and Justice: A Review of Research.* Chicago: University of Chicago Press.
Curtis, L.
  1985 *American Violence and Public Policy.* New Haven, Conn.: Yale University Press.
Dennis, J., and P. Draper
  1983 Preventive medicine. *Encyclopedia of Occupational Health and Safety* 1788.
Dodge, R.W.
  1981 *Criminal Victimization in the U.S., 1973-1979 Trends.* Bureau of Justice Statistics. Washington, D.C.: U.S. Department of Justice.
Dubowitz, H.
  1987 Child Maltreatment in the United States: Etiology, Impact and Prevention. Background paper prepared for the U.S. Congress, Office of Technology Assessment, May.
Estrich, S.R.
  1987 *Real Rape.* Cambridge, Mass.: Harvard University Press.
Fagan, J.
  1990 Intoxication and aggression. Pp. 241-320 in M. Tonry and J.Q. Wilson, eds., *Drugs and Crime,* Vol. 13 in M. Tonry and N. Morris, eds., *Crime and Justice: A Review of Research.* Chicago: University of Chicago Press.
Friedman, G.D.
  1987 *Primer of Epidemiology,* 3rd ed. New York: McGraw-Hill.
Garofalo, J.
  1981 The fear of crime: Causes and consequences. *The Journal of Criminal Law and Criminology* 72(2):839-857.

Goldstein, H.
 1990 *Problem-Oriented Policing.* New York: McGraw-Hill.
Goldstein, P.J.
 1985 Drugs and violent behavior. *Journal of Drug Issues* (Fall):493-506.
Greenwood, P.W., with Allan Abrahamse
 1982 *Selective Incapacitation.* Santa Monica, Calif.: Rand Corporation
Gregg, M.B., and B.M. Nkowane
 1986 Poliomyelitis. Pp. 173-176 in J.M. Last, ed., *Public Health and Preventive Medicine,* 12th ed. New York: Appleton-Century-Crofts.
Health Resources and Services Administration
 1986 *Report of the Surgeon General's Workshop on Violence and Public Health.* Washington, D.C.: Health Resources and Services Administration.
Henderson, D.A.
 1986 The eradication of smallpox. Pp. 129-138 in J.M. Last, ed., *Public Health and Preventive Medicine,* 12th ed. New York: Appleton-Century-Crofts.
Hindelang, M.J., M. Gottfriedson, and J. Garofalo
 1978 *Victims of Personal Crime: An Empirical Foundation for a Theory of Personal Victimization.* Cambridge, Mass.: Ballinger.
Institute of Medicine
 1988 *The Future of Public Health.* Committee for the Study of the Future of Public Health, Division of Health Care Services. Washington, D.C.: National Academy Press.
Jacobs, J.B.
 1988 *Drunk Driving: An American Dilemma.* Chicago: University of Chicago Press.
Jessor, R., and S.L. Jessor
 1977 *Problem Behavior and Psychosocial Development: A Longitudinal Study of Youth.* New York: Academic Press.
Kaplan, J., and J.H. Skolnick
 1982 *Criminal Justice: Introductory Cases and Materials,* 3rd ed. Mineola, N.Y.: The Foundation Press.
Kempe, C.H., F.N. Silverman, B.F. Steile, W. Droegemueller, and H.K. Silver
 1962 The battered child syndrome. *Journal of the American Medical Association* 17-24.
Kennedy School of Government, Harvard University
 1990 *Spreading the Gospel: The Origin and Growth of the DARE Program.* Kennedy School of Government Case Program. Cambridge, Mass.: Harvard University.
Kleck, G.
 1984 The relationship between gun ownership levels and rates of vio-

lence in the U.S. Pp. 99-135 in D.B. Kates, Jr., ed., *Firearms and Violence: Issues of Public Policy.* Cambridge, Mass.: Ballinger.

1988 Crime control through the private use of armed force. *Social Problems* 35(1, February).

Kleiman, M.
1990 State and local drug enforcement. In M. Tonry and J.Q. Wilson, eds., *Drugs and Crime.* Chicago: University of Chicago Press.

Last, J.M.
1980 Scope and methods of prevention. Pp. 3-4 in Maxcy-Rosenau, ed., *Public Health and Preventive Medicine,* 11th ed. New York: Appleton-Century-Crofts.

Mercy, J.A., and P.W. O'Carroll
1988 New directions in violence prevention: The public health arena. *Violence and Victims* 3(4).

Moore, M.H.
1983a Invisible offenses: A challenge to minimally intrusive law enforcement. Pp. 17-42 in G.M. Caplan, ed., *ABSCAM Ethics: Moral Issues and Deception in Law Enforcement.* Washington D.C.: Police Foundation.

1983b Controlling criminogenic commodities: Drugs, guns and alcohol. Pp. 125-144 in J.Q. Wilson, ed., *Crime and Public Policy.* San Francisco, Calif.: ICS Press.

1986 Purblind justice: Normative issues in the use of prediction in the criminal justice system. Pp. 314-355 in A. Blumstein, J. Cohen, J.A. Roth, and C.A. Visher, eds., *Criminal Careers and "Career Criminals",* Vol. II. Washington, D.C.: National Academy Press.

1990 Supply reduction and drug law enforcement. In M. Tonry and J.Q. Wilson, eds., *Drugs and Crime.* Chicago: University of Chicago Press.

1992 Problem solving and community policing. In M. Tonry and N. Morris, eds., *Modern Policing: Vol. 15: Crime and Justice Annual.* Chicago: University of Chicago Press.

Moore, M.H., and R.C. Trojanowicz
1988 Policing and the fear of crime. *Perspectives in Policing,* No. 3. National Institute of Justice, U.S. Department of Justice and the Program in Criminal Justice Policy and Management, Kennedy School of Government, Harvard University.

Moore, M.H., S.R. Estrich, D. McGillis, and W. Spelman
1984 *Dangerous Offenders: The Elusive Target of Justice.* Cambridge, Mass.: Harvard University Press.

Moore, M.H., with T. Bearrows, J. Bleich, F.X. Hartmann, G.L. Kelling, M. Oshima, and S. Wingart
1987 *From Children to Citizens,* Vol. 1: *The Mandate for Juvenile Justice.* New York: Springer-Verlag.

Nagel, I.H.
1990 Foreword: Structuring sentencing discretion: The new federal

sentencing guidelines. *Journal of Criminal Law and Criminology* 80(4, Winter):923.

National Committee for Injury Prevention and Control
   1989 *Injury Prevention: Meeting the Challenge.* New York: Oxford University Press.

National Institute of Justice
   1980 *Crime Prevention Through Environmental Design: An Operational Handbook.* Washington, D.C.: U.S. Department of Justice.

Newman, O.
   1972 *Defensible Space: Crime Prevention Through Urban Design.* New York: Macmillan.

Newton, G., and F. Zimring
   1969 *Firearms and Violence in American Life: A Staff Report to the National Commission on the Causes and Prevention of Violence.* Washington, D.C.: U.S. Government Printing Office.

Office of National Drug Control Policy, Executive Office of the President
   1989 *National Drug Control Strategy.* Washington, D.C.: U.S. Government Printing Office.
   1990 *National Drug Control Strategy.* Washington, D.C.: U.S. Government Printing Office.
   1991 *National Drug Control Strategy.* Washington, D.C.: U.S. Government Printing Office.

Petersilia, J.R.
   1980 Criminal career research: A review of recent evidence. In M. Tonry and N. Morris, eds., *Crime and Justice*, Vol. 2. Chicago: University of Chicago Press.

Peterson, M.A., and H.B. Braiker, with S.M. Polich
   1981 *Who Commits Crimes: A Survey of Prison Inmates.* Cambridge, Mass.: Oelgeschlager, Gunn and Hain, Publishers.

Platt, A.M.
   1969 *The Child Savers: The Invention of Delinquency.* Chicago: University of Chicago Press.

Police Executive Research Forum
   n.d. a *Summary Report on the Crime Classification System for the City of Colorado Springs, CO.* Washington, D.C.: Police Executive Research Forum.
   n.d. b *Summary Report on the Crime Classification System for the City of Peoria, IL.* Washington, D.C.: Police Executive Research Forum.

Police Foundation
   1976 *Domestic Violence and the Police: Studies in Detroit and Kansas City.* Washington, D.C.: Police Foundation.

President's Task Force on Victims of Crime
   1982 *President's Task Force on Victims of Crime: Final Report.* Washington, D.C.: U.S. Government Printing Office.

Prothrow-Stith, D.
   1987   *Violence Prevention Curriculum for Adolescents.* Newton, Mass.:
          Education Development Center.
Rosenberg, M.L., E. Stark, and M. Zahn
   1986   Interpersonal violence: Homicide and spouse abuse. In J.M.
          Last, ed., *Public Health and Preventive Medicine.* Norwalk,
          Conn.: Appleton-Century-Crofts.
Sarri, R., and Y. Hasenfeld, eds.
   1976   *Brought to Justice?: Juveniles, the Courts and the Law.* Ann
          Arbor: University of Michigan Press.
Sechrest, L., S.O. White, and E. Brown, eds.
   1979   *The Rehabilitation of Criminal Offenders: Problems and Pros-
          pects.* Washington, D.C.: National Academy Press.
Sherman, L.W., and R.A. Berk
   1984   The Minneapolis domestic violence experiment. *Police Foun-
          dation Reports* 1(April):1-8.
Sherman, L.W., P.T. Garten, and M.E. Buerger
   1989   Hot spots of predatory crime: Routine activities and the crimi-
          nology of place. *Criminology* 27(1):27-55.
Silberman, C.
   1978   *Criminal Justice, Criminal Violence.* New York: Random House.
Slaby, R.G., and W.C. Roedell
   1982   The development and regulation of aggression in young chil-
          dren. P. 119 in J. Wovell, ed., *Psychological Development in
          the Elementary Years.* New York: Academic Press.
Springer, C.E.
   1986   *Justice for Juveniles.* Washington, D.C.: Office of Juvenile Jus-
          tice and Delinquency Prevention.
von Hirsch, A.
   1976   *Doing Justice: Report of the Committee for the Study of Incar-
          ceration.* New York: Hill and Wang.
Wilson, J.Q.
   1983   Introduction. In *Crime and Public Policy.* San Francisco, Ca-
          lif.: ICS Press.
Wolfgang, M.E.
   1958a *Patterns in Criminal Homicide.* New York: John Wiley &
          Sons.
   1958b *Patterns in Criminal Homicide.* Philadelphia: University of
          Pennsylvania Press.
Zimring, F.E., and G.J. Hawkins
   1973   *Deterrence: The Legal Threat in Crime Control.* Chicago:
          University of Chicago Press.

Predicting Violent Behavior and Classifying Violent Offenders

Jan Chaiken, Marcia Chaiken, and William Rhodes

INTRODUCTION

This paper discusses the classification of *individuals* as violent persons and the prediction of *individual* acts of violence. It is based on a review of research reports that implicitly or explicitly define violence as physically harmful behavior carried out by an individual and directed against others. Thus we exclude research on such topics as collective violence (e.g., riots and wars), self-injury (e.g., suicide), and psychological violence (e.g., verbal aggression).

We further focus on research whose explanatory factors were individual characteristics, thereby excluding studies of subcultural factors, ecological factors (such as density of the population), and situational factors (such as availability of firearms). Although such factors are pertinent for predicting the occurrence of violence, this paper focuses on predicting parameters of individual criminal careers, in particular:

- the *prevalence* of violent persons in a study population (e.g., the percent of juveniles in the United States who have ever committed an act of violence) and the likelihood that any given person will be violent;

Jan Chaiken and William Rhodes were with Abt Associates in Cambridge, Massachusetts. Marcia Chaiken was at LINC, Lincoln, Massachusetts.

- the *rate* at which violent persons commit violent acts (the number of violent acts committed by a person each year);
- the *persistence* (or duration) of violent persons' histories of committing violent acts (e.g., length in years from the commission of the first act of violence to the last act of violence); and
- the *seriousness* (or harmfulness) of the violent acts committed by individuals (e.g., extent of physical harm inflicted).

Our review seeks to transcend the particular foci of the source studies (which typically concentrate on particular types of victims or forms of injury, such as spouse abuse or rape) and instead summarizes commonalities in the methods and findings of studies about violence. Considerable empirical evidence suggests that violent people frequently engage in a range of violent and other types of antisocial acts. Children who throw heavy or sharp objects at their parents are likely to hit their siblings or peers and to lie, set fires, and be truant from school (Lewis and Balla, 1976); prison inmates who are "violent predators" (they committed robbery and assault and dealt drugs prior to incarceration) are just as likely to have an arrest history including rape as are fellow inmates who are actually serving time for rape (Chaiken and Chaiken, 1982, and unpublished analysis of the same data). Thus, a focus on a narrow range of violent acts would fail to identify what is commonly perceived as violence.

Furthermore, the characteristics of victims and the forms of injury are less important for classification and prediction than are characteristics and past behavior of individuals. Although any behavioral outcome is dependent on an individual's response to the environment, including his or her access to specific classes of victims, certain biological, psychological, and social characteristics of individuals dramatically increase or decrease the probability that they will engage in specific forms of behavior, independent of environmental factors. This concept has been supported by such studies as Glaser (1964), Hare (1979), Irwin (1970), Mann et al. (1976), McCord and McCord (1959), and Robins and Wish (1977), and has guided our thinking in this review.

To carry out the review, it was useful to distinguish between classification and prediction, even in situations where this distinction is unclear in the source document. The following section explains the basis for this distinction and summarizes those methodological issues that classification and prediction have in common; it also contains a brief summary of the correlates of violence. In the following section, we turn attention to classification. There we review the purposes of classification, types of classifications, and congruent findings across studies. We then focus on prediction studies and summarize our findings about predicting violence. The last two sections present the implications for research and public policy.

TECHNICAL ASPECTS OF PREDICTION AND CLASSIFICATION

DISTINCTIONS BETWEEN PREDICTION AND CLASSIFICATION

No definitive boundaries separate classification from prediction, and they cannot be clearly distinguished by their methodology or purposes. In fact, some researchers who know they are involved in classification nonetheless state that their major purpose is prediction. For this review, however, we found that a useful and practical separation can be made by defining a prediction study as one whose underlying analysis fundamentally requires longitudinal data—*information about the same subjects' behavior at two or more points in time.*

For a work to be considered as prediction research here, the form or coefficients of the equations, models, or procedures for separating persons into subgroups must have been *initially* determined by a comparison of data at two different times. For this reason, an analysis that divides violent persons into groups by using cross-sectional data is considered to be classification, not prediction, even if the work was based on a theoretical expectation that the groups would behave differently in the future. Similarly, studies that examine subsequent data to determine outcomes of groups previously classified by use of cross-sectional data are considered classification studies (e.g., the work of Milner et al., 1984, discussed under "classification" below), as are studies in which the data collection instrument was tested for stability over time by using test-retest methods.

We also considered studies called "postdiction" by their authors (e.g., see Chaiken and Chaiken, 1990b) as classification research. In postdiction studies, data are collected describing various stages in a person's life or criminal career, but the dependent variables being estimated in the statistical analysis (e.g., individual crime commission rates during the previous year) describe behavior that is *contemporaneous with some or all of the data items used as independent variables.* In short, the behavior being estimated does not lie in the future with respect to the "predictors." A typical purpose of postdiction research is to devise ways of using officially or routinely recorded data for estimating concurrent behavior that cannot be routinely measured.

On balance we felt it is helpful to limit the term "prediction" to future-oriented research. It is immaterial whether the data for the independent variables (predictors) are collected retrospectively at one time or longitudinally.

Classification research tends to focus on dividing individuals into distinctive subgroups. In traditional classification research (e.g., Gibbons, 1975), all persons being classified are to fall in a group defined by the research, and no one is to be classified as belonging to several groups. In others, a residual group of unclassified individuals is permitted,[1] or persons are classified along several dimensions rather than in a single group (for example, as in the *Diagnostic and Statistical Manual of Mental Disorders*, Third Edition—Revised (DSM-III-R), American Psychiatric Association, 1987, discussed below).

By contrast, prediction research infrequently focuses on mutually exclusive subgroups, instead concentrating on estimating *probabilities* of future occurrences. In this framework, some or all persons could have probabilities greater than zero for several (or all) of the potential outcomes.

The purposes for undertaking classification are varied and may or may not be forward looking, whereas prediction is always forward looking by our definition. In the context of violence research, classification may be undertaken to estimate the prevalence of violent persons, or categories of violent persons, in specific populations; to construct typologies that assist in understanding personal and social characteristics of categories of violent and nonviolent persons; to learn more about causes, correlates, and stability associated with categories of violent persons; to diagnose individuals for purposes of planning treatment; and to assign individuals to groups for purposes of case management.[2]

The purposes of prediction may be similar, but prediction involves future behavior. Predictions of future violence may be made to determine whether subjects pose a risk to the community when released from criminal justice or mental health restraints; to investigate the causal relationships between events at two or more points in time; or to project future demands on criminal justice and health care resources.

Measures of Quality

The standards applicable to judging the quality of classification and prediction research are basic textbook material in the psychometric literature, but they appear to have been applied unevenly, sporadically, or incompletely in criminal justice contexts. This section discusses three important measures of quality: validity, reliability, and accuracy.[3]

Validity

Validity generally means that a variable, test, or system of equations actually measures or predicts the theoretical construct it purports to. Three dimensions of validity are considered important in the literature: content validity, construct validity, and criterion validity (Corcoran and Fischer, 1987).

Content Validity Content validity determines whether the independently measured items are a representative sample of the content area to be covered by the instrument or data collection activity. There would be little need to introduce this limited concept of "validity" except as a reminder that truly shoddy classification and prediction research is occasionally carried out. Content validity is ascertained subjectively, either by examining the items and judging if they appear to represent the content ("face validity") or by examining the procedures used in the original research to select the independent variables ("logical content validity"). Examples of procedures that may be used to quantify the validity of self-reported data are measuring consistency among responses to logically identical or reversed questions, examining the extent or pattern of missing (blank) responses, developing "lie" scales (sets of questions whose responses can be combined into an index of untruthfulness), and specifically asking respondents whether or not they are telling the truth.

Construct Validity Construct validity entails determining that the system's measured variables, or combinations of them, correlate with meaningfully related observable variables or actual behaviors, whereas dissimilar observables are not associated with scores, subgroupings, or data items in the same way. In research on violence, construct validity is often highly problematic. The variables that purport to represent the occurrence or extent of violence itself, or causative factors related to violence, are in many cases ill-defined or not representative of the intended behavior.

The reactions of other people and the institutional procedures that intervene between an occurrence of violence and a recorded instance of violence are often complex and extended in time, so that records related to violence are often difficult for researchers to interpret in the context of construct validity. For example, a past history of arrests for violent crimes is not synonymous with being a violent person, nor are recorded instances of "aggression," however defined. When histories of arrests for violent crimes are studied without addressing the question of what they represent, or by indirection leaving the implication that the data indicate whether or not the person is violent, construct validity is violated. Similarly, short follow-up periods for collecting data about persons predicted to be violent or not violent may not permit obtaining valid measures of the construct of interest.

Inadequate construct validity also occurs in independent variables used in violence research. For example, a recorded history of psychiatric treatment does not signal or characterize any clearly articulable past pattern of behavior, so its relationship to contemporaneous or future violence, if any, is difficult at best to interpret. Even many variables that superficially appear to have good construct validity because they involve "hard scientific tests" may on closer inspection be inadequate. For example a positive urine test for opiates is not a valid measure of *addiction*. A more valid but "softer" measure of addiction is a police officer's notation that an arrestee possessed "works," had recent track marks and ulcers, and showed signs of withdrawal irritability.

Criterion Validity Criterion validity deals with the existence of a relationship between test scores, subgroups, or independent variables and actual behavior, as represented by other measurements or observations (Golden et al., 1984). Criterion validity can be measured concurrently or predictively, whether or not the underlying study itself was predictive. Concurrent criterion validity involves showing that there is a relationship with an alternative method of measuring the same characteristic of interest at the same time, whereas predictive validity attempts to show a relationship with the behavior of interest at a future time. Both classification and prediction studies may be examined for their predictive validity.

Reliability

Reliability refers to the method's trustworthiness, as indicated by stability over time or among different groups, or by consistency in application by different researchers or in different contexts. Theoretically, reliability quantifies the degree to which a constructed test overlaps a perfect measure of the characteristic of interest (Golden et al., 1984).

Measures available for estimating the reliability of classification or prediction research include internal consistency, interrater reliability, and test-retest reliability.

Internal Consistency Measuring internal consistency differs from a consistency check for validity of responses to logically equivalent or reversed items, mentioned above. Coefficient alpha (Cronbach, 1951), a common measure of internal consistency, is based on the average correlations among items purporting to be related to the same theoretical construct. An alpha coefficient exceeding .80 is generally deemed to show that a measurement device is internally consistent. The Kuder-Richardson 20 formula (KR20) (Kuder and Richardson, 1937) is a similar statistical measure designed for dichotomous items.[4]

Interrater Reliability Interrater reliability is ascertained by having multiple researchers or examiners score or code the identical set of raw data or the same observed behavior. The correlations among corresponding items are then calculated, with a typical standard of acceptance being average correlations exceeding .80 and preferably above .90.

Test-Retest Reliability Test-retest reliability is determined by asking respondents the same questions twice in a single administration of a questionnaire or on two different occasions separated by days or weeks, and calculating correlations between corresponding items.[5]

Accuracy

Accuracy refers to the discriminating power of the method: the magnitude of the distinctions among subgroups or the proportion of a subgroup actually displaying the outcome predicted for them. A prediction equation is *valid* if there is some statistically significant correlation between the predictors and the actual outcomes of interest, but it is *accurate* if there is a strong or utilizable relationship, for example if a sizable proportion of persons predicted to commit violent acts turn out in fact to commit such acts, whereas a sizable proportion of the others turn out not to commit violence.

A considerable body of literature on criminal justice prediction research bemoans the typically low levels of accuracy achieved by prediction models and the lack of standardized or commonly accepted statistics for comparing the relative quality of different prediction instruments or methodologies, especially when applied to different populations. See Gottfredson and Gottfredson (1988b:252) for a good review of this literature as related to violent criminal behavior, together with an extensive bibliography; they state that "reviewing the literature concerning the prediction of dangerousness and the propensity for violence shows that there is little evidence supporting our ability to make these predictions with acceptable accuracy. The prediction of violence is exceptionally difficult, and no one seems to have done it well."

A common observation in recent literature is that predictions of violence are especially difficult due to a low base rate, namely, that in any naturally occurring population only a small proportion of individuals will commit acts of violence. However, a low base rate does not place limits on the ultimately achievable levels of prediction accuracy, which evidently can be as high as 100 percent. To illustrate the independence between base rate and prediction accuracy, consider the case of Tay-Sachs disease, whose incidence is well under 1 percent in the general population but whose occurrence can be predicted with 100 percent accuracy based on the results of appropriate tests. The persons who will develop Tay-Sachs disease (absent an intervening alternative cause of death) can all be predicted by physical tests for the absence of a specific vital enzyme, and anyone who has the enzyme will not develop the disease.[6] Of course, before the role of this enzyme was discovered, prediction of future development of Tay-Sachs disease appeared to be formidably difficult. However, the disease's low base rate was neither an obstacle to developing an accurate prediction instrument nor a bar to practical application of the prediction methodology.

A low base rate does, however, present a limitation on the *usefulness of inaccurate predictions*. If the base rate is low, the default "ignorant" hypothesis that no one in the study group will commit any acts of violence can be very close to the truth, but of course useless. Similarly, predictions of very low or very high probabilities can be accurate but useless. For example, an exactly correct prediction that 97 percent of a specific subgroup of individuals will be nonviolent is not very helpful if the base rate for nonviolence in the entire study group is 96 percent.

In the case of perfect predictions, the selection rate (proportion of the population predicted to have the characteristic in question) is the same as the base rate, but in the realm of violence classification and prediction, typical instruments have selection rates that differ from the base rate. Although often the original researcher can arrange for the selection rate to equal the base rate in the study sample, there is no guarantee that the two will be the same in subsequent applications. Comparing and making sense out of the accuracy levels of two instruments or methodologies that have different selection rates have proved problematic.

Loeber and Dishion (1983) developed the Relative Improvement Over Chance (RIOC) statistic to help permit such comparisons; RIOC calibrates a prediction's improvement in accuracy over random accuracy with respect to the constrained range between maximum accuracy and random accuracy. Farrington and Loeber (1989) present simplified formulas for calculating RIOC and its variance. The formula for IOC used in this chapter is defined in a footnote to Table 1.

CLASSIFICATION AND PREDICTION METHODS

Formal and Informal Methods

Almost all people routinely classify and predict the behavior of others on a day-to-day basis. Classification of violent behavior, as with any form of behavior, is an ongoing social process (Mead, 1934) learned early in life (Kagan, 1982). It depends on one's experience in anticipating future behavior, or behavior in related situations, based on observable acts (Weinstein, 1969) such as nonverbal gestures (Lindesmith and Strauss, 1968) and the individuals' appearance (Goffman, 1959, 1963). Some people classify persons as violent or predict their future violence based on informal processes, whereas others use highly structured statistical procedures.

Informal processes of classification occur commonly. For example, people walking in a city street at night are likely to plan their routes based on their understanding of types of violent offenders and estimates of their prevalence in certain neighborhoods; they will react to strangers in the area by crossing the street or walking faster, based on their own informal classification of the people they observe and their anticipation of possible violence from such people.

The sections that follow describe formal procedures for classifying violent offenders as developed in specific research studies. However, it should be recognized that in practice the results of even the most rigorous classification and prediction methods are interpreted in the context of the possible political, economic, and social consequences of classification decisions.[7] The informal, often hidden, methods used for classification depend as much on the organizational setting as on the characteristics of the individuals undergoing classification.

Violent persons are classified by various agencies in the criminal justice system and the public mental health system, and by private psychiatric/psychological service providers. The populations served by these classifiers often overlap, but their classification methods are typically quite different, as are the factors they consider important in regard to violent behavior. A 17-year-old male who has been convicted of rape may, for example, be sentenced to prison, to a psychiatric facility, or to probation with a stipulation of private psychological treatment or counseling in a mental health agency. Depending on where he is sentenced, he will encounter different formal and informal classification methods, and the practitioners who classify him will differ regarding the consequences of making wrong predictions and the risks they are willing accept in making classification or prediction errors.

Selection Bias

A difficulty commonly experienced in quantitatively based classification or prediction studies of violence has been the lack of a clear understanding of the selection process that produced the group under study. In many instances, the research study sample is chosen for reasons of convenience and availability to the researchers. Examples of populations of this type include incarcerated offenders, persons in treatment, or juvenile court referrals. The sequences of events through which individuals came to be members of the study population may be so remote in time and place from the research project that there is little realistic possibility of obtaining descriptions of the processes or statistical probabilities associated with selection for the study population.

Whenever there are no clear and replicable rules for selection of the study population, subsequent difficulties arise in interpreting and implementing the results of the research. Often it is not possible to specify the appropriate groups to which the prediction equations, test score cutoffs, or other classification schemes will apply. For example, the category "convicted male felons" in one state is not necessarily closely similar to the same category in another state.

Often, a research strategy is proposed in which tests, score cutoffs, or other methods are to be developed with one population and then subsequently tested on similar populations to demonstrate their robustness. However, the results to date of classification and prediction research on violence do not give much comfort to those who hope for the presence of robust findings. Instead, the sequential research strategy frequently demonstrates that the classification techniques applied to another group yield entirely different (unstable) categories, or that the classification or prediction equations are highly inaccurate when applied to different study populations.

Determining the Importance of Potential Predictive Factors

A related difficulty is that the original study population, unknown to the researchers, may differ from other populations in regard to its variance on variables strongly correlated with violence. Such variables will not emerge in the analysis as being significantly associated with violence, even if they are measured correctly in the study population. In addition, unmeasured variables pertinent to the selection process may also be predictors of violence. Such variables tend to be forgotten in interpreting the results of the analysis, especially if the researchers never had a genuine opportunity to observe or measure the variables in question. Two-stage prediction studies, in which the probability of selection is estimated first and then the outcome is estimated, can help reduce these types of ambiguities in research results. However, there are not many studies in the existing violence prediction and classification literature that control for potential selection biases in this way.

The problem of classification and prediction instruments not transporting well from one setting to another is compounded by researchers' well-intentioned efforts to maximize prediction accuracy within a construct sample. Stepwise computing algorithms and test-retest procedures used on the same set of data will typically produce predictions that maximize sample-specific correlations; such predictions are prone to *shrinkage* (reduction in prediction accuracy) when used in a second sample that does not reflect the same sample-specific correlations. Shrinkage tends to be worse in small than in large samples, a notable effect, because samples used in classification and prediction are typically small.

CORRELATES AND CAUSES OF VIOLENCE

Correlates of violence have been reported in an extensive literature reviewed by Weiner (1989) and Loeber and Stouthamer-Loeber (1987). These reviews point out that variables statistically associated with *participation in violence* (ever having committed a violent act) are not necessary the same as variables statistically associated with *persistently committing violent acts over a relatively long period of time* (the duration of the "violent career") or with the number of violent crimes committed during a specified calendar period (*crime commission rate* or *lambda*).

Participation in violence is associated with broad social categories such as sex, race, age, and socioeconomic status, but among persons who have participated in violent behavior, other factors have a stronger association with their crime commission rates and persistence. Conversely, correlates of persistence and rates of committing violent crimes—among those who engage in violent behavior—may not be correlated with participation in violent behavior. For example, many people use drugs and many have drinking problems, but most of them are not violent. However, among people who have committed violence, drug users and those with drinking problems are more likely to repeat violence, and among those who have committed a violent act and use drugs, those who frequently use heroin or other opiates are more likely than others to commit violent acts at high rates (Shaffer et al., 1984; Chaiken and Chaiken, 1982, 1987, 1990a; Johnson et al., 1985; Chaiken and Johnson, 1988; Nurco et al., 1988).

To further complicate matters, it should be noted that even the strongest *correlates* of violent behavior are not necessarily *causes* of violent behavior. Many correlates are imperfect measures of the underlying causal factors, whereas others are correlated but may actually occur *after* the commission of violent acts. For example, heroin users often decrease their heroin consumption when funds are low and increase consumption when the proceeds from robberies or other criminal activities are high (Johnson et al., 1985). Also, many violent, drug-using juveniles were delinquent before they started using drugs (see Chaiken and Chaiken, 1990a, for a summary of results showing this relationship). Moreover, participation in drug *dealing* appears to have a stronger causal relationship to violent acts than drug *use*—the correlation between frequent drug use and committing violent crimes at high rates may be in large part due to users' involvement in the systemic violence of the drug trade or participation in the symbolic violence of the urban drug culture (Goldstein, 1989; Chaiken and Chaiken, 1990a; Altschuler and Brounstein, 1989).

Similarly, the existence of causal relationships associated with other correlates of violent behavior has been questioned, including such strong correlates as alcohol (Collins, 1989), mental illness (Menzies and Webster, 1989), and child abuse (Widom, 1989a,b). The absence of proved causal relationships does not mean that these correlates are useless for classifying and predicting violent behavior. The sections that follow illustrate that noncausal correlates can provide bases for meaningful utilitarian classification and prediction. However, unlike Tay-Sachs disease, the current state of knowledge is not even close to having an adequate understanding of the causes of violence that would be needed to classify violent offenders and to predict violence with great accuracy.

CLASSIFICATION

PURPOSES AND POPULATIONS CLASSIFIED

The "art" of classifying violent offenders is reminiscent of the traditional story of the classification of the elephant by a team of blind people—each one measuring a different part and variously describing the ear, trunk, leg, tail, or torso. Not only have researchers and practitioners attempted to describe different dimensions of the same "elephant," they have also examined elephants in herds of different age mixes, sex mixes, and settings.

Populations studied for classification of violence have included nationally representative samples of adults (Gelles and Straus, 1988) and youth (Elliott et al., 1989), populations of children (Loeber and Stouthamer-Loeber, 1987), youth and adults in "high-risk" areas (Goldstein, 1989; Fagan et al., 1986; Fagan and Weis, 1990; Simcha-Fagan and Schwartz, 1986; Williams and Kornblum, 1985), clinical populations (Lewis and Balla, 1976), defendants (Chaiken and Chaiken, 1987, 1990b), institutionalized populations of convicted offenders (e.g., Megargee, 1977; Chaiken and Chaiken, 1982), and institutionalized populations of psychiatric patients (Toch and Adams, 1989; Steadman, 1987).

Researchers and practitioners carrying out these classifications have been drawn from such diverse fields as biology, mathematics, neurology, psychology, psychiatry, sociology, and statistics; their measurement techniques have included interviews, surveys, physical examinations, psychiatric examinations, ethnographic methods, and secondary analyses of data originally recorded by criminal justice and clinical practitioners. The variables they have measured have included self-reports of violent and other "deviant" behavior; reports by significant others (teachers, spouses, peers) of violent and deviant behavior; arrests, convictions, and incarcerations for violent behaviors; brain and other neurological abnormalities; and socioeconomic variables such as age, race, sex, education, and employment.

Researchers and practitioners who have different technical backgrounds or disciplinary orientations regularly disagree about the appropriateness of others' classifications, but this paper does not attempt to summarize all these variants and arguments. Rather, a description is given of the major types of methods and measures and of congruent results that have emerged from using them. The examples chosen for presentation are not meant to be comprehensive but are illustrative of methods that have experienced continued application in research or practice.

TYPES OF CLASSIFICATION

Psychological Tests—Rapid Assessments

A large number of psychological tests provide rapid diagnoses for a spectrum of psychological abnormalities (Corcoran and Fischer, 1987) by using simple univariate scaling techniques with demonstrated high reliability and validity. A few of them identify persons with violent personalities, severe psychological problems, and persistent patterns of violence. Some examples follow.

State-Trait Anger Scale (Charles Spielberger and Perry London) Respondents are asked to rank 15 specific statements as applicable to their own general feelings (e.g., "I have a fiery temper") and 15 statements about their own feeling at that moment (e.g., "I am mad"). Scaled responses are used to differentiate between anger as a state (situational response) and anger as a trait (frequent anger over time), and to differentiate between angry temperament and angry reactions. These scales, which have been tested in normal populations, have excellent reliability (.87-.93, depending on the population) and concurrent correlations with other measures of neuroticism, psychoticism, and anxiety.

Problem Solving Inventory (P. Paul Heppner) Based on 35 items about individuals' general responses to problems (e.g., "I make snap judgments and later regret them"), groups with different levels and forms of psychological disturbance are distinguished. Constructed and retested using populations of students and nonstudents, blacks and whites, a spectrum of adult age groups, and "normal" and institutionalized (alcoholic) subjects, tests of internal consistency have resulted in alphas of scales ranging from .72 to .85, and alphas of .90 for total measures.

Index of Spouse Abuse (Walter W. Hudson) Based on respondents' ranking on a five-point scale of the frequency of events described in 30 items assigned weights (e.g., "My partner belittles me"— weighted 1; "My partner becomes abusive when he drinks"—weighted 44), both physical abuse and nonphysical abuse inflicted on a woman spouse have been measured. Tested in both clinical and nonclinical samples, the instrument has good internal consistency (alpha = .90 to .94 for physical scale, .91 to .97 for nonphysical scale), with almost no measurement error, and has high correlation with factors believed to be associated with abuse.

Psychological Tests—Multivariate Scaling Techniques

Some standard psychological tests include measures of psychological or mental status associated with violent behavior, whereas other tests have been constructed specifically to classify violent persons. In clinical or correctional settings, standard tests often supplement violence-specific tests. For example, children who have displayed violent behavior may score differently from other children on portions of the Wechsler Intelligence Scale for Children, the Bender Gestalt Test, the Rorschach, or the Thematic Apperception Test. Observations of children's ability to concentrate on standard tests have also provided indicators of fluctuating attention spans that are symptomatic of neurological disorders and psychoses (Lewis and Balla, 1976).

Other standard psychological tests are administered specifically for diagnosing abnormal psychological states, including several syndromes characterized by violent behavior.

The Minnesota Multiphasic Personality Inventory (MMPI) The MMPI is one of the oldest tests still in use for classifying persons with various psychological problems. Its applicability in criminal justice contexts is enhanced by the development of a set of MMPI profiles that help classify prison inmates. Published in 1940, the MMPI was developed empirically for clinically classifying patients according to syndromes, primarily to determine treatment for a wide spectrum of behaviors (Hathaway and McKinley, 1940). The MMPI questionnaire consists of short declarative sentences in the first person singular, such as "I generally am in good health." Subjects indicate whether or not the declarations apply to them.

In all, 504 items cover 25 topics ranging from general health to phobias. After administration, yes or no responses to specific subsets of items are counted to obtain an individual's raw cumulative score on several scales. The raw scores on each scale are transformed into standard scores with a mean of 50 and a standard deviation of 10 and plotted on a standard profile sheet in which the heights of scores appear as "elevations." The profile sheet is interpreted by a psychologist who examines the highest elevation on all scales and the patterns of elevations on the scales. Scores over 70 generally are thought to be clinically significant (Butcher and Keller, 1984).

The inmate typology, which has widespread use in correctional institutions (Clements, 1986), originally was developed by using MMPI profiles of a sample of youthful offenders in a federal prison (Megaree, 1977; Megargee and Bohn, 1979). Statistical cluster analysis of the MMPI profiles was used to define 10 types of inmates. The groups were given arbitrary labels corresponding to the letters of the alphabet: Able, Baker, Charlie, Delta, Easy, Foxtrot, George, How, Item, and Jupiter.

By examining written institutional staff reports about inmates classified according to this MMPI typology, Megargee and Bohn (1979) determined the modal characteristics of individuals belonging to the various MMPI types. For example, Item (the most prevalent type in general inmate populations) is described as having these modal characteristics: "stable, effectively functioning well adjusted group with minimal problems, few authority conflicts." The most prevalent type in a population of psychiatrically disturbed inmates, How, has different modal characteristics: "unstable, agitated, disturbed, 'mental health cases.' Function ineffectively in all areas and have extensive needs."

The MMPI types were also analyzed to see whether they were distinguishable in terms of the extent of violence displayed by their members in the crimes for which they were convicted. The criterion measure was a researcher's ranking of violence as described in each person's presentence investigation report (PSI) for the crime of conviction. However, the types that scored the highest on violence in the conviction offense were a residual unclassified group (Uncle), whose modal characteristics could not be specified, and Jupiter, a type with such low prevalence that it is ordinarily excluded in other tests of the validity and reliability of the typology.

Thus the classification does not appear to yield valid indicators for distinguishing inmates who were violent in situations outside penal institutions. Nonetheless, the typology reportedly has been useful for reducing institutional violence by segregating types that are predatory from types that are prone to victimization. For example, violence within prisons appears to be reduced by segregating Deltas (amoral, hedonistic, egocentric, bright and manipulative, poor relations with peers and authorities, impulsive, sensation seeking leads to frequent infractions) from easily victimized inmates (Megargee et al., 1988).

The utility of the typology is limited by its complexity. Computer-programmed analyses of the MMPI scores were found to classify only two-thirds of the cases into the 10 types; the remaining classifications require clinical judgments for which interrater reliability is poor.

Attraction to Sexual Aggression (ASA) Scale   The ASA scale (Malamuth, 1989) instrument asks for respondents' rankings of attitudes and opinions about 13 sexual acts ranging from "necking" to rape and pedophilia. Respondents state whether or not they have ever thought about trying the activity and provide opinions on the attractiveness of the 13 acts, the percentage of males and the percentage of females who would find the acts sexually arousing, the extent to which the respondent would find the acts sexually arousing, and the likelihood of engaging in the acts if there were no negative social repercussions. The dichotomous responses of whether or not the respondent ever thought of trying the activities are combined into the ASA scale by using multivariate scaling techniques; based on the other rankings, several different scales are constructed.

A shorter version of the ASA instrument refers to six sexual behaviors. The reliability and validity of both the long and the short versions of the instrument appear to be acceptable (Malamuth, 1989). Comparisons with other measures of sexual aggression (discussed below) indicate that this scale, applied to sexually experienced men, will distinguish those who are high on sexual aggression and, applied to sexually inexperienced men, has some utility for assessing their potential future risk for sexual aggression.

Child Abuse Potential (CAP) Inventory The CAP was developed as a rapid assessment instrument for screening parents who abuse their children. The instrument's 160 items enter into construction of several scales, including a 77-item abuse scale. The instrument is self-administered, and respondents are asked to agree or disagree with statements. In addition to the diagnostic scales, items are also used to construct a lie scale. By using anonymous responses from a sample of 122 parents identified by caseworkers as physical child abusers and referred to an at-risk parent-child program for treatment, in comparison with responses from a matched control group of parents who had been referred for other agency services, the scale was found to correctly classify 82.7 percent of the abusers and 88.2 percent of the nonabusers when a 215-point cutoff was the basis for classification. The rates of correct classification were found to be higher when respondents who had a high lie scale score were omitted from classification (Milner et al., 1986). By using a lower cutoff score (166), overall classification rates were improved and false positives almost eliminated; however, the number of false negatives increased (Milner and Wimberly, 1980).

Milner and colleagues (1984) followed up 190 of 200 at-risk parents (10 refused) who had one child under 6 months and no prior history of abuse. Participants' child rearing behavior was monitored by the program staff. The analysis was limited to parent abuse as reported by program treatment staff within six months of program selection. Eleven reports of abuse were received for the 190 participants.[8] The authors report statistically significant correlations between the CAP score and the occurrence of abuse.

To summarize the findings (Milner et al., 1984): Inspection of the abuse scores indicated that 100 percent of the confirmed abuse cases had scores above the cutoff score for abuse potential reported in the CAP Inventory Manual (Milner, 1980). The 11 reported abusers, however, represent only 10.7 percent of the 103 at-risk subjects who scored above the cutoff score for abuse (Milner, 1980:881). As the authors recognized, it is difficult to know how to interpret these findings. These subjects were in treatment, so the treatment may have reduced the incidence of child abuse. Furthermore, some subjects dropped out of treatment, and other clients failed to attend all counseling sessions, but the data did not distinguish them (Milner et al., 1984).

The relationship between CAP and other measures of psychological problems has been studied (Milner et al., 1988; Robertson and Milner, 1985). Although the instrument appears to be valid and reliable for identifying physically abusive parents needing treatment, a study of the practical uses of the instrument revealed that it was being applied for inappropriate purposes such as differentiating between physically abusive parents and neglectful parents (Milner, 1989).

Psychiatric Classifications

In addition to considering psychological and psychosocial dimensions of violent behaviors, psychiatric classifications also assess organic disorders. For example, DSM-III-R recommends classification on three dimensions: clinical symptoms and conditions that are the focus of attention or treatment but are not attributable to a mental disorder (e.g., adult antisocial behavior); developmental and personality disorders; and physical disorders and conditions. For research and for some clinical settings, two additional dimensions are recommended for evaluation: severity of psychosocial stressors and global assessment of functioning. For each axis, practitioners are urged to provide assessments of their confidence in the evaluation. Some DSM-III-R classes are residual categories to be used after other diagnoses are ruled out. For example, intermittent explosive disorder, characterized by violent episodes, can only be used after ruling out "psychotic disorders, Organic Personality Syndrome, Antisocial and Borderline Personality Disorders, Conduct Disorder, or intoxication with a psychoactive substance" (American Psychiatric Association, 1987:321).

Although a primary diagnosis is recommended, the DSM-III-R classification provides for the occurrence of multiple, not necessarily discrete, disorders, and the editors (Spitzer and Williams, 1987) stress that disorders rather than people are being classified. The disorders are arranged hierarchically, with organic disorders given precedence over other types of disorders (if the organic disorder is responsible for initiating and maintaining the disturbance) and more pervasive disorders given precedence over less pervasive ones (e.g., schizophrenia over dysthymia).

The categories available in the DSM-III-R for classifying outbursts of aggression or rage include:

- Organic personality syndrome usually due to structural damage to the brain (e.g., neoplasms and head trauma)
  - Dementia (disturbance of higher cortical functioning)
  - Several categories of intoxication, including alcohol, am-

phetamines, cocaine, inhalants, and sedatives, hypnotics, or anxiolytics
  • Nicotine withdrawal
  • Late luteal phase dysphoric disorder (women) occurring a few days before or after onset of menstruation
  • Mental retardation
  • Conduct disorder (children) and antisocial personality disorder (adults)
  • Posttraumatic stress syndrome.

Other categories available for classifying violent behavior include sexual sadism. Reportedly, fewer than 10 percent of rapists are classified in this category, which is categorized by fantasies, frequently beginning in childhood, and possibly including a history of sadistic acts increasing in severity over time. Mood disorders are a residual category for classifying violent behavior not due to any other physical or mental disorder. Injurious behavior to the self or others may also be present in categories that are defined by other symptoms of elevated activity.

Categories in the DSM-III-R were revised from early instruments (the first instrument was published almost 40 years ago) on the basis of clinical experience with early instruments; research conducted to test the validity and reliability of classification; and advancement of knowledge in psychology, medicine, and social psychology.

American Psychiatric Association members instrumental in constructing the current version of the instrument strongly caution that use of the classification scheme is appropriate only if it is a first step in diagnosis, carried out by a trained clinician who is sensitive to cultural differences, and used in clinical or research settings. In particular, they caution against use of this instrument for legal decisions, especially in light of the acknowledged noncomprehensiveness of the classification categories.

Correctional Classification

The primary purposes of correctional classification are to determine the level of security necessary for an inmate and the level of his or her needs for particular services or programs within the institution. Level of security required is usually based on both public risk and institutional risk. Public risk is commonly assessed on the basis of information about the conviction crime, prior convictions for violent crimes, and history of institutional escapes. Institutional risk is assessed from information about prior institutional and custodial behaviors, psychological and mental status, and the simultaneous institutionalization of other inmates known to have a history of conflicting relations with the person undergoing classification (e.g., rival gang members).

In most states, information for risk classification is derived from presentence investigation reports, "rap sheets," and semi-structured interviews with the inmates. Classification typically is the clinical judgment of a correctional staff member, guided by the information obtained from these sources. Federal prisons and other prisons with a psychologist on staff may use standard psychological tests such as the MMPI (described above) or other multivariate scaled psychological tests; however, most jails and many prisons do not have the resources for extensive psychological or psychiatric testing of inmates for classification purposes (Clements, 1986).

Clinical Predictions

Clinical predictions are classifications carried out to identify individuals at relatively high risk of committing a specific form of violent behavior, whether or not the behavior has previously occurred. Their primary purpose generally is to permit adequate supervision or treatment that will prevent the anticipated violence. Classification can be based on a wide range of information, including factors additional to those specifically related to the individuals for whom risk is being assessed—for example, information about potential victims.

The clinical criteria developed by Ayoub and Jacewitz (Ayoub et al., 1983) to identify parents "at risk" of child abuse illustrate the kinds of factors used in clinical predictions. These include the following:

- Biological alerts: premature infants, "difficult" infants, infants with complicating medical problems, mothers with illness, recent history of sibling illness, child's physical characteristics not meeting parental expectations.
- Psychological alerts: parental childhood history, parental emotional/social isolation, history of past emotional difficulties, intellectual limitations, parental substance abuse or addiction.
- Social alerts: poor living conditions, financial difficulties, unemployment, mobility, lack of transportation, history of violent and/or illegal activities, medical conditions resulting from medical/nutritional neglect.
- Interactional alerts: marital difficulties, family difficulties, parental/infant attachment difficulties.

Official Record Data

Juvenile Arrests Perhaps the best known classification of violent offenders—that used in the Philadelphia birth cohort studies—was based on the numbers and types of police contacts accrued by 10,000 boys born in Philadelphia in 1945 and by 28,000 boys and girls born in 1958 (Wolfgang et al., 1972; Tracy et al., 1990). The findings of these seminal studies are now considered axiomatic:

• Nonwhite youths are more likely to be arrested for violent crimes than white youths: nonwhites in the 1945 cohort were arrested 15 times more often than whites for violent crime; those in the 1958 cohort, 7 times more often.

• A small subgroup of chronic offenders who were arrested for five or more offenses of any type constituted only 18 percent of the 1945 cohort but were arrested for 71 percent of the cohort's recorded murders, 73 percent of rapes, 82 percent of robberies, and 70 percent of aggravated assaults. The 1958 cohort has a smaller group of chronic offenders, but they had more violent arrests than the 1945 cohort's chronic offenders—independent of their race.

A more recent study using juvenile arrests for classification compared patterns of violent arrests among a sample of 908 children identified in court as neglected or abused, with those of a matched control group of 667 subjects (Rivera and Widom, 1991). Essentially the same racial patterns were found as in the earlier cohort studies. Blacks were much more likely than whites to be arrested for crimes of violence both as juveniles and as adults. Whereas the abused/neglected group of blacks was significantly more likely than the black control group to be arrested at some time for a violent crime (22 versus 13%), the black control group was twice as likely as the white abused/neglected group to be arrested for a violent crime, either as a juvenile or as an adult (13 versus 6.4%).

In this study, a large percentage of those who were violent early appeared to drop out of crime, but those who were persistently violent accumulated a relatively large number of arrests for a variety of crimes. Among those ever arrested for a violent crime, 17 percent had both a juvenile arrest and an adult arrest; one-third of all subjects who were arrested for a violent crime as juveniles were not arrested as adults. Those who were arrested for violence as both juveniles and adults had on the average been arrested 13.1 times for a variety of crimes (including 3.55 arrests for violent crimes); those who were arrested as juveniles for a violent crime but appeared to desist from committing violent crimes as adults had on the average only 2.32 arrests (including violent and nonviolent crimes).

Juvenile Referrals to Court A study based on the juvenile court records of 69,504 people born in Maricopa county, Arizona, and in Utah between 1962 and 1965 (Snyder, 1988) found that approximately one-third of the sample was referred to juvenile court at least once. Of these, 5 percent were charged with a violent index crime (3% aggravated assault and 2% robbery; less than 1% for aggravated rape or murder). Less than 1 percent of the sample referred to court was referred only for violent offenses, and among those referred four or more times, not one individual was referred only for violent offenses. However, although only 41 percent of referred youth had been referred a second time, more than 50 percent of those whose first referral was for robbery were returned.

Official Records of Adult Defendants in Serious Crimes A study by Chaiken and Chaiken (1987, 1990b) examined official record data available to prosecutors in two jurisdictions to learn which items of information most accurately identified offenders as high rate (committing crimes frequently) and dangerous (committing violent crimes). Although much of the information usually available to prosecutors was found useful for identifying high-rate dangerous offenders, other commonly used information proved misleading or ineffective for purposes of identification (Chaiken and Chaiken, 1987, 1990b). The research compared official record information collected from 452 case folders with defendants' self-reports of crimes including robberies and assaults. The results indicated that although some existing guidelines for identifying high-rate dangerous offenders are valid and useful, more accurate use of official data entails a two-stage screening process. In the first (but not very accurate) stage, defendants are tentatively classified as high rate or not high rate; in the second stage, those who pass the first-stage screen are classified as high-rate dangerous or not. All the studied indicators, taken together, were only weakly associated with high-rate offending. A selection rule based on an attempt to predict high-rate offending was found to have very few false positives (less than 2 percent of low-rate offenders in the sample would be classified as high-rate). However, the selection rule would have many false negatives; it would not identify most defendants who are actually high rate.

Once the offenders who passed the first-stage screen had been identified, the subset of high-rate dangerous offenders was characterized by criteria that were based on the offender's conduct in the instant crime or earlier crimes. These were found to be much more powerful than personal characteristics (e.g., age at first arrest, race, employment). Although numerous other valid indicators of dangerousness were found, five official-record items were together statistically nearly equal in value to using all valid indicators of high-rate dangerous offending in the study.

Official Records of Prisoners Aside from the MMPI profiles described above, other information collected in prisoners' case records has been used by researchers to construct typologies of different types of offenders. Numerous studies have shown that there are major differences between official-record information and prisoners' self-reports; neither source can be considered highly reliable (Marquis and Ebener, 1981; Chaiken and Chaiken, 1982). More important, typologies constructed by using self-reports cannot be replicated by using only information about arrests and convictions recorded on rap sheets for the same individuals.

Although rap sheet information, by itself, does not appear to be useful in classifying prisoners, richer information collected by criminal justice and mental health agencies does seem to provide valid and reliable data for classifying violent prisoners. For example, data obtained from public psychiatric institutions and from presentence investigation reports has been used to classify prisoners in a typology that demonstrates clear differences between inmates with histories of mental health problems and those with none (Toch and Adams, 1989).

For inmates with mental health problems, differences appeared among those with substance abuse histories, those with psychiatric histories, and those with both. Inmates with psychiatric histories were more likely than other inmates to be more serious frenzied violent offenders in terms of their conviction crimes, their chronicity of being arrested for violent crimes, and the extent of injury inflicted in their conviction crime. Inmates with substance abuse histories were more likely than other inmates to be ineffectual offenders who could not recall details of their crimes and behaved in a manner likely to lead to their arrest.

Based on cluster analyses, the largest subtype among the inmates with "pure" mental health problems consisted of "chronic disturbed exploders" who characteristically had consistent and chronic histories of extreme and uncontrolled violence. Among inmates with drug abuse treatment histories, the largest cluster consists of "drug exploders": addict inveterate recidivists with long histories of violence and other criminal involvements. Typically, this is a "career criminal with a dossier of arrests dating to adolescence ... who does well in prison ... and invariably recidivates, graduating from less serious to more serious offenses" (Toch and Adams, 1989). Among the inmates with neither substance abuse nor psychiatric histories, the largest subtype was the "early career robbers": young men who had been convicted of violent offenses in the past, started committing robberies at an early age, and were likely to be imprisoned in the past and on parole or probation at the time they were arrested. The types constructed in this study are congruent with those constructed by using self-reports of inmates (discussed below). For examples, drug exploders may be analogous to violent predators, and chronic disturbed exploders may be analogous to the high-rate "mere" assaulters discussed below.

Crime Event/Criminal Profile Data To assist its agents in identifying unapprehended violent offenders, the Federal Bureau of Investigation (FBI) typology of violent persons has been constructed to distinguish between two types of suspects in violent crimes. Based on analysis of past cases, it distinguishes between disorganized asocial offenders and organized nonsocial offenders (Holmes, 1989). The former type is below average in terms of intelligence, education, and social and employment skills, and is nocturnal and a loner. The latter type is highly intelligent, sexually adequate, charming, and socially and occupationally mobile. The crime scene is used to provide evidence about the type of violent offender involved in the case, for example, whether the event appeared to be planned, restraints were used, the crime scene was controlled or chaotic, and the weapon was removed or left behind. The resulting offender profile is used to assess actions that will be taken by the offender after the crime (e.g., the disorganized offender is more likely to attend the funeral) and the reaction during questioning if apprehended.

Similarly, based on analysis of information collected about mass murderers (defined as persons who have killed four or more people), profiles of three types have been constructed (Levin and Fox, 1991; Fox and Levin, 1994). One type commits numerous murders for economic gain, usually as adjunct to robbery, and may commit the murders either serially or in a simultaneous slaughter. The other types commit multiple murders that are not incidental to robbery.

The massacre murderer who simultaneously kills more than four people has been described as a person who does not fit any well-defined psychiatric class, although some rare cases involve serious mental disorders such as paranoia, in which victims are believed to be conspiring or voices are imagined to have suggested the crime. Massacre murderers usually have difficulty coping with failures in their own lives—often committing suicide after the event. They attribute their own misfortunes, including loss of jobs or marital difficulties, to other people. They tend to be white males between 30 and 40 who use a gun; they usually are well trained in use of firearms and have done recreational shooting under stress in the past. Typically they are loners with weak support systems who by themselves kill victims they know—family members or coworkers. Very few kill at random.

Serial murderers, on the other hand, kill to fulfill sexual fantasies, for fun, or to feel important. The motives are expressive and not, like the massacre murderer, instrumental. They rarely are recognized or diagnosed as having a serious mental disorder but frequently could be classified as having an antisocial or narcissistic personality by using DSM-III-R classifications. For the most part, they are methodical planners. They rarely use firearms and are most likely to commit strong-arm murders; stabbings are more common than gunshots but still are rare. The serial murderers predominantly are white males and vary in age, although the modal age is around 35. Their victims are usually strangers.

Self-Reports

Self-Reports Collected Through Surveys of National Samples Self-reports of violent offenses based on national samples have helped confirm many findings about the classification of violent offenders based initially on small samples or criminal justice statistics. For example, a national sample of 2,146 individual family members was interviewed in person in 1976 and asked about the frequency of violent acts between various family members ranging from shoving to using a knife or firing a gun. Among these respondents, 75 percent of parents reported striking their child at least once during the child's lifetime, whereas only 3 percent could be considered repeatedly violent, reporting that they "kick, bite, or punch their child at least once each year" (Gelles and Straus, 1988:103). Surveys based on national samples of youth have also confirmed that only a small percentage of teenage boys can be classified as persistent violent offenders, and these boys are likely to commit many violent and nonviolent delinquent acts (Elliott et al., 1989)

Self-Reports Based on Surveys of Offender Populations Self-reports of violent and nonviolent criminal behavior have provided fruitful sources of classification for a number of researchers who have studied the interrelationship between dimensions of violent behavior (rates of committing crimes, persistence, and combinations of crimes committed) and correlates of these different dimensions. Although the reliability and validity of self-reports from offenders are never close to perfect, they have been adequate to demonstrate strong relationships such as those between drug *dealing* and committing violent crimes (Chaiken and Chaiken, 1982; Nurco et al., 1988). For example, Chaiken and Chaiken (1982) classified self-reports of approximately 2,000 inmates in prisons and jails in three states and self-reports from approximately 500 defendants in two states (Chaiken and Chaiken, 1987, 1990b) according to public perception of the seriousness of crimes they had committed, with the most serious categories specifically committing violent crimes.

The types appear to differ along several dimensions of seriousness. Inmates and defendants who were classified in the most serious groups, according to the crimes they reported committing, were also on the average more serious in terms of substance abuse, irregular employment, juvenile involvement in serious crimes, early age of onset of criminal behavior, and social instability (Chaiken and Chaiken, 1982; Chaiken, 1990). In addition, the statistical association between the seriousness level of the classification and the estimated annual rates at which respondents committed specific crimes was very strong. The classification was replicated by using self-reports from unincarcerated offenders and again showed that offenders classified as violent based on types of crimes they committed were also high-rate offenders (Johnson et al., 1985).

Epidemiologic Studies

The primary purpose of recently proposed epidemiologic studies of violence is to classify groups who have a high risk of interpersonal violence, rather than violent individuals. Based on surveillance data such as the FBI Uniform Crime Reports (UCR) and the Bureau of Justice Statistics' victimization survey data, high-risk groups could be identified through simple descriptive statistics of risk factors (Mercy and O'Carroll, 1988). For example,

based on current knowledge of correlates of interpersonal violence, groups at high risk could be characterized as those in which
alcohol consumption is high, illicitly purchased handguns and drugs
are readily available, and income level is low.

Observational Studies

Observational studies have been carried out in both natural
and laboratory settings. Laboratory studies have for the most part
used as a measure of aggression, the willingness of subjects to
apply painful stimuli to others (in many studies, unknown to the
subjects, the "painful" stimuli were in fact simulated). Studies of
male sexual aggressiveness have used penile tumescence as a measure
of sexual arousal in reaction to violence.

Studies by Malamuth (1986, 1988, 1989) explored the relationship between scores on a number of dimensions of violent behaviors and psychological states. The measures used included delivery of aversive noises to female and male (confederate) subjects
(the outcome variable), penile tumescence in reaction to stories of
rape and consensual intercourse, scores on several rapid assessment tests including the Acceptance of Interpersonal Violence
Scale and the Sex-Role Stereotyping Scale; scores on several subscales
of multivariate tests including a dominance subscale and the
Psychoticism Scale of the Eysenck Personality Questionnaire and
self-reports of a variety of violent acts actually committed.

With the exception of sex-role stereotyping, all these measures were significantly correlated with the measure of aggression
toward female subjects but not toward male subjects. However,
when used in combination, other measures proved to be more
powerful discriminators than penile tumescence in response to
stories about rape. Based on these findings, Malamuth (1988:490)
concluded that "men who are aggressive toward women (e.g., rapists) are likely to commit other aggressive acts as well" and that
rape and other forms of aggression may be related to common
underlying factors.

Reports of persons who observe children in the normal course
of events are often used in research concerning classification of
violent children. For example, a review of prediction of juvenile
behavior (Loeber and Stouthamer-Loeber, 1987) indicates that 9
out of 11 longitudinal studies of delinquency used teacher ratings
of aggression; one used both teacher and peer ratings. Reports of
teachers are used frequently in court assessments of children. Data
gathered on teacher's report forms and direct observation forms,

as well as separate interviews with each parent, are integral to several standardized clinical (and forensic) assessments of children (McConaughy et al., 1988). In multiaxial approaches such as the DSM-III-R, such information can be used for classification on several axes. Moreover, interviews with the parents of children being assessed often reveal important observational information about the parents themselves.

CONGRUENT FINDINGS ABOUT INDIVIDUALS CLASSIFIED AS VIOLENT PERSONS

Although practitioners and researchers often disagree about classifying persons who have committed relatively few violent acts, congruent findings have merged across disciplines about offenders who are relatively extreme on all dimensions of violent behavior—the rates at which they commit violent acts, the seriousness of the acts they commit, and their persistence. This section summarizes the congruent findings.

(1) Although many people may at some time in their lives commit a more or less violent act, the majority of people do not repeatedly commit violent acts. Age, sex, and race are important variables in differentiating between people who have and have not committed violent acts; among people who have already committed violent acts, age, sex, and race are less helpful in differentiating those who commit many violent acts from those who commit few.

(2) Persons who are repeatedly violent typically also demonstrate other forms of antisocial or self-destructive behavior, often starting in early childhood, even more frequently than they demonstrate violence toward others. The frequency and seriousness of these other forms of socially undesirable and self-destructive behaviors are indicative of the frequency and seriousness of their violent behavior.

(3) Not surprisingly, persons who are repeatedly violent are very visible to those with whom they frequently interact: peers, family members, and (for children and youth) teachers. However, perhaps because violence is episodic, practitioners who have short-term contact with people are not likely to be able to identify the violent ones based solely on personal observations.

(4) Persons who commit violent acts over long periods of time (persistent violence) are not necessarily the same people who commit numerous violent acts in relatively short periods of time (high-rate violence). Similarly, persons who cause or attempt to cause

serious injuries to others may be neither persistent nor high rate. However, among violent persons, a subgroup has been identified by numerous researchers and practitioners as persistent, high-rate, and dangerous. In any population not selected for these characteristics, very few people would fall into this category, and even among incarcerated populations there are relatively few persistent, high-rate dangerous offenders.

(5) Violent persons may be classified into groups having different probabilities of specific behavior, but they can almost never be definitively classified as to their individual behavior. One reason that no perfect classification scheme exists is that available measures of violence are themselves imperfect. *Self-reports* are subject to both overreporting, resulting in false positives in classifications based on such data, and underreporting, resulting in false negatives. *Information collected by the criminal justice system on arrests and convictions* also does not provide reliable data for classifying violent persons. For various reasons, victims are reluctant to report persons who have abused or threatened them with violence to the police, so that many people who have committed several violent offenses are unknown to the criminal justice system and would not be correctly classified (false negatives). Conversely, many people who have committed violent crimes are either inept or uninterested in trying to conceal their crimes. These offenders are likely to be arrested for nearly every crime they commit, and classifications based on official record data are likely to falsely classify them as high-rate offenders (false positives). *Physical, psychological, and social characteristics* that are disproportionately likely to occur among specific types of violent persons nonetheless also occur among nonviolent persons and among persons who manifest other types of violence.

(6) Independent of the theoretical basis of classification and the specific measures used, classifications that explicitly or implicitly measure scaled multivariate abnormality appear to be more reliable and valid for distinguishing the most serious violent offenders from less serious offenders than classifications that depend on univariate measures or measures that do not capture associated dimensions of seriousness.

(7) Rather than being additive, there is usually collinearity between measures found useful for classifying violent offenders.

(8) The most important factor that appears to decrease the reliability of classification over time is desistance. Persons who are classified as displaying a *particular form* of violence may, for

reasons that are not as predictable, later stop committing all kinds of violent or even antisocial acts.

(9) Depending on the context, it may be desirable to reduce false positive rates in a classification system at the expense of increasing false negative rates, or alternatively to reduce or virtually eliminate false negative rates by increasing false positive rates.

(10) Independent of caveats provided by researchers and practitioners who develop classification methods, other researchers and practitioners are likely to apply readily accessible methods to achieve inappropriate objectives. For example, methods developed for diagnosis are inappropriately used for prediction.

PREDICTION

This section provides a review of selected empirical studies of predicting violent behavior. The selection was derived from articles brought to our attention by the staff and members of the Panel on the Understanding and Control of Violent Behavior, participants at the panel's sessions, a computer literature search,[9] and communications with researchers recognized for their contributions to the study of violence. With some exceptions, we limited our review to papers that have been published between 1979 and 1989. Earlier works are included in the reviews by Monahan (1981) and Klassen and O'Connor (1989a).

The studies reviewed here are all multivariate predictions, as that term was defined earlier. First, we provide a methodological critique; then we summarize results from the 19 studies that are listed in Table 1.

METHODOLOGICAL CRITIQUE

Most predictions of violence are based on occurrence models, failure-time models, or rate models. *Occurrence models* predict the probability that a violent event will occur within a specified period of time, *failure-time models* predict the length of time until occurrence of a violent event, and *rate models* predict the number of violent events to be committed within a specified time period. In any of these three approaches, the major methodological problems that arise often involve censoring events, sample selection bias, or both.

TABLE 1 Summary of Studies Predicting Violence

Key to Table:

Authors (date)

Construction	Size and composition of the construction sample
Validation	Size and composition of the validation sample
Criterion	Definition of the criterion variable
Follow-up	Length of the follow-up period
Fail rate	Percentage engaging in violence according to the criterion variable
Accuracy	Accuracy of prediction using the validation sample, when available, otherwise using the construction sample; reported as false positives, false negatives, and improvement over chance (IOC)[a]
Significant variables	Variables that were reported as being statistically significant in the prediction

Belenko, Chin, and Fagin (1989)

Construction	3,139 defendants arrested for "crack" cocaine drug law violations and 3,204 arrested for "other" cocaine drug law violations
Validation	None
Criterion	Arrest for a violent crime
Follow-up	2 years
Fail rate	Mean arrest rate of 0.17 for crack drug law violators and 0.09 for other cocaine drug law violators.
Accuracy	64% true positives, 37% false positives
Significant variables	Age, race, total prior arrests, prior arrest for violent offense, arrest for crack rather than cocaine drug law

Black and Spinks (1985)

Construction	125 mentally disordered offenders
Validation	None
Criterion	Occurrence of an assault
Follow-up	5 years
Fail rate	13 of 125 (10%)
Accuracy	44% false positives, 4% false negatives, 10% IOC
Significant variables	Prior convictions, prior psychiatric admissions for violent crimes, type of presenting offense

Cocozza and Steadman (1974)

Construction	98 middle-aged people who had been continuously hospitalized as criminally insane for an average of 14 years
Validation	None

TABLE 1 (Continued)

Criterion	Violent assaults based on arrests and hospital reports
Follow-up	Not specified
Fail rate	14 of 98 (14%)
Accuracy	69% false positives, 5% false negatives, –4% IOC[b]
Significant variables	Age, juvenile record, prior arrests, prior convictions for violent crime, severity of presenting offense

Cook and Nagin (1979)

Construction	4,154 individuals who had been arrested for a crime of violence (murder, rape, assault and robbery)
Validation	None
Criterion	Arrest for a crime of violence
Follow-up	3 years
Fail rate	14% of those charged with murder, 23% of those charged with assault, 29% of those charged with rape, and 38% of those charged with robbery
Accuracy	Not reported
Significant variables	Various, depending on criterion variable, including age and prior arrests for crimes of violence

Dembo and Colleagues (1991)

Construction	201 boys detained in a regional detention center
Validation	None
Criterion	Index of violent recidivism
Follow-up	Variable, up to 1 year
Fail rate	76%
Accuracy	$r^2 = .23$
Significant variables	Age, abuse of alcohol, number of prior self-reported crimes against persons

Farrington (1989)

Construction	411 London males
Validation	None
Criterion	Various: self-reports and reports from secondary sources
Follow-up	From age 8 until age 32
Fail rate	134 were identified as aggressive by teachers, 119 self-identified as violent during teenage years, 140 admitted getting into a fight during the five years prior to age 32, and 50 were convicted of a violent crime between the ages of 10 and 32
Accuracy	$r = .47$ for adolescent aggression, .49 for teenage violence, .44 for adult violence, and .37 for convictions for violence

continued on next page

TABLE 1 (Continued)

Significant variables	Various, depending on criterion variable, including poor school adjustment, general tendency toward delinquent behavior, family background, miscellaneous indicators of risk taking, being nervous and withdrawn, and size and intelligence

Garrison (1984)

Construction	100 male children treated in a psychiatric treatment facility
Validation	None
Criterion	Intensive physical attack on other persons
Follow-up	5 hours per week for 2 years
Fail rate	44% of 1,038 aggressive incidents were violent acts
Accuracy	Reported as "fairly low" and only marginally better than chance
Significant variables	Age, victim status, events precipitating

Holland, Holt, and Beckett (1982)

Construction	198 adult offenders placed on probation
Validation	None
Criterion	Arrest for armed robbery, aggravated assault, forcible rape, or homicide
Follow-up	32 months
Fail rate	22 of 198 (11%)
Accuracy	IOC = 1%[c]
Significant variables	Age and prior convictions for nonviolent crimes

Howell and Pugliesi (1988)

Construction	930 married and cohabitating men
Validation	None
Criterion	Minor or severe violence against a spouse
Follow-up	1 year
Fail rate	177 of 930 (19%)
Accuracy	Not reported
Significant variables	Age, occupational status (blue collar versus white collar), unemployment, parents were violent

Klassen and O'Connor (1988a-c)

Construction	239 male inpatients considered to be potentially violent
Validation	None
Criterion	Arrest for a violent crime or readmission to the mental health center for an act of violence
Follow-up	Up to 6 months

TABLE 1 (Continued)

Fail Rate	46 of 239 (29%)
Accuracy	41% false positive, 6% false negative, 18% IOC, r^2 = .34
Significant variables	Age, prior criminal record, prior arrests for violent crimes, number of prior violent incidents, assault as reason for hospitalization, family interactions, ongoing social relationships, assaultive when drinking, suicide attempts

Klassen and O'Connor (1989b)

Construction	251 male inpatients considered to be potentially violent
Validation	265 male inpatients considered to be potentially violent
Criterion	Arrest for a violent crime or readmission to the mental health center for an act of violence
Follow-up	Up to 12 months
Fail rate	74 of 251 (29%) in the construction sample
Accuracy	48% false positive, 17% false negative, 13% IOC, 0.36 RIOC
Significant variables	Early family quality, current intimate relationships, prior arrest history, admission history, assault in the presenting problem

Malamuth (1986)

Construction	155 male volunteers
Validation	None
Criterion	Self-report scale of sexual aggression
Follow-up	Not applicable
Fail rate	Not applicable
Accuracy	r^2 = .45
Significant variables	Dominance as a sexual motive, hostility toward women, attitudes facilitating violence, sexual experience, and sexual arousal in response to observed rape

Menzies, Webster, and Sepajak (1985)

Construction	211 patients at a pretrial forensic clinic
Validation	None
Criterion	11-point scale of violence
Follow-up	Variable, up to 2 years
Fail rate	Not reported
Accuracy	r^2 = .12
Significant variables	Factor scores: tolerance, capacity for empathy, capacity for change, and hostility

continued on next page

TABLE 1 (Continued)

Moss, Johnson, and Hosford (1984)

Construction	96 inmates in a federal prison
Validation	None
Criterion	(1) Participation in a major riot and (2) arrest for a violent crime
Follow-up	10 years for the arrest criterion variable
Fail rate	44 of 79 were arrested for a crime of violence (56%)
Accuracy	Variables used did not predict arrest
Significant variables	None

Rhodes (1985)

Construction	1,711 offenders released from federal prison
Validation	None
Criterion	Arrest for a crime of violence
Follow-up	5 years
Fail rate	Homicide (1.8%), kidnapping (0.3%), rape (1.1%), robbery (6.7%), and assault (7.7%)
Accuracy	Not reported
Significant variables	Age, race, gender, prior criminal record, drug use, violent offense led to conviction

Steadman and Morrissey (1982)

Construction	257 males indicted for a felony and found incompetent to stand trial
Validation	282 males who had competency hearings prior to indictment; 250 males who had been committed involuntarily
Criterion	(1) Arrest for a violent crime or rehospitalization for assaultive behavior and (2) assaultive behavior while a patient
Follow-up	Not specified
Fail rate	Construction: 28 of 154 (in the community) and 100 of 256 (in the hospital); validation 1: 39 of 227 and 85 of 282; validation 2: 22 of 117 and 11 of 147
Accuracy[d]	Validation 1: 100% false positives, 18% false negatives, and –21% IOC[e] (in the community) and 65% false positives, 27% false negatives, and 5% IOC (in the hospital); validation 2: 100% false positives, 19% false negatives, and –19% IOC[f] (in the community) and 90% false positives, 6% false negatives, and –3% IOC (in the hospital)
Significant variables	For hospital assaultiveness: age, race, alcohol problems, juvenile record; for community assaultiveness: prior arrests for violent crimes and age at first hospitalization

TABLE 1 (Continued)

Virkkunen and Colleagues (1989a, b)

Construction	36 men who attempted manslaughter and 22 who committed arson
Validation	None
Criterion	New violent offense or arson as identified by police reports
Follow-up	Variable, averaging 3 years
Fail rate	13 of 58 (22%)
Accuracy	25% false positive, 14% false negative, 0.19 IOC[g]
Significant variables	Blood glucose nadir and CSF 5-HIAA

Weiner (no date)

Construction	1,355 Philadelphia youths who had police contacts between their tenth and eighteenth birthdays
Validation	Holdout sample
Criterion	Arrest for a UCR violent offense
Follow-up	Variable length
Fail rate	Multiple, reported for different arrest transitions and for different subsets of the sample
Accuracy	Reported as very low
Significant variables	Race

Widom (1989a, b)

Construction	908 subjects who had been abused or neglected as children and a matched sample of 667 who had not been abused or neglected
Validation	None
Criterion	Officially recorded (juvenile or adult) crimes of violence
Follow-up	Variable length
Fail rate	9.8%
Accuracy	Reported as low
Significant variables	Age, race, gender, physical abuse as a child, neglect as a child

[a]To compute predictions attributable to chance, the percentage of failures in the total sample is multiplied by the number of failures in the total sample. The product is added to the percentage of successes in the sample multiplied by the number of successes in the sample. The sum is then divided by the total sample size. To compute predictions attributable to statistical analysis, the number of correct predictions (success and failure) is divided by the size of the sample. The IOC equals the percentage of correct predictions attributed to statistical analysis minus the percentage of correct predictions attributed to chance. The IOC is sensitive to the criterion used to predict a failure (i.e., the cutoff criterion). When computing IOC, we assumed that the cutoff should be set so that the predicted

continued on next page

TABLE 1 (Continued)

number of failures should equal the actual number of failures. However, published results did not always allow us to follow this rule, and alternative rules are identified with footnotes.

[b]Although only 14% of the subjects were violent, Cocozza and Steadman (1974) predicted that 37% would be violent, an assumption that likely accounts for the negative IOC. We were unable to compute IOC using alternative assumptions.

[c]The prediction was based on the number of prior nonviolent convictions only, because Holland et al. (1982) do not report regression results using violent and nonviolent convictions as independent variables with sufficient detail to compute summary statistics. The negative value for IOC appears to result from a nonlinear relationship between prior convictions and violence during the follow-up period, because we used the highest category "10 or more nonviolent convictions" as the cutoff.

[d]Statistics were reported by the authors.

[e]Only 4 of 227 were predicted to be violent. In fact, 39 were violent. The IOC is practically a product of predicting almost all subjects to succeed in the community.

[f]Only 1 of 117 were predicted to be violent. In fact, 22 were violent. The IOC is practically a product of predicting almost all subjects to succeed in the community.

Censoring Events

All empirical prediction studies examine the occurrence of violent acts during a specified follow-up period. Those follow-up periods are frequently "censored"; that is, the length of a person's follow-up period may be truncated for reasons not directly related to violence (e.g., commitment to prison for a nonviolent crime, commitment to a mental health facility, moving to another area, or death). If the probability of a violent act occurring increases with the length of time at risk to commit violent acts, controlling for each person's time at risk would seem to be important when predicting violence. Yet many studies fail to introduce adequate controls, either because the researchers did not make full use of their data or because their data are inadequate to support the necessary analysis.

The degree to which failure to adjust for censoring may affect predictions of violence varies across studies. Among the studies listed in Table 1, we note a failure to adequately adjust for censoring to be a potential problem in Weiner (no date), Klassen and O'Connor (1988a-c), Steadman and Morrissey (1982), Black and Spinks (1985), and Belenko et al. (1989).

Sample Selection Bias

One reason for predicting violence is to inform policy makers and decision makers of the likely consequences of failing to take actions to restrain individuals with violent tendencies. As examples, a psychiatrist might advise a judge about the likelihood of violence if a patient were to be released today as opposed to one year from today, and a statistician might inform a parole board of the probability of violence if an individual were to be released after five years rather than after ten years of confinement. Such predictions of violence are made *conditional* on the absence of continued social restraints.[10]

Estimating prediction equations is complicated by the fact that observations of violence made during a follow-up period are seldom untainted by social interventions into the lives of those who are being studied. As illustrations, in the criminal justice arena, individuals perceived to have a high risk of committing future violence are often subjected to more extended periods of confinement and more intensive community supervision than are individuals thought to be less violent; in the mental health field, those who appear violent may be detained longer in hospitals and receive more intensive aftercare than do those who do not appear to be violent. The data at an analyst's disposal have necessarily been "selected" by social processes that attempt to mitigate the very behavior that the analyst is attempting to predict. Unless analysts take steps to compensate for these practical responses to violence, their predictions may say less about human behavior than about processes of social control.[11]

Analyzing data to distinguish between unfettered human behavior and consequences of social control is no easy task, and there is no absolute standard to judge whether an analyst has done an adequate job. Nevertheless, ignoring the problem by simply asserting that one's analysis pertains to violent behavior, without considering or mentioning the ways in which the study subjects may have been restrained from violent acts, is almost certain to muddle predictions of violence. Incorporating in models some variables that distinguish between violent behavior and social responses is justified, even if data are uncertain and the model can merely test the predictions' sensitivity to underlying assumptions.

Some of the studies in Table 1 that are mentioned above as suffering from data censoring are also subject to selection bias: Steadman and Morrissey (1982), and Black and Spinks (1985). Selection bias problems arise also in the study by Dembo et al. (1991).

Statistical Limitations

Aside from data censoring and sample selection bias, which raise methodological suspicion about the substance of studies' conclusions about violence, many prediction studies evidence other statistical weaknesses such as use of nonrigorous or nonoptimal methods. Four of these are discussed here.

Dichotomous Dependent Variables　When researchers estimate occurrence models, the dependent variable is dichotomous, usually coded one (1) when violence occurred and zero (0) otherwise. Discriminate analysis and ordinary least squares (OLS) regression are the most frequently used methods to analyze such data, despite the fact that these tools lack strong theoretical justification in these contexts. Our own preference is for more rigorous methods such as probit, logit, or log-linear contingency tables analysis. However, because discriminate analysis and OLS regression have proved to be robust in other, similar applications, we doubt that they have any important effect on the conclusions of prediction studies.

Dependent Variables With Lower Limits　We are less sanguine about using OLS regression when the dependent variable has a lower limit, such as occurs with the number of violent events during a follow-up period. Given that OLS will yield biased parameter estimates under such conditions, our preference is for regression techniques that are suitable for censored and truncated dependent variables such as Tobit analysis (see Maddala, 1983) and for "countable" dependent variables such as Poisson regressions (see Maddala, 1983; Holden, 1985; King, 1988).

Judging how much findings would be affected by substituting more suitable estimation techniques for OLS regression is speculative, of course, and alternative techniques have their own limitations. Nevertheless, use of alternative estimating techniques can be valuable for checking the sensitivity of reported results to the statistical procedures used in reaching those results.

Stepwise Regression　Stepwise regression and related techniques, such as all-subsets regression analysis, can obscure causal relationships when independent variables are strongly correlated. It can also produce predictions that display greater shrinkage (reduction in predictive power when applied to an independent validation sample) than predictions that are not based on stepwise estimation (Copas, 1983; Copas and Tarling, 1986). This problem can be especially acute when—as is the case with many studies of predicting violence—sample sizes are small. Nevertheless, many researchers have used stepwise regression to fit their models. Given the small samples available to most analysts, stepwise regression accentuates the risk of discarding variables that are predictive of future violence, while retaining variables that have only spurious correlations with future violence and possibly overstating the power of the prediction.

Efficient Use of Data

Most studies that we reviewed were based on occurrence models. Although there is nothing wrong with a model that simply tries to predict the occurrence or nonoccurrence of a violent event during a follow-up period, it is not as powerful as methods that take into account the timing of violent events, especially when data sets include timing information. Employing survival techniques would have made fuller use of these data and perhaps would have provided a more precise, less time-dependent prediction of violent recidivism (Kalbfleish and Prentice, 1980; Maltz, 1984; Schmidt and Witte, 1988). In addition, many data bases appear to allow for records of multiple instances of violence, but the researchers focused only on the first instance of violence. Again, there is nothing wrong with such a focus, but additional information might be tapped by using panel data techniques (Heckman and Singer, 1985), Poisson regression models, or other techniques that take advantage of the information inherent in the occurrence of multiple events.

Although all predictions have inherent problems of shrinkage when moving from a prediction to a validation sample, some techniques can minimize the extent of shrinkage. One is to avoid using small samples or large numbers of predictor variables compared to the size of the sample. Another is to use a different criterion variable in the construction sample than is pertinent for the validation sample.

PREDICTING VIOLENT BEHAVIOR

The discussion of studies' substantive and statistical limitations in the previous section is not intended to condemn the existing body of literature. Although studies of the prediction of violence could be methodologically improved, the studies we reviewed are sufficient to permit meaningful interpretations. This section summarizes the content of the reviewed studies, and the sections that follow attempt to draw a cumulative picture of what variables seem to predict violence and how well those variables predict violent behavior. Given the disparity in study methods used, it was not possible to compare results from one study directly with results from another.

This section is organized around the three general empirical approaches mentioned earlier: occurrence models, failure-time models, and rate models.

Occurrence Models

As previously described, occurrence models use various statistical methods to estimate whether a violent event will or will not occur during a specified period and do not distinguish the occurrence of two or more violent events from the occurrence of a single violent event.

Klassen and O'Connor In a series of related studies, Klassen and O'Connor (1988a-c) first analyzed violence during a six-month follow-up of a group of 239 men who had been admitted as inpatients to an urban community mental health center and were considered to be potentially violent. The criterion measure was an arrest for a violent crime (simple assault, aggravated assault, arson, robbery, rape, or homicide) or readmission for violence to the mental health center during the five-month follow-up. To be counted as recidivism, the violence that led to readmission must have been judged by the researchers to have been criminal. Because most studies of violent recidivism are limited to criminal justice data, it is noteworthy that in the Klassen and O'Connor data about 60 percent of incidents recorded as violent recidivism were actually readmissions to the mental health center.

The authors were concerned specifically with short-term prediction, which—following Monahan (1984)—they argued should be the primary focus of a clinician. Given this interest in short-term prediction, the authors were especially attentive to the subject's family ties at the time of release from the hospital.

They found that several variables were correlated with future violence. Some of these were criminal record variables: number of arrests for disturbing the peace, number of arrests for violent crimes during the last year, number of violent incidents during the last year, and assault as a reason for the hospital admission.

Other variables were descriptive of the patient's family interaction during childhood: injured by a sibling before age 15, father died before age 15, parents did not provide well for needs, parents had physical fights with each other, and dissatisfaction with siblings. Still other variables characterized ongoing social relationships: never married, dissatisfaction with extended family, how often sees mother, how long ago last sexual intercourse, lives with parent, and how long ago last relationship with a woman. In addition, information about suicide attempts in the presenting problem, age, being assaultive when drinking, and abstract reasoning score strengthened the predictions of violence.

Of the 239 subjects, 46 were violent. The total correct classification was 85 percent; chance prediction would have yielded a rate of 19 percent. The false positive rate was 41 percent; the false negative rate was 6 percent.

Substantial shrinkage can be anticipated because the sample was small, the number of predictors was large, and stepwise procedures were used to estimate the model. Using a "standard formula" for preshrinking their estimates, the authors predicted a decline from .34 to .21 in the model's r^2.

In an unpublished study, Klassen and O'Connor (no date) used all-subsets regression to reanalyze the above data after the follow-up period had been extended to one year. In this reanalysis, 251 subjects had been living in the community for at least three months. Of these 251, 74 had been "violent."

The authors report that the multiple r was .45, with a correct classification of 74 percent, a false positive rate of 45 percent, and a false negative rate of 19 percent. By chance, the false positive rate would be 30 percent and the false negative rate would be 70 percent, so the predictions were considerably better than chance.

Building on these findings, Klassen and O'Connor (1989b) returned to the data still again, this time with a validation sample of 265 men who were in the community for at least three months during a one-year follow-up. Eliminating from consideration the variables that had inconsistent parameters in the two regressions in their earlier validation on 100 subjects, as well as variables that lacked a significant bivariate correlation with future violence, Klassen and O'Connor used all-subsets regression to estimate a new prediction instrument. On the basis of this analysis, they retained five scales as predictor variables: early family quality, current intimate relationships, arrest history, admission history, and assault in the presenting problem.

Applying the predictions from the construction sample to the validation sample, Klassen and O'Connor (1989b:78) report:

A total of 75.8 percent of the subjects were correctly classified. . . By chance, 63 percent would be correctly classified overall, so these results represent a 13 percent improvement over chance. . . . Calculation of [RIOC] yielded a value of .36. The false positive rate was 47.6 percent and the false negative rate was 16.8 percent. Of the violent group, 49.3 percent were correctly identified as violent. By chance, only 25 percent of the violent would be identified.

The researchers also report that, contrary to their expectations, variables that characterize ongoing social relationships played a minor role in the predictions. Among them, only family satisfaction was statistically significant.

Steadman and Morrissey (1982)   Steadman and Morrissey had data from three groups: (1) 257 persons who were indicted for a felony and found incompetent to stand trial; (2) 282 individuals who were unindicted for their felony charges and who required a psychiatric determination of competency to stand trial; and (3) 250 males who had been committed involuntarily (civil commitment) to one of six state mental hospitals.

The group of 257 persons was used to develop two prediction instruments that were tested by using data from the other two groups. There were two criterion variables: (1) rearrest for violent crime or rehospitalization for assaultive behavior, and (2) assaultive behavior while a patient, defined as a physical attack, not in self-defense, against another. Possible prediction variables included data about sociodemographic factors, criminal history, and mental hospitalizations. Discriminate analysis was used as the estimation technique.

Steadman and Morrisey (1982:477) report:

The discriminate analysis made it clear that there were major differences in the composition of the two functions for in-hospital and community assaultiveness. The equation predicting hospital assaultiveness contained four significant variables: (1) nonwhites were more likely to be violent than whites; (2) age at first mental hospitalization (the younger, the more likely to be violent); (3) history of alcohol problems before the index hospitalization (those with such a history were *less* violent); and (4) history of adjudication as a juvenile (the fewer adjudications, the *more* likely to be violent).

The equation predicting community assaultiveness included two variables: (1) number of prior arrests for violent crimes and (2) age at first mental hospitalization (again, the younger the more likely to be violent); however race and alcohol problems were not found to be statistically important. In both equations, there was no significant discrimination associated with other social, demographic, mental hospitalization, or criminal history variables.

Three of Steadman and Morrissey's findings stand out. One is that the models did not predict well. In the construction sample, the prediction of hospital assaultiveness improved 15 percent over chance (39 to 54%) and the prediction of community assaultiveness improved 32 percent over chance (18 to 50%). In the first validation sample the improvements were 5 and –21 percent; in the second, 3 and –19 percent.

Second, "no single equation can predict both types of behavior and . . . one must specify in advance the setting for which the prediction is offered" (Steadman and Morrisey, 1982:477). Finally, ". . . whether or not the person was assaultive while hospitalized had no predictive value for determining his subsequent assaultiveness in the community following release" (Steadman and Morrisey, 1982:483).

Cocozza and Steadman (1974) Cocozza and Steadman examined the postrelease behavior of 98 Baxter patients, reported to be "a group of middle-aged people who had been continuously institutionalized in hospitals for the criminally insane for an average of 14 years." They defined violent recidivism as "acts involving violent assaultiveness against persons" based on information in arrest and hospitalization reports. Each source, arrests and hospitalizations, accounted for about half the instances.

Cocozza and Steadman found that violence could be predicted using two factors: the Legal Dangerousness Scale (LDS; a composite of juvenile record, previous arrests, previous convictions for violent crimes, and the severity of the offense that resulted in confinement at Baxter) and age. Results are reproduced and presented in Table 2.

Shrinkage should not be great with this model because the prediction instrument was developed by using a different criterion variable than that used in the validation. The original prediction instrument (the LDS scale) was constructed by using all arrests as the criterion variable, and development of the original instrument did not take into account violent acts that resulted in hospitalization.

Cocozza and Steadman make several points. One is that violence is a rare event even among these patients who were institu-

TABLE 2 Dangerous Behavior of Released Patients by Combined Measures of Age and Legal Dangerousness Scale (LDS) Score (N = 98)[a]

Combined Measures	Dangerous Behavior		No Dangerous Behavior	
	N	Percent	N	Percent
Less than 50 years old and LDS score of 5 or more	11	30.6	25	69.4
50 years or older and/or LDS score of less than 5	3	4.8	59	95.2

[a]p < .001.

tionalized because of violence. A second is that the probability of a false positive is .70. The third is that this release cohort is older, and thus less likely to commit violent acts, than are other typical groups of hospitalized offenders.

Belenko, Chin, and Fagan (1989) This study used a discriminate analysis to predict a rearrest for violent crimes among 3,139 defendants who were arrested for crimes related to "crack" cocaine between August 1986 and October 1986, and among 3,204 defendants who were arrested for crimes related to cocaine between 1983 and 1984. The follow-up period was two years.

Belenko and colleagues were most interested in determining whether offenders who were involved with crack cocaine were more violent than offenders who were involved with noncrack cocaine. Their analysis seems to demonstrate that crack-involved offenders are more violent. However, according to the authors, they were unable to determine from these data which of Goldstein's (1989) explanations[12] for the relationship between drugs and violence accounted for these patterns.

After eliminating variables that were "highly correlated" and other variables that were not statistically significant, the authors report the following variables in addition to crack involvement as statistically significant: age and prior drug sales arrests (negative); male, prior violent arrests; total prior arrests; black; and Hispanic (all positive).

The authors correctly identified 64 percent of the violent recidivists. The false positive rate was 37 percent. True and false negatives are not reported.

Virkkunen and Colleagues (1989) The Virkkunen et al. (1989a) sample consisted of 58 Finnish men, 36 of whom had attempted or committed manslaughter and 22 of whom had committed arson. The researchers classified these crimes as impulsive or nonimpulsive (24 of the manslaughter crimes and all of the arson crimes were classified as impulsive). Data about each subject included age, Wechsler IQ, DSM-III scores, and abuse of alcohol. The researchers were especially interested in the predictive power of the concentration of 5-hydroxyindoleacetic acid (5-HIAA)in the cerebrospinal fluid (CSF) and of a low blood glucose nadir.[13] These variables were measured prior to the subject's release.

The follow-up period lasted 35.6 ± 18.0 months. (No explanation was provided for the variable length of the follow-up.) The Finnish Criminal Register was used to identify crimes during this period. Based on police reports, court documents, and hospital records, recidivism was defined as a new violent offense or arson.

A stepwise linear discriminate analysis was used to distinguish between recidivists (13 of 58) and nonrecidivists. The blood glucose nadir entered the model first, followed by the CSF 5-HIAA. (The researchers found no correlation between repeated violence and age or IQ, nor did these variables enter the analysis.) Using the model including both physiological variables, the group predicted to be violent had six recidivists and two nonrecidivists. The group predicted to be nonviolent had 42 nonrecidivists and 10 recidivists. The authors do not report their model's accuracy when the discriminate function is used to predict 13 recidivists (rather than the total number observed in the sample).

Virkkunen et al. (1989b:603) conclude that "the psychobiological variables as such or in combination with the behavioral variables had more predictive power for the outcome than any combination of behavioral variables." Also, consistent with the low blood glucose nadir, the researchers observed that without exception these offenders committed their crimes while under the influence of alcohol.

Black and Spinks (1985) Black and Spinks analyzed recidivism for assault during a five-year follow-up period for 125 men who were discharged into the community from Broadmore hospital (England) between 1960 and 1965. Broadmore is one of five hospitals in Great Britain for mentally disordered offenders. "In general, offender-patients have committed the kinds of offenses from which it is deemed the public need protection, and the hospital order reflects the acceptance by the court that there is some psychiatric

TABLE 3 Recidivism for Assault During Five-year Follow-Up

Predicted Probability of Failure	Success (number)	Failure (number)	Failure Rate (percent)
0 to .3	105	4	3.7
.3 to .5	6	3	33.3
.5 to .7	1	1	50.0
.7 to 1.0	0	5	100.0

SOURCE: Black and Spinks (1985).

disorder that needs treatment. Hospital orders are in effect 'indeterminate sentences,' in that the patients remain in hospital until they are thought to be fit for discharge" (Black and Spinks, 1985:177).

The dependent variable was any occurrence of an assault, as known to the hospital's research unit. The researchers used a stepwise OLS regression equation to select variables for inclusion in a final logistic regression. The regressions are not reported, but the researchers indicated that assaults could be predicted from the type of offense, age at discharge, and the MMPI scales F (a measure of neurosis) and Ex (a measure of extroversion).

Table 3 summarizes results. The instrument's predictive power appears to be considerable. However, the model was not applied to a validation sample.

Howell and Pugliesi (1988) Howell and Pugliesi analyzed self-reports of violence against a spouse by a national stratified random sample of married and cohabitating men. In the total sample, 19 percent of the men admitted "either minor or severe violence in the past year against their spouse." The authors analyzed the cases of 763 employed men and, separately, the cases of 960 men, some of whom were employed and the rest of whom were unemployed.

Variables used in this study were occupational group (blue or white collar), self-reported economic strain, age (39 or younger versus 40 or older), parental modeling (no violent model and violent model), and employment status.

Log-linear contingency tables were used to analyze these data. After conducting the analysis on employed men only, Howell and Pugliesi (1988:23) report that "having a blue collar as opposed to a white collar increases the odds of reporting spousal violence by a factor of 1.61. . . . Younger males (under 40) are almost three times (2.84) more likely to report instances of violence than are older men . . . and those who did not observe parental violence are 0.57 times as likely as those who have observed parental violence to engage in spousal violence." After including the unemployed in the analysis, the researchers report that "for those in the younger age group, being unemployed increases the odds of reporting violence by a factor of 18.61. For those in the older age group, being unemployed increases the odds of reporting violence by a factor of 2.95."

Moss, Johnson, and Hosford (1984) The researchers tested the ability of the Megargee inmate classification system (previously described in the section on classification) to predict institutional violence and violent recidivism among 96 black inmates of a federal prison in 1973. Institutional violence was limited to "participation in a major riot that occurred in 1973." Recidivism appears to have been recorded for a 10-year period, during which "44 were found to have been arrested for violent crimes and 26 for nonviolent crimes." The researchers found that the Megargee classification could not distinguish between recidivists arrested for violent and for nonviolent crimes.

As noted earlier, Megargee's inmate classification system was developed to classify inmates for management purposes, not to predict violence. It is not surprising that in this study, violence—whether measured in the institution or in the community—was not correlated with the inmate's classification. However, the outcome variables used in the study are imperfect measures of violence; riot participation is not a typical form of institutional violence, and the most active violent offenders are also those most likely to commit nonviolent crimes. Therefore, the findings do not definitively allow us to answer the question of whether the inmate classification scheme predicted violent behavior.

Moss and his colleagues cited four other unpublished studies that tested the inmate classification system's ability to predict violence within prison. According to Moss et al. (1984:227), these studies found "the system to be ineffective in predicting institutional adjustment both within a medium security setting and a penitentiary."

It is worth noting in this context that others have found that the inmate classification system does not seem to predict violence. In a review, Kennedy (1986:172) concludes:

> Findings of more recent studies . . . designed to test the efficacy
> of the Megargee topology as a predictor of inmate adjustments

and violence question its use for this purpose, however. Baum (1981) divided subjects into violence-prone and nonviolence prone groups based on their Megargee protocols. It was found that the violence-prone topology group did not commit proportionately more violent acts during confinement than did the nonviolence-prone group. It appeared that an inmate's past violent behavior (based on conviction offense) was a better predictor of violent behavior in prison than the Megargee topology. Similarly, Louscher et al. (1983) found that the Megargee topology groups were not effective in predicting which chronic and high-risk maximum security inmates . . . would be antisocial or aggressive during incarceration.

Cook and Nagin (1979) Using data from the Prosecutor's Management Information System (PROMIS) in Washington, D.C., Cook and Nagin constructed an analysis file consisting of 4,154 individuals who had been arrested for a crime of violence (murder, rape, assault, or robbery) during 1973. Also, using the prosecutor's information system, the researchers recorded rearrests for each of these individuals during a three-year follow-up. The researchers were unable to determine which of the individuals were incarcerated during the follow-up period.

Probit analysis was used to estimate the probability of being rearrested for a crime of violence. Four regressions were estimated, one for each of the four types of charges (murder, rape, robbery, and assault) at the initial arrest. The explanatory variables were type of weapon (gun, other, and none); prior arrests for violent crimes (none, 1, 2-3, and 4 or more); age (20 or younger, 21 through 29, and older); and some control variables intended to mitigate the problems of missing information about time in prison during the follow-up period.

For robbery and assault at the initial arrest, findings were statistically significant that rearrest for a violent crime increased with the number of prior arrests for crimes of violence and decreased with age. The prior arrest effect was statistically significant for rape; age mattered for neither rape[14] nor murder; the prior arrest effect was not significant for murder. The weapon type did not help to predict recidivism in any of the four regressions.

When murder was the first arrest, the offender had a .14 probability of an arrest during the three-year follow-up. Comparable figures for the other initial arrest types were .23 for assault, .29 for rape, .38 for robbery, and—for purposes of comparison with nonviolent initial offenses—.26 for burglary and .19 for weapon possession. Cook and Nagin indicate that these three-year probabilities understate the rates at which these offenders would have been arrested for violent crimes had incarcerations during the follow-up period been known and factored into the calculations.

Holland, Holt, and Beckett (1982) Holland et al. (1982) recorded the official police records of 198 adult male offenders who were released on probation. The follow-up period lasted 32 months. The dependent variable was success (no arrests); nonviolent failure (crimes against property, public order, and technical violations of supervision); and violent failure (armed robbery, aggravated assault, forcible rape, and homicide). Independent variables were the number of prior convictions for crimes of violence, the number of prior convictions for other crimes, and age.

The authors report that rearrest for a crime of violence could be predicted from prior arrests for nonviolent crimes and from the offender's age. Prior arrests for crimes of violence were not useful in predicting violence.

Widom (1989) Widom (1989b) developed a data file of 908 subjects who had been physically or sexually abused or neglected as children and 667 matched subjects who had not been abused or neglected. Abused and neglected children were identified through juvenile court and adult criminal court records. Matched subject records were identified through birth records and school records.

Physical abuse was defined as "knowingly and willfully inflicted unnecessarily severe corporal punishment" or "unnecessary physical suffering." Sexual abuse was inferred from the nature of the charge against the parent(s). Neglect meant that the child had to have "no proper parent care or guardianship, to be destitute, homeless, or to be living in a physically dangerous environment" (p. 244).

Among other dependent variables, Widom included for each subject the number of arrests for a crime of violence as recorded in juvenile court records, probation department records, and adult criminal history records. The follow-up period for collecting these data varied; about 10 percent of the subjects were under 20 at the time of follow-up and about 5 percent were over 30.

A logistic regression showed that blacks were more violent than whites, that those who had been physically abused as children were more violent than those who had not been abused physically, and that those who had been neglected as children were more violent than those who had not been neglected. Sexual abuse did not seem to predict violent behavior (Z score of 1.20). The probability of violence increased with age, but as Widom recognized, this effect might be attributed to the potentially longer follow-up of older subjects.

Widom did not present measures of association for her logistic regressions.[15] However, as she notes, only 11 percent of those children who were abused or neglected had a subsequent violent criminal record. Furthermore, the effect of being abused or neglected does not seem to be large. About 8 percent of those who had not been abused or neglected were also violent; thus, improvement over chance prediction *based on knowledge of childhood abuse alone* is negligible.

Failure Models

Failure-time models typically attempt to explain the length of time from some point M until the occurrence of a violent crime. When M corresponds to the occurrence of the nth violent crime, the analyst attempts to explain the time between the nth and $(n+1)$st violent crimes. When M corresponds to the occurrence of any crime, the analysis attempts to explain the time from that crime to a violent crime. When M corresponds to release from prison, the analyst attempts to explain the time until a violent crime once the offender is no longer restrained. When M corresponds to birth, the analyst addresses the onset of a violent criminal career.

Whatever the criterion variable, the model is typically:

$$\lambda = \text{ß}X$$

where λ is a parameter (such as the mean) of a specific distribution, ß is a row vector of parameters, and X is a column vector of explanatory variables. The problem is to estimate ß and any other parameters that may be required given the distributional assumptions.

In the violence-prediction literature to date, failure-time models have been used to estimate single transitions, that is, the occurrence of the first violent crime after M. Methods are available for jointly estimating the timing between multiple violent acts (see Heckman and Singer, 1985; Flinn, 1986), but our search did not reveal any studies that used such panel techniques when predicting violence.

Rhodes (1989) Rhodes predicted violent behavior among a random sample of 1,711 offenders who were released from federal prisons during 1979 and whose subsequent recidivism (rearrest or parole revocation) was monitored and recorded for five years. The Rhodes' model is a split-population (see Maltz, 1984; Schmidt and Witte, 1988), competing events survival model with an adjustment for selection bias.

Time until recidivism for a violent event is modeled as a latent variable distributed as log-normal, a form that is presented by Kalbfleish and Prentice (1980) and has been used by several researchers to analyze criminal recidivism (Rhodes, 1986; Schmidt and Witte, 1988). The competing events assumption permits right-hand censoring to occur for two reasons: the end of the follow-up period or incarceration for a nonviolent crime prior to any occurrence of a violent crime. In the latter case, violent recidivism is precluded by the offender's imprisonment for a nonviolent crime.

The model's correction for selection bias is particular to the nature of the data in this study. The data, based on a random sample of offenders released from prison during 1979, are intended conceptually to represent offenders entering federal prisons. However, most convicted federal offenders (roughly 70 percent) are sentenced to probation, so a study of violent recidivism based on a prison release cohort might provide a distorted representation of recidivism among federal offenders in general. Rhodes used maximum-likelihood procedures suggested by Heckman (1979) to adjust for the selection bias.

This review focuses on the portion of the study that used violent crime (robbery or assault) as the criterion variable. Rhodes reported that blacks recidivated sooner that whites, men sooner than women, and young offenders sooner than old offenders. Offenders who had prior jail or prison commitments recidivated sooner than offenders with prior convictions but no incarcerations, and they in turn recidivated earlier than offenders with no prior convictions. Offenders who had a known heroin/opiate dependence[16] recidivated sooner than those who did not. There was some tendency toward specialization: offenders who had been convicted of a violent crime or robbery prior to being released from prison were somewhat more likely to recidivate for robbery or assault than for some other crime.

Rhodes did not report the predictive accuracy of his regressions using violence as the criterion variable. However, the statistics presented permit determining his predictions' ability to distinguish between those who will and those who will not be arrested for violent crimes. Within a five-year follow-up period, the average offender (a hypothetical offender who has the mean value for all predictor variables) has a .03 probability of being arrested for a violent crime. Consider an offender who appears to be unlikely to recidivate: Caucasian, female, age 45, no prior convictions other than her federal conviction for selling drugs, not addicted to opiates, and employed at the time of her federal conviction. Her probability of being arrested for a violent crime during the five years is almost zero. Consider an offender who appears likely to recidivate: black, male, age 20, two incarcerations prior to his current federal conviction for robbery, four prior convictions not resulting in incarceration, drug dependence, under supervision at the time of this federal conviction, and unemployed at the time of this federal conviction. His probability of being arrested for a violent crime within five years is about .50.

These statistics seem to indicate that violent recidivists can be distinguished from nonviolent recidivists (and from nonrecidivists in general) with at least modest accuracy. However, the illustration exaggerates the strength of this prediction instrument because the hypothetical offenders used in the illustration are extremes.

Rhodes also ran separate regressions in which an arrest for robbery and an arrest for assault were the dependent variables (unpublished). These clarified the above results by showing there was a slight tendency for offenders who had been incarcerated for assault to commit an assault in the future, and for offenders who had been incarcerated for robbery to commit a robbery in the future.

Weiner (no date) Weiner used a failure-time model to assess violent recidivism among 1,355 boys in Philadelphia who had at least one prior police contact for a crime of violence. Weiner's data comprised three overlapping samples of boys, all of whom were born in 1958, resided continuously in Philadelphia from their tenth to their eighteenth birthdays, and had police contacts between their tenth and eighteenth birthdays. The first sample (very violent) had 1,084 observations; the second (violent) had 1,323; and the third (participated in illegal acts) had 1,100. The total sample size was 1,355.

"Very violent" delinquents were those youths who participated in at least one UCR violent index offense: criminal homicide, forcible rape, robbery, or aggravated assault. "Violent" delinquents met the criterion for a very violent delinquent or had a UCR violent nonindex offense (these include simple assault and sex offenses other than forcible rape). The third sample consisted of youths who had "participated in illegal acts in which at least one victim sustained an injury, ranging in seriousness from minor harm or treatment and discharge by a physician to hospitalization or death." Despite the different definitions, these samples were very similar, and Weiner's analysis was robust with respect to the three definitions of violence.

Data were drawn from rap sheets prepared by the Juvenile Aid Division of the Philadelphia police, police investigation reports, police arrest reports, family court records, and the census.

Weiner fit his regressions using three different failure-time distributions: Weibull, log-normal, and log-logistic. He reports that the distributional assumptions made little difference, but that the Weibull distribution provided a somewhat better fit than the other two.

Weiner used a stratified stepwise procedure to estimate his models. Twenty-one personal and delinquency history factors were grouped subjectively into four sets of decreasingly "acceptable" categories for making predictions. (Race, for example, was a member of the least acceptable category.) In the analysis, all the variables in the most acceptable category were considered for inclusion in the statistical model prior to stepping through the variables in the second group and so on.

This estimating procedure was applied separately to different violent "transitions." That is, Weiner initially examined the time from the first violent event to the second violent event, where the second event was considered censored when only one violent event had been observed prior to the subject's eighteenth birthday. Then he examined the second transition, that is, the time from the second violent event to the third, and so on. Results were reported separately for these different transitions.

Weiner found that few factors were useful in predicting recidivism. He reports that the instantaneous failure rate (the recidivism hazard) seemed to decrease over time for blacks, but not for whites. Given the unmeasured heterogeneity in these data, however, this decrease may be an artifact (see Heckman and Singer, 1985), as Weiner (no date:216) was aware.

Weiner (no date:207, 208) reports that blacks are more likely to recidivate than whites; however, few other patterns seemed to emerge:

> That several risk factors consistently failed to achieve statistical and substantive significance also bears noting: Neither the type nor gravity of a youngster's present offense, nor a selected of-

fense aggravation component, the presence of a weapon, was significant. Nor did several indices of the types and severities of the justice system response to the youngster achieve significance, such as the presence of prior UCR index offenses for which the youngster was adjudicated delinquent, the total seriousness of those offenses, and the presence of prior commitments to secure and nonsecure facilities for UCR index offenses. The extent and gravity of a youth's serious delinquent history was similarly nonsignificant. Age also failed to exhibit a relationship to recidivistic timing, including the ages at the first and last prior delinquent incident.

Consistent, then, with other research, prediction of dangerous conduct, whether assaultive or threatening, remains elusive.

A major problem with this analysis is its handling of incarceration that occurs after the first violent crime in a transition. Weiner was unable to collect data about the length of time that an offender was confined during the follow-up period, so the variable "time until recidivism for a violent crime" was likely to be measured with considerable error. Weiner (no date: 318-325) was aware of this problem and attempted to control for its effect. Although he did not know the length of time that an offender had been confined, he did know whether the youth had been confined for some period of time. Consequently, Weiner entered a dichotomous variable into his regressions whenever he had evidence that incarceration had occurred sometime during the follow-up.

It is not clear what type of a statistical model can be developed to justify the introduction of the variable "occurrence of incarceration" as an independent variable. After all, as is true of violent recidivism, a future period of incarceration is an endogenous variable. Using this endogenous variable as an explanatory variable would seem to produce biased parameter estimates. Nevertheless, it is unlikely that even this problem could have hidden a strong correlation between violence and a subject's background. Based on Weiner's analysis, we can say with some confidence that within this set of data, the ability to predict the timing of repeated violence is at best low.

Rate of Violence Models

Some researchers have attempted to predict violence by using as a dependent variable the number of violent events per time at risk (i.e., time not incarcerated) or some variant (e.g., number of events weighted by some severity index). Such studies are reviewed in this section.

Dembo and Colleagues (1991) Dembo et al. (1991) report on violent behavior during a one-year follow-up of boys who had been detained in a regional detention center in Tampa, Florida. Initial interviews were conducted with 399 boys. Of these, 305 were reinterviewed, but only 201 had been at risk of recidivism prior to the reinterview (they were either in the community at the time of the reinterview or recently detained). These 201 youths were the focus of this study.

Dembo and colleagues constructed an index of violent recidivism, which was a composite score of the following behaviors:

- Carried a hidden weapon other than a plain pocketknife
- Attacked someone with the idea of seriously hurting or killing him
- Had been involved in gang fights
- Hit (or threatened to hit) a teacher or other adult at school
- Hit (or threatened to hit) parents
- Hit (or threatened to hit) other students
- Had (or tried to have) sexual relations with someone against that person's will
- Used force (strong-arm methods) to get money or things from other students
- Used force (strong-arm methods) to get money or things from a teacher or other adult at school
- Used force (strong-arm methods) to get money or things from other people (not students or teachers)

Crimes against persons, as so defined, occurred frequently. At the time of the initial interview, only 24 percent of boys and girls reported no violent acts; 38 percent reported 1-4 acts; and another 25 percent reported 5-29 acts. At follow-up, violence was somewhat less frequent: 46 percent reported no violent acts; 27 percent reported 1-4 violent acts, and 20 percent reported 5-25 violent acts. Although the particulars are not reported for the composite score, it is apparent that the least harmful violent acts constitute most of this measure.

Youths were at risk for varying lengths of time during the follow-up period. Consequently, the authors controlled for time at risk by dividing the reported acts of violence by time not incarcerated, and the rates were then annualized. Finally, a log transform was applied, with the rate zero transformed to –1.

The dependent variable was regressed against several independent variables: age, race, gender, occupational status of the household head, recency and number of days in the previous month used alcohol, lifetime reported use of cocaine, an index for physical abuse, lifetime reported use of marijuana/hashish, an index of sexual victimization, urine test for cannabinoids, urine test for cocaine, emotional/psychological index, number of previous referrals for crimes against persons, placement in detention for crimes against persons, and self-reported crimes against persons. All variables were measured at the time of the initial interview and refer to the period just before that interview.

Only three variables were statistically significant. Violence decreased with age, increased with the abuse of alcohol, and increased with the number of self-reported crimes against persons prior to the follow-up period. Notably, violence was not predicted by the following: physical abuse, sexual abuse, drug test results, and official record of violence.

The regression predicted 23 percent of the variance in the dependent variable. Given that there were 15 independent variables and only 201 observations, significant shrinkage is likely.

Menzies, Webster, and Sepejak (1985) These researchers report on a study of recidivism among 211 patients interviewed in a pretrial forensic clinic. Two raters, who observed interviews at the forensic clinic, scored each of the subjects using the researches' Dangerous Behavior Rating Scheme (DBRS). Subjects were unaware of the raters.

Fifteen items of the DBRS were used to predict dangerousness. In addition, these fifteen items were factor analyzed, yielding four factors with eigenvalues greater than 1.0 that collectively accounted for more than 72 percent of the variance in the independent variables.

To construct a dependent variable, "for each patient a profile was constructed cataloging all (not only violent) officially recorded transactions during the two year follow-up . . . . Subsequently, these outcome danger profiles were quantified by rating the behaviors of subjects on an 11-point scale . . . . For this purpose, nine independent judges were used to assign 'danger outcome scores' to each patient" (Menzies et al., 1985:59-61). The scores were averaged across the judges, and subjects with no official incidents were assigned a score of zero.

Menzies et al. (1985:61) report that "the aggregate index of all four factors produces the most accurate prediction of dangerous behavior . . . . This complex weighing of 15 items still only accounts for 12 percent of the variance in followup violence."

Individual items with the highest Pearson product moment correlation were, in the following order, tolerance, capacity for empathy, capacity for change, and hostility. The authors do not define these terms in the text.

A serious problem is that the criterion variable was a composite of violent acts that were committed by people who, during the follow-up period, spent different times in prison, in hospitals, and on the street.[16] With such a criterion variable, it is impossible to disentangle the propensity toward violent behavior from adjustments to different institutional settings. Compounding this problem is the fact that selection into a prison setting, a hospital setting, or the community is not randomly applied to the subjects.

Farrington (1989) There appear to be few studies of early predictors of violence (Loeber and Stouthamer-Loeber, 1987). One exception is a study by Farrington of 411 London males whose criminal careers were followed for 24 years, from age 8 until age 32. The sample consisted of all boys in primary schools within a mile radius of the research office. Multiple interviews were conducted: The boys were interviewed when they were ages 8, 10, 14, 18, 21, 25, and 32; the boys' parents were interviewed yearly from the time the boys were age 8 until they were age 14-15; teachers completed questionnaires about the boys when the boys were 10, 12, and 14. The boys' official criminal records were collected throughout the 24 years.

Response rates were high. By the time the subjects were 32, interviews or questionnaires with either the subject or a proxy (such as a spouse) were completed for 94 percent of the sample.

Farrington predicted violence at four distinct points in time. The definition of violence differed at each time. "Adolescent aggression at age 12-14" was a scale developed from teachers' responses characterizing the boy as "disobedient, difficult to discipline, unduly rough during playtime, quarrelsome and aggressive, overcompetitive with other children, and unduly resentful of criticism or punishment." Teachers identified 134 boys as aggressive. "Teenage violence at age 16-18" was a scale "derived from self-reports . . . of getting into fights, starting fights, carrying and using weapons, and fighting police officers." The scale identified 119 violent males. "Adult violence at age 32" was defined as "admitting having gotten into a fight in the last five years." By this definition, 140 males were so identified. "Convictions for violence between ages 10 and 32" was the last category of violence. Fifty males had been convicted.

The predictor and criterion variables were not used in their natural scale. Rather, according to Farrington (1989:84), "each predictor and criterion variable was dichotomized, as far as possible, into the 'worst' quarter versus the remaining 3/4 of the sample." The author claims that this procedure did not lose much information, while statistics became easier to interpret.

Farrington presents both bivariate results and the forward stepwise discriminate analysis discussed here. The results demonstrate that variables describing a child's formative years can be used to predict violence during that child's youth and adult years. Some predictors would be recognized by lay persons as signs that a child has not adjusted well to school—poor attendance, behavioral problems, low academic ability, low attainment, and early dropout. Other predictors include general tendencies toward delinquent activity (hostility toward police, delinquent activities, and delinquent friends); the child's family situation (low income, authoritarian parents, and detached parents); observations of "high daring," "high aggressiveness," or "nervousness and withdrawal" by teachers and others; and the child's size and intelligence. In general, the particular variables that are pertinent vary at different times in the child's life.

Malamuth (1986) Malamuth reported on a self-report study of sexual aggression among 155 male volunteers (80 percent were college students.) The volunteers were asked to respond to a scale of sexual aggression developed by Koss and Oros (1982). Malamuth (1986:956) does not provide details of this scale in his study but states, "It assesses a continuum of sexual aggression including psychological pressure, physical coercion, attempted rape, and rape."

As explanatory variables, Malamuth uses the following: a measure of dominance as a sexual motive, a scale of hostility toward women, a scale that measured attitudes facilitating violence (Acceptance of Interpersonal Violence), a measure of antisocial characteristics, and sexual experience. A measure of sexual arousal in response to rape and to mutually consenting depictions was assessed for a subset of 95 volunteers by using penile tumescence as a gauge of arousal.

Using multiple linear regression to analyze sexual aggression among the 155 volunteers produced an r^2 of .30. All variables except the antisocial characteristics variable were significant at

.06. Using all-subsets regression methods, Malamuth added three interaction terms to his model. The r^2 increased to .453, and the variable dominance as sexual motive was no longer significant. Covariance tests indicated that sexual arousal in response to rape increased the model's explanatory power.

A related study by Ageton (1983), as reviewed by Malamuth (1988:475), found the following:

> [Ageton] . . . conducted a longitudinal study to gauge the extent to which a variety of measures including those reflecting general delinquency, attitudes about rape, and sex-role stereotyping predicted sexual aggression. Subjects, 11 to 17 years old drawn from a representative national sample, were interviewed in several consecutive years during the late 1970s. Ageton found that the general delinquency factors, such as peer support for antisocial behavior, were highly predictive of sexual assault. Attitudes regarding rape also enabled some discrimination between sexual aggressors vs nonaggressors, but sex-role stereotyping did not. She suggested that the same set of factors explains sexual assault and other delinquent behaviors.

Furby, Weinrott, and Blackshaw (1989) We reviewed no studies predicting recidivism among sex offenders. The following conclusions are from a comprehensive review of 42 selected studies by Furby et al. (1989:22, 25, 27):

- With such variability among study results, it is difficult to make any meaningful statement about the number of sex offenders who continue to commit sex offenses.
- We can at least say with confidence that no evidence exists that treatment effectively reduces sex offense recidivism.
- There is some evidence that recidivism rates may be different for different types of offenders. Those trends must be viewed as only tentative conclusions, which are based on patterns we identified across varied (and sometimes few) studies, each with its own flaws.

Garrison (1984) Among the studies that we examined, one by Garrison was unique in that it examined the events that precipitated violence. Garrison examined violent behavior among 100 males, aged 7-15, who were being treated in a psychiatric treatment facility. Over a two-year period, these children engaged in 1,038 incidents of observed, interpersonal aggression during the five hours per week that they were expected to participate in educational and social activities. Violence was defined as "intense physical attacks on other persons." Participant observers also recorded the timing, location, antecedents, choice of victim (staff or patient), objects used, immediate consequences, and staff observations regarding the presence or absence of external provocation. Antecedents were "external provocation, no external provocation, and unable to report." Victim status was "staff, peer, and combination."

Logistic regression was used to analyze the data. From this limited variable set, the author reports statistical significance among the following variables: antecedent, age group, and victim status. It is unclear why victim status was included as an independent variable, because this would seem to be a variable of choice. Garrison (1984:233) reports that the model's fit was "rather low" and that "a prediction table which employed these 1038 incidents to assess the utility of the model showed overall prediction to be only marginally better than that expected by chance."

ACCURACY OF PREDICTION

Although we could apply formal statistics, such as RIOC (Farrington and Loeber, 1989) to summarize the predictive power of the regressions that were reported above, there is little reason to do so. It is apparent that violence can be "predicted," but that for even the most recidivistic offenders, violence is less likely to occur than to not occur.

Moreover, RIOC tells only part of the story. The important question is what level of accuracy can be achieved when predicting who will and who will not be violent. However, statistical analyses generally involve officially recorded violence such as arrests and hospitalizations. Typically, we might find that for a designated class of subjects, the probability of violence, as so measured, is .3-.5. Whether such predictions are accurate or inaccurate cannot be determined from calculating a statistic such as RIOC. Instead, when interpreting accuracy, we are required to make many "leaps of faith." How likely is it that an act of violence will lead to an official record of its occurrence? How likely is it that the probability of detection is uniform across a population of subjects? Because we are interested in actual violence, not violence as revealed through officially recorded incidents, answering these questions is inescapable when judging predictive accuracy. At this time, only subjective impressions and some imprecise statistics (Blumstein et al., 1985) provide guidance. Although RIOC and similar measures give an aura of precision and science, such precision may be illusionary.

There are other problems with applying formal measures of predictive accuracy to the above studies. The criterion variable changes markedly across these studies. There are major differences in the definition of violence, in the periods during which violence might occur, in the settings in which violence might occur, in the precision with which violence is measured, in the numbers and types of explanatory variables available to the researcher, and in the availability and size of validation samples. It is not possible to make credible comparisons of statistical measures of association in the face of this diversity.

Still another problem with using measures of association to compare predictions is that any measure of association depends on the population to which it is applied. It would seem that the best way to compare the accuracy of prediction across instruments would be to use a common population (see Cohen and Zimmerman, 1990), but this raises other complications. Suppose that prediction instrument A was developed in a population X that had no variation in variable z. Then z would not appear as a predictor within population X and, of course, would not be used when predicting in population Y, despite the fact that z may in fact distinguish between those who are violent and those who are not.

Further, predictions of violent behavior are confounded with the contamination of public policy. Transporting predictions across settings where policy responses differ is not a good test of the predictors. Indeed, because public responses to violence are never absent, there may be no way to validate an instrument directly (Rhodes, 1985). As we argue above, it is important to distinguish the behavioral elements of violence from the public response elements. Most studies of violence do not allow these distinctions to be made.

SUMMARY OF OUR REVIEW OF THE PREDICTION OF VIOLENCE

1. Violence can be predicted, meaning that within a given population we can assign different probabilities of violence to population members based on the characteristics of those members. Furthermore, predictors have some roots in theory and have been replicated across studies conducted in diverse settings, leading us to believe that the predictors are manifestations of real behavior rather than pure artifacts of methodological limitations or social

responses to violence. Nevertheless, there are significant concerns with the validity, reliability, and accuracy of predictions of violence.

2. Some variables have consistently been shown to predict violent behavior. Other variables are strong in particular studies and often unmeasured in other studies. Variables that are commonly observed to predict violence, and variables that are predictive although infrequently used, provide guidance for conducting future prediction studies.

Family background variables appear to be valuable when predicting adult violence based on childhood records; they are of limited use in predicting repeated violence by adults. Criminal record variables are pertinent when predicting violent behavior within five years for offenders released from prison, but are of little use when predicting violence within a few weeks of release from a mental health clinic.

There is little doubt that criminal records (official or self-reported) are among the best predictors of violence, although there is some dispute about which aspects of criminal records have the greatest explanatory power. There is general agreement that violent offenders do not specialize in violence; nevertheless, past violence seems to be among the best predictors of future violence. There seems to be agreement that a propensity toward violence tends to be revealed prior to adulthood, but not all violent adults are known to be violent as children. There seems to be little doubt that drug involvement has some predictive power, although perhaps only for some forms of violence; the same may be true of alcohol consumption. Age, sex, and race are generally found to be predictive. Variables related to a child's development predict violence as a juvenile and as an adult. Variables such as family support can be useful when predicting violence. Although the nexus between violence and mental illness is nebulous, and it appears that health service professionals overpredict violence during clinical assessments, a history of hospitalizations has some predictive power as do some psychological scales that indicate a propensity toward violence. Violence during a period of hospitalization does not necessarily predict violence postrelease, however. The same is probably true of violence during periods of incarceration. Although the evidence from naturalistic settings is limited, biosocial variables seem to have strong predictive power.

3. Predictions are fairly accurate when violence during the short term is being predicted for a population whose past behaviors and current attitudes are well understood (e.g., people who

are admitted to a mental health clinic for recent violent behavior). Predictions may be tolerably good over a longer term among a heterogeneous population whose past behaviors and current attitudes are less well understood, provided we focus on predicting for a subset of that population (e.g., young bank robbers who have lengthy criminal records and a history of drug abuse). Predictions may be remarkably good when violent behavior is defined broadly, measured over a long period of time, and predicted from variables that reach deep into the subject's past (e.g., violence during the adult years, with early child development and delinquency used as predictors).

4. It is easier to predict repeat violence than to predict a subject's first violent act, because the best predictor of future violent behavior is past violent behavior. Given that most violent acts are not recorded in official records, we may never be able to develop predictions that do not suffer from a high proportion of false negatives.

RESEARCH AGENDA

One of our original goals for this review was to compare findings across studies and report the relative accuracy and strength of different types of factors for classification and prediction. However, the existing literature displayed so much diversity in regard to populations studied, techniques used in analysis, and measures used for validity and reliability that this comparison was not possible by using published data. Even if independent secondary data analysts could obtain the original source data for a large number of the studies, they would still be challenged to draw meaningful comparisons.

Nonetheless, it would be desirable to compare the relative strengths and reliability of different variables for classifying and predicting violence. We urge that a single study or a small number of studies be commissioned to collect data on a wide variety of types of independent variables discussed in this paper. Because biological variables appear very promising in regard to their accuracy in classification and prediction, we strongly suggest that the recommended comprehensive study or studies involve an interdisciplinary approach, including batteries of medical tests such as those used for classification on the physical disorder axis of DSM-III-R.

Secondarily, based on this review we would urge that situational variables be collected, quantified, and analyzed. Researchers have repeatedly found that classification and prediction models are not stable when applied in environments other than those in which they were developed. However, by learning which environmental factors most effect classification and prediction and by controlling for them, it may be possible to apply the same instruments across different situations. Moreover, and perhaps more important, if the situational factors that increased or decreased the probability of violent recidivism for specific types of violent persons were known, it would be possible to provide research-based policy recommendations for placement or treatment of violent persons. For example, if violent persons with certain types of brain dysfunctions were found to be more likely to recidivate in situations with a high level of sensory stimulation, a recommended treatment would be placement in a rural rather than an urban environment.

Although it may not be possible to compare previously published models across study populations, we do feel that considerable clarification of past findings could be achieved by secondary analysis that goes back to the raw data and defines comparable variables. More specifically, the definitions of outcome variables need to be standardized along the following dimensions:

- The length of time at risk (adjusting for social restraint)
- Specification of the *intended* period of prediction (short or long term)
- The extent of physical harm or potential harm associated with violent acts, if uninterrupted (e.g., distinguishing between an open-handed slap to an adult and bludgeoning with a blunt weapon)
- Specification of a relationship between the measure of violence and the actual violent behavior partially captured by the measure (e.g., adjusting for probabilities of police intervention, arrest, conviction, or self-initiated hospitalization).

Just as studies would be more comparable were the independent and criterion variables measured similarly, they would also be more comparable were statistical tools more uniformly applied. Failure-time models, occurrence models, and rate models—as defined above—are all appropriate for predicting violence, but "what" is being predicted differs so much that estimates based on one technique are difficult to compare with estimates based on another. Throughout this paper, we have emphasized the need for modeling to disentangle violent behavior from social restraints on violent behavior. We feel especially strongly that researchers should attempt to overcome censoring, selection bias, and variable length follow-up periods.

Finally, the field needs additional research on appropriate measures for statistically comparing the accuracy of predictive models. Although techniques described above have been developed for comparing the accuracy of models that divide individuals into groups (these may be classifications, or they may be predictions with cutoffs for "predicted violent" and "predicted nonviolent"), many researchers, including the authors, use these types of measures when the outcome variable being predicted is actually continuous. For example, use of the RIOC statistic requires turning a probabilistic prediction into a binary prediction by arbitrarily establishing a cutoff above which an individual is classified as violent. The literature is replete with discussions of the best or most appropriate way of establishing the cutoff, but obviously a great deal of information about the accuracy of the prediction model is being lost by summarizing the output set of probabilities into two categories.

Developing measures for comparing predictions that result in probabilistic statements is not easy for reasons explained above. Probabilistic predictions can be absolutely correct, but useless, if they are in a practical sense close to the base rate. Nonetheless, this appears to be a promising area for research.

POLICY IMPLICATIONS

Much of the research reported in this paper has been carried out in response to the need to inform policy. Practitioners need relatively quick, simple ways to decide whether a person is violent and, if so, whether treatment or special supervision is necessary. Ironically, there is a mismatch between what models can do and what we intend for them to do. Much research has been carried out to provide the types of answers we are least capable of accurately giving—unidimensional yes or no categorizations. Perhaps it is time to tell practitioners about our most accurate classification and prediction tools, and help them shape policy based on what can been done, rather than the other way around.

The types of predictions and classifications that can now be carried out most accurately are *multidimensional, probabilistic,* and *short-term.* No one can apply any known instrument to any given population and say with confidence whether or not a particular individual will commit a future violent act. However, following Gottfredson and Gottfredson (1988a), it is currently possible to give practitioners instruments to assess the *relative risks of a specific person in a specific population* being a particular type of violent offender and committing future crimes, but practitioners as the public's representatives must define the *stakes*—and make decisions based on both the probabilistic risks and the stakes. A benefit-cost analysis is an inescapable aspect of judging the adequacy of violence prediction, but when the benefits and costs are so elusive, the analysis is outside the realm of science and is appropriately in the domain of politics and public policy.

Obviously practitioners should not be expected to look at models with numerous Greek letters and parameters and then apply them correctly, but by refining instruments that help assess violent persons probabilistically along several dimensions, behavioral and medical scientists can help shape practices that consider a variety of options for dealing with violent persons rather than a simple choice of two alternatives. For example, a person with a high probability of violence related to an organic disorder but low probability of violence related to alcoholic drinking, social stress, or other factors may be a good candidate for home placement with appropriate medication and frequent medical tests, whereas a person with a moderate probability of violence related to multiple factors (social, psychological, substance abuse, and post-traumatic stress) may be a better candidate for a treatment program inside a prison setting.

It is important not only to consider risks and stakes, but also to consciously develop a wider range of options for dealing with persons classified as or predicted to be violent. Research on classification and prediction can then be more easily focused on choosing among realistic options, which will help produce results and findings that are more immediately applicable by practitioners.

NOTES

1   However, this is, in some sense, also a subgroup.

2   The distinction between case management and prediction is illustrated by the work of Megargee et al. (1988). They specifically deny that their classifications of offenders based on Minnesota Multiphasic Personality Inventory test results can be useful for predicting future violence, while at the same time they demonstrate that a reduction in the occurrence of assaults within institutions can be achieved by segregating offenders whose classification is "predatory" from those classified as likely victims of assault.

3   Megargee (1977) includes these three qualities in a list of desirable features of a classification system. Also included in the list are comprehensiveness, cost-effectiveness, and potential to reflect changes over time.

4   Dichotomous items are those having only two possible alternative responses.

5   When the separation between test and retest is as long as months or years, the comparison of test with retest is more pertinent to the temporal stability of the behavior being measured than to the reliability of the measurement instruments.

6   Tay-Sachs disease is a fatal genetic disorder that is not apparent by outward physical signs at birth. If *both* parents are carriers of the recessive gene, there is a 25 percent chance that a pregnancy will result in a Tay-Sachs baby. The blood level of the enzyme hexosaminidase A is depressed in Tay-Sachs carriers and zero in an affected person. By testing both parents' blood, it is possible to determine if both are carriers; if so, amniocentesis or other means of sampling fetal tissue permits determining with certainty whether the fetus will develop Tay-Sachs disease.

7   For an example of prosecuting attorneys' classifying defendants in the context of the local district attorney's office policy, see Chaiken and Chaiken (1987, 1990b).

8   There were an additional 15 reports of neglect and 16 reports of failure to thrive, but we do not consider these.

9   We would like to thank Joel Garner, then at the National Institute of Justice, for preparing this literature search of titles related to violence.

10   Alternatively, the prediction might be made conditional on a specific form of social constraint, such as intensive parole supervision or weekly reporting to a mental health clinic.

11   In predicting violence, one is not uninterested in social responses and whether they control or fail to control violent behavior, but it is important to distinguish the behavior itself from the effectiveness of social control. One cannot judge the effectiveness of variations in social control without independent measures of the rate at which violence would have occurred in the absence of social controls. Furthermore, development of the theory of violent behavior is retarded if empirical studies of violence are muddied with the effects of social controls of criminal behavior.

12   Goldstein (1989) advances three explanations for the relationship between drugs and violence. Drugs may have a pharmacological effect that precipitates violence; violence may be instrumental as part of property crimes committed to get funds for drug

purchases; or violence may be a systemic part of the drug distribution business.

13 From the context, we infer that the low glucose nadir indicates an abnormality in the physiological processes that keep blood sugar concentration in a normal steady state, for example, a defective system of glycogen conversion to glucose in the liver due to cirrhosis or other disease. In this case, cerebral function would be impaired in turn, because brain cells could not adequately store glucose or utilize other forms of nutrients for energy.

14 The signs of the coefficients for rape were consistent with the hypothesis that the probability of an arrest for violence decreased with age. The failure to find the difference to be statistically significant might be explained partly by the small sample size—277 for rape compared to 1,104 for robbery and 2,083 for assault.

15 The derivative of the logistic regression, when evaluated at the mean, indicates that subjects who suffered physical abuse as children were .08 more likely than others to commit violent acts, and that subjects who suffered neglect as children were .05 more likely than others to commit violent acts.

16 Other drug use was not recorded for this 1979 cohort.

17 The distribution of street time was reported as 20 or more months spent in the community ($N = 110$), 12 or more months in prison ($N = 35$), 12 or more months in a psychiatric hospital ($N = 13$), and a mixture of institutional conditions ($N = 45$).

REFERENCES

Ageton, G.
   1983 *Sexual Assault Among Adolescents.* Lexington, Mass: Heath.
Altschuler, D., and P. Brounstein
   1989 Patterns of Drug Use, Drug Trafficking, and Other Delinquency Among Inner City Adolescents in Washington, D.C. Paper presented at the annual meeting of the American Society of Criminology, Reno, Nevada, November.
American Psychiatric Association
   1987 *Diagnostic and Statistical Manual of Mental Disorders*, Third Edition-Revised. Washington, D.C.: American Psychiatric Association.
Ayoub, C., M.M. Jacewitz, R.G. Gold, and J.S. Milner
   1983 Assessment of a program's effectiveness in selecting individuals "at risk" for problems in parenting. *Journal of Clinical Psychology* 39:334-339.

Baum, M.S.
    1981 Effectiveness of the Megarege typology in predicting violent be-
          havior. Doctoral dissertation, University of California, Santa
          Barbara. (*Dissertation Abstracts International* 42/04H:1804.
          University Microfilms No. DEN81-20741.)
Belenko, S., K. Chin, and J. Fagan
    1989 Typologies of Criminal Careers Among Crack Arrestees. Paper
          presented at the annual meeting of the American Society of
          Criminology, Reno, Nevada, November.
Black, T., and P. Spinks
    1985 Predicting outcomes of mentally disordered and dangerous of-
          fenders. In D. Farrington and R. Tarling, eds., *Prediction in
          Criminology*. Albany: State University of New York Press.
Butcher, J.N., and L.S. Keller
    1984 Objective personality assessment. Pp. 307-331 in G. Goldstein
          and M. Hersen, eds., *Handbook of Psychological Assessment*.
          New York: Pergamon Press.
Chaiken, J., and M. Chaiken
    1982 *Varieties of Criminal Behavior*. Santa Monica, Calif.: The
          RAND Corporation.
    1990a Drug use and predatory crime. Pp. 203-209 in J.Q. Wilson and
          M. Tonry, eds., *Drugs and Crime*. Vol. 13 of *Crime and Justice:
          A Review of Research*. Chicago: University of Chicago Press.
Chaiken, M.
    1983 *Crime Rates and Substance Abuse Among Types of Offenders*.
          New York: The Interdisciplinary Research Center, Narcotic
          and Drug Research, Inc.
    1990 *Community or Individual Factors: What Matters More for Se-
          rious Criminal Behavior and Frequency of Arrest?* Final report
          for grant 88-IJ-CX-0022 submitted to the National Institute of
          Justice.
Chaiken, M., and J. Chaiken
    1987 *Selecting "Career Criminals" for Priority Prosecution*. NCJ 106310.
          Washington, D.C.: National Institute of Justice.
    1990b *Redefining the Career Criminal: Priority Prosecution of High-
          Rate Dangerous Offenders*. NCJ 124136. Washington, D.C.:
          National Institute of Justice.
Chaiken, M.R., and B.D. Johnson
    1988 *Characteristics of Different Types of Drug-Involved Offenders*.
          Washington, D.C.: National Institute of Justice.
Clements, C.B.
    1986 *Offender Needs Assessment*. College Park, Md.: American
          Correctional Association.
Cocozza, J., and H. Steadman
    1974 Some refinements in the measurement and prediction of dan-
          gerous behavior. *American Journal of Psychiatry* 131(9):1012-
          1014.

Cohen, J., and S.E. Zimmerman
1990 *Improved Techniques for Assessing the Accuracy of Recidivism Prediction Scales.* Pittsburgh, Pa.: School of Urban and Public Affairs, Carnegie-Mellon University.

Collins, J.
1989 Alcohol and interpersonal violence: Less than meets the eye. In N. Weiner and M. Wolfgang, eds., *Pathways to Criminal Violence.* Newbury Park, Calif.: Sage Publications.

Cook, P., and D. Nagin
1979 *Does the Weapon Matter?* Washington, D.C.: INSLAW.

Copas, J.B.
1983 Regression prediction and shrinkage. *Journal of the Royal Statistical Society* 129:311-354.

Copas, J., and R. Tarling
1986 Some methodological issues in making predictions. In J. Roth and C. Visher, eds., *Criminal Careers and "Career" Criminals.* Washington, D.C.: National Academy Press.

Corcoran, K., and J. Fischer
1987 *Measures for Clinical Practice: A Sourcebook.* New York: Free Press.

Cronbach, L.J.
1951 Coefficient alpha and the internal structure of tests. *Psychometrika* 16:297-334.

Dembo, R., L. Williams, A. Getreu, L. Genung, J. Schmeidler, E. Berry, E. Wish, and L. LaVoie
1991 A longitudinal study of the relationship among marijuana/hashish use, cocaine use and delinquency in a cohort of high risk youths. *Journal of Drug Issues* 21(2):271-312.

Elliott, D.S., D. Huiziuga, and S. Menard
1989 *Multiple Problem Youth: Delinquency, Drugs, and Mental Health Problems.* New York: Springer-Verlag.

Fagan, J., and J.G. Weis
1990 *Drug Use and Delinquency Among Inner City Youth.* New York: Springer-Verlag.

Fagan, J., E. Piper, and M. Moore
1986 Violent delinquents and urban youths. *Criminology* 24(3):439-470.

Farrington, D.
1989 Early predictors of adolescent aggression and adult violence. *Violence and Victims* 4(2):79-100.

Farrington, D., and R. Loeber
1989 Relative improvement over chance (RIOC) and phi as measures of predictive efficiency and strength of association in 2X2 tables. *Journal of Quantitative Criminology* 5(3):201-214.

Flinn, C.
1986 Dynamic models of criminal careers. Pp. 356-379 in J. Roth and

C. Visher, eds., *Criminal Careers and "Career Criminals."* Washington, D.C.: National Academy Press.

Fox, J.A., and J. Levin
1994 *Overkill: Mass Murder and Serial Killing Exposed.* New York: Plenum.

Furby, L., M. Weinrott, and L. Blackshaw
1989 Sex offender recidivism. *Psychological Bulletin* 105(1):3-30.

Garrison, W.
1984 Predicting violent behavior in psychiatrically hospitalized boys. *Journal of Youth and Adolescence* 13(3):225-238.

Gelles, R.J., and M.A. Straus
1988 *Intimate Violence.* New York: Simon and Schuster.

Gibbons, D.C.
1975 Offender typologies—Two decades later. *British Journal of Criminology* 15(2):140-156.

Glaser, D.
1964 *The Effectiveness of a Prison and Parole System.* New York: Bobbs-Merrill.

Goffman, E.
1959 *The Presentation of Self in Everyday Society.* Garden City, N.Y.: Doubleday.
1963 *Stigma.* Englewood Cliffs, N.J.: Prentice-Hall.

Golden, C.J., R.F. Sawicki, and M.D. Franzen
1984 Test construction. Chapter 2 in G. Goldstein and M. Herson, eds., *Handbook of Psychological Assessment.* New York: Pergamon Press.

Goldstein, P.
1989 Drugs and violent crime. In N. Weiner and M. Wolfgang, eds., *Pathways to Criminal Violence.* Newbury Park, Calif.: Sage Publications.

Gottfredson, D., and S. Gottfredson
1988a Stakes and risks in the prediction of violent criminal behavior. *Violence and Victims* 3(4):247-262.

Gottfredson, S., and D. Gottfredson
1988b Violence prediction methods: Statistical and clinical strategies. *Violence and Victims* 3(4):303-324.

Hare, R.D.
1979 Biological and behavioral correlates of criminal psychopathy. In L. Beliveau et al., eds., *Research on Diagnoses and Treatment.* Montreal: International Centre for Comparative Criminology.

Hathaway, S.R., and J.C. McKinley
1940 A multiphasic personality schedule (Minnesota): I. Construction of the scale. *Journal of Psychology* 10:294-354

Heckman, J.
1979 Sample selection bias as a specification error. *Econometrica* 47:153-161.

Heckman, J., and B. Singer
  1985 *Longitudinal Analysis of Labor Market Data.* Cambridge: Cambridge University Press.
Holden, R.
  1985 Failure time models for thinned crime commission data. *Sociological Methods and Research* 14(1):3-30.
Holland, T., N. Holt, and G. Beckett
  1982 Prediction of violent versus nonviolent recidivism from prior violent and nonviolent criminality. *Journal of Abnormal Psychology* 91(3):178-182.
Holmes, R.M.
  1989 *Profiling Violent Crimes: An Investigative Tool.* Newbury Park, Calif.: Sage.
Howell, M., and K. Pugliesi
  1988 Husbands who harm: Predicting spousal violence by men. *Journal of Family Violence* 3(1):15-27.
Irwin, J.
  1970 *The Felon.* Englewood Cliffs, N.J.: Prentice-Hall.
Johnson, B.D., P. Goldstein, E. Preble, J. Schmeidler, D.S. Lipton, B. Spunt, and T. Miller
  1985 *Taking Care of Business: The Economics of Crime by Heroin Abusers.* Lexington Mass.: Lexington Books.
Kagan, J.
  1982 *Psychological Research on the Human Infant: An Evaluative Study.* New York: William T. Grant Foundation.
Kalbfleish, J., and R. Prentice
  1980 *The Statistical Analysis of Failure Time Data.* New York: John Wiley & Sons.
Kennedy, T.
  1986 Trends in inmate classification: A status report of two computerized psychometric approaches. *Criminal Justice and Behavior* 13(2):165-184.
King, G.
  1988 Statistical models for political science event counts: Bias in conventional procedures and evidence for the Expontential Poisson Regression Model. *American Journal of Political Science* 32:838-863.
Klassen, D., and W. O'Connor
  1988a A prospective study of predictors of violence in adult male mental health admissions. *Law and Human Behavior* 12(2):143-158.
  1988b Crime, inpatient admissions, and violence among male mental patients. *International Journal of Law and Psychiatry* 11:305-312.
  1988c Predicting violence in schizophrenic and non-schizophrenic patients: A prospective study. *Journal of Community Psychology* 16:217-227.
  1989a Predictors of Violence: A Review. Paper presented at the Study

Group Meeting on Risk of the MacArthur Foundation Program of Research on Mental Health and the Law. Palm Beach, Florida, January.

1989b Assessing the risk of violence in released mental patients: A cross-validation study. *Psychological Assessment: A Journal of Consulting and Clinical Psychology* 1(2):75-81.

n.d. Predicting Violence in Mental Patients: Cross Validation of an Actuarial Scale. Unpublished paper, Greater Kansas City Mental Health Foundation.

Koss, M., and C. Oros
1982 Sexual experiences survey: A research instrument investigating sexual aggression and victimization. *Journal of Consulting and Clinical Psychology* 50:455-457.

Kuder, G.G., and M.W. Richardson
1937 The theory of estimation of test reliability. *Psychometrika* 2:151-160.

Levin, J., and J.A. Fox
1991 *Mass Murder: America's Growing Menace.* New York: Berkeley Books.

Lewis, D.O., and D.A. Balla
1976 *Delinquency and Psychopathology.* New York: Grune & Stratton.

Lindesmith, A.R., and A.L. Strauss
1968 *Social Psychology.* New York: Holt, Rinehart & Winston.

Loeber, R., and T. Dishion
1983 Early predictors of male delinquency: A review. *Psychological Bulletin* 94(1):68-99.

Loeber, R., and M. Stouthamer-Loeber
1987 Prediction. In H. Quay, ed., *Handbook of Juvenile Delinquency.* New York: John Wiley & Sons.

Maddala, G.
1983 *Limited-Dependent and Qualitative Variables in Econometrics.* Cambridge: Cambridge University Press.

Malamuth, N.
1986 Predictors of naturalistic sexual aggression. *Journal of Personality and Social Psychology* 50(5):953-962.

1988 Predicting laboratory aggression against females and males targets: Implications for sexual aggression. *Journal of Research in Personality* 22:474-495.

1989 The attraction to sexual aggression scale: Part one. *Journal of Sex Research* 26:26-49.

Maltz, M.
1984 *Recidivism.* New York: Academic Press.

Mann, F.C., J. Friedman, and A.S. Friedman
1976 Characteristics of self-reported violent offenders vs. court identified violent offenders. *International Journal of Criminology and Penology* 4:69-87.

Marquis, K.H., and P. Ebener
1981 *Quality of Prisoner Self-Reports: Arrest and Conviction Response Errors.* Santa Monica, Calif.: The RAND Corporation.

McConaughy, S.H., T.M. Achenbach, and C.L. Gent
1988 Multiaxial empirically based assessment: Parent, teacher, observations, cognitive and personality correlates of child behavior profiles for 6-11-year old boys. *Journal of Abnormal Child Psychology* 11:485-509.

McCord, W., and J. McCord, with I.K. Zola
1959 *Origins of Crime.* New York: Columbia University Press.

Mead, G.H.
1934 *Mind, Self and Society.* Chicago: University of Chicago Press.

Megargee, E.I.
1977 A classification system for male youthful offenders based on the MMPI. Pp. 35-60 in R.A. Keil, ed., *Mental Health for the Convicted Offender, Patient, and Prisoner.* Raleigh: North Carolina Department of Corrections.

Megargee, E.I., and M.J. Bohn
1979 *Classifying Criminal Behaviors.* Newbury Park, Calif.: Sage Publications.

Megargee, E.I., M.J. Bohn, and J.L. Carbonell
1988 A Cross-Validation and Test of the Generality of the MMPI-Based Offender Classification System. Unpublished manuscript, Florida State University, Tallahassee.

Menzies, R., and C. Webster
1989 Mental disorder and violent crime. In N. Weiner and M. Wolfgang, eds. *Pathways to Criminal Violence.* Newbury Park, Calif.: Sage Publications.

Menzies, R., C. Webster, and D. Sepajak
1985 The dimensions of dangerousness. *Law and Human Behavior* 9(1):49-70.

Mercy, J.A., and P.W. O'Carroll
1988 New directions in violence prediction: The public health arena. *Violence and Victims* 3(4):285-302.

Milner, J.
1980 *The Child Abuse Potential Inventory: Manual.* Webster, N.C.: Psytec Corporation.
1989 Additional cross-validation of the Child Abuse Potential Inventory. *Psychological Assessment: A Journal of Consulting and Clinical Psychology* 1:219-223.

Milner, J.S., and R. Wimberley
1979 An inventory for the identification of child abusers. *Journal of Clinical Psychology* 35:95-100.
1980 Prediction and explanation of child abuse. *Journal of Clinical Psychology* 35:875-884.

Milner, J., R. Gold, and R. Wimberley
1986 Prediction and explanation of child abuse: Cross validation of

the child abuse potential inventory. *Journal of Consulting Psychology* 54(6):865-866.

Milner, J.S., K.R. Robertson, and D.L. Rogers
1988 Childhood History of Abuse and Adult Abuse Potential. Paper presented at the meeting of the Midwester Psychological Association, Chicago.

Milner, J., R. Gold, C. Ayoub, and M. Jacewitz
1984 Predictive validity of the child abuse potential inventory. *Journal of Consulting and Clinical Psychology* 52(5):879-884.

Monahan, J.
1981 *Predicting Violent Behavior: An Assessment of Clinical Techniques.* Newbury Park, Calif.: Sage Publications.
1984 Prediction of violent behavior—Toward a second generation of theory and policy. *American Journal of Psychiatry* 141(1):10-15.

Moss, C., M. Johnson, and R. Hosford
1984 An assessment of the Megargee typology in lifelong criminal violence. *Criminal Justice and Behavior* 11(2):225-234.

Nurco, D., T. Hanlon, T. Kinlock, and K. Duszynski
1988 Differential criminal patterns of narcotic addicts over an addiction career. *Criminology* 26(3):407-423.

Rhodes, W.
1985 The adequacy of statistically derived prediction instruments in the face of sample selectivity. *Evaluation Review* 9:369-382.
1986 A survival model with dependent competing events and right-hand censoring: Probation and parole as an illustration. *Journal of Quantitative Criminology* 2(2):113-137.
1989 The criminal career: Estimates of the duration and frequency of crime commission. *Journal of Quantitative Criminology* 5(1):3-32.

Rivera, B., and C. Spatz Widom
1991 Childhood victimization and violent offending. *Violence and Victims* 5:19-35.

Robertson, K.R., and J.S. Milner
1985 Convergent and discriminant validity of the Child Abuse Potential Inventory. *Journal of Personality Assessment* 49:86-88.

Robins, L.N., and E. Wish
1977 Childhood deviance as a developmental process: A study of 223 urban black men from birth to 18. *Social Forces* 56(2):448-471.

Schmidt, P., and A. Witte
1988 *Predicting Recidivism Using Survival Models.* New York: Springer-Verlag.

Shaffer, J., D. Nurco, and T. Kinlock
1984 A new classification of narcotic addicts based on type and extent of criminal activity. *Comprehensive Psychiatry* 25(3).

Simcha-Fagan, O., and J.E. Schwartz
1986 Neighborhood and delinquency: An assessment of contextual effects. *Criminology* 24(4):667-695.
Snyder, H.N.
1988 *Court Careers of Juvenile Offenders.* Pittsburgh, Pa.: National Center for Juvenile Justice.
Spitzer, R.L., and J.B.W. Williams, eds.
1987 Introduction. Pp. xvii-xxvii in *Diagnostic and Statistical Manual of Mental Disorders*, Third Edition—Revised. Washington, D.C.: American Psychiatric Association.
Steadman, H.
1987 How well can we predict violence for adults? A review of the literature and some commentary. Pp. 5-17 in F. Dutile and C. Foust, eds., *The Prediction of Criminal Violence.* Springfield, Ill.: Charles C. Thomas.
Steadman, H., and J. Morrissey
1982 Predicting violent behavior: A note on a cross-validation study. *Social Forces* 61(2).
Toch, H., and K. Adams
1989 *The Disturbed Violent Offender.* New Haven, Conn.: Yale University Press.
Tracy, P., M. Wolfgang, and R. Figlio
1990 *Delinquency Careers in Two Birth Cohorts.* New York: Plenum Press.
Virkkunen, M., J. DeJong, J. Bartko, F. Goodwin, and M. Linnoila
1989a Relationship of psychobiological variables to recidivism in violence offenders and impulsive fire setters: A follow-up study. *Archives of General Psychiatry* 46:600-603.
1989b Psychobiological concomitants of history of suicide attempts among violent offenders and impulsive fire setters. *Archives of General Psychiatry* 46:604-606.
Weiner, N.
1989 Violent criminal careers and violent career criminals: An overview of the recent literature. Pp. 35-138 in *Violent Crime, Violent Criminals.* Newbury Park, Calif.: Sage Publications.
n.d. Violent Recidivism Among the 1958 Philadelphia Cohort Boys, Vol. I. Unpublished manuscript, Center for the Interdisciplinary Study of Criminal Violence, Sellin Center for Studies in Criminology and Criminal Law, The Wharton School, University of Pennsylvania, Philadelphia.
Weinstein, E.
1969 The development of interpersonal competence. Pp. 753-775 in D. Goslin, ed., *Handbook of Socialization Theory and Research.* Chicago: Rand McNally.
Widom, C.S.
1989a The intergenerational transmission of violence. In N. Weiner

and M. Wolfgang, eds., *Pathways to Criminal Violence.* Newbury Park, Calif.: Sage Publications.

1989a The cycle of violence. *Science* 244:160-166.

Williams, T.M., and W. Kornblum

1985 *Growing Up Poor.* Lexington, Mass.: Lexington Books.

Wolfgang, M., R. Figlio, and T. Sellin

1972 *Delinquency in a Birth Cohort.* Chicago: University of Chicago Press.

Incarceration and Violent Crime: 1965-1988

Jacqueline Cohen and José A. Canela-Cacho

Imprisonment rates in the United States changed dramatically from 1965 to 1988. Offenders in prison and incarceration rates per population first decreased during the late 1960s and have increased to record levels since the mid-1970s. Recent increases have continued unabated despite the severe pressures they have placed on strained prison capacities. For retributive as well as public protection reasons, the tendency in recent sentencing reforms has been to rely increasingly on longer and/or more certain incarceration terms.

This paper examines various aspects of the relationship between incarceration and levels of violent crime. We focus first on the nature of changes in the prison population from 1965 to 1988, particularly the role of incarceration for violent offenses in observed changes in the total prison population, and the relative contributions of sanction policies and levels of offending to changes in observed incarceration rates. We then explore the likely crime control effects of incarceration on levels of violent crime, espe-

Jacqueline Cohen is at the H. John Heinz III School of Public Policy and Management, Carnegie Mellon University. José Canela-Cacho is at the Graduate School of Public Policy, University of California, Berkeley.

cially the appropriateness of deterrence and incapacitation strategies as means for reducing violent offending.

Throughout the analysis, we limit consideration to incarceration in state prisons—the primary site for long-term institutionalization of violent offenders—and exclude local prisons and jails. When referring to violent offenses, we include murder (which usually includes nonnegligent homicide), aggravated assault, rape, and robbery. For purposes of comparison, we also analyze burglary and drug offenses, two nonviolent offenses that figure prominently in prison populations.[1] We rely primarily on annual data from 1965 to 1988 for selected states. State-level data are especially useful because they provide annual counts of both admissions to prison and resident populations disaggregated by crime type.

The analyses of prison populations are designed to answer three main questions:

(1) What is the contribution of incarceration for violent crimes to the changes over time in the total prison population?

(2) How have sanction policies regarding the certainty and severity of imprisonment for violent crimes changed over time?

(3) What is the contribution of changing sanction policies for violent crimes to changes in the size of the prison population?

With regard to the crime control effects of incarceration, we are especially concerned with examining whether incarceration is an effective strategy for controlling violent crimes and the merits of pursuing alternative incarceration policies.

DATA

In addition to national data, we obtained corrections data from the following states: California, Florida, Michigan, New York, Pennsylvania, and Texas.[2] These states were selected because they are geographically distributed in various regions of the United States, and together they comprised 38.5 percent of total prisoners under jurisdiction in state and federal institutions in 1988 (Bureau of Justice Statistics, 1990a). All of the states provided annual data on commitments to prison and average daily population (typically a one-day census of the resident inmate population) *disaggregated by crime type* and for the total over all crime types.[3]

The data for each state vary somewhat in the years covered. New York and California are the most complete, and cover the entire period from 1965 to 1988; the data for the remaining states

TABLE 1 State Corrections Data, 1965-1988:
Earliest Year Available for Residents and
Commitments to Prison by Crime Type

State	Residents	Commitments
California	1965	1965
Florida	1973	1965
Michigan	1973	1965
New York	1965	1965
Pennsylvania	1980	1974
Texas	1977	1977

NOTE: Corrections data end in 1987 for Michigan. Commitment data for drug offenses are not regarded as reliable for 1987 and 1988 in Florida (see note 4).

begin sometime during the 1970s and are usually more complete for commitments (see Table 1).

The data on inmates have been augmented by data on crimes reported to the police for each state available from the annual Uniform Crime Reports (UCR) published by the Federal Bureau of Investigation (FBI). We supplemented the regularly published crime data with state-level data obtained from the FBI on the numbers of total arrests and arrests of adults (age 18 or over) for each crime type for 1965 to 1988. The full data set potentially includes a maximum of 864 observations (6 states × 6 crimes × 24 years). The number of observations actually available was reduced to 723 after removing cases in which the data were obviously unreliable.[4]

PRISON POPULATIONS

Between 1975 and 1989 the total annual prison population of the United States grew from 240,593 to 679,263 inmates in custody, an increase of 182 percent. Certainly, some of this increase is due to increases in the general population over this period, and more particularly to increases in the size of the adult population. Nevertheless, the annual incarceration rate adjusted for total population rose 146 percent from 111.7 inmates per 100,000 population to a historical high of 274.4 over this same period, and the incarceration rate adjusted by adult population (age 18 or over) rose by 128 percent from 162.2 to 369.7 inmates per 100,000 adult population (Figure 1).[5] This increase is unprecedented in recent U.S. history,

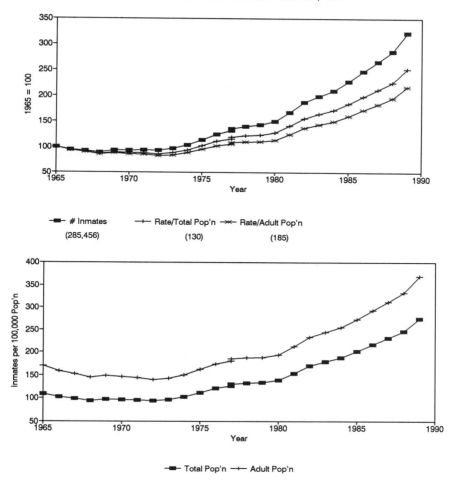

FIGURE 1 Incarceration in state and federal institutions in the United States, 1965-1989. Top. Inmate population rescaled with year 1965 = 100 (actual values for 1965 are in parentheses). Bottom. Incarceration rates.

and follows a period of relative stability in incarceration rates from 1945 to 1974 when the incarceration rate averaged 106 inmates per 100,000 total population, with a minimum rate of 93 in 1972 and a maximum rate of 119 in 1961 (Blumstein and Cohen, 1973).

The increases during the 1980s also exceed what were generally regarded as unrealistically high projections of prison populations obtained by simply extrapolating prevailing linear trends during the 1970s. The Abt Corporation's 1980 study of past prison populations in the United States (Mullen, 1980:96) was typical of a widely held view in its conclusion that

> although all prison population projections anticipate some further growth in the number of inmates in state custody, none call for continuation of the historically high rate of the mid-1970s.

In fact, as Table 2 reveals, the average annual growth from 1975 to 1980 of 5.5 percent in the number of inmates (3.7 percent in inmates per 100,000 adult population) was exceeded from 1980 to 1988, when the annual growth in the number of inmates averaged 8.0 percent (6.6% for inmates per adult population). Moreover, the one-year increase of 12.5 percent in the number of inmates in 1989 (11.3% in the rate per 100,000 adult population) was the largest increase ever.

These increases nationally are mirrored in individual states (Figure 2). By 1988 the incarceration rates, either per total population or per adult population, were close to or exceeded the corresponding national rates in five of the six states examined. Only Pennsylvania's rates remained less than 200 inmates per 100,000 population. The largest percentage increases from 1975 rates occurred in California (where the rate per total population increased more than 250%), New York (up 180%), and Pennsylvania (up 158% from 58 in 1975 to 149 in 1988). The increases in Florida and Texas were smaller, up about 60 percent from the already higher rates prevailing in those states in 1975. The six states examined are becoming more similar to one another in their incarceration rates: excluding Pennsylvania, the standard deviation in rates across the other five states drops from 33 percent of a mean rate of 120 in 1975 to only 6 percent of a mean rate of 257 in 1988.

Increases in crime—especially in violent crimes that are more likely to result in sentences to prison following conviction—are among the factors that may account for the recent rise in prison populations. Figure 3 shows the percentage of inmates incarcerated for individual crime types. Total U.S rates from the most recent 1986 inmate survey are contrasted with the corresponding range of rates found in the same year in the six study states. Although differing somewhat in absolute magnitude, the six states displayed the same relative prevalence of different crime types found in periodic national surveys of inmates in state prisons. Robbery and burglary are the most prevalent convicted offenses among resident inmates both in the United States and in indi-

UNDERSTANDING AND PREVENTING VIOLENCE

Volume 1

This landmark book offers a fresh, interdisciplinary approach to understanding and preventing interpersonal violence and its consequences. It explains how different processes interact to determine violence levels, what preventive strategies are suggested by our current knowledge, and the most critical research needs.
ISBN 0-309-04594-0; 1993, 480 pp, 6 x 9, index, hardbound with jacket, $49.95

Volume 2: Biobehavioral Influences

This volume reviews genetic contributions to the probability of violent and related behaviors; brain structure and functioning; the roles of hormonal and neurological interactions; the neurochemistry of violence and aggression and its implications for the management of those behaviors; and dietary influences.
ISBN 0-309-04649-1; 1994, 560 pp, 6 x 9, paper, $45.00

Volume 3: Social Influences

This volume examines how the risks of violent criminal offending and victimization are influenced by communities, social situations, and individuals; the role of spouses and intimates; the differences in violence levels between males and females; and the roles of psychoactive substances.
ISBN 0-309-05080-4; 1994, 592 pp, 6 x 9, paper, $45.00

Volume 4: Consequences and Control

This book analyzes public perceptions and reactions to violence; estimates of the costs; the commonalities and complementarities of criminal justice and public health responses; efforts to reduce violence through the prediction and classification of offenders; and the relationships between violence and prison population.
ISBN 0-309-05079-0; 1994, 408 pp, 6 x 9, paper, $39.00

4-volume set, $138.95 (save $40.00)
3-volume set (volumes 2-4), $99.00 (save $30.00)

ORDER CARD

UNDERSTANDING AND PREVENTING VIOLENCE

Use this card to order additional copies of the four volumes in the UNDERSTANDING AND PREVENTING VIOLENCE series described on the reverse. All orders must be prepaid. Please add $4.00 for shipping and handling for the first copy ordered and $0.50 for each additional copy. If you live in CA, DC, FL, MD, MO, TX, VA or Canada, add applicable sales tax or GST. Prices apply only in the United States, Canada, and Mexico and are subject to change without notice.

___ I am enclosing a U.S. check or money order.

___ Please charge my VISA/MasterCard/American Express account.

Number: _____

Expiration date: _____

Signature: _____

Quantity Discounts:
5-24 copies   15%
25-499 copies   25%

To be eligible for a discount, all copies must be shipped and billed to one address.

PLEASE SEND ME:

Qty.	Code	Title	Price
		Understanding and Preventing Violence:	
___	VIOL1	Volume 1	$ 49.95
___	VIOL2	Volume 2	$ 45.00
___	VIOL3	Volume 3	$ 45.00
___	VIOL4	Volume 4	$ 39.00
___	VIOSE4	4-Volume Set (Vols. 1-4)	$138.95
___	VIOSE3	3-Volume Set (Vols. 2-4)	$ 99.00

Please print.

Name _____

Address _____

City _____ State _____ Zip Code _____

To order by phone using VISA/MasterCard/American Express, call toll-free 1-800-624-6242 or call 202-334-3313 in the Washington metropolitan area.

VIOL

Return this card with your payment to NATIONAL ACADEMY PRESS, 2101 Constitution Avenue, NW, Lockbox 285, Washington, DC 20055. Customers in Japan should send their orders to: Maruzen Co., Ltd. 3-10, Nihonbashi 2-Chome, Chuo-Ku, Tokyo, Japan. Customers in the United Kingdom, Europe, Africa, and the Middle East should send their orders to: Plymbridge Distributors Ltd., Estover, Plymouth PL6 7PZ, United Kingdom.

TABLE 2 Prison Inmates in the United States, 1965 to 1989

Year	Number of Inmates	Inmates per 100,000 Total Population	Inmates per 100,000 Adult Population	Annual Change in Inmates (%)		
				Number of Inmates	Rate per Total Population	Rate per Adult Population
1965	210,895	109.0	170.3	—	—	—
1966	199,654	102.1	158.9	−5.3	−6.3	−6.7
1967	194,896	98.7	152.8	−2.4	−3.3	−3.8
1968	187,914	94.2	145.1	−3.6	−4.5	−5.1
1969	196,007	97.3	148.9	4.3	3.3	2.6
1970	196,429	96.3	146.3	0.2	−1.1	−1.7
1971	198,061	95.8	144.5	0.8	−0.6	−1.2
1972	196,092	93.7	140.2	−1.0	−2.2	−3.0
1973	204,211	96.6	143.2	4.1	3.1	2.1
1974	218,466	102.4	150.3	7.0	6.0	4.9
1975	240,593	111.7	162.2	10.1	9.0	7.9
1976	262,833	120.8	173.7	9.2	8.2	7.1
1977	278,141	126.6	180.3	5.8	4.8	3.8
1977	285,456	129.9	185.0	2.6	2.6	2.6
1978	294,396	132.6	187.1	3.1	2.0	1.2
1979	301,470	134.2	187.9	2.4	1.3	0.4
1980	315,974	139.0	193.2	4.8	3.6	2.8
1981	353,167	153.8	212.3	11.8	10.6	9.9
1982	394,374	170.0	233.3	11.7	10.5	9.9
1983	419,820	179.2	244.8	6.5	5.4	4.9
1984	443,398	187.5	255.3	5.6	4.6	4.3
1985	480,568	201.3	273.5	8.4	7.4	7.1
1986	522,084	216.8	293.8	8.6	7.7	7.5
1987	560,812	230.7	312.2	7.4	6.4	6.3
1988	603,720	246.1	332.3	7.7	6.7	6.4
1989	679,263	274.5	369.8	12.5	11.5	11.3
		1975-1980 Average		5.5	4.5	3.7
		1980-1988 Average		8.0	7.0	6.6

SOURCES: Flanagan and Maguire (1990:Table 6.43); Bureau of Justice Statistics (1990a). Adjustments to form population rates use population data from Bureau of the Census (1974, 1982, 1984, and 1986). Both custody and jurisdiction counts are reported for 1977 to facilitate year-to-year comparisons.

vidual states, whereas rape and aggravated assault are the least prevalent of the crime types compared.

When examined over time from 1975 to 1988, the crime mix of inmates in each of the six states does not display any general increases in violent offenses among either commitments to prison or resident inmates. With the exceptions of rape (which increases

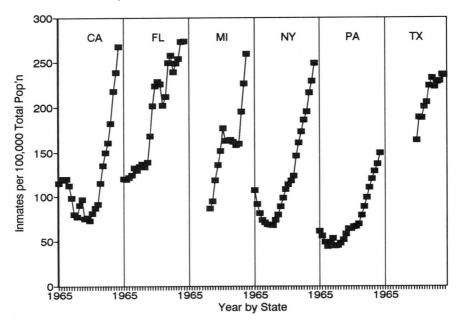

FIGURE 2 Annual total incarceration rate in individual states: inmates per total population from 1965-1988.

sharply from 4.6 to 13.8% among Michigan inmates, and more modestly in Florida from 5.0 to 9.1%) and assault (which exhibits slow but steady increases from 5.0 to 6.8% in Michigan and Pennsylvania, and from 2.1 to 4.0% in Texas), the contribution of violent offenses to the total is stable or, in the case of robbery (Figure 4-top), actually decreases during the 1980s. Only drug offenses (Figure 4-bottom) display widespread sharp increases as a percentage of total prison populations, especially after 1980.[6]

The proportional mix of crime types among inmates is a constrained relational measure: recent large increases in the proportion of inmates for drug offenses must be offset by corresponding declines in the proportions of inmates for other crime types. Such compensating changes in proportions could easily conceal real increases in incarceration for violent offenses. In order to better isolate patterns of incarceration for violent crimes, the crime-specific rate of resident inmates per 100,000 population is compared to the more commonly reported total incarceration rate.

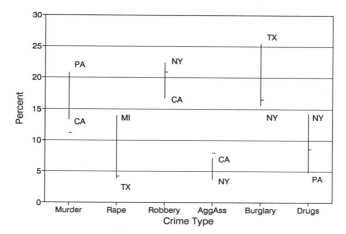

FIGURE 3 Crime mix among resident inmates in 1986: percent of total inmates by most serious convicted offense in the United States (represented by a dash), and in individual states with the lowest and highest percents among the six states in this study. SOURCE: For U.S. percents, Bureau of Justice Statistics (1988).

Figure 5 presents crime-specific incarceration rates for New York. Because the different crime types are characterized by incarceration rates that differ markedly in scale, with rates as low as 1 inmate per 100,000 population for rape or aggravated assault and as high as 60 for robbery or burglary, annual incarceration rates for each crime type are adjusted to a common scale by using the 1977 rates as a base.

Since 1977, across the six states, incarceration rates for the expressive, violent offenses of murder and aggravated assault (e.g., Figure 5-top) have increased at rates very similar to those observed for total incarceration rates in Figure 1. (The increase for aggravated assault is somewhat higher in Pennsylvania and Texas.) Similar increases in incarceration rates were also observed across the six states for the more instrumental offenses of robbery and burglary (e.g., Figure 5-bottom). The increases in total incarceration rates evident in Figures 1 and 2 thus reflect a general pattern of similar increases that occurred widely across different crime types and states. The incarceration rate for drug offenses is distinguished from other crime types by a rapid increase in the inmate population beginning in 1985.

Some interesting exceptions to the general pattern do exist. It is evident from Figure 6-top that Florida experienced distinctive

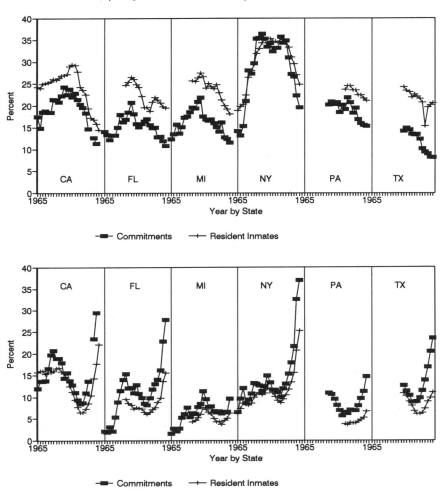

FIGURE 4 Percent of prison population serving time for robbery or drug offenses each year from 1965-1988 in individual states. Top. Commitments and resident inmates for robbery. Bottom. Commitments and resident inmates for drug offenses.

increases in incarceration rates for rape over the period under study. Similar increases in the incarceration rate of inmates serving time for rape were also observed in Michigan and Texas. Also in Florida, incarceration rates for aggravated assault, burglary, and robbery do not exhibit the same general increases observed in other states. Instead, incarceration rates for these offense types

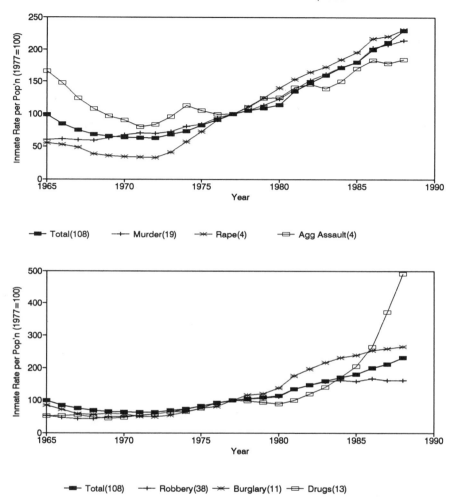

FIGURE 5 Variation over time in crime-specific incarceration rates in New York. Rates for individual crime types are rescaled using a common base rate of 100 in 1977 (actual values for 1977 are in parentheses). Values represent percentage differences from rates in 1977. Top. Violent offenses of murder, rape, and aggravated assault. Bottom. Instrumental offenses of robbery, burglary, and drugs.

recently began to stabilize or actually decline. Similar declines are also evident in incarceration rates for burglary and robbery in Texas.[7] These declines for selected crime types occur in the two states in this study whose entire correctional systems are operating under court order to relieve overcrowding and improve other

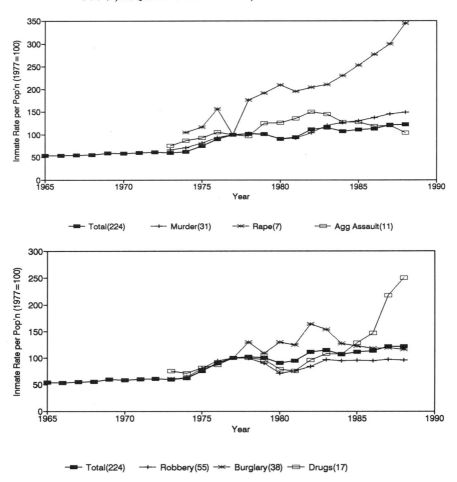

FIGURE 6 Variation over time in crime-specific incarceration rates in Florida. Rates for individual crime types are rescaled using a common base rate of 100 in 1977 (actual values for 1977 are in parentheses). Values represent percentage changes from the rates in 1977. Top. Violent offenses of murder, rape, and aggravated assault. Bottom. Instrumental offenses of robbery, burglary, and drugs.

conditions of confinement (American Correctional Association, 1989; National Conference of State Legislatures, 1989).

In the face of continuing shortages of space and other resources, one strategy to alleviate overcrowding is to reduce the number of inmates, through either reductions in the length of stay or use of alternatives to imprisonment at sentencing. Such strategies are preferably reserved for less serious or marginal cases in order to ensure sufficient prison capacity for more serious cases. In Florida, however, the escalating flow of new commitments to prison— principally for drug offenses—has resulted in early release from prison even for inmates convicted of serious violent offenses. Under a program granting "administrative gain time" (time off from the sentenced term), state prison inmates in Florida have recently had one month deducted from their sentences for every two weeks they actually serve (Isikoff, 1990).

FACTORS CONTRIBUTING TO CHANGING INCARCERATION RATES

Crime-specific incarceration rates (such as those in Figures 5 and 6) adjust for changes in the size of the base population and for changes in the crime mix that characterizes offending. Such incarceration rates are themselves influenced by changes in the underlying crime rate and in sanction policies. The standard measure of the incarceration rate as the ratio of inmates to the general population reflects the combined effects of offending rates, arrests by the police, convictions and sentences to incarceration in the courts, and release and recommitment rates by parole authorities. The separate influences on incarceration rates of these various stages of processing by the criminal justice system can be examined in the product

$$
\text{Incarceration Rate} = \text{Crime Rate} \times \frac{\text{Arrest Risk}}{\text{per Crime}} \times \frac{\text{Commitment Risk}}{\text{per Arrest}} \times \frac{\text{Time Served per Commitment}}{}
$$

or,

$$
\frac{\text{\# Inmates}}{\text{Population}} = \frac{\text{\# Crimes}}{\text{Population}} \times \frac{\text{\# Arrests}}{\text{\# Crimes}} \times \frac{\text{\# Committed}}{\text{\# Arrests}} \times \frac{\text{\# Inmates}}{\text{\# Committed}}
$$

The separate components are listed in Table 3. The appendix tables, which appear at the end of the paper, report the mean and standard deviation of each variable over time for each crime type and state. We examine the changes in individual components separately and later assess the relative contribution of these factors to the incarceration rate.

TABLE 3 Offending and Sanction Variables in Analysis of Changing Incarceration Rates

Name	Description
Incarceration rate	Number of resident inmates per 100,000 total population (inmates/population)
Crime rate, CRT	Crimes per 100,000 population for crimes known to and reported by police (reported crimes/population)
Adult percentage, ADT	Adult fraction of total crimes (estimated from adult arrests/total arrests)
Arrest risk, q_a	Probability of adult arrest per adult crime (adult arrests/adult crimes)
Imprisonment risk, Q_i	Probability of commitment to prison per adult arrest (prison commitments/adult arrests)
Average time served, S	Average total number of years served in prison per commitment from court on a new sentence (resident inmates/commitments)
Adult crime rate	Adult crimes per 100,000 total population (CRT*ADT)
QS	Expected total time served in prison per crime $(q_a{}^*Q_i{}^*S)$

NOTE: Annual estimates are obtained for all variables from 1965 to 1988 in each of six states (California, Florida, Michigan, New York, Pennsylvania, and Texas) and for each of six crime types (murder, rape, aggravated assault, robbery, burglary, and drug offenses). See appendix for the mean and standard deviation of each variable.

CHANGES IN OFFENDING

From 1965 to 1975 the total index crime rate in the United States more than doubled, from 2,445 reported index crimes per 100,000 population in 1965 to 5,284 in 1975.[8] Between 1975 and 1988 the changes in total index crime rates had slowed considerably, increasing 12 percent to a peak rate of 5,919 in 1980, declining 15 percent to a rate 5,025 in 1984, and then rising again by 13 percent to the 1988 rate of 5,664.[9] As a result, the total index crime rate in 1988 was not much higher than the same rate in 1975 (up 7.2%).

Despite the relative stability of the total index crime rate for the United States between 1975 and 1988, there are some interesting differences among the crime-type components of the total rate. Rates for violent crimes increased more than property crimes in the FBI's crime index. The modest 7.2 percent increase in the total index crime rate in the United States from 1975 to 1988 resulted from a 4.7 percent increase in the property crime rate and a much larger 32.3 percent increase in the violent crime rate.[10] If robbery (which shares features of both violent and property crimes) is excluded, the rate per total population for the remaining violent offenses increased 58.0 percent between 1975 and 1988, reflecting increases in the rates of rapes and aggravated assaults that are reported by the police;[11] murder rates actually declined by 12.5 percent between 1975 and 1988.

Changes in population crime rates may be affected by changes in the composition of the population toward increased (or decreased) representation of population subgroups that are characterized by higher (or lower) crime rates. Age, for example, is a potentially important factor distinguishing population crime rates,[12] as illustrated by age-specific arrest rates in 1988 that peaked in the late teens or early twenties and then dropped slowly through the adult years (Federal Bureau of Investigation, 1990b). The period 1965 to 1988 was characterized by a general aging of the U.S. population, with adults (age 18 and over) rising from 64 percent of the population in 1965, to 69 percent in 1975, and then to 74 percent by 1988. This population shift, combined with age-varying arrest rates, would contribute to increases in general population crime rates.

The increasing representation of adults in the total population is a particularly important factor in the differences observed between violent and property crime rates for the total population. Violent crimes are especially characteristic of adults. While the peak arrest rate for murder was at age 18 in 1988, murder rates declined slowly with age and did not reach a rate equal to one-half the peak rate until ages in the early thirties (Federal Bureau of Investigation, 1990b). Rape and aggravated assault rates peaked at ages 23 and 21, respectively, and remained above the half-peak rate into the late thirties. This contrasts with arrests for property crimes, which peaked at age 16 and reached the half-peak rate by age 23. Robbery rates fell between violent and property crimes, peaking at age 18 and reaching the half-peak rate in the late twenties.[13]

After partially controlling for age and using rates of the estimated number of crimes committed by adults per adult popula-

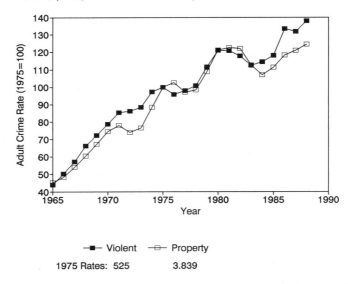

FIGURE 7 Growth in U.S. crime rate, 1965-1988, with annual adult crime rates (estimated crimes by adults per 100,000 adult population) rescaled to a common base rate of 100 in 1975 (actual values for 1975 are in parentheses). Values represent percentage differences from the rates in 1975.

tion,[14] the growth in adult crime rates through 1975 was very similar for violent and property offenses, which increased 127 and 121 percent, respectively (Figure 7). The increases in crime rates from 1975 to 1988 were smaller in magnitude for both crime types, but only slightly more pronounced for violent offenses: increasing 38 percent for adult violent crimes and 24 percent for adult property crimes. Thus, much of the larger increase over time observed in violent crime rates per total population compared to the same rates for property crimes is removed when appropriate controls for aging of the population are included.

Blumstein et al. (1991) use a richer age partition and include race differences in offending rates for a more thorough analysis of changes in total crime rates in the United States over the same period. They conclude that, on average, changes in the racial and age composition of the population accounted for about 20 percent of the total change in crime rates for robbery and burglary and almost 30 percent of the change in crime rates for murder. Changes in population composition had especially important effects on the large increases in crime rates between 1965 and 1975 for robbery and murder.

Crime rates will also be affected by changes in levels of criminality toward more or less offending. Increases in criminality—whether they result from increases in the size of the offender population or from higher frequencies of offending by individual offenders—can increase the incarceration rate independently of any changes in imprisonment policies.[15] The rise in adult crime rates illustrated in Figure 7 hints at the substantial underlying changes in criminality from 1965 to 1988 reported in Blumstein et al. (1991). Such increases in offending levels, particularly in those crime types that are more vulnerable to imprisonment, will contribute to increases in population incarceration rates.

CHANGES IN SANCTION POLICIES

The incarceration rate is influenced further by changes in sanction policies that either increase (or decrease) the risk of arrest per crime q_a, the imprisonment risk per arrest Q_i, or the average length of time served in prison S. We used data on reported crimes and arrests for each state in combination with annual data on commitments to state prisons and resident inmates to estimate the sanction variables.

Arrest Risk per Crime, q_a

The arrest risk per crime (reported in appendix Table A-2) is estimated from the ratio of adult arrests of persons age 18 and older in each state to the estimated number of adult crimes reported by the police. The arrest risk variable used here is only a proxy measure that overstates the actual risk of arrest following a crime. The upward bias in q_a arises from two sources: (1) the number of crimes in the ratio includes only crimes that are reported by the police, and (2) the number of arrests in the ratio often includes the arrest of several offenders for a single offense.

Data that are available from the annual National Crime Survey (NCS) indicate that the upward bias in q_a may be substantial. Crime victims responding to the NCS indicate that about one-half of the violent crimes they suffer are reported to the police each year. Although the reporting rate varies somewhat across offense types, it has remained fairly stable at about 55 percent per year for the more serious violent offenses of rape, robbery, and aggravated assault (Bureau of Justice Statistics, 1990b). After adjustment for unreported crimes, total crimes will increase about 1.8-fold.

The NCS also provides data on the number of offenders per crime incident. These data on multiple offenders vary considerably in availability across different offense types, but are more readily available for crimes of violence that involve direct offender-victim confrontations. By using data from Reiss (1980) on crimes committed from 1972 to 1975 in the United States, the average number of offenders per crime committed was estimated to be 1.6 for rape, 2.3 for robbery, and 2.6 for aggravated assault (Blumstein and Cohen, 1979).

Adjusting q_a for unreported crimes increases the total number of crimes about 1.8-fold, whereas adjustment for multiple offenders increases total crimes another 1.6- to 2.6-fold. The simple ratio of arrests to crimes reported by the police in q_a (Table A-2) thus overstates the arrest risk per crime committed threefold (1/[1.8*1.6]) for rape; four-fold (1/[1.8*2.3]) for robbery; and five-fold (1/[1.8*2.6]) for aggravated assault.

The arrest risk per crime (Table A-2) varies primarily by crime type. As might be expected, murder has the highest arrest risk per crime.[16] This is followed by other violent offenses with mean values of q_a that vary roughly from 0.25 to 0.35. If adjustments for unreported crimes and multiple offenders per crime incident were taken into account, the actual arrest risk per crime would be reduced to a range of 5 to 10 arrests for every 100 crimes that offenders commit for the violent offenses of rape, robbery, and aggravated assault. Some differences among states are also evident, notably, higher values of q_a in Pennsylvania for most crime types. With regard to time, q_a generally remained fairly stable from 1965 to 1988.

Certainty and Severity of Imprisonment

The decade of the 1980s was one of substantial changes in imprisonment policies effected through implementation of determinate or mandatory sentencing schemes, sentencing guidelines, and restrictions on or elimination of parole release from prison. In addition to addressing concerns about reducing judicial discretion and the variability in sentences imposed for similar offenses, these new sentencing policies entailed a shift toward more severe penalties.

Imprisonment sanctions can be distinguished in terms of the risk—or certainty—of going to prison following arrest (Q_j), and the length of time served—or severity—for those offenders who are committed to prison (S). Certainty is primarily determined by the sentencing judge, although legislatures have increasingly become involved in influencing Q_i through statutory provisions that mandate the imposition of prison terms for certain offenses. Severity, although partially the result of judicially imposed sentences, is determined primarily by administrative agencies, through the release and custody policies of corrections and parole agencies.

The partition between Q_i and S distinguishes between short-term and long-term effects of imprisonment policies on the size of the resident inmate population. Effects of Q_i on the flow of inmates into prison will be felt in the short term through immediate changes in the number of commitments to prison, whereas effects of changes in S will take longer to be manifested as substantial increases (or decreases) in the stock of resident inmates.

The prevailing levels of these imprisonment sanctions can be estimated from data on commitments to prison and the size of the resident population. The imprisonment risk per arrest (Q_i) is estimated from the ratio of commitments to prison in a year to the number of adult arrests. Data on new commitments to prison are obtained from the intake process over an entire year. Only those commitments to prison that arise from a new sentence in court are included in the count of commitments. Persons who are recommitted or returned to prison from any form of conditional release (usually parole) in order to serve additional time on a previous sentence are excluded from the commitment count. Thus, Q_i represents the risk of being sentenced to prison following an arrest.

Mean values of Q_i vary considerably by crime type (see Table A-2). The risk of prison following arrest is naturally highest for murder. Even for this most serious of violent offenses, however, imprisonment is not a certainty, due primarily to the failure of some arrests to end in conviction. Robbery and rape follow murder, with 10 to 33 percent of arrests resulting in commitment to prison for these offenses. The imprisonment risk for robbery is somewhat higher than for rape in Florida, Michigan, and New York. Q_i generally falls to a range of 2 to 5 percent for aggravated assault, burglary, and drug offenses, although the imprisonment risk for burglary is three to four times higher in Florida and Texas.

Time served in prison, S, is estimated from the ratio of the average daily census of resident inmates in a year to the number of new commitments in the same year.[17] The number and characteristics of resident inmates are obtained from a one-day census, typically conducted at the end of the fiscal year. Both new commitments from court and recommitments on the same sentence are included in the count of resident inmates. Thus, time served represents the total time an offender spends incarcerated on a sentence, including time served until first release from prison and any additional time served on the same sentence following revocation of conditional release.[18] The pattern of average time served across crime types matches that observed for Q_i, being highest for murder at 4.5 or more years per commitment, and lowest for aggravated assault, burglary, and drug offenses at 1.27 to 3.0 years (see Table A-3).

Table 4 reports the average annual percentage change in imprisonment risk per adult arrest (Q_i) and in average time served per commitment to prison (S) since 1977. Increases in both imprisonment sanctions are widespread from 1977 to 1988, although somewhat more likely for S than for Q_i.[19] Increases in time served for robbery, aggravated assault, and burglary were less than 1.5 years, whereas terms for murder increased from 2 to 4 years. Rape is the only crime type experiencing increases in both Q_i and S widely across the six states examined. For murder and robbery, by contrast, increases in S are more common than increases in Q_i.

The relative magnitudes of changes in Q_i and S vary across states.[20] In California, increases in both Q_i and S are widespread, though somewhat larger in magnitude for commitments to prison (Q_i). Increases in time served in prison, S, predominate in Michigan, New York, and Pennsylvania.[21] The increases in these four states are compatible with sentencing reforms to increase penalties in each state, especially for offenses involving violence or firearms.[22]

About one-half of all state-by-crime comparisons involve changes in opposite directions for Q_i and S. Such changes are especially characteristic of certain states and crime types. In Florida, although the risk of commitment to prison following arrest (Q_i) has been increasing for all crime types, the average time served once in prison (S) has declined for all crime types except the most serious violent offenses of murder and rape. This reflects the impact of special provisions for administrative reductions in minimum sentences in order to reduce seriously overcrowded prison populations in that state. Opposite changes in Q_i and S also predominate for robbery and burglary with Q_i declining, and for drug offenses with S declining (Table 4).[23]

TABLE 4 Average Annual Percentage Change in Imprisonment Sanctions by State and Crime Type, 1977-1988

State	Murder	Rape	Robbery	Aggravated Assault	Burglary	Drug Offenses
Imprisonment Risk per Adult Arrest, Q_i (prison commitments per adult arrest):						
California	0.9	8.2	3.5	8.4	10.9	11.5
Florida	6.0	9.1	1.8	9.8	6.7	1.9
Michigan	−0.9	6.7	−5.7	0.5	−3.4	0.5
New York	0.4	0.3	−2.7	0.1	10.7	8.3
Pennsylvania	5.5	2.7	−1.0	2.6	−1.5	0.7
Texas	−0.2	9.5	−5.1	5.6	−1.8	15.0
Average Time Served in Prison (years), S (resident inmates per prison commitment):						
California	3.5	7.0	3.6	3.5	4.6	−3.0
Florida	0.6	−0.8	−4.3	−9.3	−7.0	−6.1
Michigan	4.0	7.6	4.4	3.5	5.3	4.6
New York	7.2	7.7	3.7	2.1	2.6	−0.8
Pennsylvania	3.7	5.5	8.1	6.2	10.7	3.1
Texas	4.0	7.0	3.2	0.4	0.5	−5.7

IDENTIFYING THE COMPONENTS OF CHANGE IN INCARCERATION RATES

In this section, we aggregate the various components of the incarceration rate into two main factors: variations in the adult crime rate per population (ACR) and variations in the expected time served per adult arrest ($Q_i{}^*S$). The total incarceration rate is contrasted with these two elements to identify the relative influences of offending and sanction policies on observed changes in incarceration over time.[24]

Figures 8 to 11 present graphical displays of smoothed values of ACR and Q_iS for illustrative states and crime types. Two distinct time periods are evident in changing incarceration rates, one of relative stability or slow declines in inmate rates through the mid-1970s, followed by a period of steady growth in inmate rates through 1988. Figure 8 presents the dominant pattern of change. The early period before the mid-1970s is generally one of offsetting trends, with adult crime rate (ACR) increasing and imprisonment sanctions (Q_iS) decreasing. During the latter period of growth in incarceration rates, continued growth in adult crime rates is often compounded by rises in Q_iS as well.

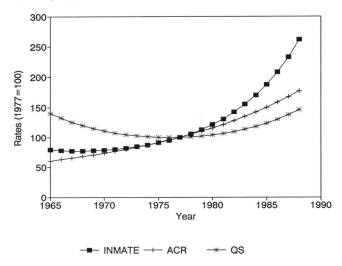

FIGURE 8 Role of crimes and imprisonment sanctions in changing incarceration rate for aggravated assault in New York (ACR = adult crimes per 100,000 population; Q_iS = expected man-years in prison per adult arrest [inmates/adult arrests]; INMATE = inmates per 100,000 total population).

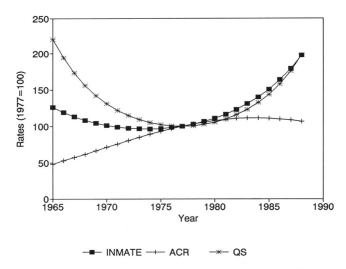

FIGURE 9 Role of crimes and imprisonment sanctions in changing incarceration rates for robbery in California (ACR = adult crimes per 100,000 population; Q_iS = expected man-years in prison per adult arrest [inmates/adult arrest]; INMATE = inmates per 100,000 total population).

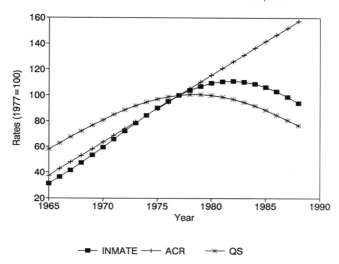

FIGURE 10   Role of crimes and imprisonment sanctions in changing incarceration rates for robbery in Florida (ACR = adult crimes per 100,000 population; Q_iS = expected man-years in prison per adult arrest [inmates/adult arrests]; INMATE = inmates per 100,000 total population).

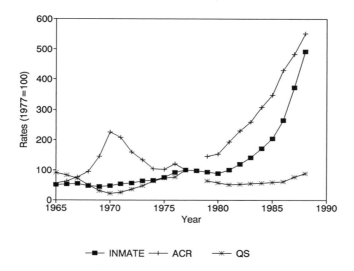

FIGURE 11   Role of crimes and imprisonment sanctions in changing incarceration rates for drug offenses in New York (ACR = adult crimes per 100,000 total population; Q_iS = expected man-years in prison per adult arrest [inmates/adult arrests]; INMATE = inmates per 100,000 total population).

TABLE 5 Average Annual Percentage Change in Crimes and Incarceration by State and Crime Type, 1977-1988

State	Murder	Rape	Robbery	Aggravated Assault	Burglary	Drug Offenses
Adult Crime Rate, ACR (adult crimes per 100,000 adult population):						
California	1.3	−1.2	1.5	5.9	−0.3	10.0
Florida	0.8	1.2	7.8	2.8	5.3	7.8
Michigan	3.8	2.4	−1.9	4.3	−0.9	8.1
New York	1.8	0.9	5.7	5.5	2.3	15.6
Pennsylvania	−1.4	2.7	2.7	3.5	1.1	9.8
Texas	−4.2	4.9	4.6	5.6	5.7	5.8
Expected Time Served per Adult Arrest, Q_iS (resident inmates per adult arrest):						
California	8.9	8.3	5.9	6.9	14.2	10.2
Florida	5.4	11.4	−3.5	−2.4	−0.8	−1.4
Michigan	0.5	16.0	0.3	3.8	7.5	11.6
New York	4.4	7.1	−2.0	0.7	11.2	4.3
Pennsylvania	11.4	10.2	7.6	10.4	10.7	5.6
Texas	2.4	16.1	−1.7	4.1	−3.1	4.3

NOTE: The average yearly percentage change in the product Q_iS does not, in general, equal the product of the average percentage change in each component, Q_i and S: $E[Q_i(t+1)S(t+1)/Q_i(t)S(t)] \neq E\ [Q_i(t+1)/Q_i(t)] \bullet E\ [S(t+1)/S(t)]$. Thus the values in this table cannot be obtained directly from the values in Table 4.

The pattern in the early period is widespread across states and crime types, as is evident in Figures 8, 9, and 11. Since the mid-1970s, imprisonment sanctions have generally increased across the states for most crime types. (Exceptions to this pattern in Florida and Texas, as well as for the crime of robbery, are discussed below.)

Table 5 reports the average annual percentage change in adult crime rates and imprisonment sanctions for the period 1977 to 1988. Increases in Q_iS are most widespread in California and Pennsylvania, where growth rates average from 5 to 15 percent per year and accompany explicit changes in sentencing policy in the two states (also see Figure 9). In 1977, California implemented a policy of determinate sentences accompanied by the elimination of early release on parole. In the early 1980s, Pennsylvania implemented new sentencing guidelines, which have frequently been augmented by special statutory provisions for mandatory minimum sentences for selected offenses. In the other four states, Q_iS actually leveled off or declined for some offenses during the later period (also see Figure 10).

The increases in Q_iS since 1977 usually accompany continued increases in adult crime rates (ACR) through the 1980s—a pattern illustrated in Figure 8. Crime rates are most stable through the 1980s in California, as illustrated in Figure 9. Since the mid-1970s, rising incarceration rates thus have resulted from upward trends in both Q_iS and ACR, or they have tracked increases in Q_iS where adult crime rates have remained relatively stable. Rape is distinguished among crime types by uniformly large increases in Q_iS across all six states (Table 5).

There are two noteworthy exceptions to the general upward trend in use of imprisonment sanctions from 1977 to 1988. First, for all crime types except murder and rape in Florida, and for selected crime types in Texas—notably robbery and burglary—Q_iS decreased, while adult crime rates continued to rise (Figure 10 and Table 5). These declines in Q_iS occur in the two states in this study whose state corrections systems are under court order to reduce prison crowding, and thus may reflect explicit changes in imprisonment policies intended to address the prison population problem.

The decrease in use of imprisonment sanctions in Florida occurs despite implementation in the early 1980s of harsh sentencing policies that abolished parole, lengthened sentences, and mandated prison terms for many offenses. Although these policies were intended to increase the use of incarceration, they quickly overburdened already strained corrections resources in that state. The problem became so acute by the late 1980s that special procedures were implemented to permit administrative reductions in sentences for most inmates serving time in Florida prisons. By 1990, sentences were being reduced by one month for every two weeks actually served (Isikoff, 1990).

The second exception to widespread increases in Q_iS is the pattern in incarceration rates for robbery. As Figure 10 illustrates (also see Table 5), Q_iS has been declining for robbery during the post-1977 period. Such declines are observed in three of the six states examined and occurred while adult crime rates (ACR) in robbery, on average, continued to increase from 1977 to 1988.

Growing at an average of about 5 to 10 percent per year, the use of imprisonment for drug offenses has increased at rates roughly comparable to those of violent offenses (Table 5). Increases in Q_iS are usually accompanied by larger increases in input to the courts from arrests of adults for drug offenses (also see Figure 11). When combined with these rising adult arrest rates for drug offenses that show no immediate indications of slowing, the recent increases in Q_iS for drug convictions forebode even larger increases expected in the inmate population for drug offenses.

SUMMARY

The data from six states illustrate the important role that changing imprisonment policies have played in rising prison populations over the last decade. Increases in the use of imprisonment, usually accompanying explicit policy changes toward harsher penalties, are widespread across states and crime types between 1977 and 1988. Policy changes that involve sentencing guidelines, statutes specifying mandatory minimum prison terms, and restrictions on parole release share a common goal of increasing the certainty and severity of prison terms imposed on offenders. The data suggest that these changes in policy have for the most part resulted in corresponding changes in practice.

Both imprisonment risk following arrest (Q_i) and time served for those committed to prison (S) have increased. Such increases were especially prevalent for rape, where both Q_i and S increased, and for murder and robbery, where time served increased while Q_i remained relatively stable or declined. Increases in the use of imprisonment sanctions also were observed broadly across crime types in California. In Florida, increases in Q_i are more common, whereas increases in S predominate in Michigan, New York, and Pennsylvania. The resulting increases in expected time served per adult arrest, Q_iS, combined with continuing increases in crime rates through the 1980s, contribute to the staggering increases in prison populations of the past decade.

Robbery and drug offenses are distinctive among the crime types examined because they involve opposite changes in Q_i and S. For robbery, increases in time served (S) were dominated by larger declines in imprisonment risk following arrest (Q_i), and robbery was the only crime type among those examined that was characterized by declining or stable levels of expected time served per adult arrest (Q_iS) during the 1980s. In the case of drug offenses, increases in Q_i were often accompanied by declines in S, which moderated somewhat the total increases in Q_iS for this offense. In Florida, the decrease in S results from an administrative program of emergency early release that is implemented as needed to offset excessive growth in prison populations in that state arising from continuing increases in Q_i.

CRIME CONTROL EFFECTS OF INCARCERATION FOR VIOLENT CRIMES

Whether measured by raw counts of inmates, by population rates, or in relation to crimes committed, the use of incarceration has increased substantially in the United States since the mid-1970s. In this section, we explore the likely impact of these changes in sanction policies on levels of violent crime. Aside from retribution (or punishment), incarceration also serves crime control purposes, operating directly through incapacitation to prevent crimes by those incarcerated offenders who are physically removed from the community, or indirectly through the deterrence (i.e., inhibiting) effects of threatened incarceration on offenders who are not now in prison.

Incapacitation and deterrence interact in important ways to reduce the overall level of crime. Despite an extensive body of empirical research, no prior studies satisfactorily estimate these two effects.[25] Numerous studies provide estimates of the elasticity of crime to changes in sanction levels. To the extent that estimates of the "deterrence" elasticity refer to imprisonment sanctions, however, they really reflect the combined effects of deterrence and incapacitation. Incapacitation estimates, by contrast, fail to incorporate deterrence effects that may substantially reduce the individual offending levels from which incapacitation is measured.

The discussion below focuses mainly on the incapacitation effects of incarceration and offers important new advances over previous estimates. We also consider, in an exploratory way, recalibrating these incapacitation estimates to accommodate the impact of deterrence on base offending levels.

INCAPACITATION OF VIOLENT CRIMES

As with other forms of crime, any single violent offense rarely leads to incarceration of its perpetrator. Thus, at any point in time, only a small fraction of offenders who engage in violent crimes are imprisoned and incapacitated from further victimizing individuals in the community. Yet, the reduction in violent crimes attributable to incapacitation need not be negligible, since a relatively small group of incarcerated offenders could, in the absence of imprisonment, substantially increase the violent crime rate.

Typically the incapacitation effect (I) of imprisonment is measured on a percentage basis by comparing the number of crimes that are prevented by incapacitation to the total number of crimes that would have been committed if offenders were fortunate enough to avoid imprisonment. Thus, I for violent offenses depends fundamentally on the number of crimes that incarcerated offenders would commit if they were to remain free in the community, which in turn rests on the mix of offense types that offenders commit, individual rates of committing violent crimes while offenders are free, and the length of time that offenders will continue to commit violent crimes.[26] Assessing the crime control effects of incapacitation in reducing violent crimes thus requires that we inquire about the general characteristics of offending careers and the role of violent offenses in those careers.

Although studies that focus exclusively on violent offenders are rare,[27] empirical evidence about violent offending can be found in cross-sectional and longitudinal studies of general offending careers. The bulk of this literature, as it applies to violent crimes, has been reviewed by Farrington (1982), Blumstein et al. (1986), and more recently Weiner (1989). We discuss briefly the empirical findings about the contributions of violent offenses in offending careers and highlight their implications for incapacitation. The results from this research generally support the conclusion that incapacitation has nontrivial consequences for the control of violent crime.

At the end of the section, we offer estimates of I for robbery in California, Michigan, and Texas. These estimates were computed based on a model that explicitly incorporates important features of the crime-generating process previously observed in empirical research. Comparable estimates for other violent offenses remain unavailable at this time.

Individual Offending Frequency (λ)

Violent offenses constitute a relatively small percentage of the total crimes generated by an offender population. For example, Tracy et al. (1990) found that violent offenses represented less than 5 percent of total police contacts in cohort studies of juvenile offending by Philadelphia boys born in 1945 and 1958. Similar results were reported by Shannon (1982, 1988) for each of three birth cohorts traced in Racine, Wisconsin. In summarizing several studies of juvenile and adult offenders, Blumstein et al. (1986:78-79) conclude that violent offenses represent only 10 to 20 percent of the criminal records of arrested or convicted offenders.

At the individual offender level, estimates of annual offending rates (λ) for selected violent crimes are typically low. The average value of λ for robbery—the violent crime most frequently analyzed—among all offenders committing that crime has been estimated to be in the interval of 1 to 3 crimes committed per year free (Peterson and Braiker, 1981; Blumstein et al., 1993). Although λ estimates of comparable accuracy for other violent crimes committed by the overall offender population have seldom been computed, existing evidence points in the direction of rates even lower than those for robbery, especially for rare offenses such as homicide and rape.[28] Extrapolating from self-reported crime rates among California prison inmates surveyed in 1976, Chaiken (1980) estimated average λ's for the general population of offenders of 0.16 crime per offender per year free for homicide, 0.92 for rape, 2.38 for aggravated assault, and 1.97 for armed robbery. Blumstein and Cohen (1979) found similar λ values for robbery and aggravated assault in samples of adult arrestees in Washington, D.C. and in the metropolitan area of Detroit.[29]

Such low offending rates would seem to suggest small to negligible incapacitation returns from incarcerating violent offenders, especially when the low risk of incarceration following most violent crimes is considered. For example, based on estimates reported in Canela-Cacho (1990:Table 6.5), the odds against imprisonment following a robbery committed during the late 1970s were 135:1 in California, 72:1 in Michigan, and 50:1 in Texas.[30] For those offenders who are caught and sent to prison, the average time served for robbery during the late 1970s was relatively constant—about 3.7 years in the three states. Over the course of a career, the average offender would only exceptionally be intercepted by the criminal justice system, and while incarcerated, fewer than a dozen robberies would be prevented. Thus, the crimes prevented by incapacitation would appear to represent only a small fraction of the total crimes that an offender would generate were he to avoid all interruptions by imprisonment.

To date, the most widely applied method to measure incapacitation is the model developed in Avi-Itzhak and Shinnar (1973) and applied in Shinnar and Shinnar (1975). This model offers a way to estimate I for the *average offender* under particular values of the sentencing parameters: $Q = q_a{}^*Q_i$ for the probability of

TABLE 6 Average Incarceration Sanctions for Robbery, 1975-1980

	California	Michigan	Texas
Imprisonment risk per robbery committed, Q	0.0074	0.0139	0.0199
Average time served (years) in prison for robbery, S	3.6	3.7	3.9
Expected time served (years) per robbery committed, QS	0.0266	0.0514	0.0776

NOTE: Q is estimated from the ratio of annual admissions to prison for robbery to the total number of robberies reported to police. This ratio is further corrected for underreporting of crimes to the police, and for multiple offenders per crime incident. S is obtained from the ratio of resident inmates to the number of commitments to prison. The average for the 1975-1980 period is used here.

incarceration following a crime, and S for the average time served among incarcerated offenders.[31] For the average Q and S values observed in California, Michigan, and Texas during the latter half of the 1970s (Table 6), and the average λ for robbery during the same period in each state estimated by Blumstein et al. (1993),[32] the Avi-Itzhak and Shinnar model yields I values of a 7.9 percent reduction from the potential number of robberies in California, 12.8 percent in Michigan, and 9.1 percent in Texas.[33] These modest reductions in crime of 5 to 15 percent are similar in magnitude to other I estimates (based on different estimating procedures), which have led some analysts to conclude that incapacitation does not contribute substantially to crime control (see, for example, Clarke, 1974; Greenberg, 1975).

Heterogeneity in Individual Offending Frequencies (λ_i)

There are, however, strong reasons for believing that these estimates suffer from a sizable downward bias. Without exception, studies of general offending, whether based on self-reports or official data, have found considerable variation in individual offending rates (Peterson and Braiker, 1981; Chaiken and Chaiken, 1982; Dunford and Elliott, 1984; English, 1990; Horney and Marshall, 1991; Miranne and Geerken, 1991). Moreover, a small subset of offenders generally accounts for a disproportionately large share of total crimes reported or recorded for the group of offenders under study (Wolfgang et al., 1972; Chaiken and Chaiken, 1982). This same general pattern also holds, but to a lesser degree, for violent offenses. For example, Piper (1985) found that 18.6 percent of violent offenders accounted for 45.2 percent of total police contacts for violent crimes in the 1958 Philadelphia cohort. These results mirror those in Miller et al. (1982:Table 4.9), in which 22.9 percent of violent offenders were responsible for 45.7 percent of all arrests for violent crimes. Such disparity in the shares of offenders and offenses reveals considerable heterogeneity in λ within the offender population.

Large variability—or heterogeneity—in individual offending rates has played a significant role in promoting policies to selectively incapacitate, typically for longer terms, only the smaller number of high-λ offenders. This same heterogeneity, however, also has important implications for existing estimates of the incapacitation effect. Although previous estimates have essentially assumed that inmates were like the average offender, heterogeneity in λ actually results in high levels of selectivity of high-λ offenders into prison.

It has been variously recognized that in the presence of λ heterogeneity, offenders in prison are not expected to be representative of all offenders (Chaiken, 1980; Blumstein et al., 1986). Even if all offenders face *identical* incarceration risks for each crime committed, and the criminal justice system does not seek to enforce any deliberate selective policies, high-λ offenders will be overrepresented among inmates. This greater *stochastic selectivity* of high-λ offenders into prison results purely from a process in which incarceration outcomes are stochastically determined. As λ increases, so does the expected number of crimes that an offender will commit, which in turn increases the risk that the offender is *eventually* incarcerated. For example, if the probability of incarceration *per robbery* is .01 for all offenders, an offender who commits robberies at an annualized Poisson rate of $\lambda = 1$ will evade incarceration during a year with probability .99, whereas an offender who commits robberies at rate of 100 per year will escape prison with the much lower probability of .37.

The bias toward high λ's among offenders sentenced to incarceration can be substantial. Blumstein et al. (1993) developed a

TABLE 7 Distribution of Robbery Rates While Free (λ) for Incoming Prison Inmates and for All Offenders In and Out of Prison

	California	Michigan	Texas
Inmate sample size	113	94	93
λ distribution of incoming inmates			
Low-λ percentage	49.7	62.9	54.4
Medium-λ percentage	30.9	25.2	38.0
High-λ percentage	19.4	11.9	7.6
Low-λ mean	3.0	2.7	1.3
Medium-λ mean	17.4	16.8	8.2
High-λ mean	193.7	294.5	137.3
λ distribution of all offenders			
Low-λ percentage	89.5	93.3	89.4
Medium-λ percentage	9.7	6.3	10.3
High-λ percentage	0.8	0.4	0.2
Low-λ mean	1.5	1.4	0.7
Medium-λ mean	9.0	8.9	4.3
High-λ mean	128.0	239.2	103.4

NOTE: The results reported here are extracted from Canela-Cacho (1990:Table 6.17). Annual individual robbery rates while free are estimated from self-reports by prison inmates of the number of robberies they committed and the time they spent free during the two years preceding a current conviction for robbery. Details about the data and the procedure for estimating the λ distribution are available in Canela-Cacho (1990).

model to infer the distribution of λ for all offenders, based on the observed distribution of λ for an entering cohort of prison inmates, and applies it to data for convicted robbers in California, Michigan, and Texas prisons who participated in a study of self-reported crimes (Chaiken and Chaiken, 1982). The results show a strikingly consistent pattern across states (see Table 7).

In all three states, the distribution of λ inferred for all robbers is a mixture of three exponential distributions representing low-, medium-, and high-λ subpopulations of offenders. The low-λ subpopulation comprises about 90 percent of the total offender population who commit robberies at a mean rate of roughly 1 per year. By contrast, the high-λ group constitutes less than 1 percent of

TABLE 8 Mean Robbery Rates While Free (λ) for Incoming Prison Inmates and All Offenders

	California	Michigan	Texas
Imprisonment risk per robbery committed, Q	0.0074	0.0139	0.0199
Overall mean annual robbery frequencies, λ			
Incoming inmates	44.44	41.10	14.28
Total offender population	3.22	2.85	1.29
Selectivity ratio [λ(inmates)/ λ(all offenders)]	13.8	14.4	11.1

NOTE: Overall mean λ's are based on the λ distributions reported in Table 7. Results are extracted from Canela-Cacho (1990:Table 6.17).

the total offender population, but they commit robberies with a mean annual λ greater than 100. The medium-λ subpopulation contributes roughly 9 percent of the offender population and has a mean rate of about 10 robberies annually per offender.

Because of selection bias toward high-λ offenders, the participation of the three subgroups is drastically different among incoming inmates. Only half of incoming inmates come from the low-λ subpopulation, whereas members of the high-λ subpopulation represent 10 to 20 percent of incoming prisoners. Thus, high-rate offenders are overrepresented among inmates by 20 to 40 times their base rate in the total offender population. The impact of this stochastic selection bias toward the most active offenders is evident in the ratio of the average λ for imprisoned offenders to that for all offenders (Table 8): 13.8 for California, 14.4 for Michigan, and 11.1 for Texas. While incarcerated robbers in California, on average, commit 44.4 robberies per year free, the mean rate for all robbers—including those who are rarely found among inmates—is just 3.2.

The implications for incapacitation of such selectivity are fully explored by Canela-Cacho (1990) and briefly summarized here. Although the homogeneous λ model of Avi-Itzhak and Shinnar

(1973) estimates I for the *average offender* in the population, the actual measure of interest is the *average value of I* across all offenders. We are interested in the average number of crimes prevented among all offenders, rather than the number of crimes prevented for an offender whose λ is equal to the population average.

It can be proved formally that unless λ is indeed constant across offenders, these alternative measures of I are not equal to one another (Canela-Cacho, 1990:Chapter 3). Whether or not their difference has any practical significance depends on the extent of the variability in λ. If the values of λ are tightly distributed around their mean, the two measures—though mathematically different—will approximate each other reasonably well. However, when the spread in the distribution of λ is of the magnitude revealed in inmate surveys, the selection bias toward high-rate offenders among inmates is sizable and I for the average offender seriously underestimates the desired average value of I across all offenders. In measuring incapacitation for robbery in California, for example, the homogeneous λ model of Avi-Itzhak and Shinnar (1973) assumes that since the average offender commits 3.22 robberies per year, every year that a robber spends incarcerated will prevent about 3.22 crimes. The fact that the average offender in prison would actually commit crimes at a rate 14 times higher is not accounted for.

Career Length (L)

Thus far, our discussion of incapacitation has ignored the possibility that some offenders in prison may have "retired" from offending and would not continue to commit crimes if they were released early from their prison terms.[34] Confinement beyond the end of offending careers for such offenders yields no incapacitation benefits to society. The duration of offending careers is thus a variable that critically affects the incapacitation returns of imprisonment. If, on admission to prison, an offender's expected residual offending career is short and his sentence is comparatively long, chances increase that the offender will end offending before he is released, thus wasting scarce prison resources.[35] The possibility of career termination lowers the expected number of crimes prevented per incarcerated offender and therefore reduces I.

Moreover, career termination could render incapacitation totally infeasible for a large number of offenders. Consider a case in which the vast majority of offenders have very short careers so that an entire career consists of only a few crimes. Obviously, an offender's first crime can never be prevented through incapacitation, since incapacitation becomes an option only after the offender commits and is convicted of that crime. Given the generally low risk of incarceration for each crime committed, it is entirely likely that offenders would also evade imprisonment following their second and third offenses.

Hence, when the offender population has a high turnover rate, with offenders committing only a few offenses before they terminate offending and are replaced by other new offenders, it is increasingly likely that a fair number of offenders would be unaffected by incapacitation. Most careers would begin and end without interruption by the criminal justice system, and the capture of a small fraction of unlucky offenders who were about to end offending soon would reduce the crime rate only marginally.[36]

Although some offenders have careers that span only a few crimes, other offenders start offending early in their lives and continue well into adulthood. Several longitudinal studies have found that between 33 and 75 percent of all delinquent youths persist into adult criminality (Blumstein et al., 1986:Table 3-13). Adult arrest history data for arrestees in Washington, D.C., Michigan, and New York State show that individuals who are arrested at least once for a serious offense accumulate an average of five to six arrests per offender in these samples.[37] Since only a small fraction of the crimes committed by offenders results in arrests—about 5 percent for robbery, aggravated assault, or burglary—the average number of crimes by these offenders is considerably higher.

Similarly, recidivism studies suggest that offenders have long rather than short careers. Most recently, for example, of 16,000 inmates released from state prisons, 62.5 percent were rearrested and 41.4 percent were recommitted to prison for a new offense within three years of their release. Among those who had served time for a violent offense, 30 percent were rearrested for another violent offense (Beck and Shipley, 1989:Table 9).

Some studies have explicitly estimated the average length of offending careers for different types of offense.[38] These studies find that careers average 5 to 10 years in length, with violent offenders—those who commit at least one violent offense during their careers—having somewhat longer careers than nonviolent offenders. Earlier attempts to approximate the length of offending careers produced similar results (Greenberg, 1975; Greene, 1977; Shinnar and Shinnar, 1975).

Thus, although the efficiency of incapacitation is reduced by career termination, which inevitably leads to some waste of prison resources from the standpoint of incapacitation, available empirical evidence on career length does not rule out incapacitation as a viable crime control strategy. Careers are sufficiently long to anticipate reasonable crime prevention from the incapacitation of some portion of the offender population.

Incapacitation Under Offender Heterogeneity and Finite Careers

Canela-Cacho (1990) generalizes the model of Avi-Itzhak and Shinnar (1973) to control simultaneously for the effects of offender heterogeneity and career termination. As in Avi-Itzhak and Shinnar, the generalized model assumes a Poisson distribution for the number of crimes committed by each offender with individual rate λ_i. The length of an offending career is modeled as an exponential random variable with a constant termination rate throughout the career. Furthermore, interactions between the criminal justice system and individual offenders are stochastic, following a homogeneous Bernoulli process: incarceration follows commission of a crime with probability Q independently of any prior outcomes, and time served (S) varies according to an exponential random variable. The expected time served per crime (QS) is assumed to be constant across offenders; thus the model excludes deliberate policies to selectively incapacitate high-rate offenders.

Unlike Avi-Itzhak and Shinnar, Canela-Cacho's model allows λ_i to vary across offenders. A continuous distribution that mixes several exponential distributions is used to represent this variability. Such mixtures are flexible enough to accommodate the high levels of skewness revealed in empirical studies of the distribution of λ, where the vast majority of offenders have low λ values, but a small subset of offenders generates crimes at unusually high rates.[39]

The model estimates the amount of time that an offender is expected to be both active and imprisoned—the only time when incapacitation occurs—as a function of the imprisonment policy parameters Q and S, and of the offending parameters λ and career length L. The incapacitation index I^* is then computed as the ratio of the average number of crimes prevented to the average total crimes that would be expected if offenders were to remain free in the community.

Table 9 presents estimates of I^* for robbery in California, Michigan, and Texas during the late 1970s. These figures are based on the distributions of λ reported in Table 7, and the values of Q and S in

TABLE 9 Estimates of the Percentage Reduction from the Potential Level of Robberies Resulting from Incapacitation in Prison Following a Robbery Conviction

	California	Michigan	Texas
I^*, heterogeneous λ	30.1	41.3	27.8
I, homogeneous λ	4.7	7.8	5.3
Incapacitative advantage, I^*/I	6.4	5.3	5.2

NOTE: Estimates of the incapacitative effects, I and I^*, assume (1) an average career length L of five years, (2) the λ distributions for all offenders reported in Table 7, and (3) the imprisonment sanction levels reported in Table 6. The estimates for homogeneous λ derive from the model in Shinnar and Shinnar (1975), with $I = \lambda QSL/(S + L + \lambda QSL)$, whereas those for heterogeneous λ are developed in Canela-Cacho (1990).

Table 6. The I^* estimates also assume an average career length of five years for robbery, which is consistent with the empirical estimates discussed above. To underscore the impact of the selection bias toward high-λ offenders that is induced by offender heterogeneity, Table 9 also includes estimates of the incapacitation effect, I, as measured by the Avi-Itzhak Shinnar model using the same sanction parameters, average career length, and mean λ that are applied in the computation of I^*.

It is evident from Table 9 that the effect of stochastic selectivity on the estimated incapacitation effect is substantial. If offender heterogeneity and the resulting selection bias toward high-rate offenders among inmates are ignored, the Avi-Itzhak and Shinnar model seriously underestimates crime reduction from incapacitation. Once we account for offender heterogeneity, the reductions in robberies that result from incapacitation are anything but negligible: of every ten potential robberies, between three and four are prevented by the incarceration of some robbers. Alternatively, whereas in the case of homogeneous λ, the number of robberies committed would be expected to increase by only 5 to 10 percent from prevailing levels if offenders were fortunate enough to avoid incarceration,[40] that increase when λ is heterogeneous would be from 39 to 70 percent.[41] This result is all the more impressive in light of an average time served (QS) of less than one month per robbery committed in the three states examined.[42]

The relationship between the composition of the offender population and incapacitation is also well illustrated by the variation in I^* across states. Texas has the highest sanction level (QS = 0.0776), but the lowest incapacitation effect. Two factors contribute to this seemingly paradoxical outcome. First, the mean λ for robbery in the total offender population in Texas is less than half of that in California or Michigan (see Table 8). Second, even high-λ robbers in Texas commit crimes at lower rates than their counterpart high-λ offenders in either California or Michigan, and they comprise a smaller proportion of the total offender population (see Table 7). It is thus not surprising that more crimes are prevented for each robber incarcerated in California than in Texas. The incapacitation index measures the fraction of potential crimes that are averted through incarceration, and as shown by Cohen (1978), the less potential crime in a community, the smaller are the returns from incapacitation.

Remaining Sources of Bias in Incapacitation Estimates

Some important potential sources of measurement bias remain in the estimates of incapacitation reported so far. We discuss these factors briefly below and indicate the direction of the biases they may introduce. Unfortunately, the models and data currently available do not permit rigorous treatment of these biases. Nevertheless, existing knowledge provides some basis for speculating on whether or not these biases are likely to be sizable.

Relationship Between λ and Q. The estimates of incapacitation—both average and marginal—assume a risk of incarceration for each crime committed, Q, that is homogeneous across all offenders. Thus, the crimes of high- and low-λ offenders alike are assumed to be equally vulnerable to interception by the criminal justice system. Heterogeneity in λ coupled with homogeneity in Q leads to overrepresentation of high-rate offenders among prison inmates, which increases the incapacitation index considerably.[43]

If λ and Q were inversely related—so that high-rate offenders were more likely to escape imprisonment following commission of a crime—the selection effect toward high-λ offenders into prison would be attenuated or could even be reversed, with obvious negative consequences for incapacitation. Consider one extreme in which the most active offenders are completely invulnerable to arrest, whereas one-time-only offenders are almost certain to be arrested. In this case, prisons would be filled with inactive offenders, and the most prolific offenders would escape incapacitation altogether.

Although empirical evidence on the relationship between λ and Q is far from conclusive, a negative association has been observed in which the probability of arrest following a crime seems to decrease as λ increases (Dunford and Elliott, 1984; Chaiken and Chaiken, 1984; Cohen, 1986; Greenwood and Turner, 1987; Blumstein et al., 1989). Ignoring this relationship will bias the I^* estimates upward. There are good reasons, however, for believing that this bias is not likely to be sizable.

First, the same evidence that suggests a negative correlation between λ and Q clearly shows that an offender's overall risk of incarceration remains an increasing function of λ (Cohen, 1986:Table B-25). In other words, although Q may be lower for each crime committed by high-λ offenders, the number of crimes that these offenders commit is sufficiently large to compensate for any reduction in Q, so that high-λ offenders still have a greater probability of eventually being incarcerated during a period of, for example, one year. Thus, although the magnitude of stochastic selectivity toward high-rate offenders is diminished, it is not completely eliminated.

Second, for the type of skewed λ distributions revealed in empirical studies, Canela-Cacho (1990:26-32) found that the crimes of low-λ offenders would have to be about 200 times more vulnerable to incarceration than the crimes of high-λ offenders before stochastic selectivity would reverse. Nothing in the available evidence suggests differentials in Q of this order of magnitude. For example, among inmates who participated in the second Rand survey, Blumstein et al. (1989) estimated that offenders who committed robberies at rates of less than 3 per year were 5 to 15 times more vulnerable to arrest per crime than those with frequency rates in excess of 100 robberies per year. Cohn (1986:Table B-25) estimates a similar differential in arrest risk per crime between high- and low-λ offenders in data from the National Youth Survey of a general population sample. Simulations in Canela-Cacho (1990) show that the stochastic bias toward high-rate offenders in prison remains sizable for differences of Q in this range, provided the distribution of λ is fairly skewed.

Finally, although the probability of arrest per crime is a decreasing function of λ, the probability of incarceration given arrest is not. An offender's prior record weighs heavily in a judge's decision to sentence a convictee to prison. Both the length and the seriousness of past recorded offenses increase the likelihood of a sentence to prison (Blumstein et al., 1983). Because high-rate offenders who remain active for long periods of time are also most likely to accumulate a prior record, it would appear that the probability of incarceration given arrest increases with λ. Thus, the range of variation in Q between high- and low-λ offenders is smaller than might be suggested by the difference in the probabilities of arrest for these two groups of offenders.

Diversity of Offending Behavior The computation of I^* for robbery, when calculating crimes prevented, includes only periods of incarceration resulting from robberies and does not account for the possibility that a "robber" could also break into a house, murder someone, or steal an automobile. Obviously, an offender who commits five robberies and three burglaries per year has a higher risk of entering prison than does an offender who commits five robberies and no other crimes. Thus, it is the total offending rate, including all crime types, that ultimately determines the fraction of a career that an offender spends in prison.

Numerous studies have looked at the issue of offender specialization in various types of crime. Overwhelmingly, the evidence indicates that exclusive specialization in any one crime type is virtually nonexistent. However, as Farrington (1982:178) concluded after reviewing the literature, "some degree of specialization [is] superimposed in a high degree of generality." So for example, Chaiken and Chaiken (1984) found a group of offenders they labeled "violent predators" who commit robbery, assault, and drug dealing at high rates. Some of these offenders, however, also regularly commit other offenses such as burglary, theft, and credit card fraud.

Although the label "violent offender" is inexact because few offenders engage exclusively in crimes of violence, it provides a useful way to distinguish offenders with some violent offenses from those who never commit violent crimes. In this respect, some interesting findings have been replicated in various studies. Violent offenders appear to have higher mean offending rates across all crime types than do nonviolent offenders. In a sample of juvenile offenders, Farrington (1978) observed that while nonviolent delinquents averaged 2.7 convictions, violent delinquents averaged 4.3. Similarly, for a cohort born in 1958 in Philadelphia, Piper (1985) found that among male delinquents, violent offenders average 4.2 arrests compared to 1.2 for nonviolent offenders. Perhaps more surprisingly, Piper also observed that although violent delinquents represented 32 percent of all offenders, they accounted for 57 percent of all offenses.

The relationship between overall offending levels and violent offending is particularly striking among male delinquents in a 1945 Philadelphia cohort. Offenders with five or more recorded police contacts of any type—violent or nonviolent—were responsible for the vast majority of violent crimes: 71.4 percent of all homicides, 72.7 percent of all rapes, 81.8 percent of all robberies, and 69.1 percent of all aggravated assaults (Weiner, 1989:Table 2.16). Although somewhat attenuated, the same pattern was also found for the 1958 Philadelphia cohort.[44]

The relationship between violent and nonviolent crimes is of paramount importance for incapacitation purposes. A nonviolent offense committed with high frequency by a violent offender can lead to incarceration, which serves just as well to incapacitate violent offending as does incarceration for violent offenses. As a matter of fact, Chaiken and Chaiken (1984) found that among inmates who participated in the second Rand survey, many of the so-called violent predators were currently serving time for a nonviolent offense, often burglary. So, even if individual offenders commit rape or homicide only rarely, incapacitation levels for these offenses can still be substantial if these offenders end up spending a large fraction of their careers behind bars as a result of other crimes they commit at much higher rates.[45]

Estimates of incapacitation based only on offending rates and incarceration for one type of violent crime, such as robbery, are biased downward because they underestimate the total amount of time that an offender serves in prison throughout his entire career. In this respect, the I^* estimates for robbery presented in the previous section should be considered conservatively low.

DETERRENCE AND INCAPACITATION

All previous estimates of incapacitation ignore the possibility that actual or threatened incarceration might alter individual propensities to commit crime. Largely for reasons of tractability, dynamic changes in offending have been ignored. The failure to address adaptive behavioral responses by offenders is especially problematic for estimates of incapacitation that are cast in terms of the proportional reduction from the potential level of crimes if incarceration were to be eliminated entirely.

Critics have rightly pointed out that even the customary estimates of the potential level of crimes at zero incarceration are themselves influenced by prevailing sanction levels. In particular, the rate at which offenders have been observed to commit crimes while they are free, λ_0 (e.g., in offender self-reports), is influenced by the sanction risks, $Q_0 S_0$, that those offenders faced while they were free. If sanctions were to change markedly from prevailing levels, it would be reasonable to expect corresponding changes in offending rates while free and thus changes in the base level of potential crimes from which incapacitation is measured.

Although changes in λ constitute a genuine cause for concern, existing estimates of incapacitation are not completely without value. In acknowledging the potential role of sanctions in determining the base level of crimes, incapacitation is measured not against a standard of crimes when incarceration is totally absent, but rather against the level of crimes that would be expected if, *despite the prevailing level of sanction risks*, offenders were to remain free. The base offending level, λ_0, is the rate at which an offender commits crimes conditional upon the prevailing risk of incarceration $Q_0 S_0$. In an expected utility formulation, λ_0 might be regarded as the rate of offending at which the expected benefits from crime equal the expected costs from incarceration for those crimes.

The estimates of incapacitation discussed in this paper should be interpreted in this way. So, for example, the 41.3 percent reduction in crime in Michigan (Table 9) is not the reduction from the expected level of crime if $Q_0 S_0$ were reduced from 0.0514 (Table 6) to zero in Michigan. Rather, it is the reduction from the level of crime that would be expected if offenders were fortunate and avoided incarceration despite a prevailing expected time served per robbery of 0.0514 year. Such conditional estimates are useful for gauging the relative magnitude of crime reduction from incapacitation in static comparisons across jurisdictions with different prevailing values of λ_0 and sanction policies, $Q_0 S_0$, and for assessing the likely impact of short-term *marginal* changes from $Q_0 S_0$. They are less well suited, however, for analyzing the impacts of substantial long-term shifts in policy, such as those observed in recent decades in the United States.

Deterrence effects that alter the size of the active offending population, the offending rates of active offenders, or the duration of offending careers will have important implications for the magnitude of crime reduction that derives from incapacitation. Because they affect the potential crime levels against which incapacitation effects are measured, decreases in the general level of offending also reduce the incapacitative effect. Although deterrence and incapacitation both contribute to crime control, they interact in complex ways, and under some circumstances their effects are negatively correlated.

When offenders are faced with a higher expected time served in prison—whether from increases in the certainty (Q) or the severity (S) of prison terms for the crimes they commit—the following behavioral responses are possible:

(1) Some offenders may reduce their offending frequencies (λ) in an effort to restore their overall incarceration risk to previous levels.

(2) Other offenders might regard the increased criminal sanctions as sufficiently severe that they withdraw from crime altogether.

(3) Some individuals who would have embarked on offending careers under previous sanctioning levels may refrain from crime because of the increased penalties.

In each case, the deterrence effects on individual offending will reduce the expected total volume of crime that is susceptible to incapacitation by depressing individual offending frequencies, reducing the number of active offenders, or both.[46]

As noted above, the smaller the total crime base is, the lower the returns from incapacitation will be. Thus, large deterrent effects would reduce the opportunities for incapacitation and result in lower incapacitation levels. In the extreme, if deterrent effects were completely successful in dissuading all offenders from further criminal involvement, prisons would have zero incapacitation returns.[47]

Estimates of the reduction in crime and increase in prison population following the introduction of tougher criminal sanctions that disregard deterrent effects and refer only to incapacitation suffer from a double distortion. On the one hand, the number of crimes prevented is *underestimated* because no correction is made for those crimes that offenders preemptively abandon in response to the threat of prison. On the other hand, prison population growth is *overestimated* because no adjustments are made for reductions in the offender population or in offending frequencies that the stiffer penalties induce.

The magnitudes of these biases depend critically on the extent to which deterrent effects are realized. Although it is virtually undisputed that criminal sanctions do deter some crime, there is considerable uncertainty about the size of these effects, particularly the marginal effects as criminal sanctions change within a reasonably small range.[48] Available estimates of the deterrence elasticity are generally in the range of –0.2 to –1.0 percent reductions in crime associated with a 1 percent increase in sanction levels.[49] These estimates are used here only as suggestive of the possible magnitude of deterrence effects.

Exploratory Estimates of Deterrence Effects

We use the following procedure to distinguish the relative magnitudes of the deterrence (D) and incapacitation (I) effects associated with a change in imprisonment policies. From an initial base level of sanctions and crimes—with total offenders N_0, average individual offending rate λ_0, and expected time served per crime $Q_0 S_0$—the potential number of crimes committed is $C_0 = \lambda_0^* N_0$.[50] An increase in imprisonment sanctions to $Q_1 S_1$ is assumed to operate through deterrence to reduce both the size of the offender population and the average offending rate, and yields a new potential number of crimes, $C_1 = \lambda_1^* N_1$.[51] Incapacitation from $Q_1 S_1$ then operates to reduce potential crimes C_1 to the expected number of crimes actually committed, O_1, where O_1 is estimated by using the model of incapacitation under offender heterogeneity and finite careers, I^*, described earlier.

The deterrence and incapacitation effects of a change in sanctions from $Q_0 S_0$ to $Q_1 S_1$ are given by

$$D_1 = \frac{C_0 - C_1}{C_0} \tag{2a}$$

$$I_1^* = \frac{C_1 - O_1}{C_1} \tag{2b}$$

where D_1 is the deterred portion of potential crimes and I_1^* is the incapacitated portion of the remaining undeterred crimes. Total crime reduction (R_1) from C_0 as a result of the increase from $Q_0 S_0$ to $Q_1 S_1$ is

$$R_1 = (C_0 - O_1)/C_0 \tag{3}$$

By substituting equation (2a) and (2b) into equation (3), R_1 can be written as

$$R_1 = D_1 + I_1^{*}(1 - D_1) \tag{4}$$

$$= \frac{C_0 - C_1}{C_0} + \frac{C_1 - O_1}{C_1} \cdot \frac{C_1}{C_0}$$

$$= \frac{C_0 - O_1}{C_0}$$

In equation (4), the expression $I_1^{*}(1 - D_1) = \dfrac{C_1 - O_1}{C_0} = I_2^{*}$ represents the incapacitated portion of the original potential level of crimes, C_0. Although the magnitues of D_1 and I_1^{*} cannot be compared directly to one another because of the different base crime levels, C_0 for D_1 and C_1 for I_1^{*}, D_1 and I_2^{*} are comparable, and indicate the relative portions of C_0 crimes that are deterred and incapacitated, respectively. The analyses of crime control effects that follow will rely on D_1 and I_2^{*}.[52]

Sanctions are assumed to be uniform for all offenders, but we allow for variation in offender taste for risk by contrasting three alternative deterrence scenarios: one in which deterrence operates equally on all offenders, a second in which only low-λ offenders are deterred, and a third in which only high-λ offenders are deterred. Under scenario 2, only the least committed, marginal offenders are deterred, whereas under scenario 3, only the worst offenders are deterred. The latter might occur, for example, if high-rate offenders are more aware of and responsive to changes in sanctions.

Values of the offending and sanction variables are chosen to closely resemble actual values estimated for violent crimes in the United States during the mid-1970s and end of the 1980s (see Table 10). The distribution of robbery offending rates estimated for all offenders in Michigan in the mid-1970s (Table 7) is used as the initial distribution of offending rates. Imprisonment sanctions are based on the numbers of inmates and total crimes for serious violent offenses in the United States in 1975 and 1989.[53]

TABLE 10 Estimated Offending Rates and Sanction Levels for Violent Crimes in the United States, 1975 and 1989

	Low-λ Offenders	Medium-λ Offenders	High-λ Offenders	Total Offenders
Mean annual offending rate while free, λ_0	1.4	8.9	239.0	2.8
Percentage of offenders in each offender group	93.3	6.3	0.4	100.0
Average career length (years)	10.0	10.0	10.0	10.0
Imprisonment risk per crime				
Q_0	0.0068	0.0068	0.0068	0.0068
Q_1	0.0123	0.0123	0.0123	0.0123
Average years served in prison				
S_0	2.5	2.5	2.5	2.5
S_1	4.0	4.0	4.0	4.0
Expected years served per crime				
$Q_0 S_0$	0.0170	0.0170	0.0170	0.0170
$Q_1 S_1$	0.0492	0.0492	0.0492	0.0492

NOTE: Offending rates are those estimated for robbery among all offenders in Michigan during the mid-1970s (Table 7). Imprisonment sanctions $Q_0 S_0$ correspond to the year 1975, and $Q_1 S_1$ to 1989.

Table 11 reports the resulting estimates of deterrence and incapacitation effects under the assumed model. Estimates are obtained by using deterrence elasticities of –0.2 and –1.0 for each scenario. In this illustration, deterrence effects increase monotonically with the contribution of $p_i \lambda_i$ to the overall mean $\lambda_0 = \Sigma p_j \lambda_j$ (with high-λ offenders contributing less than low-λ offenders, $p_{hi}\lambda_{hi} < p_{lo}\lambda_{lo}$, who in turn contribute less than the total population of offenders, $p_{lo}\lambda_{lo} < \lambda_0$). Naturally, D is also increasing monotonically, but at a decreasing rate, for larger deterrence elas-

TABLE 11 Percentage Reduction from Potential Violent Crimes Due to Incapacitation and Deterrence Under Alternative Deterrence Scenarios

	Deterrence D_1	Incapacitation I_2^*	Incapacitation I_1^*	Total $D_1 + I_2^*$
Base level crime reduction at $Q_0 S_0$	0.0	32.9	32.9	32.9
Crime reduction at $Q_1 S_1$				
No deterrence	0.0	41.9	41.9	41.9
Deter high-λ offenders				
Elasticity = −0.2	11.9	30.8	34.9	42.7
Elasticity = −1.0	30.2	14.0	20.1	44.2
Deter low-λ offenders				
Elasticity = −0.2	15.8	40.2	47.7	56.0
Elasticity = −1.0	40.1	38.3	63.9	78.4
Deter all offenders				
Elasticity = −0.2	34.7	26.0	39.8	60.7
Elasticity = −1.0	88.1	3.8	31.9	91.9

NOTE: Crime control effects are obtained from the offending and sanction levels reported in Table 10. Reductions are from the potential number of crimes $C_0 = \lambda_0 N_0$ that prevail at initial sanction levels $Q_0 S_0 = 0.017$ (i.e., *after* the base level of deterrence from sanctions $Q_0 S_0$). (The deterrence effect from the base level of potential crimes is unknown and treated as zero.)

$$D_1 = \frac{C_0 - C_1}{C_0}$$

$$I_1^* = \frac{C_1 - O_1}{C_1}$$

$$I_2^* = I_1^*(1 - D_1) = \frac{C_1 - O_1}{C_0}.$$

Deterrence from the new sanction level $Q_1 S_1$ reduces the potential level of crimes to $C_1 = \lambda_1 N_1$ by discouraging participation in crime ($N_1 < N_0$) and inhibiting the frequency of crimes committed by active offenders ($\lambda_1 < \lambda_0$). Incapacitation I_2^* at sanction level $Q_1 S_1$ further reduces potential crimes C_1 to the expected number of crimes actually committed, $\lambda_1^* < \lambda_1$. The more commonly used measure of incapacitation, I_1^*, reports the incapacitation effect relative to the new undeterred level of potential crimes, $C_1 = \lambda_1 N_1$.

ticities; in this illustration, a fivefold increase in absolute magnitude for the deterrence elasticity, $-1.0/(-0.2)$, results in only a 2.54-fold increase in crime reduction from deterrence.

The exploratory analysis manifests an interesting interaction between D and I in which the incapacitation effect is not monotonic and depends instead on how deterrence alters the distribution of offending rates. When deterrence reduces the representation and mean λ's of low-λ offenders, high-λ offenders become a greater share of the new offending distribution, and incapacitation effects are large. Deterrence of high-λ offenders has exactly the opposite effect by reducing the high end of the λ distribution. It is important to note that D and I are not necessarily inversely related. When deterrence increases the concentration of high-λ offenders, incapacitation effects will also increase. As deterrence effects become more widely spread throughout the offender population, however, incapacitation effects decline.

Under the "no-deterrence" or "deter high-λ" scenarios in Table 11, the new sanction level $Q_1 S_1$ is associated with total crime reduction in the range of 42 to 44 percent of $\lambda_0 N_0$ crimes prevented. Reflecting the decreasing marginal returns from increasing sanctions, the increment above the 32.9 percent crime reduction from incapacitation already achieved at $Q_0 S_0$ is small, especially in view of the very large increase in QS. More substantial incremental crime reduction that is similar in magnitude to the almost tripling in imprisonment sanctions between 1975 and 1989 requires large deterrence effects—an elasticity of -1.0—that apply broadly throughout the offender population.[54]

Whereas Table 11 presents the reduction in crimes relative to their potential level, we are also interested in how these crime control mechanisms affect the expected number of crimes that are actually committed. Along with observed changes in crimes and inmates, Table 12 shows the changes in crimes and inmates that would have been expected from the combination of deterrence and incapacitation, as modeled here, if observed changes in incarceration policies between 1975 and 1989 had been applied to offending levels that prevailed in the mid-1970s. Although the observed number of inmates nearly tripled (increasing by 188%) between 1975 and 1989, the observed number of violent crimes remained virtually unchanged (−1.1% in Table 12). None of the deterrence scenarios examined in Table 12 satisfactorily replicates this observed pattern in crimes and inmates. Instead, under the model analyzed here, we see that deterrence and incapacitation would have combined to transform an almost threefold increase

TABLE 12 Percentage Change in Numbers of Inmates and Crimes Actually Committed Under Alternative Deterrence Scenarios for Violent Offenses in the United States, 1975 to 1989

	Crimes	Inmates
1975 count (millions)	2.9	0.1
Observed percentage change from 1975 to 1989	−1.1	+188.3
Expected percentage change at new sanction level, Q_1S_1 in 1989		
No deterrence	−13.4	+150.3
Deter high-λ offenders		
Elasticity = −0.2	−14.5	+147.2
Elasticity = −1.0	−16.9	+140.3
Deter low-λ offenders		
Elasticity = −0.2	−34.3	+89.9
Elasticity = −1.0	−67.8	−6.9
Deter all-λ offenders		
Elasticity = −0.2	−41.4	+69.5
Elasticity = −1.0	−87.9	−65.1

NOTE: The numbers of serious violent offenses in 1975 and 1989 are obtained from the total number of rapes, robberies, and aggravated assaults reported to the National Crime Survey for those years (Bureau of Justice Statistics, 1990b, 1991), augmented by the count of homicides known to the police in the same years (Federal Bureau of Investigation, 1976, 1990a).

The number of inmates by crime type each year is estimated from the crime type distribution available from national surveys of state prison inmates in 1974 and 1986 (National Prisoner Statistics, 1976; Bureau of Justice Statistics, 1988) applied to total counts of inmates with sentences of one year or longer reported for state prisons in 1975 and 1989 (Bureau of Justice Statistics, 1990a; Flanagan and Maguire, 1990). State prison inmates are combined with annual data on the crime-type mix of inmates held in federal prisons (Callahan, 1986; Flanagan and Maguire, 1990).

Expected changes in crimes committed and in inmate population are relative to observed levels in 1975, and are associated with the changes in sanctions from Q_0S_0 to Q_1S_1 observed between 1975 and 1989 (see Table 10). All estimates derive from the model of deterrence and incapacitation specified in equations (2) and (3) and in note 51.

in imprisonment sanctions during recent years into substantial reductions from 1975 crime levels and smaller changes from the 1975 prison population.

Among the scenarios in Table 12, the two that come closest to observed rates involve either no deterrence or deterrence that operates narrowly on a very small subgroup of high-λ offenders. In the no-deterrence case, individual offending is not affected by deterrence, and potential violent crimes in 1989, $\lambda_1 N_1$, would be identical to the base level of potential crimes in 1975, $\lambda_0 N_0$. The increases in imprisonment sanctions, from $Q_0 S_0$ to $Q_1 S_1$, nevertheless, would have been expected to reduce observed crimes by 13.4 percent through increased incapacitation. If high-λ offenders were deterred by the increased imprisonment risk, slightly more crimes would have been prevented at a somewhat smaller cost in terms of increased inmates.

The other deterrence scenarios explored in Table 12 would have resulted in substantially greater crime reduction. Under the most generous deterrence assumptions—in which a deterrence elasticity of –1.0 reduces offending rates and offender numbers for most of the offending population (i.e., deter low-λ or deter all offenders)[55]—reductions in violent crimes of more than 65 percent from 1975 levels would have been accompanied by *reductions* in prison populations as fewer offenders remained active and their offending rates declined.

The near stability in crimes actually committed (which declined by only 1.1% from 1975 to 1989), despite the substantial increase in prison population (up 188.3%), is not compatible with large deterrence effects that reduced the underlying potential level of offending between 1975 and 1989. Furthermore, even in the absence of deterrence, the incapacitation effects from the observed increase in imprisonment would have reduced the number of crimes committed somewhat below the level observed in 1989 (crimes down 13.4% instead of only 1.1%). It is possible, however, that substantial crime control from deterrence and incapacitation actually did occur through a reduction in "phantom crimes" (i.e., crimes that would have been committed were it not for the deterrent and incapacitation effects associated with the increase in imprisonment sanctions from $Q_0 S_0$ to $Q_1 S_1$). Thus, the increased imprisonment between 1975 and 1989 could have contained an otherwise escalating level of offending due to factors independent of sanction levels, such as demographic changes in the population or a worsening of criminogenic factors.

Tables 13 and 14 illustrate such a process for two hypotheti-

TABLE 13 Percentage Change in Numbers of Inmates and Crimes Actually Committed Under Alternative Deterrence Scenarios in Which Underlying Potential Levels of Offending for Violent Offenses in the United States Increased Between 1975 and 1989

	Crimes	Inmates
Observed 1975 count (millions)	2.9	0.1
Observed percentage change from 1975 to 1989	−1.1	+188.3
Expected percent change at new sanction level, Q_1S_1 in 1989		
New mean $\lambda_0^* = 7.5$		
Deter high-λ offenders, elasticity = −1.0	+3.8	+200.0
Deter low-λ offenders, elasticity = −0.2	+2.1	+195.3
New mean $\lambda_0^* = 10.0$		
Deter high-λ offenders, elasticity = −1.0	+4.5	+201.9
Deter low-λ offenders, elasticity = −0.2	+3.5	+199.4

NOTE: The numbers of serious violent offenses committed and inmates held in prison for violent offenses in 1975 and 1989 are obtained as noted in Table 12.

The original base level of offending averages $\lambda_0 = 2.8$ for N_0 offenders (Table 10). The hypothesized new higher offending rates result from a shift to greater representation of high-λ offending and a higher average λ_0 for high-λ offenders at time t_1.

Expected changes in crimes committed and in inmate population are relative to levels observed in 1975, and are associated with the changes in sanctions from Q_0S_0 to Q_1S_1 observed between 1975 and 1989 (see Table 10). All estimates derive from the model of deterrence and incapacitation specified in equations (2) and (3) and in note 51.

TABLE 14 Percentage Reduction from Potential Violent Crimes Due to Incapacitation and Deterrence Under Alternative Deterrence Scenarios

	Deterrence D_1	Incapacitation I_2^*	I_1^*	Total $D_1 + I_2^*$	
New mean $\lambda_0^* = 7.5$					
Base level crime reduction at $Q_0 S_0$	0.0	59.9	59.9	⌐59.9⌐	
				+9.9	
No deterrence at $Q_1 S_1$	0.0	69.8	69.8	⌐69.8	
					+14.7
Deter high-λ offenders, elasticity = 1.0 at $Q_1 S_1$	60.9	13.3	33.9	+4.8 │ 74.2	
Deter low-λ offenders, elasticity = –0.2 at $Q_1 S_1$	5.3	69.2	73.1	⌊74.6⌋	
New Mean $\lambda_0^* = 10.0$					
Base level crime reduction at $Q_0 S_0$	0.0	69.0	69.0	⌐69.0⌐	
				+8.1	
No deterrence at $Q_1 S_1$	0.0	77.1	77.1	⌐77.1	
					+11.7
Deter high-λ offenders, elasticity = –1.0 at $Q_1 S_1$	67.7	12.8	39.6	+3.6 │ 80.5	
Deter low-λ offenders, elasticity = –0.2 at $Q_1 S_1$	4.0	76.7	79.9	⌊80.7⌋	

NOTE: Crime control effects are obtained from the sanction levels reported in Table 11 applied to hypothesized increased offending levels in 1989, represented by λ_0^*. Reductions at time 1 are from the potential number of crimes $C_0 = \lambda_0^* N_0$ that prevail at initial sanction levels $Q_0 S_0 = 0.017$ (i.e., *after* the base level of deterrence from sanctions $Q_0 S_0$). The deterrence effect from the base level of potential crimes is unknown and treated as zero.

The deterrence effect of new sanctions levels, D_1, is the percentage reduction in the potential level of crimes from $C_0 = \lambda_0^* N_0$ to $C_1 = \lambda_1 N_1$. The incapacitation effect, I_{1*}, is the percentage reduction from $C_1 = \lambda_1 N_1$ potential crimes to the expected number of crimes actually committed, $\lambda_1^* N_1^* < \lambda_1 N_1$. I_2^* recalibrates the incapacitation effect as a percentage reduction from the original potential number of crimes, $C_0 = \lambda_0^* N_0$. All estimates derive from the model of deterrence and incapacitation specified in equations (2) and (2) and in note 51.

cal scenarios of increases in the potential level of offending in 1989—one in which the overall mean rate of violent offending increased from $\lambda_0 = 2.8$ in 1975 to $\lambda_0^* = 7.5$ in 1989, and the other with $\lambda_0^* = 10.0$.[56] The results in Table 13 show that both hypothesized distributions of an increase in potential offending in 1989 are capable of reasonably reproducing the observed trends of a near zero change in crimes and a tripling in inmates between 1975 and 1989. We see in Table 14 that the observed offending levels in 1989 might result from very different deterrence scenarios—one involving a substantial deterrence effect of the high-λ offenders, and the other involving only modest deterrence of low-λ offenders but substantial incapacitation from incarceration of the new higher-λ offenders.

Under both scenarios, even if imprisonment sanctions had remained at 1975 levels of $Q_0 S_0$, the crime reduction from the new potential level of crimes due to incapacitation would be substantial—60 to 69 percent. This reflects the increase in incapacitation associated with higher crime rates. Thus, if sanction levels were to continue at $Q_0 S_0$, the dramatic increases in underlying offending rates that are explored (up 168% from 2.8 to 7.5, or up 257% from 2.8 to 10.0) would have resulted in just 61 to 66 percent more crimes expected in 1989 than were actually observed.[57] Although the relative mix of deterrence and incapacitation effects varies over the alternative deterrence scenarios examined in Table 14, the increase in total crime reduction expected from the increment in sanctions to $Q_1 S_1$ is only 8 to 15 percentage points above the base-level incapacitation effect.

It is especially noteworthy that the estimated crime reduction under a no-deterrence scenario in Table 14 (e.g., 70% for $\lambda_0^* = 7.5$) is very close to the total crime reduction achieved under either deterrence scenario (e.g., 75% for $\lambda_0^* = 7.5$). The same similarity in total crime reduction is also observed for the most likely deterrence scenarios in Table 11 (no-deterrence and deter high-λ offenders). Although the naive estimate of incapacitation that simply applies new sanctions $Q_1 S_1$ to the previously prevailing offending level $\lambda_0 N_0$ may overstate the actual incapacitation effect when there is substantial deterrence, it nevertheless provides a remarkably good estimate of the total crime reduction associated with a major shift in sanction levels. Prior concerns that incapacitation estimates seriously understate crime reduction when they ignore deterrence effects seem to be unwarranted.[58]

Remaining Sources of Bias in Deterrence Estimates

The exploratory model of deterrence that we use permits the widest possible deterrence impacts in response to sanction changes. Deterrence effects are assumed to derive equally from changes in either Q or S, and to have the same effects on both offending rates (λ) and the size of the offender population (N). Extensions to this model might selectively reduce the scope of deterrence effects, perhaps differentiating between the effects of changes in certainty and of those in severity, or limiting deterrence effects to changes in *either* N or λ. Any of these changes would reduce the total deterrence effect estimated above, but would not alter the main results.

A more interesting variant of the deterrence model would permit heterogeneity in deterrence effects across offenders. The model that we use does not vary sanction levels across offenders, but rather permits differential responsiveness of offenders to the same sanction level. We have incorporated such heterogeneity to a limited extent by selectively restricting the deterrent impact to one or another of the main λ subpopulations. The differences in impacts for the "deter high-λ" and "deter low-λ" cases were especially useful for illustrating how the partition between deterrence and incapacitation is influenced by changes in the relative representation of high-λ offenders resulting from deterrence.

Deterrence of high-λ offenders decreases both their mean and their relative representation in the population of offenders, thereby reducing the incapacitative effect below that obtained in the absence of deterrence. When the same deterrence impact is restricted to low-λ offenders, the relative representation of high-λ offenders increases, as does incapacitation's share of total crime reduction. An alternative deterrence model might provide for greater heterogeneity, with the deterrence impact varying as a function of λ. We can anticipate from the above results that cases in which the deterrence impact is a decreasing function of λ will experience the smallest losses in incapacitation effect. Such a scenario seems to be the most likely behavioral outcome, involving greater deterrence effectiveness in reducing offending at the margins (which are dominted by low-λ offenders), rather than among the most active, high-λ offenders.

POLICY CHOICES IN EXPANDING INCARCERATION

The costs and benefits of expanding incarceration beyond current levels are now considered. This is a particularly relevant policy question at a time when there seems to be broad consensus among policy makers and the public in favor of controlling rising crime rates through increased use of incarceration, but when there are serious resource constraints on available prison capacity.

To achieve higher levels of incapacitation, policy makers may increase either Q or S. For example, one option would increase the fraction of convictees who are sentenced to prison, thereby raising Q. Alternatively, the fraction of convictees committed to prison might remain constant, but those going to prison would be sentenced to longer terms, which would increase S. Of course, mixed strategies that simultaneously increase both Q and S are also possible, and the policy choice is then to specify the desired balance between broadening the offender base that goes to prison and lengthening prison terms.

Assessing incapacitation effects by analyzing the criminal histories of a sample of convictees in the Denver area, Petersilia and Greenwood (1978) found some evidence to suggest that a policy of short sentences applied to a large offender base is more efficient than a policy of long sentences applied to a small offender base. For example, they estimated that if all convictees in their sample had been given prison terms of one year, regardless of their prior criminal records, the crimes generated by the cohort would have been reduced by 15 percent at a cost of a 50 percent increase in prison population. In contrast, they found that mandatory minimum prison terms of four years imposed only on convictees who had a prior felony conviction would have resulted in the same reduction in crime, but at a cost of a 150 percent increase in the size of the prison population.

From the perspective of the separate contributions of λ and career termination to total offending, the findings of Petersilia and Greenwood are to be expected. The differential impact of Q and S on incapacitation derives fundamentally from career termination. The value of Q is critical in determining how early in an offender's criminal career incapacitation begins to operate. When Q is very small, offenders can be expected to commit numerous crimes before they are caught and incapacitated, and some offenders may survive their entire careers without a single criminal justice system intervention. As Q increases, the number of crimes before an offender's first conviction declines, so a larger Q results in earlier incapacitation following the onset of an offender's criminal career.

Incapacitation is also an increasing function of S, with long sentences preventing more crimes than short sentences. Long sentences, however, reduce the efficiency of prison resources. As time served increases, so does the expected fraction of the inmate population whose criminal careers end before they are released from prison. Thus, long sentences add to the size of the prison population, but often at the cost of increasing the number of inmates who are no longer criminally active, thereby reducing the incapacitation gains from the added inmates.

In the face of constraints on available prison resources, the problem for criminal justice policy is how to allocate a finite number of cells among competing offenders. Ideally, one would like to have the *worst active* offenders occupy those cells. This is precisely the motivation behind incapacitation policies that would deliberately select some offenders for enhanced sentences based on assessments of their future crime potential. Such a selective strategy also has initial appeal as a sensible response to deterrence impacts that are likely to be decreasing functions of λ. By selectively increasing Q and S as λ increases, it might be possible to offset expected declines in deterrence among the most active offenders. However, prevailing difficulties with accurately identifying the worst offenders and predicting when their careers will end, seriously limit the feasibility of such deliberate selective incarceration policies.[59]

The analysis of offending careers presented here indicates that even uniformly applied imprisonment policies, which make no explicit attempt to distinguish among offenders, will result in disproportionately large portions of high-λ offenders in prison. The resulting stochastic selectivity derives essentially from a form of self-selection in which offenders increase their opportunities for incarceration through the number of crimes they commit. Even if time served on each sentence is relatively short, high-λ offenders will nevertheless spend substantial portions of their careers incarcerated through the many more returns to prison that they experience.

Considerations of likely deterrence effects also favor a policy of uniformly applied imprisonment sanctions. Selection of the most active offenders into prison by explicitly varying QS to be an increasing function of λ may not be optimal. Although high-λ offenders are targeted for increased incarceration, lower QS values for low-λ offenders may have the perverse effect of increasing their levels of offending (Cook, 1986). Uniform imprisonment sanctions may actually achieve an optimal mix of crime reduction by maximizing the deterrence effects on the much larger population of low-λ offenders merely by maintaining a credible threat of incarceration, while simultaneously maximizing the incapacitative effects of limited prison resources through the naturally occurring stochastic selection of high-λ offenders into prison that results from their much higher rates of offending.

Furthermore, considerations of career termination strongly favor a policy of uniform increases in Q over corresponding changes in S. To illustrate the different impacts of Q and S, we estimated the percentage changes in crime reduction through incapacitation and in the size of the prison population that would result from a 50 percent increase in either Q or S above the base levels prevailing for robbery in the late 1970s (separate deterrence effects are not addressed here). The λ distributions remained the same as those reported in Table 7, and average career lengths continued to be five years. Only the saction variables Q and S were changed from the base values in Table 6. The results are reported in Table 15.

The cost-benefit ratio of changes in prison population relative to changes in crime reduction (in the last row of Table 15) indicates that further reductions in crime do not come cheaply, since prison populations grow at faster rates than crime reductions. Although this imbalance alone does not imply that expanded use of incarceration is unwarranted, it does raise concerns about the relative crime reduction returns of alternative policies. It is evident from Table 15 that increments in Q, the risk of incarceration per crime, are more efficient in enhancing incapacitation than the same increments in S.

The superiority of Q over S as a policy variable derives primarily from the benefit side of incapacitation. The growth in prison population is almost the same whether we increase Q or S. However, twice as much crime is prevented from a 50 percent increase in Q than from the same increase in S. These results strongly contradict the prevailing tendency to increase punitiveness by increasing time served that is evident in the widespread increases in S observed across states and crime types in Table 4.

To a large extent the tendency to increase time-served reflects important political dimensions of the sanctioning process. First, increasing time-served penalties for convicted offenders is readily obtained—at least symbolically, if not in fact—through statutory revisions and does not require improvements in the processing

TABLE 15 Percentage Increase in Crime Reduction from Incapacitation and in the Size of Prison Population Accompanying a 50 Percent Increase in Incarceration Sanctions for Robbery

	Increase in Imprisonment Risk per Robbery, Q			Increase in Average Years Served per Prison Commitment, S		
	Calif.	Mich.	Tx.	Calif.	Mich.	Tx.
Percentage increase in crime reduction from incapacitation, I^*	15	10	16	8	5	8
Percentage increase in prison population size, P	40	39	41	45	45	46
Cost-benefit ratio, P/I^*	2.6	3.9	2.6	5.6	9.0	5.8

NOTE: Estimates of the crime reduction and prison population increases arising from incapacitation (and ignoring deterrence) assume (1) an average career length of five years, (2) the λ distributions for all offenders reported in Table 7, and (3) the imprisonment sanction levels reported in Table 6. Results are extracted from Canela-Cacho (1990:Tables 7.6 and 7.7).

capabilities at various stages of the criminal justice system. Changing the statutes governing time served are a highly visible means of "getting tough on criminals." This also represents a policy that can be adopted with no immediate consequences since costs are delayed until the full impact of longer time served is felt years later in a buildup of the prison population.

Increments in Q, by contrast, are generally very difficult to attain through legislation alone. Q is usually small because the risk of arrest following a crime is low. Only about 5 robberies out of every 100 committed result in arrest. The risk of arrest per burglary is even lower at only three arrests for every 100 burglaries committed. Significant increases in Q would require immediate financial outlays to provide more police and investigation resources, more prosecutors, more criminal court judges, and more pretrial detention space. In the long run, however, greater crime reduction from incapacitation can be achieved at a lower cost by emphasizing the certainty of incarceration rather than its severity.

TABLE 16 Mean Robbery Rates While Free Among Offenders In and Out of Prison

	California	Michigan	Texas
Original incarceration levels:			
All offenders	3.2	2.9	1.3
Incoming inmates	44.4	41.1	14.3
Resident inmates	16.2	13.7	5.0
Increased incarceration:			
Additional resident inmates from 50% increase in Q	6.1	3.5	1.9
Additional resident inmates from 50% increase in S	2.9	1.5	0.9

NOTE: Estimates of mean λ's assume (1) the λ distributions reported in Table 7, (2) an average career length of five years, and (3) the imprisonment sanction levels reported in Table 6 for the original base case.

Whether changes occur in Q or S, increases in QS will increase incapacitation by raising the prison population. Offender heterogeneity, however, results in decreasing marginal returns from incapacitation as QS increases. Just as the inmate population contains a disproportionately large share of high-λ offenders, the population of free offenders contains a disproportionately large share of low-λ offenders. Thus, as the prison population grows as a result of tougher sentencing policies, it does so by extending incarceration to offenders whose average λ is lower than that of existing inmates.

The decline in λ with increasing incarceration is illustrated in Table 16, which again relies on cases of 50 percent increases in either Q or S. In addition to the mean offending rates for all offenders and for incoming inmates reported in Table 8, Table 16 includes mean λ's for a daily census of resident inmates and for the new inmates who would be added to the prison population from the increase in Q or S.[60]

We see that as the size of the prison population grows in Table 16, the average number of crimes prevented per inmate declines. In Michigan, for example, whereas resident inmates under the original sanction policies would commit on average almost 14 robberies per year if they were free, the average λ for inmates who are added to the prison population by a 50 percent increase in Q is less than 4 robberies per year free. When S is increased, which also increases the number of inmates who will terminate offending careers before they are released, new inmates would average only 1.5 robberies per year if they were to remain free. As QS increases, the mean λ for new inmates declines.

The decreasing marginal returns from incapacitation must be explicitly considered when evaluating the potential for further crime reduction from more punitive sentencing policies. In particular, the mean λ found among existing inmates cannot be applied to the new inmates that result from expanding incarceration. Failure to adjust properly for lower λ's found among free offenders will result in gross overestimates of potential additional crime reduction.[61]

CONCLUSIONS

This paper has examined the substantial increases in imprisonment policies occurring in the United States from the mid-1970s to the latter 1980s. After three decades of relatively stable incarceration rates, with the national rate of inmates per 100,000 population ranging from 93 to 119 between 1945 and 1974 (Blumstein and Cohen, 1973), the U.S. incarceration rate increased almost 2.5-fold from 112 to 274 between 1975 and 1989.

The increase in incarceration nationally mirrors similar increases that occurred widely across different crime types and states. Analyses of annual offense and incarceration data for six states indicated that rising incarceration rates since the mid-1970s were due primarily to upward trends in imprisonment sanctions over that period. Among six states examined, increases were widespread both in the risk of being committed to prison following arrest (Q_i) and in time served by those who enter prison (S), but increases in S were somewhat more likely.[62] This was especially so in Michigan, New York, and Pennsylvania, where sentencing reforms to increase penalties for certain offenses were enacted.

Increased reliance on incarceration has resulted in substantially higher costs to society in terms of prison populations. Aside from the retributive (or punitive) functions that may be served by incarceration, it is legitimate to inquire about the magnitude of crime control benefits that have accompanied these sharply rising prison populations. By invoking traditional estimation techniques in which homogeneous sanction levels are applied to the average offender, the reduction in violent crimes due to incapacitation is estimated to have been very modest—only 5 to 10 percent of potential violent crimes prevented. Strong reasons exist, however, for believing that these crude estimates vastly understate the crime reduction actually achieved by incarceration.

Numerous studies—relying on offender self-reports and official criminal histories—indicate substantial variability in offending rates among individual offenders, with a small group of especially high-rate offenders responsible for a sizable portion of all crimes committed. Through a process of *stochastic selectivity* that occurs independently of any deliberate attempts to selectively target some offenders for enhanced incarceration, high-rate offenders will be overrepresented among prison inmates. Based on their crime rates alone, high-rate offenders, in effect, self-select for greater incarceration: the more frequently an offender commits crimes during a period of length t, the more likely it is that he will end up in prison sometime during that period and will be incarcerated longer during his lifetime.

This stochastic selectivity occurs when all offenders are subject to the same expected time served for each crime they commit and persists to a considerable extent even when high-rate offenders are subject to a substantially lower risk of incarceration than are low-rate offenders. Only unrealistically large differences in incarceration risk—of a magnitude ruled out by existing empirical evidence—would seriously attenuate or reverse stochastic selectivity of high-rate offenders in prison.[63]

Consequently, the offending rates of inmates are usually many times higher than the average rate among all offenders, which increases crime reduction from incapacitation beyond that estimated for the average offender. In Michigan from 1975 to 1980, for example, the incapacitation effect for a *homogeneous* population of robbers is estimated to have been only 7.8 percent of potential robberies averted. In allowing for stochastic selectivity among offenders with *heterogeneous offending rates*, and the accompanying greater likelihood that high-rate offenders are in fact spending substantial portions of their lifetimes incarcerated, the incapacitation effect from the same size prison population is estimated to have been five times greater (41.3%; see Table 9).

Stochastic selectivity means that the incapacitation effects that prevailed during the period of low incarceration rates in the late 1970s are probably much greater than were previously estimated. The same stochastic selectivity, however, also results in decreasing marginal returns from incapacitation as increasing numbers of offenders are incarcerated. Just as high-rate offenders are overrepresented among inmates, low-rate offenders are disproportionately found among the offenders who remain free. Under these circumstances, the new inmates that result from expanding incarceration are likely to offend at lower average rates than did previous inmates.

In Michigan during the late 1970s, for example, robbers among resident inmates committed about 15 robberies per year while free, whereas the average annual rate among all robbers—in and out of prison—was only 3 (Table 16). More than doubling the prison population from 50 percent increases in both Q and S increasingly brings into prison less serious offenders whose average annual rate of only 2.4 robberies is substantially below that of robbers in the original smaller prison population.[64]

Thus, although crime control from incapacitation has undoubtedly increased from an estimated level of 32.9 percent of potential violent offenses prevented nationally in 1975 (Table 11), the marginal gains in crime control do not come close to the almost 200 percent rise in the prison population since then. Based on incapacitation alone, with no changes in individual offending, the near tripling of prison inmates convicted of violent offenses would have increased crime control from incapacitation by only 9 percentage points to 41.9 percent of potential violent crimes averted by 1989 (Table 11). This corresponds to a 13.4 percent reduction from the observed level of violent crimes in 1975 (Table 12). A combination of deterrence and incapacitation effects from rising incarceration levels would have reduced 1989 violent crimes more substantially below 1975 levels and would have resulted in much smaller increases in the prison population (Table 12).

The observation of almost stable levels of violent crimes in 1975 and 1989, in the face of a near tripling of the inmate population, is not compatible with the existence of meaningful crime control effects from deterrence and incapacitation *unless* the underlying potential level of violent crimes actually increased between 1975 and 1989. In a reasonable scenario, for example, the tripling of prison inmates by 1989 is capable of having prevented a 61 to 66 percent increase in violent crimes above the levels observed in 1975 (Table 14). It is noteworthy that in this scenario, the total crime reduction achieved by a combination of deterrence and incapacitation is not much larger than that estimated for incapacitation alone (Table 14). At least as modeled here—with offsetting trade-offs between incapacitation and deterrence—the magnitude of the estimated incapacitation effect alone provides a reasonably good estimate of the total combined effects of deterrence and incapacitation.

Aside from decreasing marginal returns of incarceration arising from stochastic selectivity, normal termination of criminal careers also reduces the crime control effects derived from increased incarceration. Short careers inhibit incapacitation in two fundamental ways. First, when careers are short, the odds that an offender is never intercepted by the criminal justice system increase. In the extreme, if offenders' careers are long enough for them to commit only one crime, incapacitation would yield zero crime control benefits.[65] Second, even for those offenders who are eventually imprisoned, the expected incapacitation benefits are limited by the possibility that an offender permanently ends offending while in prison. Thus, some of the time that offenders spend incarcerated does not result in crimes prevented, since those inmates would not have engaged in further crimes had they been free.

The effect of career termination in reducing the crime control effects of incapacitation has policy implications for the choice between increasing the certainty of incarceration following a crime (Q) and increasing the severity of prison terms (S). The longer that time served is in relation to the average length of criminal careers, the more likely are offenders to end their careers while still incarcerated. Time that is served in prison after the end of offending is "wasted" from the perspective of incapacitation because the number of no longer active offenders in prison increases, without further crime reduction from the expenditure of additional prison resources.

Career termination effectively distinguishes between the impacts of Q and S on incapacitation effects, with increases in Q dominating similar increases in S as a more effective sentencing strategy. A greater deterrent effect of certainty over severity of prison terms—as is often posed by deterrence theorists, due in part to time discounting for longer sentences—would similarly favor sentencing policies that emphasize increasing Q over similar increases in S. This policy choice runs counter to prevailing patterns of sentencing reform that have emphasized longer prison terms over more difficult to implement changes to increase the certainty of incarceration following a crime. Although strategically, increases in S are easy to implement in highly visible ways, such a strategy is likely to be less effective in the long run because the resulting increases in prison population fail to bring about substantial reductions in violent crimes.

NOTES

1   Offenders imprisoned for one or more of the offense types included in this study comprised 69.4 percent of the total inmate population in the United States in 1986, 73.9 percent in 1979, and 71.6 percent in 1973 (Bureau of Justice Statistics, 1979, 1988).

2   We are very grateful to the corrections departments in these states for their cooperation in providing us with the data.

3   Similar crime-type data are available annually for federal prisons, which represented only 8 percent of all inmates in prisons in the United States in 1988. National data on crime-type mix in state prisons are available only for the years when special surveys were conducted of national samples of state prison inmates in 1973, 1979, and 1986.

4   Certain observations were eliminated from the analysis because of problems detected in the inmate counts. The prison data for Texas prior to 1977 contained a number of anomalies, including annual growth in the number of residents that exceeded the number of commitments during the year. Officials at the Texas Department of Corrections indicated that the data before 1977 preceded computerized records and were likely to include errors. The data on the number of commitments to prison for drug offenses in Florida in 1987 and 1988 were extremely high, in relation both to earlier years and to the reported resident population at the end of each year. For these data to be correct, large numbers of the recorded commitments in these two years would have had to be released during the same year they were committed to prison.

There were also anomalies in the arrest data for some observations. Typically, the problematic state arrest counts were unusually low compared to arrests in surrounding years and to the number of reported crimes in the same year, a pattern suggesting that large police departments failed to report arrest data in selected years (Florida, 1974; Florida, 1975 and 1988 for murder; Michigan, 1979 and 1982; Pennsylvania, 1974, 1975, and 1977; Texas, 1980). There were also occasions when the number of arrests reported was substantially higher—including increases as high as 50 to 100 percent—compared to surrounding years. When the large increases in arrests were not accompanied by similar increases in the number of reported crimes in the same year, the observations were treated as suspect and eliminated from the analysis (murder arrests in California during 1981, and in Michigan during 1987 and 1988; New York aggravated assault arrests, 1966 and 1967; all arrests in New York, 1978, and in Texas, 1977 and 1978).

5   Data on total prison inmates in the United States are from Flanagan and Maguire (1990:Table 6.43). Adjustments to population rates use annual population estimates by age available in Bureau of the Census (1974, 1982, 1984, and 1986).

6   Figure 4 presents the percentage serving time for (top) robbery and (bottom) for drug offenses among resident inmates and among new commitments to prison. The relationship between these two measures provides an immediate indication of how time served for the graphed offense compares to the overall average time served by all inmates. When the percentage of commitments for an offense type exceeds the percentage for the same offense among resident inmates, time served for that offense is below the average for all offense types combined. Conversely, a higher percentage among resident inmates than among prison commitments indicates longer-than-average time served for an offense type.

In the case of robbery the percentage found among resident inmates is generally higher (by 20 to 65%) than the corresponding percentage among commitments to prison (except in New York). This indicates that time served for robbery is typically longer than the overall average time served by all inmates. For drug offenses, by contrast, the two percentages are only slightly higher among commitments to prison for most of the time period, especially in California, Michigan, and New York, and time served for drug offenses in those states is similar to the average time served by all inmates combined.

Toward the end of the 1980s, sharp increases in drug offenses as a percentage of all commitments to prison were not matched by similar increases in percentages among resident inmates for the same years. If this differential between commitments and residents were to continue into the future, it would indicate a decline in average time served for drug offenses compared to time served for other crime types. If, however, time served for drug offenses does not decline, the increases in commitments for drug offenses observed during the late 1980s would foreshadow important increases in the representation of drug offenses among the resident population of prison.

7   The similarities in incarceration rates across states and crime types were evident in simple bivariate correlations among the yearly incarceration rates for state-by-crime subgroups. In

general, the correlations of annual incarceration rates across crime types when controlling for state, or across states when controlling for crime type, exceed .73. Lower correlations are observed for the states of Florida and Texas, especially for robbery and burglary. In Texas, for example, the correlations of annual robbery incarceration rates with those of other crime types are always less than .33.

8   The index crimes, as defined by the FBI, include murder, rape, robbery, and aggravated assault as violent crimes, and burglary, larceny, auto theft, and arson as property crimes. Since arson was not included among the index crimes until 1979, it is excluded from the time series data on reported crimes to maintain comparability across years. The index rate reported here is also adjusted to include all larcenies, regardless of dollar value, from 1965 to 1988.

9   The index crime rate is calculated by using the FBI's annual estimated total index crimes in the United States—after adjusting upward for nonreporting police agencies and excluding arson (Federal Bureau of Investigation, *Uniform Crime Reports: Crime in the United States*, published annually)—combined with population estimates by age from the Bureau of the Census (1974, 1982, 1984, and 1986).

10   The differences between crime types were similar between 1965 and 1975, with total population crime rates for violent offenses increasing by 161 percent, while property crime rates increased by 99 percent.

11   The UCR crime rate does not include all crimes actually committed. Two separate reporting processes—citizen reporting to the police and police recording of citizen reports—reduce the number of crimes that are reported as known to the police in the UCR. Jencks (1991) notes that although citizen reporting to the police has been quite stable over time, the number of offenses recorded by the police in the FBI's annual UCR has increased relative to the number of offenses that victims indicate were reported to the police in the annual National Crime Survey (NCS). For aggravated assault, the ratio of UCR crime counts to NCS counts of offenses reported to the police rose from less than 50 percent in 1973 to almost 100 percent police recording of citizen-reported crimes in 1988. Jencks interprets this increase as reflecting more complete recording of these crimes by the police.

This figure reveals similar apparent increases in police recording of citizen crime reports for both violent and property crimes between 1973 and 1989 (Blumstein et al., 1992). Trends for the

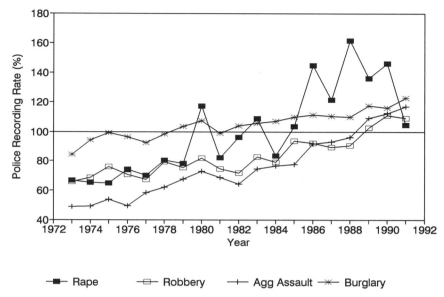

National Crime Survey (NCS) offenses reported to the police that are recorded in Uniform Crime Reports (UCR) by police. SOURCE: Blumstein et al. (1992:Figure 1). Reprinted with permission from the American Society of Criminology.

various crime types, however, suggest the need for some caution in interpreting these trends only in terms of improved police recording of crimes. By 1989 the police recording rate exceeded 100 percent for all crime types compared; for burglary the recording rate has continued to rise steadily above 100 percent since 1981. The trend in recent years is for UCR crime counts by police to exceed NCS counts from victims of crimes reported to the police.

If police counts are becoming more accurate, with more complete police recording of citizen-reported offenses, the recent excesses in UCR crime counts raise the possibility of crime undercounts by the NCS. The potential role of populations that are typically underrepresented in NCS household samples—especially transient and homeless populations and offenders, all of whom are at substantially greater risk of violence—might be an important factor in NCS crime undercounts. These same population groups, however, are also the least likely to report crimes to the police; thus the offenses they suffer are likely to be missing from both UCR and NCS crime counts.

12 See Blumstein et al. (1986) for a more extensive discus-

sion of variations in offending for different crime types by age. Race is another population attribute of interest because much higher offense rates in violent crimes and robbery are typically found among blacks than among whites. The differences between black and white crime rates are sufficiently large that even small increases in the fraction of the population who are black can produce important increases in total population rates for violent crimes (Blumstein et al., 1991).

13 These crime-type differences in age of offending are reflected in individual states by the adult fraction of crimes reported in Table A-1. The adult fraction is very high for violent offenses, averaging 0.90 for murder, 0.82 for rape, and 0.83 for aggravated assault. It was also high for drug offenses, with an average of 0.82. The two crimes involving theft of property have the lowest average adult fractions—0.71 for robbery and 0.54 for burglary. These latter two crime types also experienced the largest increases in the adult fraction of crimes over the study period, for example, up from 0.76 to 0.88 for robbery in Texas, and from 0.42 to 0.70 for burglary in Florida.

14 Throughout this analysis, we distinguish crimes by adults from total reported crimes since, with rare exception, only adults are eligible for incarceration in state prisons. The number of crimes by adults is estimated by applying the adult fraction found among arrests to total reported crimes. The annual adult fraction was obtained separately for each crime type and state in the analysis.

The adult fraction of arrests is undoubtedly somewhat different from the same fraction among reported crimes. In particular, to the extent that juveniles are more likely to commit crimes as part of a group or are more vulnerable to arrest, their representation among arrestees will overstate the proportion of crimes that are committed by juveniles. Nevertheless, the error in the adjustment that we make in estimating crimes by adults is probably smaller than the distortions that would be introduced by ignoring the changes in the adult fraction during the study period and treating all reported crimes as if they were equally vulnerable to imprisonment. The adult fraction of arrests should at least capture the direction of changes over time in the adult fraction of crimes.

15 Even if there were no change in the risk of commitment to prison *per crime*, a rise in the number of offenders would increase the number of persons who are eligible for incarceration, whereas growth in individual offending frequencies would increase the risk of incarceration *per offender*.

16   Values of q_a in Table A-2 that exceed 1.0 for murder primarily reflect the upward bias from failing to include multiple offenders per crime incident.   Although the arrest count may include more than one person arrested for the same homicide, only one crime incident is included in the crime count.

17   S is a traditional stock-over-flow estimate of time served. In steady state, this ratio provides a reasonable estimate of the average total time served per commitment to prison on a new sentence.   The ratio, however, is very sensitive to large year-to-year variations in the rate of new commitments to prison.   Based on a stochastic model, we developed an alternative measure of time served (S^*) that removes the influence of large yearly changes in the number of commitments, and relies instead on the size of the prison population that remains in prison from year to year.

A detailed analysis of S and S^* (Canela-Cacho and Cohen, 1991) reveals that the two measures differ mainly in magnitude, with S on average being somewhat lower than S^*.   The lower average values for S generally result from unusually large increases in the number of commitments to prison in some years.   Nevertheless, the patterns of change in S and S^* over time are very similar.   For this reason we are reasonably confident about the robustness of the results for S that are reported here.

18   The available data generally do not distinguish new commitments from recommitments within the resident inmate population, nor do they provide counts of the number of recommitments who enter prison each year.   Thus, it is not possible to apportion total time served between terms served following the original commitment and those served on recommitments for the same conviction.   It is also not possible to trace the impact on the size of prison populations of changes in conditional release and recommitment policies.

Data that are available for California, however, indicate that parole revocation has been a major factor contributing to rising prison populations in that state.   As the revocation rate for parolees increased from 3.5 to 33 percent between 1977 and 1988, parole violators returned to prison increased from 8 percent of total prison admissions in 1978 to 47 percent in 1988.   In 1989, parole violators comprised 16 percent of the resident inmate population in California state prisons (see California, 1990).

19   The result regarding increases in Q_i agrees with that of Langan (1991), but the finding of widespread increases in time served since 1977 using state-level data is at odds with Langan's (1991:1569) conclusion from national data that time served by

released inmates declined after 1973. Langan, however, includes only time served until first release from prison on a sentence, whereas the state data used here refer to total time served, including any time following returns to prison from conditional release.

Such returns to prison—resulting from either technical violations of release conditions or new offenses—have become an increasing factor in inmate populations. Starting in 1975 with 10 percent recommitments from conditional release among total prison admissions nationally, returns to prison increased steadily, and by 1988, 27 percent of all admissions to prison in the United States involved recommitments from some form of conditional release (see *Prisoners in State and Federal Institutions* and *Correctional Populations in the United States*, both published annually by the U.S. Department of Justice, Bureau of Justice Statistics).

The increases in recommitments to prison accompanied a substantial increase in conditional releases from prison, involving some form of postrelease supervision in the community, which rose from 54 percent of all releases in 1975 to 75 percent in 1988. The increase in conditional releases derived mainly from expansion of mandatory supervised release, which rose from only 5 percent of total releases from prisons in 1975 to 28 percent in 1988. The corresponding increase in mandatory supervised releases among conditional and unconditional releases was from 6 to 30 percent. Over this same period, parole releases declined modestly from 50 to 38 percent among total releases from prisons, but were a significantly declining fraction of conditional and unconditional releases, falling from 72 percent in 1977 to 40 percent in 1988 (Langan, 1991).

Parole release usually involves discretionary early release from prison terms based on some assessment of the risk posed by the offender. Mandatory supervised release, by contrast, automatically follows release from prison and need not involve early release from the sentence imposed in court. Under the determinate sentence provisions in California, for example, sentenced prisoners must serve the term imposed in court minus any authorized reductions granted for good behavior, and upon release from prison, all former inmates are subject to an additional three years of supervision in the community.

To some extent, rising numbers of recommitments to prison may be an expected result of the increased numbers of conditional releases. As the population of offenders under some form of supervised release (mandatory or parole) increased, simply maintaining the same revocation and recommitment policies would have increased the number of recommitments to prison. Unfortunately, national published data do not permit a more detailed examination of whether recommitment practices actually changed over time. At a minimum, such an analysis would require information about the size of the total supervised population each year.

We were also unable to analyze the nature of release practices among *recommitted* inmates, especially the extent to which recommitted inmates are released again under some form of supervised release, instead of being held until they are unconditionally released at completion of the originally sentenced term. Increased reliance on repeat supervised releases for recommitted inmates, for example, would be one possible strategy for coping with rising prison populations.

20 Such jurisdictional differences no doubt reflect the differences in imprisonment policies emerging from the body of statutory provisions and administrative practices that shape criminal sentencing in individual states. Policy changes—whether arising from sentencing guidelines, mandatory minimum sentences, or parole reforms—are generally statewide and apply broadly across crime types within a state.

21 Recent analyses of time served by prison inmates in Pennsylvania indicate that more stringent parole release policies are an important factor in rising time served in that state. Although time served by inmates paroled from Pennsylvania prisons during the early 1980s averaged 100 percent of the minimum sentence imposed in court, by the late 1980s, inmates on average were serving 125 percent of the minimum sentence before being released on parole (Pennsylvania Commission on Crime and Delinquency, 1988).

22 See Shane-Dubow et al. (1985), especially Table 36 and the discussion for individual states.

23 Changes in opposite directions may indicate a special kind of dependence of S on Q_i. On the one hand, increases in Q_i that are accompanied by declines in S need not reflect decreases in the prison terms served by individual inmates. As Q_i increases, prison sentences are imposed on a larger segment of arrested offenders. It is possible that those offenders who would have been incarcerated under previous policies continue to spend the same amount of time served in prison, whereas those newly incarcerated under an expanded Q_i serve terms that are shorter, on average, than previously incarcerated offenders, thus bringing down the overall average time served under the new higher value of Q_i. In this

case, the average S for all inmates declines, but individual offenders continue to serve the same or longer prison terms than under previous policies.

Similarly, declines in Q_i that are accompanied by increases in S need not reflect real increases in the time served by individual inmates. Instead, the decline in Q_i might arise from limiting imprisonment only to more serious offenders who continue to serve the same longer-than-average prison terms as they would have under previous values of Q_i. Since offenders who previously served shorter prison terms are no longer committed to prison, the average time served by the remaining inmates increases. In this case, although the average time served increases, individual offenders actually may be spending the same or less time in prison.

In both cases, the changes in S would result primarily from changes in the composition of inmates as Q_i changes, either increasing or decreasing the number of offenders who serve shorter-than-average prison terms. Distinguishing such composition changes from actual changes in S requires individual-level data on various attributes of inmates that are associated with the length of prison terms (e.g., prior criminal record and offense seriousness), and is beyond the scope of this paper. The key question to be answered in such an analysis would be whether or not the length of prison terms has changed, after attributes of the imprisoned offenders are controlled.

24 We ignore the arrest risk per crime, q_a, which generally remained fairly stable over the study period.

25 An earlier National Research Council panel provided an extensive review of prior deterrence and incapacitation research (Blumstein et al., 1978). Further reviews of various aspects of deterrence are available in Cook (1977, 1980); Geerken and Gove (1975); Gibbs (1975, 1986); Klepper and Nagin (1989); Paternoster (1987); Tittle (1980); Williams and Hawkins (1986); and Zimring and Hawkins (1973). Subsequent reviews of incapacitation research can be found in Blumstein et al. (1986); Cohen (1983, 1984); and Visher (1987).

26 Throughout this paper, the estimates of crime reduction from incapacitation assume that while they are incarcerated, the potential crimes of inmates are eliminated entirely. No adjustments are made for crimes that may continue in the community—perhaps because the offender is replaced or offending persists by unincarcerated members of an offending group. Such offsetting effects are likely to be small for violent offenses.

27 A notable exception is the study of violent offenders in

Franklin County, Ohio reported in Conrad (1985); Hamparian et al. (1978); Miller et al. (1982); and Van Dine et al. (1979).

28 The results from the study of violent offenders by Miller et al. (1982:55) illustrate the relative occurrence of the various violent offenses. That study was based on the criminal records of 1,591 offenders arrested at least once for murder, rape, aggravated assault, or robbery in Columbus, Ohio during 1950-1976. These offenders generated a total of 12,527 arrests, of which 23.6 percent were for violent offenses and one-half of these were the originally sampled violent offenses. Robbery and aggravated assault accounted for 73 percent of total violent crimes, with homicide and rape each contributing almost equally to the remaining 27 percent.

29 The estimated robbery offending rates were 3.4 in Washington, D.C and 4.7 in Detroit (Cohen, 1986). These higher estimates of λ in part reflect inclusion of unarmed robberies that are not included in the rates estimated by Chaiken (1980). Additionally, the estimated rates apply to *arrestees*; thus they are not representative of all offenders, and, as we explain later, high-rate offenders are overrepresented in criminal justice samples.

30 Here, the risks of imprisonment following a crime represent the risk that each offender faces for any robbery he commits, regardless of the number of offenders involved in any crime incident and whether or not the crime is reported to the police. These risks are lower than the corresponding probabilities obtained by simply multiplying the mean values of q_a and Q_i reported for robbery in each state in appendix Table A-2.

As we noted earlier, the values of q_a reported in Table A-2 *overstate* by about fourfold the actual arrest risk per crime committed for robbery. If appropriate adjustments are made to q_a for crimes that are not reported to the police and for multiple offenders involved in the same crime incident, the two estimates of imprisonment risk per crime committed become comparable in magnitude.

31 The Avi-Itzhak and Shinnar model relies on a number of parametric assumptions typical of queuing network models. They assume that each individual offender commits crimes according to a Poisson process with a constant rate λ—represented by the average value for the overall offender population—and that the length of time served in prison, S, is distributed as an exponential random variable. In addition, a crime leads to imprisonment with probability Q in a Bernoulli fashion.

32   The average λ for robbery is 3.22 robberies per offender per year free in California, 2.85 in Michigan, and 1.29 in Texas.

33   In Avi-Itzhak and Shinnar (1973) the incapacitative effect—fraction of potential crimes that are prevented by incarceration—is estimated from $I = \lambda QS/(1 + \lambda QS)$. The variation in I across states results from the variation in sentencing parameters and in average offending rates. If all other factors are held equal, I is an increasing function of λ and of QS (Cohen, 1978).

34   By termination of offending, we do not mean that offenders irrevocably cease offending. Instead, termination refers to a process by which the risk of future offenses drops to the same low trace levels that are found among nonoffenders in the population. After termination, ex-offenders are no more likely to commit future offenses than are nonoffenders.

35   We refer here only to waste from incapacitation. Besides incapacitation, prison can reduce crime through deterrence and rehabilitation functions, as well as by serving as a means for retribution. Thus, prison resources that yield zero incapacitation benefits need not be wasted from the standpoint of deterrence, rehabilitation, or retribution.

36   Gottfredson and Hirshi (1990:258-268) rule out incapacitation policies precisely on these grounds.

37   The samples were arrested in Washington, D.C., Michigan, or New York State during the mid-1970s. All offenders in these samples were arrested for homicide, rape, robbery, aggravated assault, burglary, or motor vehicle theft during the sampling period. Arrest histories included all prior arrests as adults plus subsequent arrests during follow-up periods of five years or less. The data did not follow individuals until death, so the reported average number of adult arrests is not a lifetime total.

38   Blumstein and Cohen (1982, 1985) estimate the length of offending careers using life-table analysis of cross-sectional data—a technique similar to actuarial estimates of life expectancies. Ahn et al. (1990) and Blumstein et al. (1990) develop career length estimates using competing risks models of individual offending applied to prospective longitudinal data.

39   As discussed above, Blumstein et al. (1993) found that this parametric family of distributions accounts very well for the variability in λ observed in empirical data.

40   This result relates only to the incapacitation effect of incarceration and assumes that no changes in the underlying distribution of offending result from changes up or down in incarcera-

tion levels. Later we explore the potential moderating effects of deterrence on estimated incapacitation levels.

41 The percentage increases correspond to an increase of about three crimes added to every seven already committed, or four crimes added to every six already committed, as calculated from the ratio of prevented crimes to committed crimes (.278/.722 = .385; .301/.699 = .431; .431/.587 = .704).

42 The average time served by robbers actually sentenced to prison is considerably longer at 3.6 to 3.9 years (Table 6). The very low risk of incarceration for any robbery committed (from 7 to 20 commitments per 1,000 crimes) substantially reduces the expected time served associated with each robbery that is committed.

43 The risk of imprisonment *per offender* is itself a function of the risk *per crime* and number of crimes that are committed and, thus, will vary across offenders.

44 The corresponding figures for the 1958 cohort are 60.0, 75.2, 73.2, and 65.1 percent, respectively (Weiner, 1989:Table 2.16).

45 Marital violence, especially wife battering, offers an interesting example of how general offending affects the incapacitation of a particular form of violence. As Fagan and Browne (in Volume 3) note, although wife battering is often a serious and chronically recurring violent crime, it seldom results in incarceration of the perpetrator. However, studies by Flynn (1977), Walker (1979), and White and Strauss (1981) (also see Fagan and Browne in Volume 3) report that wife batterers also commit other serious crimes against strangers for which they do spend time in prison. Obviously, while they are incarcerated for other offenses, wife batterers are also unable to victimize their spouses.

46 Cook (1986) poses a sanction process in which increased imprisonment sanctions are reserved for only the most criminally active offenders, while sentences are reduced for low-rate offenders. In this case, a negative deterrence effect, by which rising sanctions reduce crimes for high-rate offenders, is accompanied by the reverse effect of increasing offending when sanctions decline for low-rate offenders. Although Cook focuses on the potential perverse effects of these countervailing forces for selective incapacitation policies, the reverse *crime-enhancing* effects of deterrence would apply generally whenever sanction rates decrease.

47 We emphasize once again that I^* is a relative measure of the proportional reduction from the potential level of crime; so high values of I^* do not necessarily imply low crime rates, and vice versa. Large deterrent effects may lead to low values of I^*

even though the observed crime rate is quite low (i.e., a small percentage reduction from an already low potential level of crimes). Similarly, negligible deterrent effects would make high I^* values possible but still may result in a greater observed crime rate than in the previous scenario (i.e., a large percentage reduction from a high potential level of crimes). Likewise, if the potential crime base is small, even large incapacitation effects—in proportional terms—may be associated with only a small number of crimes actually prevented.

48 The formidable methodological difficulties in empirically estimating the magnitude of deterrent effects are reviewed in the report of a previous National Research Council panel (Blumstein et al., 1978). See also the discussion of future prospects for deterrence research in Cook (1980).

49 The estimates typically derive from empirical studies of cross-sectional variation in sanctions and crimes. Imprisonment sanctions are variously measured by the incarceration rate (inmates per population), imprisonment risk per crime (Q), and time served (S). Findings are mixed with regard to both the direction and the statistical significance of the estimated deterrence coefficients.

50 Recall that the potential level of crime refers to the number of crimes that would have been committed if offenders were to remain free despite a prevailing imprisonment risk, QS.

51 The change in the number of offenders N, and in λ from deterrence, $r = \lambda_1/\lambda_0 = N_1/N_0$, is assumed to be proportional to the increase in sanctions, with $r = [Q_1S_1/Q_0S_0]^b$ where b is the deterrence elasticity (-1.0 or -0.2).

52 The more commonly reported incapacitative effect relative to the new potential level of crimes, C_1, can be obtained easily from $I_1^* = I_2^*/(1 - D_1)$.

53 The distribution of inmates by crime type is available from periodic national surveys of inmates in state prisons in 1974 and 1986, and annual data for federal prisons (Bureau of Justice Statistics, 1979, 1988). By applying the crime-type distribution in 1974 to inmates in 1975, 100,082 inmates are estimated to have been incarcerated in 1975 for a serious violent crime—homicide, rape, robbery, or aggravated assault. The crime-type distribution from the 1986 survey is applied to total state prison inmates in 1989 to yield an estimated total of 288,566 inmates incarcerated for a serious violent crime in 1989—an increase of 188 percent from 1975 to 1989.

The counts of the violent crimes of rape, robbery, and aggravated assault are estimated from annual data from the National Crime Survey. The NCS crime count includes all crime incidents, whether or not they are reported to police. The NCS crime count is augmented by the annual UCR count of homicides known to the police, to yield a total of 2,944,500 violent crimes in 1975 and 2,937,500 in 1989. To properly represent the incarceration risk faced by all offenders for the crimes they commit, the NCS crime count is doubled to reflect an average of two offenders per crime incident (Reiss, 1980). The resulting ratios of inmates to total offender crimes are applied homogeneously to all active offenders.

54 The prevailing expected level of crimes is 67.1 percent (100 –32.9 crimes prevented) of $\lambda_0 N_0$ potential crimes at $Q_0 S_0$. Tripling imprisonment sanctions corresponds to a proportionate crime reduction when expected crimes are reduced to no more than one-third this level, or 22.4 percent of potential crimes (i.e., a total crime reduction of $D + I_2^* \geq 77.6$ in Table 11).

55 Recall that an elasticity of -1.0 represents a 1 percent reduction in crimes associated with a 1 percent increase in imprisonment sanctions. The marginal returns in terms of proportional reductions in crimes decrease with proportional increases in sanctions greater than 1 percent. For $K = Q_1 S_1/Q_0 S_0$, and a change in λ or N such that

$$r = \lambda_1/\lambda_0 = N_1/N_0 = K^b$$

a proportional change in sanctions of $K - 1$ (e.g., for $K = 1.5$, the proportional change in sanctions is +0.5, or a 50% increase) is associated with a proportional change in λ or N of $r - 1 = K^b - 1 \leq K-1$ when $b < 0$. So, for example, if $b = -1.0$, a 50 percent increase in sanctions ($K = 1.5$) is associated with a 33 percent decrease from λ_0 and N_0 ($r - 1 = K^b - 1 = 1.5^{-1} - 1 = -0.33$).

56 The two scenarios result from slight modifications to the distribution of offending presented in Table 10 that increase the representation of high-λ offenders. The percentage distribution is changed to 85, 13, and 2 percent for low-, medium-, and high-λ offenders, respectively. Also the mean λ for high-rate offenders is increased from 239 to 259 for an overall mean λ_0^* of 7.5, and to 384 for $\lambda_0^* = 10.0$. The selected increases in potential crimes reflected in λ_0^* are hypothetical. They are used here for illustrative purposes to show how the observed small change in crimes between 1975 and 1989, while prison inmates nearly tripled, nevertheless, might be compatible with deterrent effects associated with the substantial increase in sanction risks.

57   Under sanction level $Q_0 S_0$ applied to the offending distribution in Table 10, offenders are expected to commit an average of 1.87 of 2.79 potential crimes (i.e., $\lambda_0^*[1 - I_1^*] = 2.79[1 - I_1^*] = 2.79[1 - 0.329] = 1.87$ from Table 11). If the offending distribution shifts to the larger shares and increased means for high-λ offenders described in note 56, offenders will commit an average of 3.01 crimes ($\lambda_0^*[1 - I_1^*] = 7.5[1 - 0.599]$) or 3.10 crimes ($\lambda_0^*[1 - I_1^*] = 10.0[1 - 0.690]$) (from Table 14) under the same $Q_0 S_0$ sanction levels, representing a 61 to 66 percent increase over the 1.87 crimes committed in the base case scenario.

Such an increase is certainly a possibility. A total increase of 60 percent over 15 years corresponds to an average annual increase of about 3 percent in observed crimes, and is very close to the total increase in violent crimes from 1,039,710 in 1975 to 1,646,040 in 1989 reported by police in the FBI's Uniform Crime Reports program (Federal Bureau of Investigation, 1985, 1990a).

58   At least with respect to the model of deterrence examined here, total crime reduction is reasonably well estimated even when the mix between deterrence and incapacitation effects is seriously in error. Since the assumptions of the present model are quite generous with respect to the range of possible deterrence effects, we are reasonably confident that this finding will also generalize to other formulations of deterrence.

59   See the report of an earlier National Research Council panel on criminal careers for a review of predictive accuracy (Blumstein et al., 1986). Farrington and Tarling (1985) and Gottfredson and Tonry (1987) also provide comprehensive treatments of prediction issues in criminal justice applications.

60   The number of resident inmates represents the number of inmates found in prison on any day. This resident population reflects the buildup in prison population associated with time served and includes disproportionately more offenders serving long prison terms than are found in an incoming cohort.

61   Such overestimates are evident in Zedlewski (1987) and Abel (1989); also see Zimring and Hawkins (1988) for a critique of these estimates.

62   The risk of arrest following a crime, q_a, remained reasonably constant over the same time period.

63   For example, consider a population of offenders comprised of two subpopulations, one low-λ and the other high-λ, who together commit an average of three offenses per offender annually while they are free (similar to robbers in California and Michigan

in Table 8). The risk of commitment to prison per crime (Q) for low-rate offenders would have to exceed 100 times the same risk for high-rate offenders before reversing the overrepresentation of high-rate offenders among incoming inmates. Such a differential far exceeds the variations in sanction levels that have been observed within offending populations. (See discussion of the relationship between λ and Q earlier in this paper.)

64 Fifty percent increases in Q and S in Michigan are estimated to increase the prison population by 39 and 45 percent, respectively, for a total increase of 102 percent (1.39*1.45 = 2.02 from Table 15). The weighted average offending rate of these added prisoners is estimated from Table 16 to be 2.4 = (0.464*3.5) + (0.536*1.5).

65 In general, offenders are vulnerable to incarceration only *after* they commit a crime, so the first crime they commit is not subject to incapacitation. Only a policy of preventive incapacitation that incarcerates nonoffending individuals based on the expectation that they will eventually commit crimes could prevent the first crime an offender commits.

REFERENCES

Abel, R.B.
  1989 Beyond Willie Horton. The battle of the prison bulge. *Policy Review* 47(4):32-35.
Ahn, C.W., A. Blumstein, and M. Schervish
  1990 Estimation of arrest careers using hierarchical stochastic models. *Journal of Quantitative Criminology* 6(2):131-152.
American Correctional Association
  1989 *Vital Statistics in Corrections.* Laurel, Md.: American Correctional Association.
Avi-Itzhak, B., and R. Shinnar
  1973 Quantitative models in crime control. *Journal of Criminal Justice* 1:185-217.
Beck, A.J., and B.E. Shipley
  1989 *Recidivism of Prisoners Released in 1983.* Bureau of Justice Statistics. Washington, D.C.: U.S. Department of Justice..
Blumstein, A., and J. Cohen
  1973 A theory of the stability of punishment. *Journal of Criminal Law and Criminology* 64:198-207.
  1979 Estimation of individual crime rates from arrest records. *Journal of Criminal Law and Criminology* 70:561-585.
  1985 Estimating the duration of adult criminal careers. *Proceedings of International Statistical Institute Annual Meeting.* Amsterdam: International Statistical Institute.

Blumstein, A., and J. Cohen (with P. Hsieh)
1982 The Duration of Adult Criminal Careers. Final Report submitted to the National Institute of Justice, August 1982. School of Urban and Public Affairs, Carnegie-Mellon University.

Blumstein, A., J. Cohen, and D. Nagin, eds.
1978 *Deterrence and Incapacitation: Estimating the Effects of Criminal Sanctions on Crime Rates.* Panel on Research on Deterrent and Incapacitative Effects, Committee on Law Enforcement and the Administration of Justice, Assembly of Behavioral and Social Sciences, National Research Council. Washington, D.C.: National Academy of Sciences.

Blumstein, A., J. Cohen, S. Martin, and M. Tonry, eds.
1983 *Research on Sentencing: The Search for Reform*, 2 vols. Panel on Research on Sentencing, Committee on Law Enforcement and the Administration of Justice, Commission on Behavioral and Social Sciences and Education, National Research Council. Washington, D.C.: National Academy Press.

Blumstein, A., J. Cohen, J. Roth, and C.A. Visher, eds.
1986 *Criminal Careers and "Career Criminals,"* 2 vols. Panel on Research on Criminal Careers, Committee on Research on Law Enforcement and the Administration of Justice, Commission on Behavioral and Social Sciences and Education, National Research Council. Washington, D.C.: National Academy Press.

Blumstein, A., J. Cohen, and C.A. Visher
1989 Linking the Crime and Arrest Process to Measure Individual Crime Rates: Variations in Individual Arrest Risk per Crime. Working paper, School of Urban and Public Affairs, Carnegie-Mellon University.

Blumstein, A., J. Cohen, and A. Golub
1990 A Comparison of Termination Rates of Adult Criminal Careers Across Offender Characteristics and Jurisdictions. Paper presented at the annual meeting of American Society of Criminology, Baltimore, Md., November.

Blumstein, A., J. Cohen, and R. Rosenfeld
1991 Effects of Demography and Criminality on Crime Rates. Working paper, School of Urban and Public Affairs, Carnegie-Mellon University.
1992 The UCR-NCS relationship revisited: A reply to Menard. *Criminology* 3(1):115-124.

Blumstein, A., J.A. Canela-Cacho, and J. Cohen
1993 Filtered sampling from populations with heterogeneous event frequencies. *Management Sciences* 39(7):886-899.

Bureau of the Census
1969 *Estimates of Population of States by Age, 1965 to 1967 with Provisional Estimates for July 1, 1968.* Current Population Reports, Series P-25 Number 420. Washington, D.C.: U.S. Department of Commerce.

1970   *Estimate of the Population of States by Age, 1968.* Current Population Reports, Series P-25 Number 437. Washington, D.C.: U.S. Department of Commerce.

1974   *Estimates of the Population of the U.S. by Age, Race, and Sex.* Current Population Reports, Series P-25 Number 519. Washington, D.C.: U.S. Department of Commerce.

1980   *Estimates of the Population of States by Age, July 1, 1971 to 1979.* Current Population Reports, Series P-25 Number 875. Washington, D.C.: U.S. Department of Commerce.

1982   *Preliminary Estimates of the Population of the U.S. by Age, Sex, and Race, 1970-1981.* Current Population Reports, Series P-25 Number 917. Washington, D.C.: U.S. Department of Commerce.

1984   *Projections of the Population of the U.S. by Age, Sex, and Race: 1983-2080.* Current Population Reports, Series P-25 Number 952. Washington, D.C.: U.S. Department of Commerce.

1986   *Estimates of the Population of the U.S. by Age, Sex, and Race 1980-85.* Current Population Reports, Series P-25 Number 985. Washington, D.C.: U.S. Department of Commerce.

1988   *State Population and Household Estimates with Age, Sex, and Components of Change 1981-87.* Current Population Reports, Series P-25 Number 1024. Washington, D.C.: U.S. Department of Commerce.

1989   *State Population and Household Estimates with Age, Sex, and Components of Change 1981-88.* Current Population Reports, Series P-25 Number 1044. Washington, D.C.: U.S. Department of Commerce.

Bureau of Justice Statistics

1979   *Profile of State Prison Inmates: Sociodemographic Findings from the 1974 Survey of Inmates of State Correctional Facilities.* Washington, D.C.: U.S. Department of Justice.

1988   *Profile of State Prison Inmates, 1986.* Washington, D.C.: U.S. Department of Justice.

1990a   *Prisoners in 1989.* Washington, D.C.: U.S. Department of Justice.

1990b   *Criminal Victimization 1989.* Washington, D.C.: U.S. Department of Justice.

1991   *Criminal Victimization in the United States: 1973-88 Trends.* Washington, D.C.: U.S. Department of Justice.

California

1990   *Report of the Blue Ribbon Commission on Inmate Population Management.* Sacramento, Calif.: California Prison Industry Authority.

Callahan, M.

1986   *Historical Corrections Statistics in the United States, 1850-1984.* Bureau of Justice Statistics. Washington, D.C.: U.S. Department of Justice.

Canela-Cacho, J.A.
  1990   Incapacitative Effect and Prison Population Under Offender Het-
          erogeneity. Unpublished Ph.D. dissertation, School of Urban
          and Public Affairs, Carnegie-Mellon University, Pittsburgh.
Canela-Cacho, J.A., and J. Cohen
  1991   Measuring Time Served in State Prisons. Working paper, School
          of Urban and Public Affairs, Carnegie-Mellon University.
Chaiken, J.M.
  1980   Models for estimating crime rates. In M. Peterson and H. Braiker
          (with S. Polich) *Doing Crime: A Survey of California Inmates.*
          Santa Monica, Calif.: RAND Corporation.
Chaiken, J.M., and M. Chaiken
  1982   *Varieties of Criminal Behavior.* Report R-2814-NIJ. Santa Monica,
          Calif.: RAND Corporation.
  1984   Offender types and public policy. *Crime and Delinquency* 30(2):195-
          226.
Clarke, S.H.
  1974   Getting 'em out of circulation: Does incarceration of juvenile
          offenders reduce crime? *Journal of Criminal Law and Crimi-
          nology* 65(4):528-535.
Cohen, J.
  1978   The incapacitative effect of imprisonment: A critical review of
          the literature. In A. Blumstein, J. Cohen, and D. Nagin, eds.,
          *Deterrence and Incapacitation: Estimating the Effects of Criminal
          Sanctions on Crime Rates.* Panel on Research on Deterrent and
          Incapacitative Effects, Committee on Research on Law Enforce-
          ment and Criminal Justice, National Research Council. Wash-
          ington, D.C.: National Academy of Sciences.
  1983   Incapacitation as a strategy for crime control: Possibilities and
          pitfalls. In M. Tonry and N. Morris, eds., *Crime and Justice:
          An Annual Review of Research*, Vol. 5. Chicago: University of
          Chicago Press.
  1984   Selective incapacitation: An assessment. *University of Illinois
          Law Review* 1984(2):253-290.
  1986   Research on criminal careers: Individual frequency rates and
          offense seriousness. Appendix B in A. Blumstein, J. Cohen, J.
          Roth, and C.A. Visher, eds., *Criminal Careers and "Career Crimi-
          nals,"* Vol. 1. Panel on Research on Criminal Careers, Commit-
          tee on Research on Law Enforcement and the Administration of
          Justice, Commission on Behavioral and Social Sciences and Edu-
          cation, National Research Council. Washington, D.C.: Na-
          tional Academy Press.
Conrad, J.P.
  1985   *The Dangerous and the Endangered.* Lexington, Mass.: Lexing-
          ton Books.
Cook, P.J.
  1977   Punishment and crime: A critique of recent findings on the
          preventive effects of punishment. *Law and Contemporary Problems*

(winter):164-204; pp.137-180 in R. Andreano and J. Siegfried, eds., *The Economics of Crime*. New York: John Wiley & Sons.

1980   Research in criminal deterrence: Laying the groundwork for the second decade. In N. Morris and M. Tonry, eds., *Crime and Justice: An Annual Review of Research*, Vol. 2. Chicago: University of Chicago Press.

1986   Criminal incapacitation effects considered in an adaptive choice framework. In D. Cornish and R. Clarke, eds., *The Reasoning Criminal*. New York: Springer-Verlag.

Dunford, F.W., and D.S. Elliott
1984   Identifying career offenders using self-report data. *Journal of Research in Crime and Delinquency* 21:57-87.

English, K.
1990   Measuring Crime Rates in Colorado: 1988-89. Paper presented at the annual meeting of the American Society of Criminology, Baltimore, Md., November.

Farrington, D.P.
1978   The family background of aggressive youths. In L. Hersov, M. Berger, and D. Shaffer, eds., *Aggression and Anti-Social Behavior in Childhood and Adolescence*. Oxford: Pergamon Press.

1982   Longitudinal analysis of criminal violence. In M.E. Wolfgang and N.A. Weiner, eds., *Criminal Violence*. Beverly Hills, Calif.: Sage Publications.

Farrington, D.P., and R. Tarling, eds.
1985   *Prediction in Criminology*. Albany: State University of New York Press.

Federal Bureau of Investigation
annual *Uniform Crime Reports: Crime in the United States*. Washington, D.C.: U.S. Department of Justice.

1976   *Crime in the United States—1975*. Washington, D.C.: U.S. Department of Justice.

1985   *Crime in the United States—1984*. Washington, D.C.: U.S. Department of Justice.

1990a   *Crime in the United States—1989*. Washington, D.C.: U.S. Department of Justice.

1990b   *Age-Specific Arrest Rates and Race-Specific Arrest Rates for Selected Offenses 1965-1988*. Washington, D.C.: U.S. Department of Justice.

Flanagan, T.J., and K. Maguire
1990   *Sourcebook of Criminal Justice Statistics 1989*. Bureau of Justice Statistics. Washington, D.C.: U.S. Department of Justice.

Flynn, J.D.
1977   Recent findings related to wife abuse. *Social Case Work* 58:17-18.

Geerken, M.R., and W.R. Gove
1975   Deterrence: Some theoretical considerations. *Law and Society Review* 9:497-513.

Gibbs, J.P.
1975   *Crime, Punishment, and Deterrence.* New York: Elsevier.
1986   Deterrence theory and research. In G.B. Melton, ed., *The Law as a Behavioral Instrument: Nebraska Symposium on Motivation.* Lincoln: University of Nebraska Press.

Gottfredson, D.M., and M. Tonry
1987   *Prediction and Classification: Criminal Justice Decision Making.* Chicago: University of Chicago Press.

Gottfredson, M.R., and T. Hirschi
1990   *A General Theory of Crime.* Stanford, Calif.: Stanford University Press.

Greenberg, D.
1975   The incapacitative effect of imprisonment: Some estimates. *Law and Society Review* 9:541-580.

Greene, M.A.
1977   The Incapacitative Effect of Imprisonment Policies on Crime. Unpublished Ph.D. dissertation, School of Urban and Public Affairs, Carnegie-Mellon University.

Greenwood, P.W., and S. Turner
1987   *Selective Incapacitation Revisited: Why the High-Rate Offenders are Hard to Predict.* Report R-3397-NIJ. Santa Monica, Calif.: RAND Corporation.

Hamparian, D.N., R. Schuster, S. Dinitz, and J.P. Conrad
1978   *The Violent Few. A Study of Dangerous Juvenile Offenders.* Lexington, Mass.: Lexington Books.

Horney, J., and I.H. Marshall
1991   Measuring lambda through self-reports. *Criminology* 29(3):471-496.

Isikoff, M.
1990   Florida's crime crackdown is freeing felons early. *Washington Post,* December 28.

Jencks, C.
1991   Is violent crime increasing? *American Prospect* (winter):98-109.

Klepper, S., and D. Nagin
1989   The deterrent effect of perceived certainty and severity of punishment revisited. *Criminology* 27(4):721-746.

Langan, P.
1991   America's soaring prison population. *Science* 25:1568-1573.

Miller, S.J., S. Dinitz, and J.P. Conrad
1982   *Careers of the Violent.* Lexington, Mass.: Lexington Books.

Miranne, A.C., and M.R. Geerken
1991   The New Orleans inmate survey: A test of Greenwood's predictive scale. *Criminology* 29(3):497-578.

Mullen, J. (with K. Carlson and B. Smith)
1980   *American Prisons and Jails,* Vol I. National Institute of Justice. Washington, D.C.: U.S. Department of Justice.

National Conference of State Legislatures
  1989   *State Legislatures and Corrections Policy: An Overview.* Denver, Colo.: National Conference of State Legislatures.
National Prisoner Statistics
  1976   *Survey of Inmates of State Correctional Facilities, 1974.* National Criminal Justice Information and Statistics Service. Washington, D.C.: U.S. Department of Justice.
Paternoster, R.
  1987   The deterrent effect of perceived certainty and severity of punishment: A review of the evidence and issues. *Justice Quarterly* 42:173-217.
Pennsylvania Commission on Crime and Delinquency
  1988   *Trends and Issues in Pennsylvania's Criminal Justice System.* Harrisburg: Pennsylvania Commission on Crime and Delinquency.
Petersilia, J., and P.W. Greenwood
  1978   Mandatory prison sentences: Their projected effects on crime and prison population. *Journal of Criminal Law and Criminology* 69(4):604-615.
Peterson, M.A., and H.B. Braiker (with S. Polich)
  1981   *Who Commits Crime.* Cambridge, Mass.: Oelgeschlager, Gunn, and Hain Publishers. (Also available in 1980 publication *Doing Crime: A Survey of California Prison Inmates*, Report R-2200-DOJ. Santa Monica, Calif.: RAND Corporation.)
Piper, E.S.
  1985   Violent recidivism and chronicity in the 1958 Philadelphia cohort. *Journal of Quantitative Criminology* 1(4):319-344.
Reiss, A.J., Jr.
  1980   Understanding changes in crime rates. In S.E. Fienberg and A.J. Reiss, eds., *Indicators of Crime and Criminal Justice: Quantitative Studies.* Bureau of Justice Statistics. Washington, D.C.: U.S. Department of Justice.
Shane-Dubow, S., A.P. Brown, and E. Olsen
  1985   *Sentencing Reform in the United States: History, Content, and Effect.* National Institute of Justice. Washington, D.C.: U.S. Department of Justice.
Shannon, L.W.
  1982   *Assessing the Relationship of Adult Criminal Careers to Juvenile Careers.* Iowa City: Iowa Urban Community Research Center, University of Iowa.
  1988   *Criminal Career Continuity: Its Social Context.* New York: Human Sciences Press.
Shinnar, R., and S. Shinnar
  1975   The effect of the criminal justice system on the control of crime: A quantitative approach. *Law and Society Review* 9:581-612.

Tittle, C.R.
  1980   *Sanctions and Social Deviance: The Question of Deterrence.*
         New York: Praeger.
Tracy, P.E., M.E. Wolfgang, and R.M. Figlio
  1990   *Delinquency Careers in Two Birth Cohorts.* New York: Plenum Press.
Van Dine, S., J.P. Conrad, and S. Dinitz
  1979   *Restraining the Wicked. The Incapacitation of the Dangerous
         Criminal.* Lexington, Mass.: Lexington Books.
Visher, C.A.
  1987   Incapacitation and crime control: Does a "lock 'em up" strategy reduce crime? *Justice Quarterly* 4(4):514-543.
Walker, L.E.
  1979   *The Battered Woman.* New York: Harper and Row.
Weiner, N.A.
  1989   Violent criminal careers and "violent career criminals." In N.A.
         Weiner and M.E. Wolfgang, eds., *Violent Crime, Violent Criminals.* Newbury Park, Calif.: Sage Publications.
White, S.O., and M.A. Strauss
  1981   The implications of family violence for rehabilitation strategies. In S.E. Martin, L. Sechrest, and R. Redner, eds., *New
         Directions in the Rehabilitation of Criminal Offenders.* Washington, D.C.: National Academy Press.
Williams, K., and R. Hawkins
  1986   Perceptual research on general deterrence: A critical review.
         Law and Society Review 20(4):545-572.
Wolfgang, M.E., R.M. Figlio, and T. Sellin
  1972   *Delinquency in a Birth Cohort.* Chicago: University of Chicago Press.
Zedlewski, D.W.
  1987   *Making Confinement Decisions.* National Institute of Justice.
         Washington, D.C.: U.S. Department of Justice.
Zimring, F.E., and G.J. Hawkins
  1973   *Deterrence.* Chicago: University of Chicago Press.
  1988   The New Mathematics of Imprisonment. Working paper No. 8,
         Earl Warren Legal Institute, School of Law, University of California, Berkeley.

TABLE A-1 Descriptive Statistics for Offending Variables

Crime Type and State	Reported Crimes per 100,000 Population[a](CRT)			Adult Fraction of Crimes[b] (ADT)		
	n	Mean	SD	n	Mean	SD
Murder						
California	23	9.413	2.584	23	0.891	0.019
Florida	21	11.900	1.599	21	0.930	0.019
Michigan	20	9.551	2.384	20	0.901	0.022
New York	23	9.812	2.451	23	0.895	0.036
Pennsylvania	21	5.229	1.044	21	0.873	0.057
Texas	9	14.075	1.923	9	0.916	0.016
Rape						
California	24	41.658	9.696	24	0.859	0.034
Florida	23	37.293	15.026	23	0.817	0.050
Michigan	22	41.325	16.762	22	0.812	0.050
New York	23	24.819	7.237	23	0.824	0.046
Pennsylvania	21	17.776	5.878	21	0.790	0.047
Texas	9	46.696	3.545	9	0.889	0.020
Robbery						
California	24	271.505	78.001	24	0.754	0.055
Florida	23	235.886	85.813	23	0.753	0.052
Michigan	22	267.332	63.825	22	0.697	0.098
New York	23	462.591	141.094	23	0.649	0.102
Pennsylvania	21	129.545	41.438	21	0.642	0.057
Texas	9	206.934	22.719	9	0.839	0.029
Aggravated assault						
California	24	333.190	119.661	24	0.831	0.038
Florida	23	422.622	139.843	23	0.843	0.024
Michigan	22	276.383	93.965	22	0.774	0.076
New York	21	310.615	92.158	21	0.848	0.045
Pennsylvania	21	125.923	41.206	21	0.782	0.069
Texas	9	300.022	39.893	9	0.886	0.018
Burglary						
California	24	1841.936	310.668	24	0.564	0.081
Florida	23	1827.666	431.777	23	0.492	0.113
Michigan	22	1480.715	312.157	22	0.510	0.129
New York	23	1422.106	301.340	23	0.593	0.109
Pennsylvania	21	733.388	182.121	21	0.532	0.065
Texas	9	1879.704	186.837	9	0.636	0.060
Drug offenses[c]						
California	24	519.247	265.595	24	0.808	0.071
Florida	21	238.553	141.086	21	0.806	0.088

continued on next page

TABLE A-1 Continued

Crime Type and State	Reported Crimes per 100,000 Population[a] (CRT)			Adult Fraction of Crimes[b] (ADT)		
	n	Mean	SD	n	Mean	SD
Michigan	22	175.690	105.093	22	0.807	0.085
New York	23	298.523	176.242	23	0.869	0.058
Pennsylvania	21	105.363	51.907	21	0.814	0.086
Texas	9	334.005	32.468	9	0.901	0.038

NOTE: SD = standard deviation.

[a]The *crime rate* is estimated from the ratio of the number of crimes reported by police to the total population in each state. Data on reported crimes in each state were obtained from the Federal Bureau of Investigation (annual) *Uniform Crime Reports*. Annual population estimates for each state were obtained from Bureau of the Census (1969, 1970, 1980, 1988, and 1989).

[b]The *adult fraction of crimes* (adult %) is estimated from the adult fraction of arrests in each state obtained from unpublished supplementary tables of statewide arrest counts from the FBI annual Uniform Crime Reports program.

[c]Independent data are not available on the number of crimes committed for drug offenses, and the "crime rate" reported here is the number of arrests per 100,000 population.

TABLE A-2 Descriptive Statistics for Sanction Risk Variables

Crime Type and State	Arrest Risk per Reported Crime, $q_a{}^a$			Incarceration Risk per Arrest, $Q_i{}^b$		
	n	Mean	SD	n	Mean	SD
Murder						
California	23	1.070	0.114	22	0.372	0.073
Florida	21	0.769	0.122	21	0.765	0.211
Michigan	20	0.915	0.156	20	0.433	0.070
New York	23	0.789	0.095	23	0.628	0.129
Pennsylvania	21	0.983	0.119	12	0.671	0.128
Texas	9	0.810	0.070	9	0.625	0.051
Rape						
California	24	0.356	0.033	23	0.107	0.043
Florida	23	0.351	0.065	21	0.261	0.091
Michigan	22	0.358	0.037	21	0.268	0.113
New York	23	0.454	0.060	23	0.097	0.039
Pennsylvania	21	0.613	0.085	12	0.152	0.021
Texas	9	0.278	0.028	9	0.341	0.097
Robbery						
California	24	0.340	0.062	23	0.116	0.031
Florida	23	0.254	0.039	23	0.336	0.071
Michigan	22	0.188	0.028	21	0.304	0.062
New York	23	0.241	0.033	23	0.186	0.043
Pennsylvania	21	0.404	0.039	12	0.135	0.020
Texas	9	0.213	0.021	9	0.322	0.051
Aggravated assault						
California	24	0.477	0.041	23	0.026	0.008
Florida	23	0.343	0.077	23	0.055	0.019
Michigan	22	0.291	0.035	21	0.059	0.010
New York	21	0.419	0.043	21	0.022	0.004
Pennsylvania	21	0.507	0.044	12	0.032	0.006
Texas	9	0.299	0.013	9	0.059	0.009
Burglary						
California	24	0.165	0.010	23	0.049	0.023
Florida	23	0.133	0.019	23	0.220	0.086
Michigan	22	0.116	0.024	21	0.139	0.027
New York	23	0.108	0.019	23	0.071	0.041
Pennsylvania	21	0.182	0.022	12	0.073	0.012
Texas	9	0.108	0.009	9	0.237	0.019
Drug offenses[c]						
California	24	1.000	0.000	23	0.020	0.014
Florida	21	1.000	0.000	21	0.073	0.064

continued on next page

TABLE A-2 Continued

Crime Type and State	Arrest Risk per Reported Crime, $q_a{}^a$			Incarceration Risk per Arrest, $Q_i{}^b$		
	n	Mean	SD	n	Mean	SD
Michigan	22	1.000	0.000	21	0.063	0.074
New York	23	1.000	0.000	23	0.028	0.011
Pennsylvania	21	1.000	0.000	12	0.025	0.003
Texas	9	1.000	0.000	9	0.050	0.021

NOTE: SD = standard deviation.

^{a}The *arrest risk per crime* (q_a) is estimated from the ratio of adult arrests (>18 years of age) in each state to the estimated number of adult crimes reported by police. Adult crimes in each state are estimated from the product of adult % and crime rate (see Table A-1). Arrest data by state were obtained from unpublished supplementary tables from the FBI Uniform Crime Reports program.

The arrest risk per crime reported here overstates the actual risk of arrest per crime by about threefold for rape, fourfold for robbery, and fivefold for aggravated assault (see discussion of q_a in the main text.) Appropriate adjustments for crimes that are not reported to police and for multiple offenders per crime incident will have similar impacts in reducing q_a for burglary and drug offenses.

^{b}The *incarceration risk per arrest* (Q_i) is estimated from the ratio of annual commitments to prison on a new conviction to the number of adult arrests in each state. Arrest data for each state were obtained from unpublished supplementary tables from the FBI Uniform Crime Reports program, and data on the number of commitments to prison are from annual published reports of the corrections department in each state.

^{c}Separate crime and arrest data are not available for drug offenses. Annual arrest counts are used in the crime rate variable (Table A-1), and the arrest risk per crime is set to 1.0.

TABLE A-3 Descriptive Statistics for Average Time (years) Served in Prison[a]

Crime Type and State	Mean Time (years) Served per Prison Commitment, S[b]		
	n	Mean	SD
Murder			
California	22	5.04	0.88
Florida	13	4.50	0.65
Michigan	12	5.70	1.23
New York	23	5.02	1.39
Pennsylvania	9	7.29	1.18
Texas	9	4.83	0.54
Rape			
California	23	4.18	1.22
Florida	13	3.89	0.48
Michigan	13	2.96	0.55
New York	23	4.57	1.35
Pennsylvania	9	5.36	0.68
Texas	9	3.76	1.00
Robbery			
California	23	3.95	1.39
Florida	15	2.83	0.56
Michigan	13	3.10	0.66
New York	23	2.88	0.76
Pennsylvania	9	4.24	1.17
Texas	9	3.92	0.43
Aggravated assault			
California	23	2.80	0.77
Florida	15	1.79	0.46
Michigan	13	2.22	0.35
New York	21	2.30	0.33
Pennsylvania	9	2.60	0.54
Texas	9	1.56	0.12
Burglary			
California	23	2.64	1.06
Florida	15	1.57	0.29
Michigan	13	1.89	0.39
New York	23	2.36	0.66
Pennsylvania	9	2.99	0.96
Texas	9	1.84	0.15

continued on next page

TABLE A-3 Continued

Crime Type and State	Mean Time (years) Served per Prison Commitment, S^b		
	n	Mean	SD
Drug offenses			
California	22	2.71	1.30
Florida	13	1.36	0.21
Michigan	13	1.51	0.28
New York	23	2.13	0.36
Pennsylvania	9	1.72	0.17
Texas	9	1.27	0.37

NOTE: SD = standard deviation.

[a]*Average time served in prison* (years) is the total time served from the original commitment from court on a new conviction until an inmate is unconditionally released, including time served until first release from prison and any time served following parole revocation. Data on commitments to prison and resident inmates were obtained from annual published reports of the corrections department in each state.

[b]The *measure of time served* (S) is obtained from the ratio of the number of resident inmates (available from a daily census of prison populations) to the number of new commitments to prison each year. This stock-over-flow measure is reasonable when commitments to prison and time served are stable over time, but is vulnerable to error when there are large variations in these data from year to year.

An alternative measure of time served, S^*, incorporates data from several years on the number of inmates remaining in prison at the end of a year, thus smoothing unusual changes in the annual number of commitments to prison (Canela-Cacho and Cohen, 1991). Although differing somewhat in magnitude—with S generally lower than S^* due to unusually large increases in commitments to prison in some years—the two estimates nevertheless change similarly over time.

TABLE A-4 Descriptive Statistics for Imprisonment Variables

Crime Type and State	Incarceration Rate per 100,000 Population[a]			Expected Time Served (person-years) per 100 Arrests, Q_iS [b]		
	n	Mean	SD	n	Mean	SD
Murder						
California	23	17.094	7.242	23	193.16	59.89
Florida	13	34.053	6.965	12	373.49	103.85
Michigan	12	23.294	6.334	12	244.63	57.32
New York	23	21.841	10.355	23	313.64	102.92
Pennsylvania	9	23.447	4.975	9	509.34	153.12
Texas	9	30.951	2.047	9	302.04	41.14
Rape						
California	24	5.423	2.520	24	42.30	14.19
Florida	14	15.272	4.821	14	113.26	28.41
Michigan	13	16.160	10.343	13	98.50	38.13
New York	23	4.284	2.778	23	43.20	19.27
Pennsylvania	9	8.770	2.709	9	81.20	20.69
Texas	9	14.399	5.564	9	125.38	46.46
Robbery						
California	24	27.766	5.466	24	42.89	10.08
Florida	15	49.109	6.670	15	90.99	23.80
Michigan	13	36.597	7.178	13	95.84	28.00
New York	23	37.749	18.131	23	53.03	16.23
Pennsylvania	9	24.867	5.006	9	53.42	11.27
Texas	9	45.696	4.607	9	125.15	17.07
Aggravated assault						
California	24	9.143	4.129	24	7.22	2.39
Florida	15	12.852	2.258	15	8.00	1.27
Michigan	13	9.506	3.891	13	12.65	3.10
New York	21	5.326	1.436	21	5.06	1.45
Pennsylvania	9	6.184	2.336	9	8.61	2.31
Texas	9	7.297	1.450	9	9.13	0.99
Burglary						
California	24	20.704	11.496	24	12.12	5.80
Florida	15	43.941	10.128	15	27.30	4.10
Michigan	13	24.762	7.579	13	26.71	7.65
New York	23	14.752	9.225	23	16.12	8.44
Pennsylvania	9	17.597	3.581	9	21.60	5.88
Texas	9	55.826	4.581	9	43.79	5.46

continued on next page

TABLE A-4 Continued

Crime Type and State	Incarceration Rate per 100,000 Population[a]			Expected Time Served (person-years) per 100 Arrests, $Q_i S$ [b]		
	n	Mean	SD	n	Mean	SD
Drug offenses						
California	24	17.132	11.840	24	6.00	7.32
Florida	13	16.671	3.588	13	6.09	0.88
Michigan	13	8.788	3.566	13	5.15	2.26
New York	23	15.835	14.446	23	5.90	2.02
Pennsylvania	9	5.089	2.354	9	4.20	0.60
Texas	9	17.717	4.649	9	5.82	0.94

NOTE: SD = standard deviation.

[a]The *incarceration rate* is obtained from the ratio of the number of resident inmates in a daily census of prison populations each year to the total population of each state. Inmate data were obtained from annual published reports of the corrections department in each state. Annual population estimates for each state were obtained from Bureau of Census (1969, 1970, 1980, 1988, and 1989).

[b]The *expected time served per arrest* ($Q_i S$) reflects the number of person-years served in prison per 100 adult arrests in a year. It is obtained from the ratio of the number of resident inmates from a daily census of prison populations to the number of arrests of adults. Inmate data were obtained from annual published reports of the corrections department in each state. Arrest data by state were obtained from unpublished supplementary tables from the FBI Uniform Crime Reports program.

Index

A

ABC News survey, 34-35, 53
Accuracy of prediction, 223-225,
    227-228, 278-279, 280
Adolescents. *See* Youth
Age, 245, 280
    and confidence in criminal justice
        system, 53
    and fear of violence, 11-14, 34
    and incarceration and sentencing,
        51, 309
    and perceived seriousness of violent
        acts, 48
    see also Juvenile delinquency; Older
        persons; Youth
Aggression, 235-236
Alarms, 23
Alcohol abuse, 180, 190, 196, 197-198,
    280
Altruistic fear, 56-57
American Psychiatric Association, 220,
    236
Animal models, 25-26
Antisocial personality disorder, 236,
    242, 245
Anxiety, 4-5, 96
Arrest, 168, 222
    risk of, 311-312, 332-334, 336

B

Assault, 35, 86, 92, 93, 99, 105, 107,
    142, 151n:16, 173-174, 301, 302,
    303, 309
    mental health impacts, 96, 98
    perceived seriousness of, 46
Attraction to Sexual Aggression (ASA)
    Scale, 233
Avoidance behaviors, 20, 21-22, 23-24,
    26, 54, 55-56

Battered women's centers, 101
Behavior. *See* Lifestyle; Offenders and
    criminal behavior
Behavioral science model, 188
Benefit-cost analyses, 71-72, 147
    of incarceration policies, 71, 132,
        349-354
Black population
    confidence in criminal justice
        system, 53-54
    fear of, 18-19
    homicides, 168
    knowledge of others' victimization,
        34, 36
    and perceived seriousness of violent
        acts, 47-48
Blood glucose levels, 263, 286n:13

Bureau of Justice Statistics, 87, 243
Burglary, 18, 20, 30, 35, 36, 177, 300, 303

C

California, 136, 300, 318, 319, 320, 363n:18
Case management, 220, 284n:2
Censoring events, 247, 254, 283
Chicago, Ill., 18-19, 22
Chicago Tribune, 29, 30
Child abuse and neglect, 92, 148, 151n:16, 179, 200-201
  classification instruments, 234-235, 242
  false accusations of, 139-140
  later violent behavior by victims, 81, 122, 180, 201, 238
  mental health impacts, 98, 179-180
  psychological testing for, 234-235
  risk factors, 237
Child Abuse Potential (CAP) Inventory, 234-235
Cities. *See* Neighborhoods; Urban areas
Citizen patrols and crime-reporting programs, 24
Classification of violent behavior, 217-219, 226-228, 229-247
  informal methods, 225-226
  research needs, 281-283
  types of, 230-245
Clinical predictions, 237
Coefficient alpha, 223
Community treatment facilities, 83
Companionship, 19, 22
  loss of, 81, 119
Compensatory value. *See* Willingness to accept
Conduct disorder, 236
Consequences of violent behavior, 1, 67-69. *See also* Costs of violent behavior; Injuries
Construct validity, 221-222
Consumer product injuries, 89-90
Content validity, 221
Contingent valuation surveys, 85
Corporal punishment, 204
Correctional institutions and inmates, 296-298, 354-358
  classification systems, 231-233, 236-237

costs of incarceration, 71-72, 73, 83, 131-134, 136-139
fear of victimization in, 56
offense rates and mix, 307-321
official records, 240-241
overcrowding, 305-307
populations, 298-307, 320-321
public opinion on, 49-50
rates of incarceration, 131-132, 315-320
risk and severity of imprisonment, 312-314
Costs of violent behavior, 67-70, 75, 76, 87-89, 91-122, 141-145
  comparisons among offenses, 70-71
  conceptual framework, 72-79
  criminal justice system, 83, 125-135
  death risk, 86, 117-118
  direct, 72, 79, 79-81, 80, 85, 87, 91-101
  emergency response, 101-106
  estimation, 69-72, 78-79, 84-87, 189
  to family members, 81, 118-121
  fear of crime, 83, 88, 125
  fixed, average, and marginal, 76-77
  imprisonment, 71-72, 73, 83, 131-134, 136-139
  indirect, 85-86, 99-101
  injuries, 82, 84-87, 89-91, 91-94, 145-146
  literature review, 84-91
  medical, 73, 79, 88, 89-94, 145
  mental health, 79, 88, 98-99, 114-115, 121, 122, 152n:24-25
  monetary, 73-74, 87, 99-101
  nonmonetary, 72, 73-74, 79, 81, 85-86, 87-89, 101, 150n:8
  to offenders, 73, 83, 84, 136-139, 141
  offsetting benefits, 75-76
  overdeterrence, 83-84, 139-140
  pain, suffering, and quality of life, 73-74, 81, 88, 89, 90, 112-117
  and policy analysis, 71-72
  preventive measures, 70, 87, 123-125, 135-136
  reduction measures, 77-78
  research needs, 99, 146-148
  and seriousness of acts, 37, 70, 149n:3
  societal, 72-73, 82-84, 122-140, 144, 145

torts, 81, 111-112
victim assistance, 77-78, 101-103, 104
see also Productivity losses
Courts
costs, 83, 126
public confidence in, 49, 53
Crime. *See* Criminal justice system;
Mass media *(for news coverage)*;
Nonviolent crime; Offenders and
criminal behavior
Crime event/criminal profile data,
241-242
Crime seriousness index, 70
"Crime stoppers" programs, 136
Criminal intent, 58-59, 182-183
Criminal justice system
case processing, 126-129, 130, 131
costs, 83, 125-135, 147
legal fees, 83, 129, 131, 132
public confidence in, 49, 53-54
versus public health perspectives,
167-183, 191-210
public opinion, 27-28, 48-54, 59
research activities and researchers,
172, 188-191
sanction policies, 311-321
see also Correctional institutions
and inmates
Criminogenic commodities, 170,
190-191, 196-198, 202, 206
Criterion validity, 222
Cross-sectional studies, 219
Cultural influences
and perceived seriousness of crimes,
37
and violence prevention, 171,
203-205, 207, 209-210
Cycle of violence. *See*
Intergenerational violence

D

Dallas, Tex., 16, 17, 21, 22
Dangerous persons, 18-19
Dangerous places, 15-18, 21-22, 24,
55-56
Darkness, 19, 22
Death penalty, 133-134
Deaths, 81
risk, 86, 117-118
Dementia, 235

Demographic characteristics
and confidence in criminal justice
system, 53-54
and fear of victimization, 11-15,
33-34
and knowledge of others'
victimization, 34, 36
offenders, 228, 245
and perceived seriousness of violent
acts, 47-48, 51
and punishments preferred, 51-52
see also Age; Employment status;
Females; Gender differences;
Income level; Males; Older
persons; Race and ethnicity;
Youth
Desistance, 246-247, 328-330
Deterrence, 49, 52, 59, 71-72, 73, 168,
182, 183, 194, 321, 336-348,
350-351, 356-357
*Diagnostic and Statistical Manual of
Mental Disorders* (DSM-III-R),
220, 235-236, 245
Dichotomous dependent variables, 256
Discount rates, 78-79
Discriminate analysis, 256
Disorganized asocial offenders, 241
Dogs, for personal security, 23, 123
Domestic violence, 92, 151n:16, 170,
179, 199, 200-201
mental health impacts, 179-180
see also Child abuse and neglect;
Spousal abuse
Downtown areas, 16
Dramatization of crime, 31-32, 204
Driving while intoxicated, 58, 197-198
Drug abuse, 180, 190, 196-197, 228,
235-236, 240-241, 262, 280,
285-286n:12
Drug offenses, 45, 302, 303, 320,
359n:6
dealers, 86, 87, 150n:10, 228-229, 243
Durkheim, Emile, 26-27

E

Early release programs, 72, 307,
320-321, 328
Economics. *See* Costs of violent
behavior
Educational level, and sentencing, 51
Educational programs, 135, 201, 205-206

Elderly. *See* Older persons
Electronic monitoring of offenders, 71
Emergency medical treatment, 89
  transport costs, 73, 105-106
Employer costs of injuries, 107
Employment status
  prior to offense, 136-137
  and victimization risk, 86
Engraving of valuables, 21, 23
Entertainment, crime as, 31-32, 204
Environmental influences, 184-188
  fear reactions, 4, 5, 15-19, 57-58
  and violence prevention, 201-203
Epidemiological studies, 168-169,
    183-188, 243-244
Escorts, 22, 24
Ethnopenologies, 49, 52
Expressive violence, 186
Extortion, 178

F

Failure-time models, 247, 268-272, 282
False imprisonment, 138, 139-140
Family members
  of offenders, 138
  quality of life costs, 118-121
  see also Child abuse and neglect;
    Domestic violence; Spousal
    abuse
Fear of victimization, 2, 3-28, 167
  biological bases, 25-26
  community responses, 24-25, 26-28
  conceptual issues, 3-5
  consequences of, 20-24, 26-27,
    177-178
  costs, 83, 88, 125
  and cues to danger, 4, 5, 15-19,
    57-58
  and knowledge of others'
    victimization, 36
  lifestyle changes, 26, 83, 124-125
  for loved ones, 56-57
  measurement of, 5-6
  offense-specific, 7-11
  physiological indicators, 3, 5-6
  and prior victimization, 19-20,
    54-55, 96
  research needs, 54-57
  social distribution, 1, 11-15
  sociological impacts, 26-27

surveys of, 3, 6-7, 21-24, 57
  see also Public opinion and
    perception
Federal Bureau of Investigation (FBI)
  crime statistics, 7, 31, 92, 117, 243
  offender typologies, 241-242
Females
  and fear of violence, 11-14, 18
  mental health impacts of
    victimization, 96, 98
  risk reduction measures, 23-24
  see also Gender differences; Rape
Fictional crime, 31-32
Fines, 137
Firearms. *See* Weapons
Fixed costs, 76, 77
Florida, 300, 302, 303-305, 319, 320
Folk theories. *See* Ethnopenologies
Frontier justice, 27-28

G

Gallup Surveys, 6, 7, 9, 53
Gangs, 178
Gender differences, 245, 280
  fear of violence, 11-14, 18
  and perceived seriousness of violent
    acts, 48
  risk reduction measures, 23-24
  and sentencing, 51
General Social Survey (GSS), 2, 6, 7,
    23, 36, 53
Goetz, Bernard, 28
Gresham's Law, 31
Guns. *See* Weapons

H

"Habilitation" programs, 135
Haddon matrix, 184, 185, 187
Health consequences. *See* Injuries
Health insurance, 79, 109-110, 145,
    153n:30-31
Hedonic pricing models, 85-86, 87
Home detention, 134
Homicide, 86, 138-139, 168, 173, 266,
    303, 309, 320
  child witnesses of, 120, 121
  costs of, 92, 94, 106, 108-109
  family impacts of, 120-121, 145-146

interpersonal diffusion of
knowledge of, 35-36
mass murderers, 191, 241-242
news coverage, 30
perceived seriousness of, 38
risk of, 2, 9, 117-118
in television dramas, 32
"Hosts," 184-187, 191
Household characteristics, 55
Household duties, loss of, 79, 81, 88,
107-108, 118, 153n:28-29
"Human capital" valuation, 74

I

Imprisonment. *See* Correctional
institutions and inmates
Incapacitation of offenders, 49, 52,
71-72, 73, 75-76, 168, 182, 183,
194, 321-336, 341, 344, 346,
349-354, 356-357
Incest, 98
Incidence-based cost estimates, 78-79
Income level
of incarcerated offenders, 137
and knowledge of others'
victimization, 36
and victimization risk, 86
Income transfer programs, 110
Index crime rate, 308-309, 360n:8-9
Index of Spouse Abuse, 231
Indigent defense, 83, 129, 131
Information sources, on violence, 1, 2,
28-38, 57-58. *See also* Mass
media
Injuries, 167-168, 173, 175-176
costs, 82, 84-87, 89-91, 91-94,
145-146
see also Mental health injuries;
Risk of injury and victimization
Innocent parties, 84
Instrumental violence, 186
Insurance, 21, 23, 109-111, 145-146,
153n:30-31
Intergenerational violence, 122, 180
Internal consistency, 223
Interpersonal diffusion of crime news,
34-36, 57
Interrater reliability, 223

J

Jury awards, 85, 86, 88, 89, 98, 114,
115-116, 119
Jury Verdict Research, Inc., 111,
114-115
Juvenile delinquency
arrest records, 238-239
referrals to court, 239
sentencing, 51

K

Kuder-Richardson formula (KR20), 223

L

Laboratory studies, 244
Lambda. *See* Rate of commission
Late luteal phase dysphoric disorder, 236
Law. *See* Criminal justice system; Torts
Life insurance, 110, 145-146
Lifestyle, 55, 99, 101
Longitudinal studies, 219, 244
fear of victimization, 54-55
perceived seriousness of violent
acts, 58
Losses. *See* Costs of violent behavior

M

Males
in crime dramas, 32
fear of, 18, 19
and fear of violence, 11, 13
homicides, 168
mental health impacts of
victimization, 96
risk reduction measures, 24
see also Gender differences
Marginal costs, 70, 76-77
of incarceration, 73
Mass media, 1, 2, 28-34, 57
and community programs, 25
crime as entertainment, 31-32, 204
crime as filler material, 31
criticisms of crime news coverage,
29-31
Mass murderers, 241-242
Media General/Associated Press
survey, 53

Medical costs, 73, 79, 88, 89-94, 145
Mental health injuries, 94-99, 167, 181
  costs, 79, 88, 98-99, 114-115, 121,
  122, 152n:24-25
  to family members, 119-121
  to witnesses, 121-122
Mental retardation, 236
Michigan, 302, 320
Minnesota Multiphasic Personality
  Inventory (MMPI), 231-233,
  284n:2
"Mirror image" model, 30-31, 33
Molestation, 96, 97
Moral judgments, 167, 191, 204-205.
  See also Normative evaluations
Mothers Against Drunk Driving
  (MADD), 58
Multiple personality disorder, 98
Multiplicative model of fear, 8-9
Multivariate scaling techniques,
  231-235, 246
Murder. *See* Homicide

N

National Accident Sampling System
  (NASS), 93
National Council on Compensation
  Insurance (NCCI) data base,
  93-94, 151-152n:19
National Crime Survey (NCS), 7, 23,
  26, 57, 87, 88, 92-93, 95,
  127-129, 148, 150-151n:14-17,
  311-312
National Electronic Injury Surveillance
  System (NEISS), 93
National Health Interview Survey
  (NHIS), 93
National Hospital Discharge Survey
  (NHDS), 93
National Survey of Crime Severity,
  38-48
National Survey of Punishment for
  Criminal Offenses, 50
Neighborhoods, 15-18, 21, 87
  and conversations about crime, 34
Neighborhood watch programs, 24-25,
  27, 136
News coverage. *See* Mass media
Newspapers, 28-29, 30
New York, 300, 303, 320
Nicotine withdrawal, 236

Nighttime, 19, 22, 24, 26, 83
Nonviolent crime
  interpersonal diffusion of
    knowledge of, 35-36
  news coverage, 30-31
  perceived seriousness of, 38, 46
  and potential for violence, 176-178,
    180-181
Normative evaluations, 49-51, 58

O

Observational studies, 244-245
Occurrence models, 247, 257, 258-268,
  282
Offenders and criminal behavior,
  174-175, 182-183
  career lengths, 328-332, 351, 357
  characteristics of, 48-49, 51-52,
    228-229, 245
  classification of, 217-219, 226-228,
    229-247
  costs to, 73, 83, 84, 136-139, 141
  defendant records, 239-240
  disorganized asocial, 241
  FBI typology, 239-240
  former victims, 122
  organized asocial, 241
  prediction of, 217, 218-220,
    247-281, 284n:2
  relationship to victim, 46-47
  victimization of, 56, 75-76, 86-87
  see also Correctional institutions
    and inmates; Criminal intent;
    Criminal justice system; Juvenile
    delinquency; Recidivism and
    recidivists
Official record data, 238-242, 246, 280
Older persons
  and fear of violence, 11-14, 22
  mental health impacts of
    victimization, 96
  and perceived seriousness of violent
    acts, 48
  risk reduction measures, 23
  sentencing of, 51
Opportunity costs, 73, 77
Ordinary least squares (OLS)
  regression, 256
Organic personality syndrome, 235
Overdeterrence, 83-84, 139-140

P

Pain and suffering, 73-74, 81, 88, 89, 90, 99, 112-116, 114, 116
Paranoia, 242
Parole, 133
Pennsylvania, 51, 300, 302, 318-319, 320, 365*n:21*
Perceptions of violence. *See* Fear of victimization; Public opinion and perception
Persistence of violence, 218, 228, 245-246
Philadelphia, Pa., 15-16, 17, 22
Police
    community relations, 24
    confidence in, 23, 27-28, 49, 53-54
    costs, 73, 83, 103-105, 126, 147
    preventive patrols, 71
Policy. *See* Public policy
Postdiction studies, 219-220
Post-traumatic stress disorder (PTSD), 94-97, 120-121, 236
Poverty, 203, 207
Predatory behavior, 284*n:2*
Prediction of violent behavior, 217, 218-220, 247-281, 284*n:2*
    accuracy, 223-225, 227-228, 278-279, 280
    methodological problems, 222, 224-228, 247, 254-257
    research needs, 281-283
    review of studies, 248-254, 257-278
President's Commission on Law Enforcement and Administration, 3
Pretrial detention, 126
Prevalence, 2, 217, 220
Prevalence-based cost estimates, 78, 149*n:6*
Preventive and precautionary measures, 192-193
    costs, 70, 87, 123-125, 135-136
    criminal justice approaches, 194-200
    juvenile delinquency, 195-196
    personal strategies, 20-21, 22-24, 25-26, 54, 55, 72-73, 123-125
    public health approaches, 169, 200-205, 206-207
    timing of, 186-187
    see also Deterrence
Primary prevention, 193

Prisons. *See* Correctional institutions and inmates
Probation, 71, 83, 131, 133, 134, 138
Productivity losses, 73, 74, 79, 83, 90, 98, 106-109, 108-109, 135
    of incarcerated offenders, 136-137
Property losses, 73, 79, 88-89, 99, 149-150*n:7*
Property-marking projects, 24, 25
Prosecution, 83, 126
Psychiatric classifications, 235-236
Psychological injury. *See* Mental health injuries
Psychological tests, 230-235
Public defenders, 83, 129, 131
Public health system, 168
    and epidemiological analyses, 168-169, 183-188
    operational resources, 207-209
Public opinion and perception, 1-3
    of criminal justice system, 27-28, 48-54, 59
    effects of victim, offender, and respondent characteristics, 51-52
    seriousness of violent acts, 37-48, 58-59
    see also Fear of victimization
Public policy
    and cost analyses, 69-70, 71-72, 147
    criminal justice and public health dichotomy, 192-207
    and incarceration, 349-354
    policing, 9, 11
    and seriousness of violent acts, 37
    and violence classification and prediction, 279, 283-284
Public service announcements, 83
Punishment. *See* Criminal justice system; Deterrence; Incapacitation of offenders; Rehabilitation of offenders; Retributive justice; Sentences to prison

Q

Quality of life, 73, 81, 90, 112-113, 116-117, 118-121

R

Race and ethnicity, 203, 207, 209, 245, 280, 362*n:12*

and confidence in criminal justice
system, 53-54
and fear, 14-15, 18-19
and juvenile arrests, 238
and knowledge of others'
victimization, 36
and perceived seriousness of violent
acts, 47-48
and sentencing, 51
Rage, classification of, 235-236
"Ransom" value. *See* Willingness to
pay
Rape, 35, 92, 93, 94, 99, 101, 105, 107,
142, 266, 286n:14, 301-302, 304,
309
child witnesses of, 120, 121
fear of, 14
mental health impacts, 95-98, 179
perceived seriousness of, 38, 45,
46-47, 58
and sadism, 236
tort actions, 111, 112
Rapid assessments, 230-231
Rap sheets. *See* Official record data
Rate models, 247, 272-278, 282
Rate of commission, 218, 228, 245-246,
322-328, 350-351
Reactive approaches, 192-193
Recidivism and recidivists, 72, 83, 138,
174-175, 191, 241, 364-365n:19
career termination, 328-330
drug abusers, 241
juvenile, 238, 329
sentencing of, 51
Regression analysis, 256-257
Rehabilitation of offenders, 49, 52, 72,
135, 168, 182-183, 194
Relative Improvement Over Chance
(RIOC) statistic, 225, 278-279,
283
Reliability, 223, 246, 280
Repeat offenders. *See* Recidivism and
recidivists
Research activities and needs, 219-220,
281-283
costs and consequences, 99, 146-148
criminal justice system, 172,
188-191
prediction, 217, 218-220, 247-283,
284n:2
quality measures, 221-225, 279-280
Restitution, 49

Retail businesses, 55-56
Retributive justice, 49, 52, 167, 204
costs, 73, 83
Risk of injury and victimization,
11-12, 177
and fear, 8-9, 10, 12-15, 125
to inmates, 138
public health approaches, 169, 171,
183-184, 187, 202, 203
Robbery, 21, 34, 35, 45, 92, 93, 99,
105, 107, 142, 177, 300, 303,
309, 320, 359n:6
mental health impacts, 95, 96, 98

S

Sadism, 236
Safe School Study, 17
Samples. *See* Selection bias; Surveys
School days lost, 81, 88, 108
Schools, 17
Seattle, Wash., 17, 21, 22
Secondary prevention, 193
Security systems and devices, 21,
22-23, 25, 56, 83, 125
Selection bias, 226-227, 247, 255, 283
Self-destructive behavior, 245
Self-reports, offender, 240, 242-245,
246, 280. *See also* Surveys
Sentences to prison, 50-51, 59, 173,
296, 312-314, 318-319, 320, 337,
349
costs and benefits, 71, 132, 349-354
Serial killings, 191, 241, 242
Seriousness of violent acts, 218
as determinant of fear, 8-9, 10, 37
and interpersonal diffusion of crime
news, 35-36
and news reporting, 30-31
public opinion, 37-48, 58-59
and punishment, public preferences
for, 37, 49-50
surveys of, 38-48, 70-71
"Seven-stitch rule," 173-174
Sex. *See* Females; Gender differences;
Males
Sexual violence
psychological testing for, 233, 244
public health perspectives, 178-180
sadism, 236
tort actions, 111
see also Rape

Shock incarceration programs, 71
Shrinkage, 227-228
Situational analyses and approaches, 170-171, 189, 198-200
Social institutions, public confidence in, 27-28
Sociological analysis, 188-191
Spatial avoidance, 21-22, 26
Spousal abuse, 178, 369n:45
   later violent behavior by victims, 122
   misdemeanor arrest programs, 71
   perceived seriousness of, 46, 47
   psychological testing for, 231
Standard psychological tests, 231-235
States victim aid funding, 102-103
State-Trait Anger Scale, 230-231
Statistical limitations, of predictive models, 256-257, 282
Stepwise regression, 227, 256-257
Stochastic selectivity, 355-357
Stress, 96, 180
Stuart, Carol, murder case, 67-68
Suicides, 138-139, 168
Supported Work experiment, 71
Surveys, 188
   interpersonal diffusion of crime news, 34-36
   of medical costs, 93
   offender self-reports, 240, 242-246, 280
   of preferred punishments, 49-51
   see also National Crime Survey

T

Tay-Sachs disease, 224, 285n:6
Teacher observation studies, 244-245
Teenagers. *See* Youth
Television, 28-29, 30, 31, 32, 33, 204
Tertiary prevention, 193
Test-retest reliability, 219, 223
Texas, 300, 302, 305, 319
Theft, 35, 36. *See also* Burglary; Robbery
Times of danger, 19, 22
Torts, 81, 111-112

U

Unemployment, 86, 136-137

Uniform Crime Reports (UCR), 7, 92, 117, 127-129, 189, 243, 360-361n:11
Urban areas, 15, 229

V

Validity of research, 221-222, 279-280
Vandalism, 35
"Vectors", 184-187, 191
Victim assistance programs, 77-78, 101-103, 104
Victimization
   careers, 55
   lifestyle changes, 99, 101
   offsetting benefits of, 75
   personal knowledge of others', 34-36
   See also Fear of victimization
Victims, 174-175, 181, 218
   characteristics and public opinion, 47, 51-52
   later violent behavior by, 122
   prior criminal behavior of, 86
   ratings of seriousness of violent acts, 48
   relationship to offender, 46-47
Victims of Crime Act (VOCA), 101-102
Vigilantism, 27-28

W

Wage losses, 73, 79, 83
Wealth effect, 149n:4
Weapons, 190-191, 196, 198, 202-203
   injuries, 150n:13
   for personal security, 21, 22, 23, 83, 123, 190
White-collar crimes, 46, 58
Willingness to accept (WTA), 74, 85-86, 113, 149n:4
Willingness to pay (WTP), 74, 85-87, 112-113, 116-117, 159n:4
Witnesses, 120, 121-122, 134, 135, 174

Y

Youth
   fear of, 18, 19, 22
   homicides, 168
   violence prevention programs, 201
   see also Juvenile delinquency